India's Democracy

Written under the auspices of
the Center of International Studies,
Woodrow Wilson School, Princeton University

A list of other Center of International Studies
publications appears at the back of the book.

India's Democracy

An Analysis of Changing State-Society Relations

Edited by Atul Kohli

CONTRIBUTORS
Pranab Bardhan · Paul R. Brass
Stephen P. Cohen · Jyotirindra Das Gupta
Francine R. Frankel · Henry C. Hart
James Manor · Ghanshyam Shah

Foreword by John P. Lewis

PRINCETON UNIVERSITY PRESS
PRINCETON, NEW JERSEY

Copyright © 1988 by Princeton University Press

Epilogue © 1990 by Princeton University Press
Published by Princeton University Press, 41 William Street,
Princeton, New Jersey 08540
In the United Kingdom: Princeton University Press, Oxford

ISBN 0–691–07760–6
ISBN 0–691–02333–6 (pbk.)

Publication of this book has been aided by a grant from the
Center of International Studies, Woodrow Wilson School, Princeton University

First Princeton Paperback printing, with epilogue, 1990

This book has been composed in Linotron Sabon

Printed in the United States of America by Princeton University Press,
Princeton, New Jersey

10   9   8   7   6   5   4   3   2

CONTENTS

TABLES AND FIGURES

PREFACE TO THE 1990 EDITION

A number of important political changes have taken place in India since the first edition of this volume went to press in mid-1986 and was published in early 1988. In the ninth general election held in late 1989, India's premier political organization, the Congress party, lost power for only the second time in the last forty years, and in early 1990 India is being governed for the first time by a minority government. Other significant developments included the stalled efforts of Rajiv Gandhi, India's Prime Minister from 1984 to 1989, to liberalize India's economy, rebuild the Congress party, and find a solution to the ethnic strife in the Punjab. New political problems have also arisen from the reassertion of religious and communal conflicts. These and other major developments are interpreted within the general framework of this volume in an epilogue written especially for this new edition.

PREFACE

This volume analyzes state-society relations in India's democracy. The issues discussed concern the changing nature of India's political institutions and the role of organized social groups in Indian politics. The central theme of the volume is: How have India's democratic institutions altered while accommodating new demands for political participation and while solving serious socio-economic problems?

The papers brought together here are all original scholarly contributions commissioned for this volume. They were first presented and discussed at a conference on "India's Democracy" held at the Woodrow Wilson School of Public and International Affairs, Princeton University, on March 14 through 16, 1985. A list of the invited conference participants follows.

The conference at Princeton University was organized in connection with the Festival of India celebrations in the United States during 1985–1986. The ad hoc organizing committee consisted of four faculty members of the Woodrow Wilson School: Robert Goheen, Atul Kohli, John Lewis, and Donald Stokes. The Ford Foundation, through the auspices of the American Institute of Indian Studies, provided part of the funding for the conference. The Woodrow Wilson School covered the remaining costs. Travel costs of a few participants from India were borne by the government of India.

The support of a number of individuals was crucial throughout this project. The conference and, therefore, this volume would not have been possible without the full support of Donald Stokes, dean of the Woodrow Wilson School. Robert Goheen, former United States ambassador to India and now a senior fellow at the Woodrow Wilson School, consistently helped solve the numerous problems that any such large organizational effort creates. The support of John Lewis, professor of economics and international affairs at the Woodrow Wilson School, was indispensable; from the very early decisions of how to secure funding and whom to invite, to the production of this volume, he was always available for both scholarly and collegial advice. I owe him a special thanks. Finally, Henry Bienen, director of the Center of International Studies, Princeton University, deserves thanks. A grant from the Center via Johnson and Higgins has facilitated the publication of this volume.

The help of several other individuals was crucial to the completion of this project. Jayashree Balchander and Caren McGuiness helped organize the conference. Rocco Rossi and Peggy Ricardi played an important part in editing the papers. Supriya Roy Chowdhry helped with the preparation of the index. The comments of Paul Wallace and other anonymous reviewers were very useful. Margaret Case of the Princeton University Press helped the project along with her friendly advice on numerous issues. Patricia Zimmer of the Center of International Studies, Princeton University, typed and retyped the manuscript with great skill. I would also like to note that the editing work on this volume was completed while I was on leave from Princeton University. This leave year was partly supported by a grant from the Ford Foundation.

Although a number of organizations and individuals have been connected with this project, none of them is responsible for the views expressed in this volume; the views are those of the individual authors. I, as editor, take the responsibility for giving the authors and their views a chance to appear in this volume.

Princeton
July 1986

ATUL KOHLI

List of Invited Participants at the Conference on "India's Democracy," held at the Woodrow Wilson School of Public and International Affairs, Princeton University, March 14–16, 1985

BASHIRUDDIN AHMED	Centre for the Study of Developing Societies, Delhi, India
PRANAB BARDHAN	University of California, Berkeley, U.S.A.
JAGDISH BHAGWATI	Columbia University, U.S.A.
PAUL R. BRASS	University of Washington, U.S.A.
STEPHEN P. COHEN	University of Illinois, Urbana-Champaign, U.S.A.
PRAN CHOPRA	Centre for Policy Research, Delhi, India
JYOTIRINDRA DAS GUPTA	University of California, Berkeley, U.S.A.
FRANCINE R. FRANKEL	University of Pennsylvania, U.S.A.
ROBERT HARDGRAVE	University of Texas, Austin, U.S.A.
HENRY C. HART	University of Wisconsin, U.S.A.
RONALD HERRING	Northwestern University, U.S.A.
ALBERT HIRSCHMAN	Institute for Advanced Study, Princeton, U.S.A.
GIRILAL JAIN	Editor, *Times of India*, India
L. K. JHA	Economic Administration Reforms Commission, Delhi, India
W. H. MORRIS-JONES	Institute for Commonwealth Studies, London, England
STANLEY KOCHANEK	Pennsylvania State University, U.S.A.
JAMES MANOR	University of Leicester, England (Visiting Professor, Harvard University, U.S.A.)
PHILIP OLDENBURG	Columbia University, U.S.A.
BALDEV RAJ NAYAR	McGill University, Montreal, Canada
NORMAN PALMER	University of Pennsylvania, U.S.A.
RAMESHRAY ROY	Centre for the Study of Developing Societies, Delhi, India

LLOYD RUDOLPH	University of Chicago, U.S.A.
SUSANNE RUDOLPH	University of Chicago, U.S.A.
BARNETT RUBEN	Yale University, U.S.A.
GHANSHYAM SHAH	Centre for Social Studies, Surat, India
T. N. SRINIVASAN	Yale University, U.S.A.
K. SUBRAHMANYAM	Institute of Defense Studies & Analysis, Delhi, India
ELLIOT TEPPER	Carleton University, Ottawa, Canada
PAUL WALLACE	University of Missouri, U.S.A.
MYRON WEINER	Massachusetts Institute of Technology, U.S.A.
JOHN WOOD	University of British Columbia, Vancouver, Canada
HOWARD WRIGGINS	Columbia University, U.S.A.

This list does not include the names of the numerous participants who are on the faculty of Princeton University. Many of them came in and out of seminars. An incomplete list of those who participated actively would include Robert Goheen, Atul Kohli, John Lewis, Donald Stokes, John Waterbury and Lynn White. The list also does not include the names of many who contributed to the success of the conference by participating as active audience, or of those who were invited but could not attend.

FOREWORD

This volume is one of the lasting products of a major public relations event, the year-long Festival of India, which began in the United States in 1985. Some of us at the Woodrow Wilson School thought right away that this was an appropriate time and opportunity to organize a conference on Indian politics.

Princeton has some important ties to India. Though the University does not have a formal South Asian regional studies program, it does have a good number of Indian undergraduate and graduate students, especially at the Wilson School. Several of us on the faculty have served in India, including Robert Goheen, a native of India, and President Emeritus of the University, who was the U.S. ambassador to India from 1977 to 1980. A few members of our faculty are Indian by origin, including continuing members like Atul Kohli and other visiting scholars. Moreover, our political scientists in the School and the Politics Department have a strong tradition of interest in Third World affairs, including Indian politics.

The four of us involved in the initial conversations about the projected conference—Goheen, Kohli, myself and Donald Stokes, the dean of the Woodrow Wilson School—quickly decided that the focus should indeed be on politics. I think we shared the sense that the United States, presumed by many to be a partisan of democratic modes of development, has been relatively inattentive to this aspect of the Indian experiment.

With the subject set and support for the conference secured, the rest of us left the arrangements for the affair largely to Kohli. He must be given most of the credit for assembling an outstanding assortment of specialists on Indian politics—Indians, Americans, British, Canadians, academics, journalists and ex-officials. Those who were invited to present papers at the conference are named in this volume. Others who attended added to the richness of what proved to be a spirited debate.

With his skillful editing and his overview at the end of the volume, Atul Kohli has fashioned these proceedings into a thoughtful and penetrating commentary on India's contemporary politics. As a non-specialist, I welcome and recommend it. I would add only a few quibbles.

The conference occurred in March 1985. The time turned out to be one of unexpected interest in the subject. It was too early to have much of a reading on Rajiv Gandhi and his era. His mother's assassination was still fresh, as was the Bhopal tragedy. Feelings regarding the Punjab issue remained highly inflamed. Since the conference this last set of tensions has not receded nearly as much as one had hoped. The euphoria about the new prime minister has also come and gone. The essays in this volume have been revised to take account of these changes. The point that remains, however, is simply that events have moved on from where they were when the present perceptions were initially conceived.

There is a related point. What made this an exciting conference was that it was one of aficionados. They were full of their subject, arguing over all the warts, at each others' throats (mostly good-naturedly). An outsider might have thought he was listening to a set of doomsday disclosures, but this was not the mood of the group at all. These are people fascinated by India's democracy. Among themselves they linger over its problems, pitfalls, and reversals. But, quite clearly, they expect the subject of their study to persist. Most of them attribute a basic vitality and a capacity of improvement to Indian democracy, which their in-group critiques may not always convey.

Finally, I have a related semantic quibble: I am a bit bothered by the references these political scientists make to political "decay" in India. "Decay" is a strong metaphor. Any organ or organism that is decaying surely is dead; it has no possibility of revival. Institutions do, of course, die and decay from time to time and are replaced by others. But to imply that the whole system, in this case, the Indian democratic system has succumbed would be a far more extreme claim. It is not a claim that, as I read these essays, the authors of this volume mean to make. Kohli's preferred phrase—that the system is under great strain—implies the possibility of recovery and thus it is more apt.

As an economist, I find an upbeat perspective to be eminently reasonable just now. Pranab Bardhan, the one economist among the authors, is quite right to highlight and seek to explain the inefficiency with which India is using capital. But even so, during the five years leading up to our conference, the country's sluggish output growth had picked up enough so that, with a little accompanying slowdown in population growth, the annual improvement in output per capita was double its level of ten years earlier. The country also had become self-sufficient in food. Although limited, these were major gains. The present volume makes it clear that an improving economic situation is no guarantor of an improving political situation. But I will still prefer to think that the relationship is not necessarily inverse.

JOHN P. LEWIS

India's Democracy

INDIA *as of* 1985

U.T.   Union Territories

•••••   Line of control between India and
        Pakistan in Jammu and Kashmir

CHINA

AFGHANISTAN

JAMMU AND KASHMIR

TIBET

PUNJAB
HIMACHAL PRADESH

Chandigarh (U.T.)

BHUTAN

ARUNACHAL
PRADESH (U.T.)

PAKISTAN

HARYANA

NEPAL

SIKKIM

Delhi (U.T.)

RAJASTHAN

UTTAR
PRADESH

ASSAM
NAGALAND

BIHAR

BANGLA-
DESH

MANIPUR

GUJARAT

WEST
BENGAL

MEGHALAYA

MIZORAM (U.T.)

MADHYA PRADESH

Calcutta

Diu (U.T.)

TRIPURA

Daman (U.T.)

MAHARASHTRA

ORISSA

BURMA

DADRA AND
NAGAR HAVELI (U.T.)

Bombay

BAY OF BENGAL

ANDHRA
PRADESH

GOA (U.T.)

KARNATAKA

Madras

Pondicherry (U.T.)

LAKSHADWEEP
ISLANDS (U.T.)

ANDAMAN
AND
NICOBAR ISLANDS (U.T.)

TAMIL NADU

KERALA

SRI LANKA

Richard Boscarino

Interpreting India's Democracy: A State-Society Framework

ATUL KOHLI

For nearly four decades now democracy in India has appeared somewhat of an anomaly. India is a multinational, agrarian society with a rigid and hierarchical social structure. The existence in such a setting of periodic elections, constitutional government, and freedom of expression and association has posed an intellectual puzzle. In a world where most stable democracies have industrialized and capitalist economies, some observers have felt that India's democracy is either not genuine or that it is likely to falter soon. Others have been convinced of its authenticity and have wondered if the assumptions that make democracy in India seem anomalous are valid. Whether one believes India's democracy to be deep or superficial, the analysis of political strains within that country has always had to be balanced against a tendency toward resilience.

During the last decade of Indira Gandhi's rule, the troubles of India's democracy grew. The precarious balance between strains and resilience appeared once again to have tilted toward the emergence of multiple strains. Considerable evidence has accumulated in recent years to support this judgment: The significance of political parties has declined. Personal rule has come to replace party rule both at the center and in many of the states. The public bureaucracies are under pressure at all levels, with the relatively "neutral" civil service becoming more and more politicized, and the police often proving ineffective in the face of civil disorder. Violence, corruption, and crime have come to be associated with political life at all levels, and, as state institutions have eroded and new social forces have become politicized, armed forces have frequently been used to maintain order.

These trends raise doubts—some say serious doubts—about the future of India's democracy. An analysis of social and political trends cannot alone, however, predict the future of strained political regimes. As Indira Gandhi's Emergency in 1975–1977 illustrated, leadership actions are as much responsible for the breakdown of a democracy as are underlying social trends. The ascendance of Rajiv Gandhi to the prime ministership and his decision to use his considerable popularity to pursue a more compromising approach had similarly highlighted the significance of leadership actions. It is far too early to assess the institutional impact of Rajiv Gandhi's policies, but his reconciliatory stance had altered, at least for the short run, India's mood of political pessimism.

This volume brings together eight essays that document and explain changing state-society relations within India's democracy. The essays share the general view that changes in political-economic outcomes have been caused both by long-term social structural changes within India and by specific actions of the national leadership.

India's nationalist leaders have, over the last few decades, sought to promote economic development within the framework of an elite-dominated democracy. The resulting forces of commercialization and politicization have thrown up new social groups demanding a share of the society's power and wealth. A competitive and factionalized elite has successfully mobilized these new groups in the political arena. Access to the state as a source of power and wealth has thus come to be fiercely contested.

Faced with the recurring choice between accommodation with, and exclusion of, new demands, Indira Gandhi, especially during the last decade of her rule, adopted a recalcitrant stance. Instead of institutional accommodation of new demands, an accommodation that might not have been easy in any case, she established a pattern of personal rule: the Congress party organization was downgraded; the Cabinet, the Parliament, and even the constitution were bypassed; routine administration came to be executed by a "loyal" and politicized bureaucracy; and elections were contested by populist mobilization. These leadership strategies hastened the long-term "structural" trend toward erosion of institutional rule in India.

Rajiv Gandhi had adopted a more accommodating political approach than that of his mother. Although his position of political power was unassailable, in 1985, he had given concessions to the forces of opposition. It is difficult to predict what Rajiv Gandhi will be like when pressed against the wall. That answer will only be provided by scholars who write a volume similar to this one, at least a decade from now.

Meanwhile, the pressing question of long-term significance is: can India's democratic institutions survive while accommodating new demands and solving the multiple problems of socio-economic development? The question is important for both normative and analytical reasons.

Liberals of various hues do not need to be convinced that a study of the erosion of democracy in India is worthy of scholarly attention. Those on the left, however, may well be suspicious. Defense of democracy for many on the left is a defense of "bourgeois interests." To the extent that democratic regimes protect and help reproduce socio-economic systems based on private property and, therefore, "bourgeois interests," radical critics of democracy cannot be dismissed lightly. Under Indian conditions, however, the alternative to "bourgeois democracy" is not likely to be revolutionary socialism. The much more plausible alternative is counterrevolutionary authoritarianism. India's poor and underprivileged, therefore, need democracy. Organized political change under democracy offers limited, but probably the only realistic, hope of mildly egalitarian socio-economic development for modern India.

The central issue posed by the erosion of institutional politics in India concerns the causes of such political change. What forces are responsible for the decay? Is it the result of increasing demands of new social groups propelled by socio-economic development; are its roots located in the inability of a class-dominated state to solve the problems of economic development; or has it been hastened by competitive politics and power-hungry leaders?

Explanations vary with the theoretical assumptions scholars make. Some of the main theoretical issues relevant to the analysis of India's democracy in general, and to the issue of institutional decay in particular, are discussed below in this introduction. The following eight essays then analyze various aspects of India's changing state-society relations.

THEORIES OF DEMOCRACY AND OF DEMOCRACY'S TROUBLES

The analysis of contemporary state-society relations in India leads to a concern with the twin issues of increasing social pressures on the state and the capacity of the battered state to accommodate new demands and stimulate economic development. These issues can be approached from a number of different perspectives. Marxists, liberals, and conservatives, for example, are bound to differ in their understanding of why India's political institutions are not functioning effectively and, even more, on what the future implications of such instability are.

Differences in the underlying assumptions made by scholars pose a special problem for the coherence of edited volumes. Instead of imposing an artificial unity, however, I shall outline here the main alternative approaches to the analysis of 1) why and how democracies come into being; and 2) why and how democracies break down, especially in a developmental setting. The discussion is intended to provide a conceptual umbrella for the essays that follow. It is suggested that the analysis of India's democracy proceeds best by focusing on the mutual interaction of the Indian state and society.

Theories of Democracy and India's Democracy

Three theories continue to be relevant for understanding the conditions for democracy.[1] First, and probably most important, is the theory that conceives of democracy as a form of government likely only in market or capitalist economies. Second is an old and interesting theory that views democracy as more likely to be sustained in wealthy or economically developed societies. And third is the theory that suggests that well-established traditions of compromise politics, and of acceptance of checks and balances on central power, help countries evolve into democracies. Taken together, these theories suggest that democracy is most likely in wealthy capitalist countries with traditions of protodemocracy. Because these theories are generally based on Western experiences, they do not easily explain why democracy has taken root in India. Nevertheless, an understanding of why these conditions might generally be conducive to democratic government provides insights into the questions of why India has a democracy and why its maintenance remains an uphill battle.

Whatever evaluation Marxists, liberals, or conservatives may make of the democratic form of government, most of them would readily admit the historic and logical connection between capitalism and democracy.[2] The historical analysis of European democracies has often stressed the rise of a victorious bourgeoisie. The rising business classes, according to this view, successfully tamed the monarchical state, challenging the aristocratic claim of government as a prerogative of birth and slowly replacing it by the principle of government as a natural domain of wealthy "commoners." Later, under pressure from organized working classes, legitimacy in Western democracies came to rest on the notion that government

[1] This brief discussion on theories of democracy also appears in Atul Kohli, "Democracy and Development," in *Development Strategies Reconsidered*, edited by John P. Lewis and Valeriana Kallab, New Brunswick: Transaction, 1986, pp. 164–167.

[2] Contemporary scholars as diverse as Charles Lindblom, Samuel Huntington and Barrington Moore have posited this link. See Charles Lindblom, *Politics and Markets: The World's Political-Economic Systems*, New York: Basic, 1977, especially pt. 5; Samuel Huntington, "Will More Counties Become Democratic," *Political Science Quarterly* 99, no. 2 (Summer 1984), pp. 203–205; and Barrington Moore, Jr., *Social Origins of Dictatorship and Democracy*. Boston: Beacon, 1966, especially chap. 7.

representatives have to be elected by a legally equal citizenry.[3] This historical sequence in several countries led Barrington Moore Jr. to the succinct
conclusion, "No bourgeois, no democracy."[4]

The logical links between democracy and capitalism are also apparent
in this historical process. Capitalism, as an economic system based on private property, provides a fundamental check on state power by generating
a "private sphere" of social and economic activity separate from the
"public sphere." It is this separation between public and private realms
that is an initial and necessary condition for the evolution of democracy
as a form of limited government. This division, moreover, sets the sphere
of legal and political equality somewhat apart from that of substantial social and economic inequalities. Separating political equality from economic inequalities, in turn, not only lays the basis for legitimate elected
governments in inegalitarian societies, but also opens up the hope and opportunity—though radical critics of democracy may with some legitimacy
call it a false hope—of modifying inherited inequalities through the use of
democratic state power.

The general statement that democracy is positively related to economic
development has over the years often been criticized.[5] Not only have critics noted that the process of economic development can create "political
decay,"[6] but also that many industrialized Communist countries are not
about to become democratic. A more limited version of this old general
position, however, still merits attention. The simple and overwhelming
fact remains that most of the industrialized, capitalist countries of the
world today are democratic. Democracy has clearly not been a "home-
grown" affair in many of these countries, but, once installed, it has found
a hospitable environment in industrialized capitalism.

Political theorists have delineated a number of characteristics of industrial economies that may help democracy.[7] One factor, however, shared

[3] For example, see Barrington Moore (n. 2), chap. 7; Reinhard Bendix, *Nation-Building and Citizenship*, Berkeley: University of California Press, 1977, especially chap. 3; and T. H. Marshall, *Class, Citizenship and Social Development*, New York: Doubleday, 1964.

[4] Moore (n. 2), p. 418.

[5] One of the most influential and systematic statements relating economic development to democracy is that of Seymour Martin Lipset, "Some Social Requisites of Democracy: Eco-nomic Development and Political Legitimacy," *American Political Science Review* 53 (March 1959), pp. 69–105.

[6] See Samuel Huntington, *Political Order in Changing Societies*, New Haven: Yale Uni-versity Press, 1968, especially chap. 1.

[7] In addition to the Lipset article quoted above (n. 5), see Karl Deutsch, "Social Mobili-zation and Political Development," *American Political Science Review* 55 (September 1961), pp. 493–514; and Alex Inkles, "Participant Citizenship in Six Developing Countries," *Amer-ican Political Science Review* 63 (December 1969), pp. 1120–1141.

by all industrial capitalist societies, is relative wealth. Economic wealth—absolute levels and rates of change—help ease both intra-elite and elite-mass political strains. Prolonged periods of steady economic growth laid the basis for welfare states in Western capitalist economies. The welfare state, in turn, helped ease and tame class conflict in early industrial capitalism. The fact that prolonged economic recession can contribute to political and social polarization even in a democracy is well established. Modern Britain is evidence for this historical point.

Wealthy capitalism, moreover, helps ease the intensity of intra-elite conflict. The stakes of the political game are lower when the losers have alternate channels of social and economic mobility. Access to the state, under these conditions, is not necessarily viewed as the only route for upward mobility. The struggle for power is not viewed as a zero-sum game. As a result, losers in the power game are less likely to attempt extrasystemic political mobilization such as mass demonstrations, riots, or participation in underground terrorist activities. Wealth, in other words, helps create boundaries within which elites choose to fight. Disruption of these boundaries damages the system that creates the wealth and thus curtails opportunities for advancement. This bounded struggle, in turn, is crucial for initiating and sustaining democracy.

Some political theorists have pointed out that democratic institutions often took root prior to the age of capitalism and industrialization. German scholars have been especially struck by the contribution of England's feudal past to its later democratic evolution.[8] Feudalism in England bequeathed a legacy of power-sharing arrangements rooted in the principles of political compromise and checks and balances. Although the evolution of democracy in England was slow and often tortuous, the early establishment of protodemocratic institutions was, according to this influential line of thinking, critical. These institutions provided a framework to accommodate the demands of new social classes in a democratic manner. This historic argument suggests that the ruling traditions of a nation are important for understanding how authority is organized during the process of significant socio-economic change. Countries with protodemocratic pasts are more likely to deal with political challenges in a democratic manner.

These three theories highlight some general factors that contribute to the evolution of democratic politics—capitalism, high levels of economic

[8] These scholars generally build on the work of Max Weber. For example, see Felix Gilbert, ed., *The Historical Essays of Otto Hintze*, New York: Oxford University Press, 1975, chap. 8; and Reinhard Bendix, *Kings or People: Power and the Mandate to Rule*, Berkeley: University of California Press, 1978, especially chaps. 6 and 9.

development, and protodemocratic political traditions. How well do these theories illuminate, and how well do they stand up when juxtaposed against, India's experiment with democracy?

The Indian case suggests that the theories that focus attention on the political, rather than the socio-economic, origins of democracy are the most helpful. Democracy in India took root in the first half of this century, at a time when modern capitalist enterprises contributed only a small fraction of India's economic production. Moreover, even today India remains a largely poor, agrarian society; nearly three-quarters of its population lives in villages, and the majority of production and employment is generated through agriculture. Thus, neither capitalism nor industrialization can be considered the primary force behind India's democracy.

Democracy in India is understood better by examining India's modern political traditions. Colonialism was the crucible of India's democracy. Early manifestations of colonial influences included the democratic inclinations of Western-educated leaders like Nehru, internal democracy within the Congress-led nationalist movement, and the participation of Congressmen in elections and legislatures prior to independence. Other lasting contributions of colonialism were traditions of constitutional government, freedom of the press, an effective civil service, and an "apolitical" armed force. It is not surprising, therefore, that when a panel of India experts—W. H. Morris-Jones, Girilal Jain, Rameshray Roy, and Susanne Rudolph—were asked during the Princeton conference to comment on the factors relevant to India's democracy, all of them considered the political traditions inherited from a colonial past to be important.[9]

Considering the fatality rate of democracies in post-colonial settings, the political traditions inherited from the colonial past are clearly not a sufficient explanation. The democratic commitment of India's leaders since independence has also made a major contribution to the survival of democracy in India. Immediately after independence, India's democracy could be characterized as a "gift" of the elite to the masses. This is not to deny or ignore the self-serving aspect of an elitist democracy; the democratic system did enable a group of competing elites to collectively share privilege and power. Nevertheless, these very leaders offered democracy to the Indian masses as a means of incorporating them into the decision-making process. The significance of this benign role of the early leaders is

[9] The Princeton conference mentioned here has been described in the preface to this volume. The comments of the panel participants appear under "Opening Roundtable: Why and How have Democratic Institutions Survived in India," in *Summary of the Proceedings of the Conference on "India's Democracy,"* mimeo., Woodrow Wilson School, Princeton University, pp. 1–11.

highlighted by the contrasting situation later created by Indira Gandhi's Emergency.[10]

The longer democracy has been practiced in India, the lower down in the social strata has penetrated the urge for an enhanced share of power and wealth. The long-run consequences of such a "spread effect" may or may not be to strengthen stable democracy. Much will depend on the modes and intensity with which new demands are made and on the willingness of the pressed elite to make timely concessions. Over the short run, however, the spread of democracy has brought many more than just the Western-educated elite into a participatory political system. As Susanne Rudolph eloquently put it during the Princeton conference:

> After the experience of 37 years of democracy in India, one may say that to learn democracy is to play democracy. . . . The way to qualify for democracy is to operate democratic instrumentalities and thereby learn to become competent craftsmen at operating them. India has shown that the so-called prerequisites may not in fact be essential for democracy. . . . Indians, as they went through a series of elections and socializing experience, have picked up a great deal of values and ideologies that lie beneath the institutions that are there.[11]

When India's political practices are set against its socio-economic structure, it appears that politics can indeed be considerably more autonomous than is suggested by developmental and Marxist theories of democracy. Any general perspective on Indian democracy, then, must assume that politics and the state in India cannot be fully understood by reductionist socio-economic analysis. However, to avoid overemphasizing the "autonomy of the political," it is necessary to simultaneously stress the significant impact of socio-economic conditions.

Although capitalism has not been the driving force of India's democracy, the "elective affinity" between capitalism and democracy in India can hardly be denied. Over a few decades, by trial and error, even the "socialistically" inclined Indian leaders have realized that a democratic political order needs a "working arrangement" with those who control property and production.[12] This "alliance" was clear with regard to the

---

[10] Commenting on Mrs. Gandhi's role, Myron Weiner was thus led to an eloquent generalization: "Societies do not destroy their democratic institutions. States do." Myron Weiner, "The Wounded Tiger: Maintaining India's Democratic Institutions," in *Transfer and Transformation: Political Institutions in the New Commonwealth*, edited by Peter Lyon and Jim Manor, Leicester: Leicester University Press, 1983.

[11] See *Summary of the Proceedings* (n. 5), pp. 8–9.

[12] I have developed this argument at greater length elsewhere. See Atul Kohli, *The State and Poverty in India: The Politics of Reform*, Cambridge: Cambridge University Press, 1987, chap. 2.

industrial sector even before independence; since independence, India's industrial and business houses have often benefited from the government's economic activities. And, although governmental support of private economic activity in agriculture has been, by contrast, slow in coming, by the middle of the 1960s, even in agriculture land reforms were abandoned in favor of the Green Revolution.[13] It would be absurd in the face of such evidence to suggest that India's economic order does not influence its political activity. Those who are not convinced should ponder the counterfactual: what would have happened to Indian democracy if the "socialist" leaders of that country had seriously pursued policies detrimental to the interests of the property-controlling classes?

The low level of India's economic development has also been politically consequential for it has been necessary for the state to promote development. For a democratic state, this creates a special problem: how to incorporate diverse interests while simultaneously standing above them to steer and guide socio-economic change? We see in India a repeated struggle among those who seek to justify policies on the grounds of "economic rationality" and those whose diverse political interests are affected by these policies. Specific manifestations of this struggle include a series of recurring conflicts: for example, those over the share of public resources allocated between the center and the states, among those who favor the agrarian over the industrial sector, and of late, those involving the proponents and the opponents of a more liberal development strategy.

The political significance of low levels of economic development is further transmitted through the scarcity of available economic resources. Conflicts in mobilized democracies like India's are harder to manage when the economic pie is relatively small, and both intra-elite and elite-mass conflicts have been exacerbated by scarcity. Moreover, the process of economic development has mobilized people out of their traditional social niches. Whatever the problems with "developmental theory," and there are many, there can be little doubt that a society in which the prevailing values and the changing patterns of stratification are not synchronized is difficult to govern. High levels of economic development may not create democracy, but it would be foolish to assume that economic scarcity and low levels of economic development do not create problems for a democracy.

To summarize, India's democracy is best analyzed from a perspective that highlights state-society interaction. Patterns of political behavior, as

---

[13] How this policy shift came about has been discussed in detail by Francine R. Frankel, *India's Political Economy, 1947–1977: The Gradual Revolution*, Princeton: Princeton University Press, 1978, chaps. 5, 6, and 7.

well as the choices of state authorities, cannot be reduced to the underlying socio-economic forces. At the same time, patterns of economic organization, conflicting interests of socio-economic groups, and changing values of the society continuously influence the political structures and processes. A focus on state-society relations does not eliminate the old debates between developmentalists and Marxists, but the recognition of the "autonomy of the political" blunts their sharpness. Developmentalists and Marxists may still differ sharply over the relative significance of culture, values, and status considerations, on the one hand, and of economic interests and class conflict, on the other. In the Indian case, however, neither set of variables is decisive for political analysis; the political arena has its own life. The task of empirical analysis must be to unravel various aspects of the mutual interaction between society and the Indian state.

Theories of Democracy's Troubles and India's Troubles

Paralleling the theories of democracies discussed above are alternative sets of explanations of why democracies in a developing country, like India, tend to break down.[14] Marxists and developmentalists, for example, differ as to which aspects of social organization—class conflict or value disequilibrium—are more important for the analysis of political decay. Those who take the "autonomy of the political" seriously, by contrast, tend to view the process of breakdown as rooted more in the crises of political order and less in socio-economic conflict.

A popular and well-established line of thinking suggests that the process of industrialization and economic development is an inherently unstable one. From Durkheim, through Parsons and Smelser to Huntington, numerous scholars have been struck by the fact that transitional stages between "tradition" and "modernity" are often characterized by anomie, social disorganization, and political decay.[15] The explanation for this state of affairs is thought to rest on the corrosive impact of economic development on a society's established beliefs and patterned behavior. In-

[14] These issues are discussed in greater detail in chapter 2 of a book that I am currently writing. The tentative title of this book is *Erosion of Authority in India: A Study of Political Change.*

[15] For one of many general reviews of the "developmental" or the "modernization" literature on these themes, see Richard A. Higgott, *Political Development Theory*, New York: St. Martin's, 1983, chap. 2. One of the original formulations that stressed the gap between the forces of "integration" and "differentiation" as root of developmental instability was, Neil Smelser, "Mechanisms of Change and Adjustment to Change," in *Political Development and Social Change*, edited by Jason Finkle and Richard Gable, New York: John Wiley, 1971, pp. 27–43; and Huntington, *Political Order* (n. 6), especially chap 1.

dustrialization "differentiates" the "traditional" society. If new patterns of "integration" do not keep up with the process of "differentiation," social disorganization results. The more politically oriented arguments from this tradition, such as Huntington's, propose that political decay results from the failure of political institutions to accommodate social groups that are mobilized by economic development.

What appears as general social disorganization to "modernization" scholars looks like intensified class conflict to scholars in the Marxist tradition. The development of capitalism, according to Marxists, generates pressures for increases in "surplus appropriation." Because the coercive power of the state is necessary to facilitate such increases, politics based on compromise and consensus is not likely in early capitalism.

An influential and more specific argument originating from this tradition traces the roots of authoritarianism to the requirements of the "deepening of industrialization" in "dependent capitalist" countries.[16] The argument is that, as one moves beyond superficial industrialization, which can occur even under the auspices of open regimes and import substitution policies, governmental capacity for facilitating economic development is increasingly strained. Sustained industrialization requires a disciplined working class and political stability. It also needs foreign capital and the imposition of austere economic policies. What is especially pressing is the need to shift away from an inward-oriented growth model—which cannot be sustained in the absence of income redistribution—to an export-oriented approach. Such daunting economic tasks can, according to this argument, overwhelm fragile democratic regimes. Technocratic and authoritarian regimes—the bureaucratic-authoritarian regimes—thus emerge as a consequence of the requirements of sustained capitalist economic development.

A number of other scholars have suggested that the breakdown of democracies is a result not only, or even primarily, of socio-economic crises but that the troubles of democracies are, rather, political in origin and represent crises of legitimacy.[17] Loss of legitimacy, in turn—an elusive condition—is only partly a result of social and economic problems. Various

[16] This well-known argument is associated with Guillermo O'Donnell, *Modernization and Bureaucratic-Authoritarianism: Studies in South American Politics*, Berkeley: Institute of International Studies, University of California, 1973. For a critical review of O'Donnell's hypothesis, see David Collier, ed., *The New Authoritarianism in Latin America*, Princeton: Princeton University Press, 1979, especially the chapters by Albert Hirschman, Jose Serra, and Robert Kaufman.

[17] The most sustained attention to the political causes of the breakdown of democracies has been given in a series of volumes organized by Juan Linz. For a general discussion of this subject, see Juan Linz, *The Breakdown of Democratic Regimes*, Baltimore: Johns Hopkins University Press, 1978.

regimes, although existing under fairly similar socio-economic conditions, may be deemed more or less legitimate by the ruled.

A number of purely political variables influence how well a democratic state is governed: quality of leadership, leadership choices, prevailing ideology, degree of intra-elite harmony and the design of such dominant political institutions as the party system and legislative-executive relations. Demagogic leaders, for example, can easily exacerbate political tensions within a democracy. Widely divergent ideological beliefs and/or a fragmented political elite can similarly make stable political rule difficult. Most important, democratic values and behavior take root only over time and only after repeated practice. The best-designed democracies are thus fragile over the short run. Even established democracies can be threatened by increases in extrasystemic protests and/or by leaders who do not cherish democratic norms.

The troubles of democracy in developing countries can thus be analyzed alternatively from a modernization or Marxist perspective or from a standpoint that emphasizes political variables. India's political economy presents a tapestry rich enough to provide evidence to buttress a number of competing claims. For example, it would be difficult to argue against the observation that the demands of newly mobilized social groups are exacerbating the problems of India's democracy; or that India's democratic state caters primarily to the socio-economic interests of India's privileged and, as a consequence, is often hamstrung in its capacity to take difficult developmental decisions; or that the recalcitrance of such leaders as Indira Gandhi brought India's democracy to the brink of extinction. Each of these trends has been of considerable significance in Indian politics in recent years.

Over the last decade or two, numerous social groups in India have made their political presence felt.[18] Some of these groups are primarily products of economic development; others, already in existence, have become politically conscious and active with the spread of democracy. Particularly significant with regard to political development has been the role of those generally in the middle of India's hierarchical social structure. The "middle peasants" have enhanced their economic status through the Green Revolution in a number of states. They have, in turn, sought to turn this wealth into commensurate political power. Moreover, a number of intermediate castes—often called the "Backwards"—who were traditionally ignored by the elite-dominated Congress, have also in recent years thrown

---

[18] The consequences of the role of the new "demand" groups for Indian politics are analyzed in Lloyd L. and Susanne Hoeber Rudolph, *In Pursuit of Lakshmi: The Political Economy of the Indian State*, Chicago: University of Chicago Press, forthcoming.

their weight behind various opposition parties. They have provided a formidable opposition to the old and established ruling alliances. Violent conflicts between the "Backwards" and the "Forwards" over "reservation" policies are one of the many manifestations of the new role of these "middle" groups.

Those at the bottom of the social hierarchy have posed less of a political challenge to the established elite. However, as economic development and the spread of egalitarian values have slowly undermined the hold of the traditional elite over its numerous dependents, these groups are increasingly emerging as a "free-floating political resource." Organized and sustained political activity by these groups is still rare, but their presence has encouraged a populist and personalistic leadership style. Because there are few organizational mechanisms available in India to systematically incorporate the poor, the establishment of a direct relation between the leader and the masses has become a tempting alternative. Although this appeal generates a political following over the short run, the long-run consequences for institutionalized politics of enormous power vested in individuals are at best, unhealthy.

If the politically corrosive impact of social mobilization seems considerable, so have been the consequences of the actions of a "soft" state. Among developing countries, India's democratic state has been remarkable for its systematic capacity to accommodate diverse interests. The flip side of this accommodating capacity, however, has been that difficult developmental decisions have been hard to make, especially decisions that would adversely affect entrenched class interests.

The failure of the leadership to translate into action ideological commitments to socialism and redistribution is a consequence of both organizational weakness and the class alliances underlying governmental power.[19] India's diverse and dominant social classes have also staked out their share of public resources in exchange for political support. The greater the share has been of governmental resources used in "buying" support, the smaller the share that has been available for economic development.[20] Slow economic growth and considerable poverty are, in turn, likely to remain politically damaging economic conditions for quite some time to come.

No analysis of India's changing democracy would be adequate if it did not go beyond the socio-economic trends mentioned above to include purely political changes. The most significant of these has been the role of

[19] This is one of the themes developed in Kohli, *The State and Poverty in India* (n. 8).

[20] This argument is developed in Pranab Bardhan, *The Political Economy of Development in India*, Oxford: Basil Blackwell, 1984.

Indira Gandhi. Although Mrs. Gandhi clearly confronted an India that was increasingly difficult to govern, her intense desire for personal power may have cost India's democracy dearly. A number of Mrs. Gandhi's "deinstitutionalizing" actions have already been mentioned.[21] In addition to these, the failure of other "leaders" to provide leadership, as during the Janata period, further heightened the sense of the fragility at the apex of the Indian polity. Below the center, moreover, rampant corruption, the breakdown of law and order in a number of states, and the entry into politics of criminals sponsored by Sanjay Gandhi were hardly "sociological necessities." The contrast that Rajiv Gandhi's leadership has provided only lends support to the general contention.

This brief overview clearly suggests that a number of sets of variables have influenced political change in India. If the primary goal of scholarly endeavor were to choose from among alternate theoretical perspectives, selected evidence could easily be used from India to develop such a case. By contrast, however, if the primary purpose is to unravel the complex empirical puzzle of India's democracy—and that is the primary purpose of this volume—it is difficult to exclude any of the significant theoretical insights on a priori grounds.

A focus on the mutual interaction of state and society provides a synthetic theoretical perspective. In this volume, we begin with the assumption that political structures and processes enjoy a degree of autonomy from the social structure. Thus, not only can states influence socio-economic change, but power struggles are also not reducible to socio-economic struggles. Conversely, it would be absurd to underemphasize the significant impact that cultural and class variables have on a society's politics. The task of empirical analysis within a state-society framework must be to assess the relative significance of competing variables and how they mix.

THE PLAN OF THE VOLUME

The volume is organized on a state-society framework. Each contributing scholar was asked to analyze a specific facet of India's state-society relations. The focus of some articles is thus more on state institutions; of others, on social groups; and of yet others, on the interaction of state and society. All the papers are concerned with, on the one hand, the changing nature of India's ruling institutions and, on the other, with the role of

---

[21] Rajni Kothari and James Manor have both developed this theme in their recent writings. For example, see their essays in *Transfer and Transformation* (n. 6). Also see Manor's essay below.

newly organized groups in Indian politics and the capacity of India's rulers to deal with emerging socio-economic challenges.

The first three essays analyze three of India's important state institutions: leadership, the major parties and the party system, and the armed forces. Henry Hart was invited to analyze the significance of leadership in India in general, and the impact of Indira Gandhi's style and actions in particular. His essay also provides a good picture of India's changing civil and police bureaucracy.

At the heart of India's contemporary political turmoil is the changing role of political parties and the party system. Jim Manor ably analyzes this complex picture in Chapter Two.

The fact that India's military has been relatively apolitical is a puzzle worthy of serious scholarly attention. Stephen Cohen's interesting essay in Chapter Three unravels this puzzle and in addition analyzes the recent changes in the civilian and political roles of the Indian armed forces.

Because issues of ethnicity and the related topic of center-state relations have played such a significant role in India recently, we solicited two essays on this subject. Jyotirindra Das Gupta's insightful essay addresses generally the problem of accommodating ethnic political demands and specifically Assam's relations with New Delhi. Paul Brass's essay, in turn, addresses the turbulent Punjab issue. He provides a persuasive explanation of why the separatist demands of the Sikhs were successfully dealt with under Nehru, but were not during the tenure of Indira Gandhi.

In the last three essays the focus shifts away from state institutions and toward society. The political economist Pranab Bardhan analyzes the role of the dominant social classes in India's democracy. His provocative essay links what he calls the "heterogeneity" of the dominant proprietary classes to the survival of India's democracy.

The role of the newly politicized social groups in India is analyzed in the last two essays. Francine Frankel's paper deals with the newly emergent "middle" castes and classes in Indian politics. She contrasts the role of these groups in the North with their role in the South. What emerges is an interesting explanation for political turbulence in such states as Bihar. Ghanshyam Shah's essay surveys the political activities of those at the bottom of the social hierarchy, dispelling the widespread belief that India's downtrodden are inactive.

I shall return to the general picture of India's democracy that emerges from these essays in the concluding chapter of the volume.

ONE

Political Leadership in India: Dimensions and Limits

HENRY C. HART

Political leadership has been a perennial concern among evaluators of Indian democracy. It was addressed in 1956 at the first international conference of such evaluators, convened in Berkeley by the late Richard L. Park,[1]
although it was not then a conventional category of political analysis,[2]
and it remains a concern today. Why has the subject of leadership occupied observers of India and why does it recur today with new urgency?
Some assert that India is well-nigh ungovernable, that no system can suf-
fice, and that only superhuman leaders can, for a time, hold the reins.[3] Yet
this is certainly not the premise that guided the 1956 conference, and it is
not supported by fact. India's constitution and her established rules of
power, formal and informal, have been working longer, arguably, than
those of any developing nation.

The leadership problems examined during the 1956 conference differ
from those confronting analysts today. In 1956, toward the end of its first
decade of independence, India had already lost some of its political
giants—Gandhi, Patel, Subhas Chandra Bose, and Ambedkar—but those
who remained far exceeded the top leadership cadre of other new nations—Jawaharlal Nehru, Rajendra Prasad, Abul Kalam Azad, Govind
Ballabh Pant, C. Rajagopalachari, Jayaprakash Narayan, and Vinoba
Bhave. They were men who differed in intellectual outlook and leadership
style and whose followings were complementary rather than common.

[1] Richard L. Park and Irene Tinker, eds. *Leadership and Political Institutions in India*,
Princeton: Princeton University Press, 1959.

[2] As late as 1977, Glenn D. Paige characterized the state of leadership studies in political
science as "Past neglect. Present emergence. Future potential," *The Scientific Study of Political Leadership*, New York: The Free Press, 1977, p. 61. Note also his earlier *Political Leadership: Readings For an Emerging Field*, New York: The Free Press, 1972.

[3] For such a radical view, see a recent letter to the *New York Times* by an Indian professor
of philosophy and political science living in the United States. Anand Mohan, *New York
Times*, 28 November 1984.

Yet, it was remarked by the 1956 conferees, these leaders shared a single vision of the system of rule that must guide the new nation. It was a parliamentary system, its leaders answerable to the people through elections.[4] The entire existing network of power was manned by a "Westernized minority," whose aim was to make over society in its own image, using the state as its main instrument.[5] Those manifestations of leadership operating outside the elective/parliamentary sphere (labeled "nonconventional" by the 1956 conference) could enter that sphere in the roles of "interest groups."[6] The leaders who rejected Western models of society—Shyama Prasad Mookerjee, though dead, had left his Jan Sangh party in place—were increasingly drawn into the orbit of the elective/parliamentary system as opposition parties.

The great unknown, in the perspective of the 1956 conferees, was the response of the people themselves. Would the hundreds of millions, suddenly drawn into politics beyond the horizons of their villages, non-Western in culture, and innocent of English or of any written language, accept the patterns of leadership prepared for them by an elite very different from themselves?[7] To this gigantic challenge the leaders of the 1950s were perceived as bringing two mighty resources: the civil services and the Indian National Congress. Both institutions were in the midst of vast and rapid extensions into the villages, and through them leaders were able to keep in touch with the Indian people, and even to work their will.

In 1986 India recognized in Rajiv Gandhi a true political leader, but he stood alone on the plateau of national eminence and public trust. The legitimacy of his entitlement to lead has been tested and vindicated by the now familiar elective/parliamentary process, but that process had little to do with his emergence. During his first year in office he has grasped firmly the nettles of crisis, but it is not yet apparent how he will cope with less clearly defined chronic problems. We need both historical and theoretical perspective to assess a leadership function and capability that is evidently in transition.

Robert C. Tucker provides a helpful scheme for categorizing the functions of leadership.[8] As a scholar of Soviet politics, he is concerned with

[4] Granville Austin, *The Indian Constitution: Cornerstone of a Nation*. Oxford: Clarendon, 1966. As to panchayat raj, of course, Ambedkar dissented.

[5] Myron Weiner, "Some Hypotheses on the Politics of Modernization in India," in Park and Tinker (n. 1), p. 36.

[6] Ibid., pt. 5.

[7] See the papers of Selig S. Harrison, "Leadership and Language Policy in India," pp. 151–165; Myron Weiner (n. 5), pp. 20–22; and Richard D. Lambert, "Hindu Groups in Indian Politics," pp. 211–224, in Park and Tinker (n. 1).

[8] Robert C. Tucker, *Politics as Leadership*, Columbia: University of Missouri Press, 1981.

more than mere Westminister conventions. Yet, we must stretch his list to contain the Indian experience.[9] This done, we can order the tasks of Indian leadership under three headings: 1. maintaining political and administrative institutions; 2. diagnosing problems and formulating policy responses; and 3. integrating the nation as a political community. In a democracy, as opposed to a totalitarian or authoritarian system, access to leadership is as well structured and open to scrutiny as are the tasks to be performed, and the ways in which leadership is gained throw light on how leaders perform their functions. The path taken to leadership in some part determines the power held by the leader, the legitimacy of his leadership, and, to some extent, support for his policies. It provides, also, a test of whether established routes to the top tend to select and prepare men and women who can carry the leadership load. Two added categories with which to assess the Indian experience are, thus, 4. winning mandates; and 5. pathways to power. Using these five categories, our task is to scan thirty-six years of Indian political experience to determine the characteristics of leadership in India's democracy.

Maintaining Political and Administrative Institutions

The Indian republic was born with governing institutions fully grown, institutions remarkable for their strength and, even more, for their deep roots in Indian society. The Indian National Congress and its rival parties comprise the most remarkable of these. As to administrative institutions, Paul Appleby, a senior American practitioner and teacher of administration, rated them in 1953 as among the world's best.[10] Although a foreign observer might be judged a bit generous, the process of constitution making, which proceeded right through the trauma of partition, provided unassailable evidence that the political leaders maintained full confidence in the very apparatus that had recently been locking them in jail. They retained intact the tools by which the great subcontinent could initially be governed.

Changes in Indian society and in the tasks imposed on the administrative institutions, however, soon began to undermine the basis of that con-

[9] Tucker's categories are: "diagnosing the situation authoritatively, devising a course of action designed to resolve . . . the problem, and mobilizing the political community's support for the leaders' definition and their prescribed policy response," ibid., p. 31. His first and second categories are collapsed in our second; his third category is elaborated in our third and fourth.

[10] Paul Appleby, *Public Administration in India: Report of a Survey*, New Delhi: Government of India, 1953.

fidence. The state, guided by Nehru's socialist vision, took on itself the responsibility for transforming the economy. Even more ambitious, it sought to deliver new services—education, public health, sophisticated agricultural technology, cooperative marketing—to half a million villages. The very structure of power in these isolated communities was to be remade by reforms of land tenure and credit. These heavy new burdens overstressed the old imperialist bureaucracy. Nehru intervened episodically in program implementation, but his principal structural change was to counterpose to the lower reaches of the bureaucracy several tiers of elected councils, panchayat raj. The effect was both democratizing and divisive, and stresses on field administration increased. According to Nehru's sympathetic biographer, "The failure to dismantle the civil services and to replace them with a new machinery of administration suited to the objectives of free India set up unnecessary hurdles."[11]

Police Reforms: Aborted

We can observe a further cycle of the breakdown by examining the key state institution of the police, by noting how the needs of leaders have added to the burden of an admittedly obsolete machinery, and by understanding what the obstacles to reform have been. The Indian government has, with characteristic candor, detailed the shortcomings of the police system in its report of the National Police Commission.[12]

The commission was convened just after Indira Gandhi's Emergency was lifted. Police abuses of power were among the deep grievances that had animated voters to reject her continued control. The commission found, however, that several sources of stress on the encrusted police apparatus would not disappear with the end of Emergency rule. The opening of higher education, for example, in the context of capital-intensive industrialization providing few jobs, had created career dead ends for many young people. In only seven years, 1972 to 1979, the number of educated unemployed doubled, from 3.2 million to 6.9 million. The number of "public order" incidents recorded by the police as arising from student unrest grew apace during a corresponding period, from 3,861 in 1970 to 7,520 seven years later.[13]

Likewise, the nation's principal efforts toward righting injustices and

[11] Sarvepalli Gopal, *Jawaharlal Nehru: A Biography*, Cambridge: Harvard University Press, 1984, vol. 3, p. 282; see also p. 300.

[12] Indian National Police Commission (hereafter N. P. C.), *First Report*, New Delhi: Government of India, 1979. This was followed by seven additional reports from 1979 through 1981 and by the *Compendium of Observations and Recommendations*, 1981.

[13] N. P. C., *First Report*, 1979, p. 10.

opening opportunity in the countryside aroused violent responses. Untouchables slowly awakened to their new legal rights: annual prosecutions under the Untouchability (Offenses) Act rose from an average of fewer than 500 per year in the 1950s, when the law was passed, to over 3,000 per year in the 1970s. Backlash took bloody forms. Atrocities against Untouchables rose from 5,968 in 1976 to 14,571 in 1978. In these clashes the police characteristically did the will of powerful landholders in the villages, not of the national leaders who had championed the new charters of rights. The commission was forthright on this point: "The poor who seek police help are rebuffed by the influence of village power on the police." So it was, too, with the long series of programs to redistribute power in land.[14]

The stresses were largely qualitative, government responses were wholly quantitative. State police forces were expanded. Central forces swelled even more; by the mid-1970s these latter numbered 800,000 men, three-quarters the size of the Indian army.[15] Chances of promotion for constables, nine-tenths of the state forces, were almost nil. Sixty-two percent were still at the bottom rank when they retired, 28 percent advanced to head constable, only 10 percent moved up even to assistant sub-inspector.[16] Alienated from their officers, aggrieved over low pay and status, the constabulary, defying the prohibition of law and regulations, began to form unions. Total collapse of control from the top was signaled in 1973 by the notorious episode in Uttar Pradesh, when the Indian army had to be called in to disarm and relieve the Provincial Armed Constabulary (PAC), which had joined the student demonstrators it had been sent to quell. Discontent over pay was part of the problem, so was perceived weakness on the part of politicians in charge. Stephen Cohen has pointed out that this was only the second instance since 1857 of military or police rebellion in India.[17]

Any assessment of Indian democracy must take into account the interaction of the steady decomposition of the chain of command in the agencies of government with the progressive intervention of elected politicians in bureaucratic affairs. Even as compared with representatives in other mass democracies, Indian legislators have been occupied more with servicing their constituents than with struggling over policy decisions. As one

[14] N. P. C., *Third Report*, 1980, pp. 2–7.
[15] *Economic and Political Weekly* (Bombay), 1 June 1974, pp. 846–847. See also, on police expenditures, a report of the Public Accounts Committee cited in the *New York Times*, 24 October 1974.
[16] N. P. C., *Seventh Report*, 1981, p. 10.
[17] Stephen P. Cohen, "The Military," in *Indira Gandhi's India*, edited by Henry C. Hart, Boulder: Westview, 1976, pp. 224–225.

scholar of Indian administration reported, "Most party leaders strove for positions as ministers not so they could provide executive leadership for agencies, but so that they would be in strong positions to penetrate those agencies' lower ranks on behalf of their constituencies."[18] Such politicians found field administrators and constabulary prepared to make deals with incumbent politicians to protect and advance their careers. As parties or factions within parties altered in office, such alignments produced divided field forces.

Politicians had a powerful weapon with which to enforce their will upon officers of all ranks: summary transfers of station. Over four years in the mid-1970s, the National Police Commission found that transfers for other than normal administrative reasons created average tenures of twenty months for inspectors general (top state police officers), nineteen months for district superintendents, and fourteen months for sub-inspectors. Over half of all constables had been transferred within a year in Uttar Pradesh, 43 percent, in Delhi.[19] Politicians needed to control the police to protect bootleggers, black marketeers, local toughs, and other lawless elements in their vote-delivery apparatuses, to blunt the effect of redistributive laws upon their powerful local supporters, and to suppress agitations by opposition parties or movements. On occasion, the substitution of party control of the police for the rule of law became a matter of high policy. In March 1967, the Communist party (Marxist) government of West Bengal ordered that the police must first get orders from the labor ministers of their government before arresting for trespass employees who were *gheraoing*, or sitting in, in the offices of factory managers.[20] This was a rare exception to the tendency of political intervention to serve particularistic motives. The nationwide situation was summarized by David Bayley in a letter to the commission: "Police officers throughout India have grown accustomed to calculating the likely political effect of any enforcement action they contemplate. . . . Altogether, then, the rule of law in modern India, the frame upon which justice hangs, has been undermined by the rule of politics."[21] Quite logically, such interventions have subverted the chain of command. "Subordinate officers see . . . that their superior officers count for very little . . . ," observed the police commission.[22]

West Bengal provides a recent example. The state deputy commissioner of police was killed when a party of constables he commanded were afraid

[18] Stanley J. Heginbotham, "The Civil Service and the Emergency," in Hart (n. 17), p. 79.
[19] N. P. C., *Second Report*, 1979, p. 24.
[20] Ibid., p. 25.
[21] Ibid.
[22] N. P. C., *Eighth Report*, 1981, p. 5.

to follow him into a hostile neighborhood to arrest a fugitive. His accused killer was then beaten to death by the constables in the nearest police station. The government hesitated to bring action against either group of offending constables, *India Today* reported, "because of fear of the Non-Gazetted Police Karmachari Samiti (Worker's Association), 42,000 strong throughout the state."[23]

Why Political Leaders Have Not Acted

The diagnosis and prescription for police reform run remarkably parallel to the findings of an earlier commission on the civil services in general.[24] The Administrative Reforms Commission found need for "radical change." Among its many recommendations, however, only the most easily implemented were put into effect. Deeper restructuring to open competition for topmost policy-recommending posts, to end invidious differences among career lines of generalists and more specialized professionals, and to fix responsibility for performance and appropriately to reward or penalize it was never accomplished. Ten years after the Administrative Reforms Commission report, the man who had directed the Indian Institute of Public Administration still found a "crisis" in India's administrative institutions.[25] What had happened, of course, was that new stresses on institutions had overtaken halting changes in them.

Why have top political leaders not instituted reforms so insistently and authoritatively pressed? Are these matters beneath their levels of concern? Perhaps, but a closer look suggests that decomposition of the institutions of government threatens leadership from four directions.

1. Corruption of office-holding has become an industry in many sectors of government. The turning point is reached when middle-level executives pay large sums for the purchase of office. They then count on the systematic taking of bribes by those at the bottom and on an orderly division of the spoils. The National Police Commission found just such an industry of corruption in the police; Robert Wade has found it in delivery of water from irrigation canals; and these are certainly not the most vulnerable sectors.[26] Government forces so tainted will obviously not effectuate any program that will redistribute benefits from those who pay, and they cannot

[23] *India Today*, 15 May 1984, pp. 38–39.
[24] India Administrative Reforms Commission (hereafter A. R. C.), The *A. R. C. and Its Work, A Brief Survey*, New Delhi: Government of India, 1970.
[25] J. N. Khosla, *Crisis in India's Development and Administration* (Hanumanthaiah Lectures, 1977), Bangalore: Bangalore University, 1979.
[26] N. P. C., *Third Report*, 1980, p. 28.

be expected to enforce equal justice. "When you want to use an arm of the state," Arun Shourie writes, "the arm is limp."[27]

2. Police forces, armed with coercive powers and operating as a law unto themselves, inflict upon weaker members of society abuses so heinous that they represent political liabilities to some leaders, even though others appear callous to the ugliest of official crimes. Jagannath Mishra, chief minister of Bihar, strove mightily to cover up the involvement of most of his police establishment in the blinding of thirty-one, perhaps thirty-four, supposed bandits who had fallen into the hands of the police. The victims' eyes were punctured with the coarse needles used to sew up gunny bags, then filled with acid. Indira Gandhi, who discovered the atrocity through photographs in the *Indian Express*, was, she said later, physically sick. She could not believe that such things could happen in India. She telephoned Mishra. "She was so upset," the chief minister told Arun Shourie of the *Express*, "she talked to me for fifteen minutes." But it was only a series of coincidences, involving whistle-blowing by a handful of principled jail and police officers, and dogged perseverence by the *Express*, that uncovered the official guilt.[28] Lest anyone conclude that such abuses are a monopoly of one backward state, consider the record in Tamil Nadu. *India Today* reports the recent record of brutality there toward suspects not yet produced for trial. "Once every ten days for five years, on the average, an under-trial has died in agony. . . ."[29]

3. Where communal violence tears at the fabric of the nation, leaders find those groups assigned to protect that fabric acting, or perceived to be acting, as partisans in the struggle. State police forces are almost everywhere losing their legitimacy as guardians of national unity. K. F. Rustamji, after a distinguished career as a police administrator and member of the National Police Commission, recently lamented: "I have watched with dismay during the year 1982 the conversion of the U.P. PAC [Provincial Armed Constabulary] from the model force I worked with in the fifties to a unit which is feted by the Hindus and hated by the Muslims."[30] How immediately this sort of partisanship may weaken the prime minister's leadership was shown in 1985 in the assassination of the respected Sikh leader with whom Rajiv Gandhi had just signed a settlement of Sikh grievances in the Punjab. Harchand Singh Longowal's police guard was under the command of an officer, who, although suspected by the state

---

[27] Arun Shourie, *Mrs. Gandhi's Second Reign*, New Delhi: Vikas, 1983, p. 46.

[28] Ibid., pp. 322–375.

[29] *India Today*, 30 September 1982, p. 46.

[30] K. M. Rustamji, "New Wave of Violence," *Seminar*, no. 281 (January 1983), pp. 46–47. For a case in point, see "Meerut Riots: A Crisis in Faith," *India Today*, 31 October 1982, pp. 46–51.

government of complicity with the terrorists, was yet left in charge and was absent from his post when the gunmen struck.[31]

4. Leaders of nations need information beyond their personal experiences and contacts in order to identify problems and to determine whether effect is being given to the solutions they have devised. Tucker calls the process of obtaining this information "signalizing." Bureaucracies are meant to do it, but they tend, characteristically, to distort information flows when truth makes them look bad or if the leader penalizes deliverers of bad news.[32] Blockages of both kinds vitiated the final thrust of Mrs. Gandhi's Emergency. It is arguable that they cost her her office in 1977, for it is logical to assume that she would not have called the 1977 election had she not received utterly erroneous intelligence predicting her victory at the polls. More basically, she would probably not have acquiesced in her son Sanjay's bullying tactics to compel sterilizations all across North India had she been informed of the bitterness of public reaction to that campaign.

There is evidence that top leaders have, on occasion, perceived the weaknesses of their instruments of rule and have intervened. Mrs. Gandhi sought change twice: once in the Congress party when, while her father was still prime minister, she assumed the party presidency, and again in the bureaucracy, as she tackled the problems of eliminating poverty in the early 1970s. She was diverted from the first effort by a combination of a crisis in the state of Kerala and by illness.[33] The second reform she pursued vigorously, for it was evident that an "irresponsible" bureaucracy would not implement her redistributive programs. She demanded "committed administration," and pursued it by threatening, even prematurely retiring, a handful of officers close to the top.[34] Pressure from the top was only effective, however, to the extent that blame could be fixed, and the structure was resistant to that. Emergency rule further stifled information flows upward. The intervention ended by weakening, not reforming, administrative structures.

Reform has been frustrated simply because it is much more difficult to effect than is usually supposed. Let us first be clear as to what is needed. A commentator on the difficulties of leadership in the United Kingdom

[31] *India Today*, 30 September 1985. See also *New York Times*, 1 September 1985.

[32] Tucker (n. 8), pp. 31–35.

[33] H. C. Hart, "Indira Gandhi: Determined Not to Be Hurt," in Hart (n. 17), p. 258.

[34] C. P. Bhambri, *Bureaucracy and Politics in India*, Delhi: Vikas, 1971, p. 62. Twelve officers each in the Indian Administrative Service and Indian Police Service were dismissed in the first year of the Emergency. *Data India*, New Delhi: Press Institute of India, 1976, p. 436. Of course, the ultimate effect was to dismiss hundreds at lower levels.

writes that policy innovation ". . . requires more than pushing buttons; it requires both knowledge and constant maintenance of the wiring itself."[35] The electrical metaphor is apt; certainly in India the circuits are often blocked or shorted out, and energy does not flow. But the need in India is not for maintenance of existing circuits; it is for rewiring. So far as the bureaucracy is concerned, design defects stand in the way of capturing and transmitting the new energies of an increasingly participative society. It would be easy, here, to mistake the trouble. Indian civil services, schools, universities, and courts are conventionally criticized, even condemned, as vestiges, transplants, of British rule. This would not, however, render them unusually difficult to transform. The stability, but now also the invulnerability to structural change, of these institutions derives, it seems to me, from the resonance that colonial institutions evoked from some of the enduring structures of Indian society. Some such explanations were entertained during the deliberations occasioned by the Administrative Reforms Commission twenty years ago. "We still seem to rely a great deal on human docility," said a study team. "Social distance" prevails over "team spirit."[36] The cadre system, the criterion of admission to which is an academic examination taken "5 or 25 years ago," fixing the course of an individual's entire working life, "is very much a reflection of our caste and hierarchy ridden society." So are vast differentials in compensation and promotion prospects between classes of staff.[37] To the extent that they are rooted in old and pervasive societal norms, such features of governing institutions must certainly provide stubborn resistance to "rewiring."

There is no reason to think the cause hopeless, however. One has to reassess the difficulty of reform and the duration of the problem. It is comparable to the continuing efforts of British reformers to free their civil service from class distinctions and of American reformers to get rid of spoils. One such fundamental reform was accomplished in India with the thoroughgoing restructuring of the Indian National Congress in 1920, when Gandhi assumed leadership. It is unlikely that such an opening will recur, that even informed and patient leadership can match what such a man at such a moment accomplished at a stroke.

[35] Dennis Kavanagh, "Party Politics in Question," in *New Trends in British Politics: Issues for Research*, edited by D. K. and R. Rose, London: Sage, 1977, pp. 191–220. On the United States, see Richard E. Neustadt, *Presidential Power: The Politics of Leadership from F.D.R. to Carter*, New York: John Wiley, 1980.

[36] India, A. R. C., *Report of a Study Team on Promotion Policies, Conduct Rules, Discipline and Morale*, New Delhi: Government of India, 1967, pp. 202–203.

[37] Conference on Personnel Administration, *Personnel Administration: The Need for Change*, New Delhi: Indian Institute of Public Administration, 1968, p. 18.

Diagnosing Problems and Formulating Policy Responses

A leader, Tucker tells us, diagnoses a problem authoritatively and lays out a course of action for the nation. How well have India's leaders discharged this responsibility? In what ways have they succeeded, in what ways failed? The clearest answers come from the examination of cases of high policy critical to the nation. Two examples, taken from a series of annual reviews of the state of Indian politics from 1962 to 1983[38] can be used to test the effectiveness of the steering function under stress. Both cases represent flawed diagnoses, leading to courses of action that failed to reach the announced goals. Although it would have been possible to select more successful cases, or more thoroughly failed ones, shortcomings in these situations defined by India's leaders as crucial to the nation may well suggest *system* limitations.

The first case deals with foreign affairs and shows the leadership of Jawaharlal Nehru, well along in his prime ministership. The second is concerned with an overarching domestic problem faced by Nehru's daughter, Indira Gandhi. Although the steering errors revealed had rather different consequences, the causes of errors partly correspond.

Nehru's China War

Leaders never make policy on a clean slate; their decisions come tangled in the history of previous actions. But the results of even the most intricate and incremental policy have a way of standing evident at one time and place. Such a time and place was 19 September 1962, beneath Thagla Ridge on India's northeastern frontier with China. The Indian brigade commander there received an order to seize a position on the 14,000-foot ridge that very day. He estimated that the Chinese occupying it equaled his men in number and vastly outgunned them. Chinese reinforcements were three hours away, his were five days. The Indian commander flatly refused the order, his division commander supported the refusal.[39] Unfortunately for India's military performance, further rash orders in the 1962 war could not be disobeyed.

Nehru's stewardship of the national interest in the Himalayan border is generally faulted; a detailed reexamination of the record that has become available does not alter that assessment. India inherited from the British

---

[38] These are published annually in *Asian Survey*, usually in the February issue.

[39] For events in the battle for Thagla Ridge, I have relied primarily on the testimony of the Indian officer in charge, J. P. Dalvi, *Himalayan Blunder*, Bombay: Thacker, 1969. This can be cross-checked with Neville Maxwell, *India's China War*, London: Jonathan Cape, 1970, and D. R. Mankekar, *The Guilty Men of 1962*, Bombay: Tulsi Shah, 1968.

empire Himalayan boundaries unmarked on the bleak landscape and never formally accepted by China. Tibet, which the British could prudently regard as a buffer zone, was occupied by the People's Army in 1950. India recognized the occupation in a 1954 treaty with China, but without settling the disputed border. What Nehru got in return was Chinese subscription to Panch Shila, his five abstract principles of peaceful coexistence.[40] For five years China consolidated control of Tibet without any public issue being raised in India. But in 1959 the flight of the Dalai Lama into India captured public sympathy and focused attention on the ruthlessness of the Chinese occupation. Nehru forthrightly welcomed the fugitive, and in the new public attentiveness, had to disclose that the Chinese had already built a road right across the most significant piece of disputed territory, the Aksai Chin plateau in the northwest. The fraternal pretense (*"Hindi-Chini bhai, bhai"*) was dead. Sporadic outpost clashes followed in 1959; in one of them an Indian patrol, daring to traverse disputed terrain near Aksai Chin, was captured by the Chinese and nine of its members killed.[41]

The border issue could no longer be finessed. Either India would have to negotiate a compromise settlement or prepare for a trial of military strength. A chance came for diplomacy early in 1960 when Chou En-lai, on a visit to New Delhi, made it evident that China would accept India's version of the northeastern Himalayan boundary provided India relinquish claim to the Aksai Chin, which China apparently needed as a supply route into Tibet. But in 1960 the settlement, which would have been perfectly acceptable had Nehru negotiated it in 1950 or 1954, lay outside Indian public tolerance. The Chinese were perceived as aggressors, Indian blood had been shed, national honor was at stake. Willy-nilly, Nehru had to reject Chou's overture.[42]

Meantime, Nehru's top officers specified that defense of the border required more men, mountain equipment (even woolen uniforms were lacking, let alone mule-drawn artillery), and retraining of troops who so far had been prepared to face Pakistan on the plains. To honor these requests would have required a shift in the planned use of the nation's resources

[40] Dorothy Woodman, *Himalayan Frontiers: A Political Review of British, Chinese, Indian and Russian Rivalries*, London: Barrie and Rockliff, 1969, pp. 224–225. The Dutch diplomat W. F. van Eekelen concluded, "It seems almost incredible that in 1954 India gave up her treaty rights in Tibet without trying to obtain Chinese endorsement of the McMahon Line." *Indian Foreign Policy and the Border Dispute with China*, The Hague: Martinus Nijhoff, 1964, p. 193.

[41] John Rowland, *A History of Sino-Indian Relations*, Princeton: D. Van Nostrand, 1967, p. 129.

[42] Maxwell (n. 39), pp. 150–170.

from economic growth to defense; in the main, Nehru turned them down. What he did instead was to order a "forward policy" of occupying or patrolling up to India's claim line, but without the military means to withstand a Chinese challenge.[43] It was a policy he maintained up to the day of Thagla Ridge. By the fall of 1962 the Chinese were thoroughly prepared in Tibet, and they struck with devastating might.

The consequences for India were heavy. Two thousand men were lost at Thagla Ridge when the Chinese poured down; 6,765 casualties followed. India sustained its greatest humiliation since it had appeared on the world scene. Nehru's leadership was challenged within his own party when the executive committee of the Congress party in Parliament flatly rejected his insistence on keeping his failed defense minister, V. K. Krishna Menon. Nehru had to yield. The personal blow to him must have been painful. Characteristically, he was honest enough to admit it: "We are getting out of touch . . . we are living in a world of our own creation, and we have been shaken out of it."[44]

As it turned out, India was saved the worst possible consequence of defeat by the Chinese decision to withdraw her troops, once they had routed Indian border defenses, to the Tibetan boundary she had proposed in 1960. That remains, de facto, the boundary today, with no settled part of India occupied.[45] The Indian policy failure is all the clearer, however, as no doubt some Chinese strategists intended, for, humiliated militarily, India had to accept boundaries she could evidently have gained by treaty two years before. The leader, quite clearly, had lost his function of guiding his people's reaction to events.

We can find in the boundary conflict a few tentative generalizations about leadership in the Indian context:

1. Diagnosis and prescription may address a situation that exists only as conceived by a top leader, however belied by events. In Nehru's case there were two such concepts. One was of India and China, the awakening giants of Asia, shaking off the bonds of Western capitalist domination and moving side by side in the quest for a better life for their impoverished millions. Nehru had written as a young man from prison that, "the future of which I dream is inextricably interwoven with close friendship and some-

[43] Mankekar (n. 39), p. 39. The tactful reference to this Nehru-Menon policy in the published part of the official commission inquiry report reads: "[P]olicy guidance . . . must bear a reasonable relation to the size of the army and the state of its equipment." Statement of the Defense Minister in Parliament, 2 September 1963, published in G. S. Bhargava, *The Battle of NEFA*, New Delhi: Allied, 1964, Appendix 2, p. 178.

[44] *Times* (London), 26 October 1962.

[45] India continues to assert her pre-1962 claim.

thing almost approaching union with China."[46] Even after patrols had exchanged fire in 1959, Nehru clung to a vestige of the dream. He premised his "forward policy" on the assumption that, whatever her military advantage, China would not make war.

Nehru's second concept was of India as the leader of many nonaligned nations, which, though militarily weak, were strong in the moral claims of their vast populations and would serve as peacemakers between the nuclear superpowers. He was ready, therefore, to trade Indian recognition of the Chinese occupation of Tibet for Chinese endorsement of the peace-making tenets of *Panch Shila*. The shattering of these dreams must have seemed doubly cruel to Nehru. The nonaligned nations did not, with a few exceptions, rally to India's support in 1962–1963, when Nehru charged China with aggression. Worse, in the extremity of the military debacle, Nehru felt constrained to call on the superpowers for arms. He appealed to both Russia and the West, but only the United States responded in a substantial way.

2. Unreal premises might be revised in time to prevent miscarriage of policy prescriptions if leaders have continually to face powerful challenges by coleaders possessed of independent minds. While he lived, Vallabhbhai Patel was such a critic for Nehru. In 1950 he wrote the prime minister that, ". . . even though we regard ourselves as friends of China, the Chinese do not regard us as their friends. . . . Chinese irredentism and communist imperialism has a cloak of ideology which makes it ten times more damaging."[47] That was Patel's last year. Nehru's advice, when he took the final rash decisions of 1960 to 1962, was coming from the intellectually congenial V. K. Krishna Menon and from B. M. Kaul, a politically ambitious general.[48]

3. Public demands upon policy, once evoked by the illusory premises of a leader, may in a later phase of decision making lock him into disagreeable options. Public revulsion at the events of 1959 must have been intensified by the previous image of *Hindi-Chini bhai, bhai*. The problem of the Himalayan boundary, which might once have been approached as a bilateral search for clarification of historical and geographic ambiguity had, by the time the decision was faced, turned into what Nehru had ruefully to admit "now became homeland, testing national honor and the worth of soldier's lives."[49]

[46] Woodman (n. 40), p. 302.
[47] Published by Dalvi (n. 39), pp. 490–491.
[48] Cohen (n. 17), pp. 218, 221. Kaul published his version in *The Untold Story*, New Delhi: Allied, 1967.
[49] In the Lok Sabha, 4 September 1959. Quoted by Maxwell (n. 39), frontispiece.

Garibi Hatao

Early in 1971, Indira Gandhi, who had been elevated to the prime ministership by party managers unable to choose among "stronger" contenders, called a special parliamentary election. With her simple appeal of
Garibi Hatao (Out with Poverty), she drew a line all could understand.[50]
The opposition alliance, pieced together from rightist opposition parties
and from the rump of the Congress party left behind by Mrs. Gandhi's
leftward split, squarely joined the contest. Mrs. Gandhi's overwhelming
victory gave a clear mandate to her new government. Reinforced by India's victorious war against Pakistan later in the year, she probably held
as much power as had ever been in her father's hands. Her use of that
power toward her announced goal of eradicating poverty poses, therefore,
a second searching test of the policy-forming capability of political leadership in India.

There can be no faulting the diagnosis of poverty as an urgent problem
of the Indian polity. At least 40 percent, or even half, of Indian families
were judged to have insufficient food.[51] For twenty years Indian government planning had been aimed at improving per capita income and, even
intermittently, at rapidly raising the level of the poorest. To many people,
results must have seemed overdue.

At the close of the sixties, there were worrisome signals that the poorest
sensed their deprivation. Capital-intensive industrial development had
created well-paid jobs in large factories, but these were very few. The new
strategy of concentrating agricultural development in resource-rich (well-
irrigated) districts may also have given ammunition to organizers of protest, including violent protest, among the landless poor in marginal and
tribal areas. In 1969 the home ministry diagnosed the nondelivery of
promised services and reforms, especially the failure of land redistribution, as an underlying cause not only of a rash of "land grab" movements,
but also of the violent Maoist *Naxalbari* uprisings.[52] We must acknowledge that a strong current in contemporary social science (in these years
American ghetto uprisings were being authoritatively diagnosed as due to

---

[50] For the facts in this section, I have relied primarily on Francine R. Frankel, *India's Political Economy, 1947–1977: The Gradual Revolution*, Princeton: Princeton University
Press, 1978, pp. 434ff.

[51] B. S. Minhas, "Mass Poverty and Strategy of Rural Development in India," Economic
Development Institute, International Bank for Reconstruction and Development, 1971 (mi-
meographed). V. M. Dandekar and Nilakantha Rath, "Poverty in India," *Economic and Political Weekly*, February 1973, pp. 245–254.

[52] India, Home Ministry, Research and Policy Division, "The Causes and Nature of Current Agrarian Tensions," New Delhi, 1969 (unpublished).

"relative deprivation") warned that the Green Revolution would turn into red revolution if India did not radically improve redistributive measures.[53]

Once her power was secure, Mrs. Gandhi addressed the issue of poverty, first, by the familiar, but intensified, targeting of public sector programs toward the poor. These soon ran into limits upon the government's capacity to deliver. Food grain distribution to "vulnerable sections of the community" was stopped far short of its goals by failures to procure enough grain from farmers. An innovative "Crash Scheme for Rural Employment" began producing good results but would have required six times the funds allotted to complete the programs.[54] A progressive tax on agriculture had been officially recommended to raise revenues of this magnitude, but it ran directly counter to the political support of the Congress in the states.[55] Lack of financial resources also thwarted an innovative policy proposal of C. Subramanium, then Mrs. Gandhi's representative on the Planning Commission. His parallel system of agricultural credit for tenants and marginal farmers, secured by crops, rather than lands, might have encouraged these hard-pressed farmers to adopt some of the new productive practices.

An acid test of *Garibi Hatao* was the redistribution of farmland held in excess of prescribed ceilings to tillers of substandard holdings.[56] Under Mrs. Gandhi's prodding, the Congress party set up the Central Land Reforms Committee; the idea was to commit Congress leaders in the states, where they had blocked previous efforts. After a struggle, the committee adopted a tough ceiling, twenty-seven acres for a family of five on land irrigated for a single crop. Where chief ministers who derived their power from large classes of land-owning cultivators dragged their feet, Mrs. Gandhi undermined them politically. But actual transfers were even more miniscule than before: 25,000 hectares nationwide from 1972 to 1975.

The immediate reasons for failure were plain enough, bogus deeds to relatives or dependents, corruption of village recordkeepers, and unending lawsuits. That these ploys worked, ingenious though they sometimes were, revealed a deeper weakness. The Congress party had adopted a policy its field leaders had no intention of honoring; Mrs. Gandhi had tried

[53] Francine Frankel, *India's Green Revolution: Economic Gains and Political Costs*, Princeton: Princeton University Press, 1971. This interpretation was challenged by Donald Zagoria, "The Ecology of Peasant Communism in India," *American Political Science Review* 65 (March 1971), pp. 145–149.

[54] Frankel (n. 50), pp. 508–509.

[55] India, Ministry of Finance, *Report of the Committee on Taxation of Agricultural Wealth and Income*, New Delhi, 1972.

[56] An exhaustive and comparative assessment is in Ronald J. Herring, *Land to the Tiller: The Political Economy of Agrarian Reform in South Asia*, New Haven: Yale University Press, 1983, pp. 135–138.

but failed to substitute her will for a fabric of joint decision and shared commitment. The formal power of the courts to defend property rights against legislated redistribution might be cut away at the top by constitutional amendment piled on amendment, but the small-town courts would still halt the redistribution for months or years to hear the landlord. Late in 1975 there were 800,000 cases pending, more than the number of acres scheduled for redistribution.[57] India's villages remained semiautonomous structures of power, economic power fused with political and social. Upsetting these structures in a quarter of a million villages would have required a talented staff, backed politically and motivated for the long term by career rewards. To set forth the specifications is to remind ourselves how far India was from being equipped in the 1970s for redistribution of resources to the poor.[58]

Two situations confronting Mrs. Gandhi had an indirect bearing on her attack upon poverty. One she diagnosed accurately and addressed successfully, though it was of no help to her politically. The other she neglected, and it contributed to her loss of office. The first was the Green Revolution, effected by a bundle of new agricultural practices centered on high yielding grain varieties grown under chemical fertilization and irrigation. Jawaharlal Nehru was not interested in modernizing Indian farm technology. Mrs. Gandhi saw it as a way of meeting the nation's food needs on fixed farm acreage. She accepted the findings of the plant breeders in India and abroad and the policy recommendations of her agriculture minister, now C. Subramanium, including the licensing in the private sector of large fertilizer plants using foreign technology. Twenty years later, the policy had made a much enlarged Indian population self-sufficient in food, even in a failed monsoon. "What has happened in India is a tribute to the policies of Indira Gandhi," said Maurice Williams, executive director of the United Nations World Food Council at the close of 1984.[59] By then, of course, Mrs. Gandhi had been assassinated. Her slow-maturing policy had apparently, by 1985, permitted the first reduction in the percentage of Indians too poor to eat enough. But no one sensed that success during her 1971 term of office; indeed, two years of scant rainfall in 1972–1973 and 1973–1974 raised grain prices 13 and 29 percent, respectively.[60] It was the immediate privation, not the invisible solution, that was credited to Mrs. Gandhi politically.

[57] *Economic Times* (Bombay), 26 December 1975.

[58] Susanne Hoeber Rudolph, "The Writ from Delhi: The Indian Government's Capabilities after the 1971 Election," *Asian Survey* 11 (October 1971), p. 961; Ramashray Roy, "India 1972: Fissure in the Fortress," *Asian Survey* 13, no. 2 (February 1972), pp. 239–242; Frankel (n. 50), pp. 502–504.

[59] *New York Times*, 2 December 1984.

[60] Frankel (n. 50), p. 508.

The situation that Mrs. Gandhi neglected and that contributed to her fall from office was the remorseless growth of high school and college graduates unable to find work. Between 1971 when she was re-elected and 1975 when her crisis of support came, the number of educated youths actually registered with the employment exchanges had grown from 1.8 million to 4.1 million. A sample survey showed one out of four urban literate youths unemployed.[61] Facts were available for diagnosis. In 1966 the Education Commission had found the school system virtually useless in preparing youth for scientific agriculture or technical employment, fields in which opportunities existed.[62] The five-year plans had regularly reported entrants into the labor market far outpacing the creation of jobs in the capital-intensive economy being promoted.

It was not the rural poor, whom Mrs. Gandhi had promised but failed to help, who agitated against her in 1974 and 1975. It was the students and the jobless ex-students in Bihar and Gujarat. Price rises for their hostel meals were the triggering grievances, corruption in government the target of their slogans, the frustration of their careers perhaps the underlying cause. The inability to fulfill her 1971 election promise to abolish poverty gave credibility to the charge of opposition leaders, notably Jayaprakash Narayan, that she was interested only in clinging to office.[63] The failure of *Garibi Hatao* made it easy for voters in the special elections of 1975 to turn their grievance over high food costs on Mrs. Gandhi.

Statistically, poverty remained constant in the six years of Mrs. Gandhi's term. To some among the poorest, one or two of the specific measures she pressed during the semidictatorship of the Emergency brought relief. Distribution of government lands to Untouchables, a moratorium on debt repayment, and the outlawing of debt slavery helped some. But there were others, perhaps equal in number across North India, who were coerced into vasectomies by officials intimidated by Mrs. Gandhi's son Sanjay. Some of these humble villagers escaped the sterilization teams only by hiding in the grain fields. And in Delhi it was the poorest, the shanty dwellers, whom the police herded into trucks on Sanjay's orders, to be deposited out of sight across the Jamuna River. To these people, *Garibi Hatao* ("Out with Poverty") had turned into *garib hatao*, "out with the poor."

If *Garibi Hatao* had been only an electoral strategy, it could be said to have succeeded famously. But Mrs. Gandhi said she intended more. "My government has been returned to office on the clear pledge that the central

[61] H. C. Hart, "Explanations," in Hart (n. 17), pp. 282–283.

[62] India, Education Commission, *Report, 1964–66: Education and National Development*, Delhi: Manager of Publications, 1966. See the entire "Minute of Supplementation" for its remarkable foresight.

[63] H. C. Hart, "Introduction," in Hart (n. 17), pp. 5–6, 8–12.

objective of our policy must be the abolition of poverty," she said to the new Parliament through the president's address. The picture of poverty must be altered "swiftly and visibly."[64] A share of the public disillusion that followed must, therefore, be charged to her leadership. On the other hand, she must be credited with pointing the nation's political energies at an overarching problem insoluble in the short run. Americans are, in the 1980s, familiar with the political use of economic illusion.

Reviewing these two cases of diagnosis and policy prescription we see, with Nehru, a clear failure of leadership and, with Indira Gandhi, an ambiguous performance. What are important for us are the characteristics of leadership that, occurring as they do in such very different individuals and situations, appear to be system tendencies.

Most striking is how nearly alone both leaders were, over long periods, in making complex, broadly consequential decisions. Career officers, of course, shaped specifics of diagnoses and programs. Gone is the time when service traditions required civil or military careerists to resign upon receiving indisputably unworkable or unconstitutional orders. Political associates, also, might exercise independent judgment involving no high political stakes for the leader; C. Subramanium did so with the agricultural productivity program. Otherwise, they functioned as subordinates. No senior cabinet or party colleagues challenged either leader's judgment from positions of independent information or as tribunes of India's diverse publics. There was no Sardar. Worse, both leaders, squeezed between intransigent situations and hardening public demands, gave power to persons whose political strength derived wholly from the leaders themselves—to Krishna Menon and Kaul on the one hand, and to Sanjay Gandhi, on the other. These parasitic colleagues reinforced the leaders' weaknesses, isolating each more completely from the nation.

But in India, the isolation comes to a crashing end. The leader faces the voters at last. Diagnosis and prescription in this system become a test of how rightly or wrongly the leader has, startlingly alone, anticipated what the voters will accept. How insignificant the Cabinet and Parliament have become. Even in Nehru's time these formal institutions of collective responsibility seldom hammered out policy under the pressure of conflicting currents of public opinion, but they did call policy to account after the people had felt the weight of its implementation.[65] When, in early 1975, a

[64] President's address to the joint session: India, *Parliamentary Debates, Rajya Sabha, Official Report* (23 March 1971), 75:1, p. 5.

[65] The Congress party in Parliament forcing Nehru to fire V. K. Krishna Menon as defense minister after the Chinese attack is one example. Another is the shelving of the policy of forced public deposits with the government to help pay for that war. See Henry C. Hart, "In-

weak and tentative signal was given to Mrs. Gandhi that such a midcourse correction might be required, she cowed Parliament, as well as other sources of criticism, through the police state. Course correction by subsequent leader displacement proved costly for the nation as well as for Mrs. Gandhi.

We can find another pattern in the unmediated, highly episodic encounter of leader with voters. The expectations by which voters in the end test leader stewardship may be an exaggeration of the leader's own earlier misdiagnosis—China as brother, poverty as "swiftly" eradicable. Indian prime ministers exhibit mighty powers to implant pictures in the heads of citizens; solitary leaders are free to implant pictures unique to themselves. The visions of India's future held by Jawaharlal Nehru and his daughter were not mean visions, only sometimes illusory. One might find a thread of Greek tragedy running through the denouements. One might, alternatively, take a more mundane view: that these admittedly unrepresentative failures of strong leaders signal the decay of a corrective fabric that had earlier begun to be woven in India's working constitution, a fabric of conciliar decision interacting repeatedly with spreading circles of concerned publics.

INTEGRATING THE NATION AS A POLITICAL COMMUNITY

Nation *building* is not a leadership function distinguished by Robert Tucker. Thinking perhaps of the established nations in Europe and America, he could take for granted the existence of political communities available for leadership. In India, of course, this function takes on special weight. India emerged as a nation-state from the condition of being an empire of diverse peoples. The resulting situation was thus characterized by Ashok Mitra, a minister in the Communist government of West Bengal:

> All the while, we talk of the national tradition and of the national heritage. . . . [T]here is . . . the affection for, and allegiance to, a common corpus of classics, of mythology and music, of literature and architecture, and so on. It would, however, be straining credibility to claim that, qualitatively, this commonality of Indian tradition and of our national consciousness is of a deeper genre than what is supposed to be represented by, say, the European tradition. The European tradition is a collage. . . . [O]ur model, which excludes the concept of such sub-sets of sovereign entities, has a unique delicacy. . . . We are grap-

dia after the Chinese Attack," *The Annals of the American Academy of Political and Social Science* 351 (1964), pp. 50–57.

pling with not just the fact of enormous disparities in the levels of awareness as well as in the levels of social and economic development; the linguistic, cultural and religious divides are of acute order, as are the heterogeneities in ethnic stocks and societal attitudes and behaviors.[66]

The Indian political leader has special resources, however, with which to address the challenge of national diversity. India was defined not only territorially at independence, but also morally. Although Gandhi's definition of nationhood failed to capture the newly unleashed political energies of a majority of Indian Muslims, it was, in the entire array of twentieth-century nationalisms, uniquely ecumenical. To be sure, in a nation possessed of neither much weight of habit nor anything like cultural homogeneity, that definition has been perennially questioned.

It is to be expected, then, that cleavages will appear in the fabric of national unity, not, as in the history of the United States, bipolar and episodic cleavages, but chronic and multiplex breaks.[67] It can also be expected that the fabric will be most vulnerable at the edges. Two different subnationalisms challenging two different leaders illustrate the potential for such breaks in the Indian national fabric: the case of the Tamils in the 1960s and of the Sikhs in the current period.

Tamil Subnationalism

Certainly, linguistic identity was, by the mid-sixties, an overwhelming force among the Tamils. It had ridden piggyback upon the earlier demand of the non-Brahman castes to seize their fair share of the opportunities of modernization, opportunities they saw as monopolized by the Brahman cultural imperialists from the north.[68] The fervor of the Tamil grievance is captured by C. N. Annadurai, who mobilized it into a political party, the Dravida Munnetra Kazhagam (DMK): "The Aryans who came in the middle ages polluted the Tamilian culture and resorted to many devices to perpetrate their own glory and their own supremacy, pushing to the background the Tamilian civilization."[69] By the early 1960s, the non-Brahmans had won their fight for education and economic opportunity, led not

[66] Ashok Mitra, "The Center," in *Seminar*, no. 281 (January 1983), p. 41.

[67] An excellent assessment of the problem worldwide can be found in Crawford Young, *The Politics of Cultural Pluralism*, Madison: University of Wisconsin Press, 1976, pp. 13ff.

[68] Robert L. Hardgrave, Jr., "The Riots in Tamil Nadu: Problems and Prospects of India's Language Crisis," *Asian Survey* 8 (August 1965), p. 404.

[69] In his key book *The Aryan Illusion*, quoted by Marguerite R. Barnett, "The Politics of Cultural Nationalism: The D. M. K. in Tamil Nadu, South India," Ph.D. dissertation, University of Chicago, 1972, p. 136.

only by the DMK, but shrewdly, too, by their own Kamaraj within the Congress. Then the door to their highest aspirations seemed suddenly to shut. According to a provision of the original constitution, on 26 January 1965, fifteen years after promulgation of the constitution, Hindi would replace English as the official language of the union. It meant that the work of the central government would progressively shift to Hindi. Most chilling to the students in the mushrooming colleges in the state was the realization that, although they could still compete in the all-India civil service examinations in English, their counterparts in North India could answer the questions in their mother tongue, Hindi. The DMK organized massive protests, but they underestimated the passion of their student followers. Five Tamil students burned themselves to death in protest against the "imposition" of Hindi; in two weeks police firings had killed sixty rioters.

Nehru had promised that Hindi would not be "imposed" in the non-Hindi speaking states against their will; Nehru was dead. The new prime minister, Lal Bahadur Shastri, held no such trust from the non-Hindi states. From apparent weakness in Delhi came responsiveness. In the aftermath of the riots, the Congress Working Committee was persuaded by its strongest state bosses (Kamaraj, Sanjiva Reddy, S. Nijalingappa, and Atulya Ghosh), all from non-Hindi speaking states, that holding to the present policy would cost the party the South. That diagnosis was reinforced when two Tamilians in Shastri's cabinet resigned. But there was, equally plainly, the threat in the North that opposition parties, most notably the Jan Sangh, could capitalize on an outright reversal of course. Negotiation was extended to opposition parties and to the chief ministers of all states. In June the party working committee produced a resolution that proved to be a minimally acceptable compromise. It was hotly debated in the Parliament and eventually became law. Its major component was the three-language formula of mother tongue for primary instruction, state language for secondary school and university instruction, and a third language—English or Hindi, or in the North, a South Indian language—available for high school study. English would continue to be used for communication between the central government and non-Hindi states until the latter should accept Hindi. At the time of its implementation the policy was judged to be "perhaps the most workable, and the one more nearly acceptable to both North and South."[70]

The results have been impressive. Threats of secession, earlier presented formally by the DMK, had so alarmed Nehru's leadership that in the crisis of the Chinese border war the constitution was amended to make advocacy of secession a crime. Now language as a cause vanished utterly from

[70] Hardgrave (n. 50), p. 407.

campaigns in Tamil Nadu. The DMK found more enticing immediate objectives. In the 1967 election they rode their tide of popularity to outright victory in the state elections, Kamaraj himself being unseated by a DMK student who had led the anti-Hindi agitation. For individual Tamilians the ceilings of opportunity were manifestly higher in the union than out, and they could harness the political power inherent in their collective Tamil subnationalism by governing their own state.[71]

Sikh Subnationalism

The substance of the Sikh challenge to Indian nationalism is dealt with in other chapters, but the test it has posed to national leadership is too severe to be ignored here. It is a test more exacting than the Tamil one, for it arises from differences of religion as well as language. Like Dravidian or Tamil subnationalists, Sikhs have entertained the idea of separate nationhood.[72] Sikh separatism has received two specifically political stimuli. A movement of the 1920s to rid Sikh gurdwaras of corrupt priests left behind a gurdwara management committee chosen by the Sikh electorate and a party, open only to Sikhs, to contest these elections. That party, the Akali Dal, has long since entered the general political struggle for control of the Punjab government.[73] Subnationalism has, in addition, been stimulated by the chronic factionalism that is characteristic, perhaps, of religions stressing the brotherhood of believers. A frequent consequence in the Sikh community has been competition among factions for the most militant defense of the religious community. "*Panth* in danger" is the rallying cry.

We need not explain here why Sikh subnationalism crystallized into specific demands for an autonomous theocratic state. Let us assume, in order to appreciate the full challenge to India's leaders, that these demands tended toward Khalistan, a sovereign Sikh state, though it be more chimerical, even, than Dravidistan. All we need acknowledge is that these demands have been compounded in unknown proportions from political and economic grievances and from religious concerns difficult or impossible for a secular state to resolve. Sikh subnationalists have demanded a larger share of interstate irrigation flows, exclusive possession of Chan-

---

[71] The case is interpreted from the perspective of crises in nation-building by Thomas E. Headrick, "Crises and Continuity: India in the Mid-1960s," in *Crisis, Choice and Change, Historical Studies of Political Development*, edited by Gabriel A. Almond, Scott C. Flanagan, and Robert J. Mundt, Boston: Little, Brown, 1972, chap. 9.

[72] Khushwant Singh, *A History of the Sikhs*, Princeton: Princeton University Press, 1966, vol. 2, pp. 3, 303.

[73] Mohinder Singh, *The Akali Movement*, Delhi: Macmillan, 1978, p. 18.

digarh (the state capital shared with Haryana), and relief from the handicaps felt by Sikh farmers who find their markets and banks run by Hindus. Sikh religious concerns have included not only the old "Raj karega Khalsa," but the new fear of Sikh fathers that their educated, urbanized sons may stray from orthodoxy, and the prospect that demographic increases in the Punjab's Hindu population might deprive Sikh institutions of state protection.[74]

National leaders have responded to these tangled, in some respects dangerous, demands in two ways. Indira Gandhi's initial response appears to have been to "divide and rule," a response Arun Bose called "Chanakyan realism."[75] Some commentators believe that Mrs. Gandhi gave unpublicized support to the extremist wing of Sikh leadership in order to weaken the more moderate, but politically competitive, Akali Dal.[76] However that may be, it is difficult to understand how the master terrorist among Sikh militants, Jarnail Singh Bhindranwale, arrested for the murder of a moderate Akali, could be released on bail, publicly violate the terms of his bail, be rearrested in the most provocative public setting—precipitating a riot in which seventeen were killed—and then once more be released on Mrs. Gandhi's order, if he were being treated as a simple threat to the peace. It was only at the end of this bizarre sequence that Bhindranwale converted the Golden Temple into the heavily armed headquarters of his death squads. Whatever the truth of Mrs. Gandhi's support of Sikh extremism, the leadership of Sikh subnationalism was, by October 1983, bitterly divided between violent extremists and Akali leaders interested in political solutions.

There was relief in Punjab when Mrs. Gandhi superseded the helpless state government with president's rule.[77] The momentary security felt among both Sikhs and Hindus created an opening for peacemaking, but the contradictions between a policy responsive to subnationalism and a policy of "Chanakyan realism" quickly surfaced. Mrs. Gandhi's home minister invited the Akali leaders to Delhi for talks without preconditions. Three days later he was castigated in the Cabinet for having "without authorization" omitted the previous proviso that Akali negotiators must first publicly condemn Sikh terrorist tactics. Journalists reporting the abrupt about-face speculated that Mrs. Gandhi was unwilling to jeopardize her much larger Hindu following across North India for a Sikh subnationalism now partly expressed through violence.

[74] Sunil Sethi, "Journey in Punjab," *India Today*, 30 September 1983, p. 102.

[75] "Diversities in Our Politics," *Seminar*, no. 288 (August 1983), p. 19.

[76] Ibid., p. 419; and Balraj Puri, "Understanding Punjab," *Economic and Political Weekly*, 21 July 1984, pp. 1126–1129.

[77] *India Today*, 31 October 1983, p. 15.

Bhindranwale scoffed at the moderate Akalis who had trusted the Delhi government to negotiate and sent his death squads out again. A further opening for negotiation early in February 1984 was disrupted by an outburst of killings by both Sikh and Hindu extremists on the day negotiations started. The political opening for talks, which this time had included members of the national opposition parties with government and Akali leaders, did not recur. Violence and fear escalated,[78] and in June Mrs. Gandhi sent the Indian army into the Golden Temple to rout out Bhindranwale's forces.

Little more than a year later a new prime minister signed with the president of the Akali Dal a settlement of all Akali grievances. How did Rajiv Gandhi, and equally remarkable, Harchand Singh Longowal, resolve the most dangerous threat to the unity of India since independence?

It was not resolved by a cessation of obstructive violence. Sikh extremists had, in the intervening year, killed Prime Minister Indira Gandhi and Hindus had taken bloodthirsty revenge on whole communities of Sikhs in North India. When the new prime minister made overtures to Akali moderates by releasing some of their members, including Longowal, from jail, Sikh terrorists countered by blowing up passengers in Delhi buses with booby-trapped transistor radios. The destruction of an Air India jet over the North Atlantic and the death of all those on board may also have been the work of Sikh terrorists.

Nor were the terms of the settlement particularly new. The concessions made, for example, Chandigarh as the exclusive capital of Punjab, or slight boundary changes intended to put a few more Sikhs in Punjab and Hindus in Haryana, with referral of some of the stickiest questions to commissions of inquiry, had long been under discussion within the government and in the press.

What was new was the determination to negotiate an agreement, whatever the pressures acts of terrorism put on each side. The contrast with Indira Gandhi's stance was dramatic. A Sikh who followed the earlier talks, during which Mrs. Gandhi declined to meet personally with the Akalis, told Pranay Gupte that, "the Akalis and others familiar with the on-again-off-again negotiations suspected that Mrs. Gandhi was being reluctant because she had an ulterior motive. She let the Punjab crisis drag on, they suspected, in order to rally the state's Hindus behind her and in order to unify the Hindu majority of the north Indian states."[79] What had changed was not Chanakyan realism. Rajiv Gandhi proved to be as shrewd and, in

[78] For this account I have relied on the *Indian Express*, New Delhi, from 9 February 1984; and on *India Today*, 15 March and 30 April 1984.

[79] Pranay Gupte, *Vengeance: India after the Assassination of Indira Gandhi*, New York: W. W. Norton, 1985, p. 127.

the service of his objectives, as ruthless as his mother. A few months before he signed the agreement with the Akalis he had campaigned for votes in Hindu constituencies by raising the spectre of Sikh "secessionists." And Longowal, on his side, in a desperate contest with the extremists for leadership of the Akali party, had, a few months before he sat down to negotiate with Rajiv Gandhi, spoken favorably of the Sikhs who shot Rajiv's mother. What had changed, rather, was the target of these manipulative maneuvers, each leader outflanking potential obstructionists in his own camp, not undermining the legitimacy of the other. Steven R. Weisman reported to the *New York Times* from New Delhi that the political leader of Haryana, a Hindu of Mr. Gandhi's party, had not roused passions in his state against the loss of a share of Chandigarh simply because he was under investigation for corruption "and Mr. Gandhi was reportedly not above using these charges for leverage."[80]

Conditions of Nation-Building Leadership

Examined together, the two cases suggest the conditions for leadership toward national unity. Three of the conditions are plain enough. The fourth is a bit obscure and, perhaps, debatable.

1. Civil peace must be secured, at least against the systematic killing of moderates by extremists. This was done in the Tamil country in the sixties; it was not done by a corrupt, demoralized, communally compromised police in Punjab.[81] When the terrorists accomplished their completely predictable assassination of Longowal, peace in the Punjab was saved, at least momentarily, only by the accident that he had already won Akali endorsement of the settlement, and by Rajiv Gandhi's bold decision to proceed with the state election. No nation can count on such long chances.

2. National leaders must be staunch in their desire to solve problems. They must respond to subnational demands as stubborn facts of political life. Such a responsive posture has come from two very different political situations in New Delhi. Twenty years ago in Tamil Nadu, all-India leadership was too tentative, too plural, to take a hard line. Subnationalist sentiment was, moreover, accurately registered within the wide circle of leadership. In 1985, Rajiv Gandhi could, with a fresh election mandate, approach the Punjab from a position of strength, secure against Hindu communal attack.

[80] *New York Times*, 30 July 1985. It is important to keep in mind that these lines were written in early 1986. As the book goes to press in 1987, Punjab's fluid situation has already undergone some important changes.

[81] Shourie (n. 27), pp. 425–426; and Sunil Sethi (n. 74), pp. 102–103.

3. Subnational leaders must, in the end, prefer a place in the Indian system to the chimera of sovereignty, a position they come to partly because their people, in overwhelming majority, can appreciate the opportunities in terms of careers, markets, defense, and technological progress that are available to them as citizens of a great nation. Even the students come to see that. The subnationalist leaders have, in addition, a more tangible lure. Elective power to control their state beckons them as soon as the conflict can be settled. It is no coincidence that the Tamil subnationalist party won control of Tamil Nadu in 1967, and the Akali Dal, of Punjab in 1985. The power available through open elections in a federal system creates a powerful pull.

4. Underlying both conflicts, both settlements, is a final and surprising commonality. Key demands of the subnationalists characteristically contradicted vital principles hitherto deemed by national leaders to be essential to the integrity of the nation. Development of one indigenous language as the eventual common language of the nation was contradicted by the Tamil agitators, India as a secular state by the Sikhs. But far-sighted national leaders understood that what was contradictory in form might, in the human drama of political aspirations, admit of reconciliation. The Tamil and the Sikh lessons go even further, for at certain phases of their histories, each subnationalism called for separate sovereignty: Dravidistan unequivocally, Khalistan ambiguously.

Some of the most discerning intellectual champions of the multicultural integration of India have, in considering the Akali's Anandpur Resolution of 1973, diagnosed the Akali movement as tragically, but inevitably, anticonstitutional.[82] Rajiv Gandhi has not. His resolution of the arguably antinational posture of a subnational group stands as a paradigm for nation-building leaders. The memorandum of settlement he signed with Sant Harchand Singh Longowal specified that "Shiromani Akali Dal states that the Anandpur Sahib Resolution is entirely within the framework of the Indian constitution . . . that the purpose of the Resolution is to provide greater autonomy to the State with a view to strengthen the unity and integrity of the country. . . ."[83] Thus defused by the testimony of the legitimate spokesman for the subnationalists, the supposed bomb represented by the 1973 resolution was deftly passed to the unemotional arena of the Sarkaria Commission, a body already established to examine grievances of various states against central domination. Accommodations can be made by leaders convinced that they need each other to realize the intertwined destinies of their peoples.

[82] Arun Shourie argues the divisive content of official Akali demands in (n. 27), pp. 433ff. Their political meaning is seen as more ambiguous by Pranay Gupte (n. 79), pp. 124–125.

[83] Published in *India News* (Washington), 29 July 1985.

Winning Mandates

All national leaders, including authoritarian ones, need entitlement to their leadership position; they need legitimacy. They also need to be able to persuade citizens, as well as intermediate leaders, to follow the courses of action they lay down. As Tucker says, coercion may produce grudging and minimal compliance; active and creative support of leaders requires intercommunication and some consciousness of shared goals between leaders and citizens.[84] In democracies, elections are the vehicles for both the legitimation of leaders and persuasion of voters. It is not too pretentious to say that India has demonstrated to the world that these connective functions are available to poor, largely illiterate, and highly diverse populations, provided their leaders trust them at the polls. Equally valuable, the Indian experience with elections can tell us what they cannot contribute to leadership.

Designating Leaders

India's eight general elections give ample evidence that they designate leaders in four ways.

1. They settle preeminence upon one among rival claimants to lead. Jawaharlal Nehru and Lal Bahadur Shastri, in quite different ways, came to their positions by choices made in leadership circles.[85] But it is clear in Indira Gandhi's case that, although she became prime minister by elite selection, she did not obtain preeminence, the ability to direct the political community, until some of her powerful rivals had lost election in 1967, and she had won decisively in 1971.

2. They legitimize a leader. Having won an election, the leader is known to lead by right. The function could not be clearer than in the case of Rajiv Gandhi. Prior to December 1984 he was an heir, of questionable qualification and, at worst, a makeshift successor. In a month's feverish action centered on an election to which he chose to submit, he acquired full status as prime minister, party head, spokesman and symbol of the nation. He is empowered at least as fully as was his mother in her final years. If we consider these uses of elections together, we can see characteristic advantages and disadvantages of the electoral route to legitimate leadership. An ad-

[84] Tucker (n. 8), p. 62.

[85] Michael Brecher, *Nehru's Mantel: The Politics of Succession*, New York: Praeger, 1955; and Brecher, "Succession in India: The Routinization of Political Charisma," *Asian Survey* 7 (July 1967), pp. 423–443.

vantage is that elections provide the opportunity for power to men and women otherwise without hope of getting uncontested control. Both Rajiv Gandhi and his mother illustrate this point. A disadvantage is that the ability to win office by election is only weakly connected with whatever other criteria of fitness might, as abstract propositions, be brought forward. One might think of others among the powerful personalities of Indian politics who *at particular times* might have brought more to the office of prime minister—Maulana Azad, Pandit Pant, Kamaraj, Y. B. Chavan—but each carried severe handicaps as national election candidates. Each had, moreover, to contend with incumbents whose overwhelming popularity had already been established by election. Elections test and confirm choices of leaders that have initially to be made by ancillary processes.

3. The election campaign tests qualities relevant to the duties of leadership. This is especially true of the Indian general election contest. Although it is brief by American standards, it is hectic. The candidate who does not offer extraordinary energy, organizing ability, tactful dealing with allies, articulateness, and above all a feel for what is of overriding importance to men and women of all kinds reveals his weaknesses in the ordeal.

4. Elections provide a training institute for democratic leadership, especially leadership of a diverse people. Nehru credited his election experiences with bringing him close to peasants, tribesmen, manual workers, and people of low caste, so that he could "commune" with them.[86] He felt this even though he had already gone through many struggles in the Gandhian campaign that drew him outside his Harrow-Cambridge-Inns of Court education and his elite family and caste. His grandson, without the benefit of such struggles, may owe his leadership skills even more to the sensitizing effects of a general election campaign and to the confidence gained during campaigning.

As soon as the contributions that the elective process makes to leader selection are noted, however, a limitation must be registered. In the main, these contributions are not available to leaders at the state level, except to those in states where opposition parties have a serious chance to win, for example, in Tamil Nadu, Andhra Pradesh, West Bengal, Manipur, and now Punjab. Under Indira Gandhi's leadership, the chief ministers of solidly Congress states came to and kept office by maintaining favor with the prime minister. Elections only registered her selection. Mrs. Gandhi ex-

[86] Jawaharlal Nehru, *The Discovery of India*, Calcutta: Orient Longmans, 1946, pp. 58–65; and Michael Brecher, *Nehru: A Political Biography*, London: Oxford, 1959, p. 228.

ploited an existing vulnerability of the electoral link between voters and heads of state governments by inducing state legislators to desert disfavored leaders, thus, in the parliamentary system, toppling the chief minister. The practice came to be known during her time as "the politics of defection."[87] One of her son's early, and promising, initiatives was to get national legislation discouraging this practice. Should his reform succeed, it would remove three crippling effects of the manipulation of state leadership choices from New Delhi.

First, leaders whose tenure depends on the national leader are not apt to confront and lay out solutions to problems peculiar to their own states. A disjunction develops, too, between state and national leaders in diagnosing and resolving national problems that affect different states differently. Second, chief ministers of the states are no longer forceful, well-informed counselors who can say how a proposed policy will be received in their states, or even whether it will be enforced if adopted. Mrs. Gandhi's manipulation of state leaders had already proceeded so far in 1971 that they did not confront her with the unenforceable aspects of her land reform policies.[88] Third, the politics of defection denies national leadership selection one of its great potential strengths, use of state office and state political leadership to test and prove candidates for minister in Delhi, or prime minister. No Pandit Pant, Morarji Desai, Y. B. Chavan, or Kamaraj will emerge from a system of toppling noncompliant state leaders.

Mobilizing Support for Policies

Potentially, elections have another vital use in democratic politics. They can rally public support behind the course of action laid out by the leader.[89] This function operates in two phases. In the policy-formulating phase, voters' demands register themselves on the policy agenda. Situations are diagnosed as politically salient problems; solutions are compared for their relevance and viability. The democratically chosen legislature is the primary institution at this stage. In the second phase, politically responsive leaders' diagnoses of problems and proposed courses of action come under fire in competitive elections. Victory means the identification of a very large body of voters and intermediate political activists who now regard themselves as champions of the contested policy.

[87] Subhas C. Kashyap, *The Politics of Defection: A Study of State Politics in India*, Delhi: National, 1969; Shourie (n. 27), pp. 44–89. To gauge the peremptoriness of some of Mrs. Gandhi's decisions, see *India Today*, (16–30 June 1980), p. 47.

[88] Herring (n. 56), p. 136.

[89] Tucker (n. 8), pp. 19, 61, 68.

The mandate to legislate becomes a mandate to implement. Always basic to the Indian system, this function of elective representation has shriveled in the 1970s and 1980s.

The difficulty begins with the atrophy of *parliamentary* policy making. The design assumption of India's constitution is that problem diagnosis and problem solving would occur in Parliament.[90] Plural representatives would contend; government initiatives would run the gauntlet of compatibility to the full range of interest and regional concerns. Decisions would proceed by stages: several times, government initiatives and parliamentary debate upon them would be circulated to the political public through the media. The final product would thus represent the reactions of a wider public than was initially concerned. Something like this happened in the formulation of the Hindu Code Bill. In the reworking of the official language formula in the mid-sixties, central decision was indeed plurally representative, and multistaged, but only *after* the initial policy had been subjected to violent protest in the streets of Tamil Nadu. This latter pattern characterized the making of controversial policy in the fifties and sixties. Controversial legislation was almost casually approved, only then subjected to wide and intensive protest, and then was drastically modified or abandoned. But much controversial and consequential policy, especially that having to do with the economic transformation of the country, was all along made outside parliamentary legislation. The five-year plans, land reform, division of fiscal resources between the center and the states illustrate the point.

Under Indira Gandhi's leadership, the whole spectrum of redistributive policy upon which she wished to be judged was articulated outside Parliament. There was one interesting regression. *Garibi Hatao* was, indeed, submitted to the voters in 1971 and approved. But, although the mandate was powerful, it was ineffective, for no one could be clear what, specifically, had been endorsed. Later Mrs. Gandhi's redistributive program was made specific enough in the Twenty Points, but there could be no serious claim of electoral endorsement or rejection because the overriding issue became the sincerity of her claim of implementing these specifics, and her claim to need quasi-dictatorial powers to do it. Finally, voters were asked to endorse only "a government that works." The precedents now are for national leaders to diagnose problems and lay down courses of action unilaterally and at a single stage of the representative process, and thus to do without the essence of parliamentary representation in policy. Parliament

[90] To an important degree Jawaharlal Nehru gave life to the constitutional assumption. Sarvepalli Gopal, *Jawaharlal Nehru, A Biography*, Cambridge: Harvard University Press, 1984, vol. 3, pp. 278–279.

only questions and criticizes. The *directive* function of leadership is a monopoly of the leader, consented to, or rejected by, the voters only in toto and after the fact.

A corresponding limit upon the uses of elections occurs when the leader's policies are to be put into effect. Programs that have not been articulated in a combat among supporters and opponents lack mobilized political troops to watch over and push forward implementation. This limitation is particularly serious under Indian conditions, for society in India is not a mesh of politically oriented organized interests. Despite claims from the center that national policies are erasing human inequalities, most villages still function as autonomous domains of power, with that power still partly denominated by caste and firmly entrenched in the control of land. In this setting, a struggle that polarizes society is to be won only in a struggle that polarizes politics.

The exception that proves the rule shows up in the states ruled by the Communist party (Marxist). In these we have seen the most controversial of all internal economic policies being made in mighty battles of which elections register popular mandates. In Kerala the arenas were the legislature, where party and factional coalitions had to be pieced together to enact bills, and the streets, the workplaces, and the fields, where organized cadremen and workers demonstrated the intensity of their demands. In West Bengal, election of panchayats was deliberately set to draw conflicting forces into the policy-implementation struggle from within the tight inequalities of village power structures.[91]

The uses of elections, and their limits, have never been clearer than in the case of the 1977 poll. By external indicators, Indira Gandhi's power had already been secured. She had crushed her opponents in the parties, the press, and the streets; she had made the constitution safe for her quasi-dictatorship through amendments. Why did she choose to submit to the judgment of the voters? Mixed with whatever misinformation she held or Machiavellian strategy she intended, one motive had to be simply that elections were, for her, an indispensable test of legitimacy.[92] And only an election that was competitive—with competitors released from jail, the press uncensored, the ballots counted straight—could provide that test.

There was, equally plainly in 1977, the limit of the mandate. Using the unreformed policy and legal machinery, the victors could not even bring

[91] Atul Kohli, "Parliamentary Communism and Agrarian Reform," *Asian Survey* 23 (July 1983), pp. 783–809.

[92] For contemporaneous speculation regarding Mrs. Gandhi's motives, see *India Today*, (1–15 February 1977), p. 35. So unexpected was the decision that George Fernandes, released from jail, advised boycotting the election.

the judgment of law upon those who had inflicted personal suffering on them and their adherents.[93] Atrophy of conciliar conventions of leadership placed all the stakes upon the newly chosen prime minister. Under that stress, opposition unity collapsed as the threat of imprisonment receded. The broadest lesson of 1977 for India is this: Election is necessary to permit a man or woman to lead the country, yet elective representation does not, as currently practiced, empower the leader to move the country to any particular destination.

PATHWAYS TO POWER

As has been stressed, the ability to lead India politically depends on having a network of institutions capable of bringing problems to the leader's attention and of making decisions operational in people's lives. Leadership is, of course, also a personal ability, developed as one develops a personality. Early and intimate experiences shape the core but are given political form by one's experiences in political arenas, or arenas of action relevant to politics.[94] We are concerned here only with the political system, with the way it selects some aspirants for top power and excludes others, and with the way it reinforces certain personal traits and inhibits others. As to the inner core of personality we see the system acting only as screen, not as shaper, yet the relevance and effectiveness of that screen may be vital to the preservation of the system. Ashis Nandy wrote, in a most thoughtful article on the occasion of Indira Gandhi's assassination, that he had once, during the Emergency, characterized her as "an imperfect autocrat," though now he considers her "an imperfect democrat." Recognizing her "authoritarian politics and personality," he finds the common basis for two such different appraisals in ". . . her role in Indian political culture as a person who, often in spite of herself, abided by democratic values . . . her instincts might have been authoritarian, but her values were democratic."[95]

Accepting that judgment, we are driven to ask: Can political culture be counted on to overcome political instincts, the authoritarian instincts of *every* leader who might reach the top, of a *succession* of such leaders? Thus we must examine the conditioning and the screening function of the

---

[93] Arun Shourie, *Institutions in the Janata Phase*, New Delhi: Popular, 1980, pp. 73–78; and Shourie (n. 27), pp. 32–36.

[94] Hart (n. 33), pp. 241–274.

[95] Ashis Nandy, "Mrs. Gandhi and the Indian State," *Indian Express Magazine*, 25 November 1984.

system's routes to power. Do they open the way for strong leaders? Do they inhibit autocrats?

The Indian democracy demonstrates three very different paths to top leadership: the institutional ladder, the transfer to politics of the culture hero, and dynastic succession. I doubt that any system offers such diverse routes. Let us assess each in turn.

The Institutional Ladder

At the national level, this is the route followed by Lal Bahadur Shastri. Quite aside from his considerable role in the Gandhian movement,[96] he had demonstrated his abilities in his own state of Uttar Pradesh as party secretary and minister, had managed the 1952 general election campaign as national party secretary, and had further served Nehru as minister of railways, of industry and commerce, and of home affairs. His sense of public accountability was thoroughly tested in the railways post, from which he resigned in 1956, taking upon himself as minister responsibility for a series of accidents. Finally, Nehru, in the months before his own death, brought him back into the Cabinet as minister without portfolio, not by any means settling the succession upon him, but placing him on the rung of the ladder next below.

This route to the top operates today only at the state level, and there only for chief ministers of parties not in power in Delhi. For instance, Ramakrishna Hegde came to the chief ministership of Karnataka in this way. He had been a minister in several Congress governments of the state from 1957 to 1971, toward the end of that time acting almost as de facto chief minister. He had shown his mettle within his party, too. Jailed for fourteen months during the Emergency, he helped found the Janata party and served as its secretary for a time. When, however, he stood for election to Parliament in 1977, he lost to a candidate backed by Indira Gandhi, who carried Karnataka while losing nationwide. Hegde's is an interesting case of the institutional ladder reaching the top, for it makes quite clear that the path is available even in the absence of the sort of towering patronage that Nehru might be thought (probably incorrectly) to have represented for Lal Bahadur Shastri.[97]

Shastri's and Hegde's successes demonstrate career ladders climbed through both party and government posts. The institutional ladder works for Communist leaders largely on the strength of party and mass agita-

[96] On this phase, see Gayanendra Pandy, "The Shastris of Kashi and Lahore; The Making of Congress Leaders," in *The Making of Politicians: Studies from Africa and Asia*, edited by W. H. Morris-Jones, London: Athlone, 1976, pp. 123–125.

[97] Kuldip Nayar, *Between the Lines*, p. 8.

tional work, although electoral campaigning is important there, too. Jyoti Basu and, earlier, E.M.S. Namboodiripad both became chief ministers upon a record of party work so exemplary as to leave them unquestioned candidates for chief minister when the Communists won legislative control.[98] The institutional ladder to top political leadership does not, these last illustrations should make clear, comprise fixed steps, much less criteria of advancement established by rule, as for civil service or military promotions. But this route does require the aspirant to show what he or she can do in progressively more demanding roles, which, taken together, represent most of the tasks or duties required in leadership at the top. Along the way there are apt to be tests of commitment to the values of the system, as in Shastri's case, and also in Namboodiripad's and Basu's when they willingly relinquished power upon central government intervention, even though they questioned the fairness of that exercise of constitutional authority.

The institutional route to power has, not coincidentally, given India leaders who appreciate the need for vigorous party organization reaching to the voters, for bureaucratic staffs and procedures capable of delivering services and carrying policies into execution, and for drawing a wide range of other leaders into a ministry and keeping them on the team. A candidate not demonstrating these orientations and skills does not climb the ladder. There is another advantage to this route. Because each step up is in some measure competitive and is somewhat representative of the requirements of the top post, there is a good chance that other contenders for the top position will recognize the legitimacy of the candidate's claim to lead. To the extent that the party is truly autonomous from the government, there is even the possibility that the party can translate this recognized claim into an agreed party choice, obviating factional struggle over the succession. That is what Kamaraj arranged in the otherwise contentious succession to Nehru's leadership.[99]

Climbing the institutional ladder does not by itself measure what is,

[98] Namboodiripad was a founder of the Communist party in Kerala from within the Indian National Congress, a member of the CPI central committee beginning in 1943 and of the politburo from 1950; he was elected to the legislative assembly of Madras in 1939, and of Kerala in 1957, before being chosen chief minister by his party. Basu had been a member of the politboro of his state's CPM since its founding; earlier in 1951 he entered the CPI Central Committee. He was elected to the state legislature in 1946 and again in 1957, led the opposition for fourteen years and had served as minister and deputy chief minister before reaching the top in 1977.

[99] Gopal Krishna saw "The traditions of the Congress party as the stabilizing factor in the 1964 and 1966 successions to Nehru's leadership," in *Asian Political Systems: Readings on China, Japan, India, Pakistan,* edited by Betty B. Burch and Allan B. Cole, Princeton: D. Van Nostrand, 1968, p. 261.

perhaps, the most important quality of national leadership, the ability to galvanize the people around a course of action or a definition of nationhood. But, as we have seen, once a leader is in position, a general election fought under his or her banner will bring out this dimension clearly enough. (In Shastri's case, a war did it.) In such an election, the voters are provided with a choice within their competence to judge; the top candidate is a known quantity whose future performance is predictable from his or her past political record.

Culture Hero to Political Leader

N. T. Rama Rao's election victory in Andhra Pradesh in January 1983 showed that, under certain conditions, a career as film superstar may provide entree to political leadership, that the model of M. G. Ramachandran in Tamil Nadu is no longer a fluke. What are the conditions under which this route is open, and what does this phenomenon tell us about leadership in Indian democratic politics?

First, film stardom, coupled with the right personality, can provide a combination capable of overcoming great odds. Rama Rao won against every resource of money, nationwide political talent, experience, and personal charisma that Mrs. Gandhi could mobilize against him. Film stardom could, of course, be transferred into the election campaign in the form of a ready-made charisma, anticipating, not yet reflecting the power of office. There was evidence of this in the display on street corners of man-sized cardboard effigies of Lord Krishna holding aloft yellow flags bearing Rama Rao's election symbol, the bicycle. Telugus, who had watched many of his 300 films, could readily identify him with the god. In his campaign appearances, attended by perhaps three million people, his body language, the timing of his phrases, the incorporation into the pageantry of the crowds streaming after his battered campaign van—all were translations of film into electoral image.[100]

But, second, the cinema star identified himself with the masses. His aim was candidly revealed in his own early description of his model, M. G. Ramachandran, whom he described as "able to successfully project himself as a hero standing on the side of suffering people."[101] A few populist promises—rice at two rupees per kilo, free midday meals for school children—gave substance to the image. In addition, Rama Rao identified a specific focus for Andhra voters' frustrations. It was expressed in the single word "imposition," a word that evoked two kinds of yearnings in the

[100] *India Today*, 15 January 1983, pp. 23–24.
[101] Ibid., 16–30 April 1982, pp. 55–56.

state.[102] One was for political dignity. The prime minister had intervened unrestrainedly in state government, imposing four chief ministers in two years. The least competent among them, T. Anjiah, himself said, "I came in because of Madam, and I am going because of her. I do not even know how I came here."[103] Against the impositions of "Amma," Mother, the frustrated citizens could turn to "Anna," Elder Brother. There was also the yearning to vindicate the "3,000-year-old culture of the Telugus." New strata had come into politics since the cosmopolitan elite of the independence movement. For reasons set forth by Selig Harrison thirty years ago,[104] a latent linguistic patriotism awaited Rama Rao's call. A professor at Osmania commented, "So what if he does not have a political ideology. He still has a cultural ideology; the glory of the Telugu heritage."[105] In this context, much of Mrs. Gandhi's campaign played into his hands. Congress notables from Uttar Pradesh and Delhi bustling about the state and Arun Nehru's dictation to Andhra Pradesh campaign organizers were interpreted in the Telugu language press as further insults to Telugu identity. Rama Rao's appeal was not anti-India ("We must . . . make everybody feel proud of being an Indian"),[106] but it touched a chord of subnational loyalty.

So he won. Governing the state without a corps of experienced political executives was a more difficult translation of a film-acting experience, but he has worked at organizing his hold into institutional form. He called his party, founded even before he announced his campaign, Telugu Desam (Telugu Land), and he instituted a three-year training course stressing Telugu history and culture for several hundred full-time party cadremen. His political hold on the state has proved durable. When Mrs. Gandhi tried to topple him from power by the familiar defection ploy, he appeared before the president in Delhi with a solid majority of the state legislators, forcing her capitulation, and in the 1984–1985 general elections, he was reelected to office.

Some of Rama Rao's qualities have no evident connection with his particular route to power through super stardom, his concern, for example, for institutionalizing his party.[107] But he has deployed as political leader dimensions of charisma from his earlier career. At his inaugural he appeared in shaved head; later he adopted saffron robes. At the outset of the campaign he said, "I have got enough money, enough fame, enough patronage and enough of everything. I can expect nothing more. . . . After

[102] Ibid., 15 September 1982, pp. 31ff; 11 January 1983, p. 25.
[103] Ibid., 1–15 March 1982, p. 24.
[104] "Leadership and Language Policy in India," in Park and Tinker (n. 1), pp. 151–166.
[105] India Today, 15 January 1983, p. 23.
[106] Ibid., 15 October 1982, p. 61.
[107] Ibid., 15 September 15 1982, p. 31ff.

entering my 60th year, I thought of devoting a certain part of my life to public good and social service."[108] A journalist who accompanied him in the campaign concluded: "They believe that . . . if NTR comes to power there won't be corruption."[109] There is, of course, nothing in a film star's rise to eminence that tests the inner qualities of character. In a state legislature by-election where he had spent an enormous sum to secure a seat for his son-in-law, an opponent asked Rama Rao publicly how much he had contributed to his own charitable relief fund. He answered simply, "I am a *sanyasi*."[110]

Defining the conditions of success by this route suggests a limit upon its availability. It has been open so far in clearly defined linguistic states, states quite conscious of their cultural distance from Delhi. Hindi film stars have won elections, but they have not evoked followings prepared to follow them against the government in power.

Dynastic Succession

Little need be said of the now familiar path of dynastic succession. One who enters top leadership by inheritance alone need demonstrate very little in the way of character, very little in the way of performance in prior political roles. This statement is less true if succession by inheritance is contested, as it was for Indira Gandhi in the period from 1966 to 1971. She wrested de facto control from what was intended to be a mere formal and perhaps temporary tenure by showing extraordinary will, strategic skill, and popular appeal. But where succession is prearranged, neither character nor ability is tested. Inheritance poses no test of faithfulness to the constitution, to its conventions, or to its law. For democracy it is a risky path. To be sure, there is still the hurdle of election, the hurdle and the training experience. But elections test only if there are worthy opponents.

One can judge Rajiv Gandhi as committed to the constitution, as a capable manager determined to cleanse government and invigorate the party, and as dedicated to the welfare of the people of India without judging that he is all these because he is Indira Gandhi's son and won an overwhelming electoral victory. Might it not have been Sanjay?

A few general comments on the three routes to leadership in the Indian system might be advanced. Clearly, to produce leaders to fill the roles we have defined, the first path, up the *institutional* ladder, is most valid; the

[108] Ibid.
[109] Ibid.
[110] Dhiren Bhagat, "Elites and the Notion of Satisfaction," *Seminar*, no. 293 (January 1984), p. 86.

third, dynastic succession, is the most risky. The first is not, unfortunately, now open to national leadership. The obstacles are obvious but formidable. The ruling party, now deinstitutionalized, neither builds nor tests the capabilities of a candidate to link citizens' concerns to government programs and party purposes or ideology. Opposition parties cannot place their leaders in the prime ministership. The power of both Parliament and ministers has declined so that the strongest minister still seems well out of reach of succession. This would hold true even if one assumed an end to the kind of capricious appointments made by Mrs. Gandhi.[111] Chief ministers, once a prime source of strong central ministers and of possible successors to the prime ministership, have lately been mere creatures of the prime minister if not of the nationally dominant party, or disqualified from upward succession if leaders of a minority party, which often lacks appeal outside a particular state. For quite different reasons, arising from India's cultural diversity and varying stages of societal development, route two is not likely to connect with national power. Dynastic succession occurs in India, not because it serves the system, but for want of a present alternative.

REFLECTIONS OF 1986

We have reviewed a record of thirty-five years in the life of a political system. Now things are changing. A time of transition calls out for predictions, but predictions now are even more vulnerable than they were. The patterns of the past can be used most prudently, I think, to raise questions about some of the hopes and expectations that have become current in this expectant time.

The Leader as Manager

A leader in control of events is the need of the mid-eighties. Just as people voted for, but did not see, the abolition of poverty in the seventies, they voted for, but did not get, "a government that works" in 1980. In Rajiv Gandhi they see a manager,[112] a leader who faces problems and solves them in order of priority, who monitors compliance, using computers to feed him information, who replaces unproductive officials, who unburdens the central government of impossible tasks both in the economy and

---

[111] "Mindless Management of Government," *Economic and Political Weekly*, 8 September 1984, p. 1560.

[112] Pranay Gupte (n. 79), p. 324. Rajni Kothari had a more skeptical view of this development in his "The Politicians," *Seminar*, no. 299 (July 1984), pp. 20–23.

the federal system, and who sets a model of tireless coping. One can accept all these characterizations of the new prime minister, accept them with enthusiasm, but question whether the leadership he must exert, or in several crucial tests has exerted, is adequately conceived as that of a manager. Consider his most remarkable achievement: he held the confidence of Hindu-oriented politicians while he negotiated a thoroughgoing settlement with the Sikh Akalis. It was an exercise in adroit political management. But was it more than that? Was it that trust, perhaps a kind of charisma, accrued to a son who had lost his mother to this tragic conflict? The question is asked, not to disparage the leader as manager, but to inquire what it may take to permit him to manage.

It will take, first, we have seen, a reconstruction of the institutions of politics and government. This must have been evident to Rajiv Gandhi when he assumed office. The desperate need of leadership was to bind up the deep wound to India's unity. What he saw was the killing of Sikhs, fomented by his own party stalwarts and watched, even in his own capital, by the police. However manifest the need, however, reconstruction of institutions requires more than managerial attention. The institutions to be reformed are webs of power entrenched in thousands of towns, hundreds of thousands of villages. Elective and bureaucratic authority will join in defense of profitable connections with businessmen and landowners. Citizens, who are exercised episodically over the corrupt use of office to deny service to nonpaying customers, do not understand the interior working of institutions well enough to press through painful changes. The manager, if he wants to get to the sources of institutional palsy, must be at it for years; the struggle is not a blitzkrieg but a war of attrition. Yet, he will be judged by the voters in five years. What rational manager will pay the price of near-term controversy and division in his own camp for slow-maturing benefits?

One can think of two partial solutions to making the management of the government manageable. One is to lighten the substantive burdens carried by government. This can be done, first, by leaving to the energy and the controls of the market significant sets of economic decisions. One whole class of corrupt activities might be dispensed with by a renunciation of the "license-permit raj." And from the prime minister's viewpoint, great areas of decision might be returned to his counterparts in the states, for example, decisions on what development projects deserve what priority, and whether they are worth burdening taxpayers to obtain, decisions for which responsibility is not confused and hidden. There are signs that Rajiv Gandhi is moving in both these ways to make his role manageable.

As a leader moves beyond lightening his load, he thinks about which institution to tackle first. The need of reform is most manifest in the police establishment. Yet, the political party is the institution that, once animated and oriented, has the potential for energizing reform in other sectors of government. This is so because the party can, as once before the Congress did, evoke and channel energies from among the people, a force that will be necessary to overcome the natural resistance of placeholders to changes of their roles. There is another strategic advantage of beginning reform in the party. Because it is a bottom-to-top process, it can proceed state by state. The national leadership can progressively devolve responsibility upon state units—for example, in the designation of bearers of the party label in elections—as reform proceeds. The readiness of any unit of the party to manage its own affairs can be tested: Is its membership base sufficiently well defined that contests for leadership within it can be settled by internal election? Gaining the support of more and more such self-managing party units, the national leadership will have a source of power to concentrate on moving the nation.

This was, of course, the way M. K. Gandhi approached the leadership role when he assumed it in 1920. It is in such a sense that the Indian leader needs to be a manager in 1986.

The Solo Leader

Two months after his mother's death, Rajiv Gandhi had become "India's hope for the future."[113] Some irony might be found here. Rajiv's grandfather, Jawaharlal, was not, when Indian leadership was assessed by scholars thirty years ago, so sole a hope, though he had received the mantle of leadership from the father of the country and had more than anyone else formed its constitution and government. Like Rajiv, his mother had been the object of her nation's hopes after her triumph in 1971, but it was she, more than any Indian leader, who demonstrated the limits and risk of sole leadership, even by a leader of "effortless grace, style, stamina . . . and guts."[114] If the grandfather has been likened to a great banyan tree, in whose shade other trees are stunted, then the mother must be compared to a permanently fixed storm cloud, shading the growth of alternative leaders over most of a nation. When she fell, there was no alternative to her son; not only was there no rival for succession, there was no Kamaraj to preside over the formation of a considered party consensus, or even a Nanda to serve as acting prime minister. That the succession could be arranged informally and ratified quickly by the president, as Pranay Gupte

[113] Gupte (n. 79), p. 30.
[114] Editor, *India Today*, in Gupte (n. 79), p. 279.

tells us it was,[115] demonstrates how solitary was the model of leadership Rajiv Gandhi inherited.

The disadvantages of solo leadership are evident. We know that a leader who can diagnose far-reaching national problems single-handedly can diagnose them according to an idiosyncratic picture of the real world. Both Indira Gandhi and Jawaharlal Nehru did so. We know that policy prescriptions may, when they are effectuated in the lives of the diverse people of India, have untoward consequences. A parliament is needed to anticipate those consequences in hundreds of constituencies, to insist that they be taken early into account. A cabinet of ministers, protected by a circle of shared confidence and prepared to press alternative pictures of the world upon the prime minister, is needed. Civil servants are needed to focus the information flows from the candid observations of their field people upon the formulation of those pictures. The network of leadership must include the party, the state leaders, and the well-informed and interested spokesmen from outside government, scientists, businessmen, and leaders of causes. In the history of leadership successes in India there have been plenty of tangled strands to be rewoven, but few Gordian knots to be cut.

India has two significant advantages. The skeletons of all these institutions of conciliar leadership remain. They have merely to be fleshed out again with vigorous and enterprising men and women and given life by being drawn into the circles of decision and effectuation. In addition, all citizens are free to express themselves. The question is, as Pranay Gupte puts it, "Will Rajiv Gandhi be willing to devolve power . . . ?"[116] The power to lead is so concentrated now that we look to one leader to distribute it, not to many to use it together.

Leadership of a New Generation

> The political aspirations of the post-Independence generation have now found expression in the ascendency of Rajiv Gandhi, forty years old. . . .[117]

That a generational change in leadership has occurred, and that it is an enormously hopeful change, one can agree. That it also carries with it entirely new burdens for leadership may not be so evident.

Men and women who were fifteen years old when Mahatma Gandhi led his nationwide salt satyagraha are, if alive, seventy years old today. Those

[115] Ibid., pp. 93–94.
[116] Ibid., p. 33.
[117] Ibid., p. 272.

who could in any sense have participated in his campaign against untouchability would be sixty-eight. The generation that has taken over has not lived through the experiences that formed the nation. They are ready to pioneer new paths of technology, productivity, artistic creativity, and pragmatic government policy making. They also man the motorcycle gangs of assassins that have survived Bhindranwale in Punjab, the "sons of the soil" mobs in Bombay, and the strikes of medical students in enlightened Gujarat demanding an end to the preferred admission of Untouchables to medical colleges.

Every nation must commend itself afresh to each cohort of its young people. If there remains still some lack of fit between the principles justifying the nation and the institutions and mores that condition the young—between, for example, nonparticipative schoolrooms and participative elections, between unemployment and the "Directive Principles" of the constitution, between the unequal worth of men before the village accountant and the equal worth of men in the words of the law—then the nonhabituated minds of the young can be expected to challenge one or the other. Nehru, who was conscious of his responsibilities as builder of a new and somewhat exotic political, economic, and social order, took seriously the need to socialize the incoming generation. He commended to his education minister an idea he said he had held for some time: all Indian youths, finishing secondary school or higher education, should spend a year in the nation's service.[118] It would have been a sort of domestic, compulsory peace corps. Nehru could, we have observed, base policy on illusion. We are entitled to ask whether such a prescription would deal with the yearnings of the Punjab, Bombay, or Assam graduates, or those seeking admission to medical college in Baroda. We may ask who would conduct the national service projects: university administrators, civil servants, party officers? Yet we may concede that some such need exists; indeed, in the postsatyagraha generation, it is more acute. Again, India is fortunate. One of the less dramatic yet pervasive tendencies of the new generation is to initiate voluntary projects, often relating the aspirations of the young to the hard realities of traditional life.[119] There are projects for village self-help, small-scale technology, environmental protection, vocational training for illiterate women, and hundreds of other nonconventional pursuits. Even the movements prompted by economic grievances (for example, farmer protest movements) or subnationalism (the old Tamil language movement, or the contemporary cause of the Assamese

[118] Gopal (n. 11), p. 169.
[119] Rajni Kothari, "Grass Roots," *Seminar*, no. 293 (30 January 1984), pp. 47–52; Arun Shourie (n. 27), pp. 487–492.

students) represent potential arenas in which aspirations may be brought to confront the realities of political and economic options. That assumes, of course, that national leaders are prepared to tackle the underlying problems, such as unemployment and dead-end education that now frustrate these aspirations.

A generation does not learn its political values from texts or speeches or even from the achievements of its parents retold. It learns from what it does. "Constructive work" or sarvodaya year in, year out, and satyagraha once in a long while—these were the schools of a generation now gone, a generation of leaders and followers who had worked together in pursuit of a common vision. What of the new generation? Does it share with its forty-year-old leader anything more orienting than its age and its innocence of those old formative experiences? Will leadership today mean the involvement of leader and led in new experiences oriented toward that old, or perhaps a revised, vision?

TWO

Parties and
the Party System

JAMES MANOR

Political systems in which diverse parties compete freely for mass electoral support are increasingly hard to find in the less developed nations,
even in those that experienced British rule—for a long time thought to
yield durable systems of liberal, representative government. But India,
after nearly four decades of self-government and eight general elections,
and despite hair-raising traumas and persisting threats to open, competitive politics, still qualifies. Nevertheless, in recent years, decay within parties and increasingly destructive conflict among parties have so eroded the
strength of the open political system that its survival is in question.

There is consequently an urgent need for rebuilding, both within individual parties and in relations among them. Since his election victory in
the last week of 1984, Prime Minister Rajiv Gandhi has begun, somewhat
hesitantly, the process of rebuilding within the formal institutions of state.
He has also, at least for the time being, restored a modicum of civility to
relations between his ruling Congress–I party and the opposition, and this
has in turn led to an improvement in relations between the central government in New Delhi and opposition-controlled governments at the state
level. Rajiv Gandhi has also indicated, through scorching criticisms, that
he is well aware of the wretched condition of his own party.[1] But he may
also have missed his opportunity to rebuild it. If that is indeed true, then
he could eventually experience the kind of vulnerability that caused him
and his mother before him to seek all-out confrontation with opposition
parties. It could even lead civilian elites to abandon hope in parties and in
open, competitive politics.

This chapter seeks to delineate the changes that have occurred within
India's parties, especially the Congress party, and within the party system
since independence, and to explain how forces within the sphere of party
competition have contributed to those changes. For a full understanding
of how all of this came about, it will be necessary to look beyond that lim-

---

[1] *Times of India* (Delhi), 29 December 1985, and *Times* (London), 30 December 1985.

ited sphere and to consider the question from the various perspectives represented in this volume.

At first glance, it may seem that few dramatic changes have actually occurred within and among India's parties. It may appear that the victory of the Congress party in the 1984 general election closely resembles all but one of those that have come before—the aberration being 1977—and that one need only dust off and update the classic studies of the party system that Rajni Kothari and W. H. Morris-Jones produced some years ago.[2] To adopt that view, however, is to overlook a number of basic changes in Indian politics over the last two decades that have substantially altered conditions within parties, relations among parties, and, partly because parties have provided the main links between state and society, state-society relations. Some of these changes were disguised by the result of the 1984 election, but they remain realities nonetheless.

To emphasize the changes that have taken place, this chapter is divided into four sections that deal with the three main phases in the evolution of India's parties and party systems, the periods from 1947 to 1960, from 1967 to 1977, from 1977 to 1984, and the year following the election in the last week of 1984. It is not yet clear whether this last period should be seen as a fourth distinct phase in the process, but enough has changed since the election to justify a separate discussion.

From 1947 to 1967

To understand India's parties and party system from independence in 1947 to 1967, just after Indira Gandhi first became prime minister and the year of the fourth general election, we can do no better than to turn to the accounts that Kothari and Morris-Jones provided. Their views are sufficiently similar, though they are developed independently, to be considered together here. They described a "dominant party system," that is, a multiparty system, in which free competition among parties occurred but in which the Indian National Congress enjoyed a dominant position, both in terms of the number of seats that it held in Parliament in New Delhi and

---

[2] Rajni Kothari, "The Congress 'System' in India," *Asian Survey* (December 1964), pp. 1161–1173, much of which was foreshadowed in his "Form and Substance in Indian Politics," *Economic Weekly* (April-May 1961), pp. 846–863; Wyndraeth H. Morris-Jones, "Parliament and Dominant Party: The Indian Experience," and "Dominance and Dissent: Their Inter-relations in the Indian Party System," in Morris-Jones, *Politics Mainly Indian*, Madras: Orient Longman 1978, pp. 196–232. Both Kothari and Morris-Jones provided helpful suggestions during the preparation of this paper. I am also grateful to Stanley A. Kochanek for many useful comments on the initial draft.

the state legislative assemblies, and in terms of its immense organizational strength outside the legislatures. It is extremely important that we recognize that Congress was dominant in both spheres. Indeed, it was its dominance at the organizational level that was more important, for on that rested its legislative superiority. The might, the reach, and the subtlety of its organization also enabled it to dominate the actions of bureaucrats who were charged with the implementation of policies and laws at regional and, especially, at subregional levels.

In this first period, India had a party system characterized by "dominance coexisting with competition but without a trace of alternation,"[3] because opposition parties had little hope of preventing the Congress from obtaining sizable majorities in the legislatures despite the ruling party's failure on most occasions to gain a majority of valid votes cast. Neither, by and large, did opposition parties share power in coalitions with Congress at the state level. So here was a "competitive party system . . . in which the competing parts play rather dissimilar roles." The ruling Congress party was "a party of consensus" and the opposition parties were "parties of pressure."[4] That is to say, the opposition parties played a role that was "quite distinctive. . . . Instead of providing an alternative to the Congress party, they function by influencing sections within the Congress. They oppose by making Congressmen oppose. Groups within the ruling party assume the role of opposition parties, often quite openly, reflecting the ideologies and interests of other parties. The latter influence political decision-making at the margin."[5]

In other words, there was "a most important 'openness' in the relations between Congress and the other parties . . . a positive communication and interaction between them." This meant that the main hope that opposition leaders had of exercising political influence was to "address themselves . . . to like-minded . . . groups in the dominant party."[6] Those efforts by opposition groups generated ideas and pressure within the ruling party's organization, which was sophisticated enough to detect them and communicate them upward to the leaders who could respond to them.[7]

These comments begin to reveal the extraordinary dimensions of Congress dominance in that period. It was within Congress, and not between Congress and the opposition parties, that the major conflicts within In-

[3] Morris-Jones, "Dominance and Dissent" (n. 2), p. 217.
[4] Kothari, "The Congress 'System' " (n. 2), p. 1162.
[5] Kothari, "Form and Substance" (n. 2), p. 849.
[6] Morris-Jones, "Dominance and Dissent" (n. 2), p. 218.
[7] Kothari, "The Congress 'System' " (n. 2), p. 1163, and Morris-Jones, "Parliament" (n. 2), pp. 207–208.

dian politics occurred.[8] It was within Congress that nearly all of the groups that mattered in Indian politics could be found. The party possessed a large number of skilled operatives who were able to arrange bargains between important social groups, to interpret the logic of politics at one level of the system to people at higher and lower levels, and to knit together the varied regions and subcultures of the subcontinent. The Congress organization was also the main instrument that knit together state and society, which is to say that it was India's central integrating institution.[9] As a consequence, one did not find in India, as in the West, "a relationship between the government and the party organization in which the latter plays an instrumental and subsidiary role."[10] Congress was more important than that, and arguably more important than all of the formal institutions of state put together.

Congress occupied not only the broad center of the political spectrum, but most of the left and right as well. This relegated the opposition parties not only to the margins of Congress, but to the margins of the political and party systems as well. To make matters worse, these parties often found themselves on opposite sides of the Congress, which killed any hope of their making common cause against it.[11] To save themselves from absorption by or the loss of defectors to the Congress, opposition parties tended to develop rigorous ideologies and tightly disciplined organizations.

Congress was able to maintain its position as a party occupying most of the space in the political system because "there [was] plurality within the dominant party which [made] it more representative, [provided] flexibility, and [sustained] internal competition. At the same time, it [was] prepared to absorb groups and movements from outside the party and thus prevent other parties from gaining strength."[12] The task of creating and sustaining the immensely broad Congress coalition in that first phase was, at least in the view of Morris-Jones, facilitated by the complexities and ambiguities of Indian society, which prevented polarization (in class terms or any other terms) and the formation of contradictions that might fracture such an all-embracing alliance of interests. This insight differs from but complements Myron Weiner's argument that the task of building the Congress coalition was eased by traditional values and roles of concilia-

   [8] Kothari, "The Congress 'System' " (n. 2), p. 1163.
   [9] I have set this argument out more fully in two articles: "Indira and After: The Decay of Party Organization in India," *The Round Table* (October 1978), pp. 315–324; and "Party Decay and Political Crisis in India," *The Washington Quarterly* (Summer 1981), pp. 25–40.
   [10] Kothari, "The Congress 'System' " (n. 2), p. 1162.
   [11] Morris-Jones, "Dominance and Dissent" (n. 2), pp. 219–220.
   [12] Kothari, "The Congress 'System' " (n. 2), pp. 1164–1165.

tion that Congressmen astutely took up,[13] and the Rudolphs' contention that traditional elements of the caste system assisted the development of modern, representative politics in India.[14]

But however much the social background may have helped, and however important Congress' role in the winning of independence may have been in placing the party in a dominant position in the first place, the survival of Congress dominance depended on the efficient functioning of the party organization. Of crucial importance was its effectiveness in distributing the resources, which it acquired from its control of state power, among existing and potential clients in exchange for their political support. This management of resources, at which many within the Congress organization excelled, was essential to the proper functioning of the "conciliation machinery within the Congress, at various levels and for different tasks, which [was] almost constantly in operation, mediating in factional disputes, influencing political decisions in the States and districts."[15]

The same skill at allotting patronage also enabled Congress to co-opt and absorb within itself groups whose grievances had "been ventilated through agitations launched by the opposition parties." This was reinforced by Congress' "policy of neutralizing some of the more important sources of cleavage and disaffection" and by the leadership's tendency "to preserve democratic forms, to respect the rule of law, to avoid undue strife," and to show "great sensitivity on the question of respect for minorities . . . ."[16]

FROM 1967 TO 1977

The second phase extended from 1967 to the defeat of the Congress party at the general election of 1977, which occurred in the immediate aftermath of the Emergency. It is of course possible to see the Emergency, which extended over nineteen months from 26 June 1975, as a separate phase in this story. But a chapter-length study cannot do justice to a more elaborate disaggregation. It is nevertheless worth noting that the Emergency constituted both an intensification of certain trends from the period between 1969 and 1975 and, at the same time, something of a hiatus between phases two and three, during which opposition leaders were jailed,

[13] Myron Weiner, "Traditional Role Performance and The Development of Modern Political Parties: The Indian Case," *Journal of Politics* (November 1964), pp. 830–849.

[14] Lloyd I. and Susanne Hoeber Rudolph, *The Modernity of Tradition: Political Development in India*, Chicago: University of Chicago Press, 1967, p. 1.

[15] Kothari, "The Congress 'System' " (n. 2), p. 1168.

[16] Ibid., pp. 1168–1170.

the party system and open politics were closed down, even Congress leaders were intimidated, and Mrs. Gandhi attempted, only partly successfully, to centralize power within the ruling party.

Some of the earliest and most perceptive comments on the party system between 1967 and 1977 came from studies by Morris-Jones and Kothari after the 1967 general election, which occasioned important changes.[17] One important feature of the old system that persisted was, in Kothari's words, "the central role of the Congress in maintaining and restructuring political consensus." But he also argued that:

> The socio-economic and demographic profile of the polity is changing rather fast. . . . The mobilization of new recruits and groups into the political process . . . has given rise to the development of new and more differentiated identities and patterns of political cleavage. . . . [This gave rise to] the expectation of freer political access . . . and a greater insistence on government performance. Intermediaries and vote banks, while of continuing importance, have become increasingly circumvented as citizens search for more effective participation in the political market place and develop an ability to evaluate and make choices.[18]

As a result, "the dominant party model has started to give way to a more differentiated structure of party competition. . . ."[19]

Morris-Jones also emphasized the emergence of "a market polity" in India. This was, of course, nothing very new. "There was plenty of competition and bargaining before 1967 . . . ," but it had taken place "largely within the Congress, between groups and in semi-institutionalized form."[20] In the 1967 election, however, which saw Congress lose power in six states, the competition had grown too severe to be contained by the party's internal bargaining, so that "dissident Congressmen played an important role in the weakening of the party . . . in perhaps every 'lost' State except Tamil Nadu."[21] This brought a number of opposition parties fully into the market place, and competition that had previously occurred within the Congress was now brought into the realm of interparty conflict. Competition also increased inasmuch as opposition parties formed

---

[17] Rajni Kothari, "Continuity and Change in the Indian Party System," *Asian Survey* (November 1970), pp. 937–948; and W. H. Morris-Jones, "From Monopoly to Competition in India's Politics," in Morris-Jones, *Politics Mainly Indian* (n. 2), pp. 144–159.

[18] Kothari (n. 17), p. 939.

[19] Ibid. Morris-Jones also noted that "the market of politics has expanded by the participation of new groups in government" (n. 17), p. 156.

[20] Morris-Jones (n. 17), p. 154.

[21] Ibid.

coalition governments in every state they controlled except Tamil Nadu, and "coalition governments are themselves small markets."[22]

That election also made center-state relations an important feature of interparty competition. Bargaining had long been an important element of relations between New Delhi and the states, even in Nehru's day when Congressmen held sway at both levels. After Nehru's death, the power of state-level Congress leaders had become both greater and more apparent. The 1967 election created conditions in which quite serious conflict might have arisen between center and states, but, thanks mainly to the finesse of Union Home Minister Y. B. Chavan, this did not occur.[23]

Another new phenomenon after 1967 was a "pretty regular and continuous 'defectors market.' "[24] It is easy to forget that this was so, for our minds tend to rush onward to the dramatic splitting of the Congress in 1969 and Mrs. Gandhi's subsequent surprises, which gained her the political initiative and the great election victory of 1971. But defection was an important element in the aftermath of the 1967 election, and two points should be made about it. First, defectors flowed both ways, both into and out of Congress. More flowed out, however, than in, causing the fall of Congress governments in three states.[25] Second, the highly disciplined, ideologically oriented parties of the Marxist left and the Hindu chauvinist right remained almost entirely immune to this new trend. (The Communists experienced a split over ideological issues in 1969, but that was different from defection.)

In other words, the parties to the far right and left tended to remain "hard" in that they retained tough shells through which people did not pass in and out, and in that they maintained their organizational integrity through centralization, discipline, and ideological consistency. They also retained narrower social bases than most of the other parties in that period and narrower bases than the Communist party of India–(Marxist) (CPI[M]) and the Jan Sangh/Bharatiya Janata Party (BJP) have developed in the post-1977 years. They nonetheless moved very cautiously along the road to more moderate policies, a road down which, Stanley A. Kochanek observed, other opposition parties were motoring once the possibility of power presented itself.[26]

The 1967 election had created a situation in which Congress "dominance was strikingly diminished" because its "performance in the art of

[22] Ibid.

[23] Ibid., p. 153.

[24] Ibid., p. 155.

[25] Ibid., and Kothari (n. 17), p. 946.

[26] Stanley A. Kochanek, *The Congress Party of India*, Princeton: Princeton University Press, 1968, p. 446.

governance was subjected to harsh judgment by supporters and opposition alike."[27] It was a situation marked by "ambiguity, blurred lines, flexibility and flux . . . ," but this was not seen to represent disintegration. Indeed, the actors in the system had adjusted with such "amazingly little difficulty" that "the stability of the regime appears more assured than ever before." This was true because the regime had, among other things, "moved away from any degree of dependence on one outstanding leader." If this raised questions about the need for "clarity and firmness of decision," it was reassuring inasmuch as decisions "also require reconciliation of very varied interests if they are to succeed."[28]

The schism in the Congress in 1969 was a major shock to the political system in India. Partly as a result, Mrs. Gandhi's version of the party faced a largely united opposition in the general election of 1971. B. D. Graham has compared the polarization of India's parties into something close to two opposing blocs in 1971 (and 1977) to a few key elections in the Third French Republic when similar polar blocs emerged. This did not occur often in France, but when it did, it indicated that a "crisis of regime" had developed and that the two blocs were disputing fundamental issues about the nature of the political order.[29] Mrs. Gandhi's decision to split her country's central political institution produced such conditions in India in 1971, conditions that altered the shape of the party system at that election. This happened again in 1977 when the threat to all liberal institutions created a widely shared perception that a "crisis of regime" had occurred. Such perceptions did not arise among most opposition leaders in 1980, as I have argued elsewhere, or in 1984.[30]

Mrs. Gandhi's victory in the 1971 election made it appear, in words Morris-Jones used soon afterward, that "the end of the dominant party had been too readily proclaimed in 1967" and that "now it is back." This led him naturally to expect that the opposition parties would be "forced to operate less by confrontation than by interaction with segments of the centre mass."[31] They were not, however, given many opportunities for interaction by the new Congress. Mrs. Gandhi adopted a more confrontational posture, both toward opposition parties at the national level and

[27] Kothari (n. 17), p. 947.

[28] Morris-Jones (n. 17), pp. 158–159. Kothari was slightly less optimistic than Morris-Jones on this count. Ibid., p. 948.

[29] I am grateful to B. D. Graham for bringing his argument to my attention in numerous conversations. See also Graham, "Theories of the French Party System under the Third Republic," *Political Studies* (February 1964), pp. 21–32.

[30] James Manor, "The Electoral Process amid Awakening and Decay," in *Transfer and Transformation: Political Institutions in the New Commonwealth*, edited by Peter Lyon and James Manor, Leicester: Leicester University Press, 1983, pp. 87–116.

[31] Morris-Jones (n. 17), p. 187.

toward opposition-controlled governments in various states.[32] She also took a more aggressive line with her own party, and this soon produced what Kochanek has rightly called "a new political process" as the prime minister created "a pyramidical decision-making structure in party and government." Although this "prevented threats to her personal power, it tended to centralize decision making, weaken institutionalization, and create an overly personalized regime. Moreover, the new political process proved unable to manage the tensions and cleavages of a heterogeneous party operating in a heterogeneous society, federally governed. A major crisis in the system followed."[33]

The new system entailed, crucially, the abandonment of intraparty democracy, a change that has never been reversed. Positions in the Congress organization at all levels were filled by appointment from above rather than by election from below. This change caused people at all levels to tend to tell people above them what they thought those people wanted to hear, so that the organization's once formidable powers as an information-gathering agency soon wasted away.[34] The centralization of power within the party did not, however, mean that factionalism ceased to be a problem. Instead, partly because centralization reduced the leaders' ability to manage conflict, partly because Mrs. Gandhi set leaders and factions at the regional level against one another, and partly because she had largely abandoned the use of bargaining, conflict within the organization grew more severe and dysfunctional. All of this reduced the party's ability to cope creatively or even adequately with conflicts that arose from a society facing increasing economic hardship.[35]

Not surprisingly, this created openings for the opposition, and by 1974, under Jayaprakash Narayan's leadership, an opposition movement had acquired real substance and momentum. Mrs. Gandhi's reaction, which set the tone of relations between her Congress and nearly all opposition parties (with the exceptions of the Communist party of India and, at times, one or the other of the two main parties in Tamil Nadu) for many years to come, was severe. As Kochanek put it: "Dissent within the Congress, party opposition and press criticism ceased to function as thermostats measuring discontent. They were now interpreted as anti-party, anti-national, and traitorous, or even foreign-inspired. . . . Opposition party

---

[32] Bhagwan D. Dua, *Presidential Rule in India, 1950–1974: A Study in Crisis Politics*, New Delhi: S. Chand, 1979.

[33] Stanley A. Kochanek, "Mrs. Gandhi's Pyramid: The New Congress," in *Indira Gandhi's India*, edited by Henry C. Hart, Boulder: Westview, 1976, pp. 104–105.

[34] This is developed further in Manor, "Party Decay" (n. 9).

[35] Kochanek, "Mrs. Gandhi's Pyramid" (n. 33), pp. 109–111.

attempts to mobilize and express local grievances, valid or not, were perceived as law and order problems."[36]

The opposition's response was similarly forceful and stubborn, with fasting and agitational techniques brought to the fore. Mrs. Gandhi, who found herself under growing pressure from within her own party (indeed, it was thence that the main threat came in mid-1975), turned increasingly to a small circle of confidants in which her son Sanjay figured most prominently. He began to treat the opposition to the threats, smears, and organized violence that remained his trademark until his death in mid–1980.

There followed the Emergency, during which relations between Congress and the opposition reached their nadir. Not only were opposition activists faced with imprisonment, but power within Congress was further centralized. The organization of the Congress itself, in some regions where it provided a base for potential rivals to Mrs. Gandhi, was systematically dismantled—the most vivid example being the Maharashtra machine that had been created by Y. B. Chavan.

But the centralizing often had the opposite effect to that which was intended. It cut off still further Mrs. Gandhi and her circle from reliable information from states beyond the Hindi belt, so that, for example, the chief ministers of Karnataka and Andhra Pradesh were repeatedly able to submit reports of huge numbers of vasectomies, none of which had occurred. And instead of homogenizing the regions as intended, centralization made possible the assertion of their natural heterogeneity, so that they actually diverged from one another.[37] Mrs. Gandhi's centralizing violated the basic logic by which India had been governed under both the Crown and Nehru's Congress. According to that logic, the influence of people at the apex of national and regional political systems penetrates down through the systems most effectively by means of compromise. Attempts to rule by diktat paradoxically weaken the centralizers, as happened to Mrs. Gandhi.[38]

FROM 1977 TO 1984

The third phase in the evolution of India's parties and party system extends from the defeat of Indira Gandhi's Congress in the election of March 1977 to the election victory of the Congress led by her son Rajiv in the last

[36] Ibid., p. 114.
[37] James Manor, "Where Congress Survived: Five States in the Indian General Election of 1977," *Asian Survey* (August 1978) pp. 785–803.
[38] Manor, "Party Decay . . ." (n. 9).

week of 1984, following her assassination. I choose the 1984 election and not the assassination as the end of this phase because it is only thereafter that a set of new and quite different trends emerge. The years from 1977 to 1984 were, broadly speaking, a time of abrasive conflict and bad feeling between political parties and a period marked by decay and fragmentation within parties. I will deal with all of that presently, but first it is necessary to identify several larger themes in this period of India's politics that provide the context essential to an understanding of the changes within parties and the party system.

Two great themes, which had become plainly evident before 1977 and which dominated the phase thereafter were awakening and decay. The awakening occurred among the great mass of India's voters, as people at all levels of society became increasingly aware of the logic of electoral politics, of the secrecy of the ballot, and of the notion that parties and leaders should respond to those whom they represented. It was more advanced among prosperous groups, but it also occurred among the poor.[39] As a result, disadvantaged rural dwellers largely ceased to vote according to the wishes of the landowning groups that continued to dominate life in the villages. Voters became more assertive and competitive, and their appetites for resources from politicians grew. Interest groups crystallized and came increasingly into conflict, so that it became harder to operate a political machine that could cater to every organized interest, as Congress had very nearly done in the Nehru years. India became increasingly democratic and increasingly difficult to govern.

The second great theme that marked this period was the decay of political institutions, which is to say, a decline in the capacity of institutions to respond rationally, creatively, or even adequately to pressures from society.[40] This decay affected both the formal institutions of state and most political parties, including, above all, the Congress party. It was partly the result of systemic problems of ossification within the party. But it was quite substantially the result of the tendency of Indira Gandhi and her associates to centralize power and to deinstitutionalize. The awakening of the electorate and the decay of institutions combined to generate five further changes as by-products.

The first of these was a change in the way that elections are won and lost, or to put it more plainly, a change from the days before 1972, when incumbent governments at the state and national levels usually won re-

---

[39] See, for example, John O. Field, *Consolidating Democracy: Politicization and Partisanship in India*, New Delhi: Manohar, 1980; and D. L. Sheth, ed., *Citizens and Parties: Aspects of Competitive Politics in India*, Bombay: Allied, 1975.

[40] Samuel P. Huntington, "Political Development and Political Decay," *World Politics* (April 1965), pp. 386–430.

election, to a period in which they usually lost.[41] This follows quite logically, for the decay of ruling parties and the formal institutions through which they govern has meant that incumbents have been less able to respond to society at a time when the expectations and assertiveness of the electorate have increasingly demanded responses.

The second change was a marked decline in confidence in the state as an agency capable of creative social action (as opposed to an agency with the coercive power to maintain order). This occurred within the Congress led by both Gandhis. It was demonstrated by Indira Gandhi's abandonment of reformist rhetoric in the election of 1980 and of serious attempts to create legislation for the betterment of society between 1980 and 1984, and by Rajiv Gandhi's preference for the private sector. But this decline was also observable within many opposition parties, among many intellectuals who were critical of Mrs. Gandhi, and among large numbers of people in local arenas all across the subcontinent. There were exceptions—notably on the Marxist left, among certain elements of the Hindu chauvinist right, and in some parties at the regional level—but the predominant trend was nonetheless clear.

The third change, which was closely related to the second, was the tendency for society and politics to diverge. As political institutions, especially parties, became less able to respond rationally to appeals that arose from society, social groups tended to give up on politics and politicians and to turn inward, battening on parochial sentiments and whatever internal resources they possessed. This led to an increase in conflict between social groups as the social-political divergence and the decay of political institutions reduced the state's capacity to manage and defuse conflict.[42]

A fourth change entailed the blurring of the relatively clear lines that had existed between many political parties and their social bases, both at the national level and in many Indian states. This was a destabilizing, and potentially destructive, trend, particularly as the awakening of the electorate made it more important than ever that parties develop solid, clearly perceived links to social bases of manageable size.[43]

The last of the five changes was a growing divergence between the logic of politics at the national level and the political logic in various state-level

[41] This had clearly been the predominant trend since the state assembly elections of 1972. The general election of 1984 is an exception to this pattern, but it occurred under extraordinary and emotionally charged circumstances that are unlikely to occur again.

[42] See *Times* (London), 18 May 1984. I have developed this further in *New Society*, 12 August 1982.

[43] James Manor, "Blurring the Lines between Parties and Social Bases: Gundu Rao and the Emergence of a Janata Government in Karnataka," in *State Politics in Contemporary India: Crisis or Continuity?* edited by John R. Wood, Boulder: Westview, 1984, pp. 139–168.

arenas. The most obvious sign of this was the emergence in the early 1980s of regional parties in several states. But even within the Congress party, during the Emergency, state-level units often went their own way.[44] This, like the appearance of regional opposition parties, was an unintended result of the excessive centralization of power by Mrs. Gandhi.

With these themes in mind, let us now consider the third phase in the evolution of India's parties and party system. This period, from 1977 to December 1984, was marked by freer competition between political parties but also by greater instability in the party system and within many parties. It was a time characterized by abundant alternation between parties in power at the state and national levels, by continued decay and fragmentation within parties, by a tendency toward personalized control of parties or splinters by eminent and not-so-eminent politicians, and by great fluidity within the party system as factions and rumps and individuals defected or realigned themselves this way and that.

The defeat of the Congress led by Mrs. Gandhi in 1977 and the election of the Janata party—which was actually a motley coalition of parties—brought immense changes to the party system. Defeat caused the Congress to disintegrate. Some Congress activists left Mrs. Gandhi because they had secretly disapproved of the Emergency, others because they had had enough of her son Sanjay's bizarre and often vicious egotism. Some believed that they could revive the "real" Congress in the absence of its former and supposedly discredited leader, whereas others saw little reason to stay now that Congress had lost access to the political patronage that had been its life's blood.

Even before her defeat, Mrs. Gandhi had imposed something very close to personal and dynastic rule on the political system and the party. Defeat only intensified this tendency within the Congress, or her version of it. At a time when so many were deserting her, her already extravagant distrust of other politicians intensified, and personal loyalty became an even more precious commodity. The reconstitution of her version of the Congress party in January 1978 under the label of the "Indian National Congress–Indira," or the "Congress–I," was emblematic of this increased personalization. As the badly divided Janata party increasingly demonstrated its incapacity to govern satisfactorily and Mrs. Gandhi's prospects improved, waves of deserters redefected back to her camp. Each wave tended to operate as a new faction in an already factionalized Congress–I, and the inability of Indira and Sanjay Gandhi to apply standards consistently to these returnees actually catalyzed further division and strife. Latecomers

[44] Manor (n. 37). I have also dealt with this in "Where the Gandhi Writ Doesn't Run," *The Economist*, 15 May 1982, pp. 55–56.

were sometimes humiliated or sometimes inexplicably promoted over the heads of old loyalists. In this atmosphere, every group thought it had a chance and so remained a contentious force. This process continued even after Mrs. Gandhi's return to power in January 1980 and Sanjay's death six months later.

The Janata government that held power between March 1977 and July 1979 was a hastily assembled coalition of quite different opposition groups united mainly by their opposition to Mrs. Gandhi and the Emergency. Victory at the polls meant that those objectives had been realized, and the natural divisions among them then began to emerge. The Janata party contained elements of the old Congress–O, the mainly conservative but secularist remainder of the out-faction after the 1969 Congress split. Alongside it stood the Jan Sangh, a party of the Hindu chauvinist right, whose main support came from high caste, middle-class people in urban areas, particularly in the Hindi-speaking states of North and Central India. Third was the Bharatiya Lok Dal (BLD), mainly representing prosperous small peasant proprietors in the Hindi belt. It sought to reallocate resources away from the urban, industrial sector toward agriculture. Fourth was the Socialist party, whose base included some of the rural poor of North India and sizable but scattered pockets of support among urban labor unions. Finally, there was the Congress for Democracy, a group led out of Mrs. Gandhi's Congress after the Emergency by Jagjivan Ram, one of her most formidable ministers and the leading Scheduled Caste ("ex"-Untouchable) politician. Its support was greatest among poor, low caste rural dwellers.

Given the heterogeneous composition of Janata and the fierce ambitions of its three leading figures—Morarji Desai, Jagjivan Ram, and BLD leader Charan Singh—it is no surprise that the government was unable to achieve much cohesion. One result was a loosening of ties between the national and state levels within both the Janata party and the political system. The factions that tended to dominate the Janata party in the national Parliament were antagonistic to those that held sway in several Janata-controlled states. This antagonism set the national and state governments at loggerheads on some important questions, a trend that was reinforced by friction between the Janata regime in New Delhi and opposition-controlled governments in several other states. This made it impossible to reverse the tendency of the Indian federation to become an increasingly loose union. It was not that secession threatened national unity. That problem has always been greatly exaggerated by observers who have failed to see that insufficient solidarity exists at the state level to fuel separatism. But the threat of secession prepared the ground for further deterioration of center-state relations when Mrs. Gandhi, returning to over-centralization after 1980, generated regional movements in reaction and then dealt even more aggressively—and unconstitutionally—with those movements when they had taken power in several states.

When the Janata government disintegrated in mid-1979, many of the elements that had formed it also splintered. This paralleled the disintegration that had occurred on the Congress side after the 1977 election, and the result was a confusing array of fragmentary parties, many of which were little more than personal cliques presided over by individual politicians. In this context, Mrs. Gandhi's Congress–I appeared to be the only coherent national party—even though its own organization was in considerable disarray—and this image enabled it to take advantage of the strong popular reaction against the Janata government and win the 1980 election. The difficulties of the anti-Congress–I parties at making common cause persisted from the early 1980s through the election preparations during the third quarter of 1984. The assassination of Mrs. Gandhi on 31 October 1984 seemed to ensure an emotion-based victory for her son and party, making opposition unity still more difficult to achieve.

This victory has led many observers to write off the opposition over the middle and even the long term, but such a judgment is premature, as the evidence from 1967 to 1984 shows. It should first be recalled that Mrs. Gandhi appeared to be in a similarly unassailable position in 1972, and that mismanagement led her into severe political trouble within only three years. If such errors should recur, the Indian electorate, which is even more aware and assertive today than in the early 1970s, is unlikely to be any more patient than on that occasion. Every state in India, like the nation as a whole, has now had at least one spell of non-Congress government. Opposition rule is no longer unthinkable anywhere. Misgovernment will generate a credible opposition.

Second, some opposition parties possessed greater promise and substance (real or, in some cases, potential substance) than the 1980 and 1984 election results implied. These parties retained either the support of important groups or ideological resources and respectable organizations or both. Stanley Kochanek has usefully identified four broad *tendencies* in Indian politics that unite particular elements in society around certain sets of ideas.[45] These are a communist tendency, a socialist tendency, a non-confessional rightist tendency, and a confessional rightist tendency. All of these have at times been represented by non-Congress political parties. The Congress has at times allied itself with and borrowed a limited number of ideas from the communist tendency. It has also at times moved into the territory on the political spectrum normally inhabited by the other

---

[45] I am grateful to Stanley A. Kochanek for suggesting this approach to me.

three tendencies and in so doing has drawn support away from opposition parties there. In recent years, the socialist tendency can be said to have been somewhat in eclipse, both within Congress and in the opposition. The main party of the nonconfessional right, the Swatantra, has long since passed away, but Congress under Indira Gandhi, and especially under her son Rajiv, has begun to give assertive expression to views associated with that tendency. We shall see presently how the parties of the confessional right and the communist left have fared in recent years and how the Congress–I has moved into the territory traditionally occupied by the former.

Let us first note, however, that one other possible tendency is also unlikely to pass from the scene: that represented by the peasant proprietary group in the Hindi-speaking areas and championed by Charan Singh under various labels (Lok Dal, Bharatiya Lok Dal, Dalit Mazdoor Kisan party). Charan Singh himself is aged and infirm and unlikely to play an important role again. But this force has sufficient cohesion to figure in future anti-Congress–I alliances unless Rajiv Gandhi's new economic policies develop in ways that attract it to his party.

We should pay particular attention to the Communist party of India (Marxist) (CPI[M]), and the Bharatiya Janata party (BJP), which is a successor to the old Hindu chauvinist Jan Sangh. These were the two most potent "hard" parties of the late 1960s, and they are the only two opposition parties that are patently able to rejuvenate themselves by recruiting large numbers of young idealists. They have also managed to broaden their bases. This last comment may sound strange in the aftermath of the 1984 election, in which the CPI(M) lost ground in West Bengal and suffered embarrassments in Kerala, and in which the BJP was reduced to a parliamentary delegation of two. But it should be noted that the CPI(M) still came first in a solid majority of assembly segments in West Bengal, and it did so because it has managed, since coming to power there in 1977, to cultivate a solid base among the rural majority, a success managed partly because it has organizational efficiency in West Bengal that is said to surpass even that of the party in Kerala.[46] If the decay of other parties and some sort of socio-economic crisis should make it possible for the CPI(M) to extend the West Bengal model to other states—an eventuality that seems highly unlikely at present—we may look back on this acquisition of a rural base as a crucial change. The CPI(M) has also managed this broadening without ceasing to be a "hard" party, without losing or gaining people through defections, and without suffering too much erosion of discipline or ideology. It is nonetheless more flexible and pragmatic than

[46] I base this on conversations with Thomas J. Nossiter.

it used to be, as is exemplified by electoral pacts in states where it is a minor party.

The BJP presents a different picture. It remains a corporate entity of real institutional sinew and has not suffered from the drift toward personal rule that has done so much damage to many other opposition parties and, of course, to the Congress–I. And although it lost a large number of Rashtriya Swayamsevak Sangha (RSS) activists to the Congress–I during the 1984 election, it is generally agreed by most observers in India that it retained a majority of these and that many who decamped to the ruling party are likely to return, especially after Rajiv Gandhi's moves away from Hindu chauvinism in 1985. To put that statement into perspective, it helps to recall that the RSS has no fewer than 700,000 swayamsevaks, or full-time activists, in the field.[47] The figure dwarfs that of any other party, including the Congress–I, which has surprisingly few people spending most of their time working for the organization. In addition, in many states, Congress personnel are startlingly ineffective. In Karnataka, for example, the Congress president had to go outside the party to find an efficient organizing general secretary.[48] A large minority of the RSS swayamsevaks are adolescents, but many of them are capable of important political work.[49]

The BJP has not, however, remained the kind of "hard" party that it once was and that the CPI(M) largely remains. It is far less penetrable than the other non-Communist parties, but it has become less parochial and uncompromising in its tactics and ideology, and hence more porous than it used to be. It has both lost and accepted a surprising number of defectors in the last five years, and it was possible to identify a number of people during the 1984 election campaign who had one foot in the BJP and another in other non-Congress and non-Communist parties, so that the boundaries between it and some other parties became slightly blurred.[50]

This political straddling is a logical result of a fundamental change of outlook among some BJP members, and a third reason why the opposition should not be written off. B. D. Graham, who knew the old Jan Sangh

[47] I am grateful to B. D. Graham for confirming reports that I received in India on this matter.

[48] Interview with a high official of the Karnataka Congress-I, 8 January 1985, in Bangalore.

[49] Interview with B. D. Graham, London, 8 February 1985.

[50] Widespread RSS support for the Congress-I became apparent from numerous interviews with BJP and Congress-I activists in several Indian states during December 1984 and January 1985. See also *Times of India* (Delhi), 23 December 1984; the report from Ambala in the *Hindustan Times* (Delhi), 14 December 1984, and the discussion of the open letter by veteran RSS leader Nanaji Deshmukh offering support to the prime minister in the *Indian Express* (Bombay), 26 January 1985.

well, became convinced on a visit to India in mid-1984 that the BJP is a genuinely new entity, both in terms of organization—their party constitution is modeled on that of the post-1977 Janata party rather than that of the Jan Sangh—and in terms of ideas. BJP views on economic issues are less market-oriented than social democratic and suggest a return to the reformism introduced in the fifties by Nehru, although party members tend to describe themselves as "neo-Gandhians" and to avoid references to Nehru.

Graham also found common ground between the outlook of the BJP and other non-Communist opposition parties, although they were probably less than fully aware of this themselves. There was a nostalgia among many of them for several of the themes and conditions that had characterized the Nehru era. This was true even within Charan Singh's Lok Dal where the name of Nehru was distinctly unpopular, and there was a fondness for the constitution as it had been, and as it was implemented during the fifties, when, for example, emergency powers were used with restraint. There were in addition, warm memories of the more balanced center-state relations of that period and a longing, too, for the days when the state was less intrusive in rural life, when peasant landholders got what they regard as more realistic prices for their produce. Ethics seemed more clearly defined and more commonly applied during the fifties, when disadvantaged social groups were just awakening, and Nehru's reformism appeared sufficient to meet their demands. Many felt an urge to return to genuine non-alignment in foreign relations and a desire to re-establish more civilized interactions between the ruling party and the opposition at home. On each of these counts, however, it was possible to find at least one opposition party that did not share in the nostalgia. Atul Kohli has recently found BJP activists at the state level to be far less liberal in outlook than the national leaders Graham encountered. But there may now be enough common ground to suggest that if compelling reasons were to arise for cooperation among opposition parties at the national level, there would be some basis for it, at least at the level of ideas and party programs.[51]

It is of course true that the opposition to the Congress–I did not achieve much unity in 1980 or 1984. There are at least two ways to view its failure to do so. Those who lean toward Graham's view can argue that, in 1980, the wounds from the internecine squabbles of the Janata years were too fresh and that, in 1984, popular sympathy for Rajiv Gandhi in the wake of the assassination rendered opposition actions irrelevant so that there was no incentive to unite. There are, on the other hand, those who doubt that the shared views that Graham encountered will outweigh the per-

[51] Interview with B. D. Graham, Brighton, 12 October 1984.

sonal bitterness among opposition leaders and the antagonisms between groups of their supporters. They point to the lack of progress in opposition unity in 1984 even *before* the murder of Mrs. Gandhi. At this writing, I remain ambivalent on the matter.

Let us now turn to an astonishing development of the early 1980s, the adoption by Indira Gandhi of themes that have traditionally belonged to the Hindu chauvinist right. To many who are familiar with Congress in Nehru's time or in Mrs. Gandhi's earlier years as prime minister, it may be difficult to believe that this happened. Yet, it appears that at some point during 1982, Congress–I leaders recognized that a confrontational posture toward the overwhelmingly Muslim National Conference party in Kashmir and the Sikh extremists in Punjab (whom Mrs. Gandhi's confidants, Sanjay Gandhi and Zail Singh, had initially encouraged in order to divide the opposition Akalis) might gain them the support of many Hindus in the Kashmir and Delhi elections. When numerous activists of the RSS deserted the increasingly liberal BJP to support Congress–I candidates in those elections, the tactic seemed to have worked surprisingly well.

It began to seem an even more attractive option after the defeat of the Congress–I in the southern states of Karnataka and Andhra Pradesh in January 1983. That defeat led Congress–I leaders to suspect that the south might not support them at the next parliamentary election, and that they would therefore need to look to northern and central India for most of their Lok Sabha seats. Because their party organization was in such disarray that it could not cultivate much of a following through patronage— the main mode of operation during the 1960s—an evocative theme like Hindu chauvinism, which could be conveyed to voters through talk of threats to national unity from anti-national minorities, began to seem all the more useful.

It is impossible to regard this rightward shift as an accident, as something that happened with Congress–I leaders realizing too late that it was occurring and merely acquiescing. Too much of what took place required willful action by Mrs. Gandhi and then her son Rajiv. Indeed, as early as August 1982, after commentators like Pran Chopra had warned against the dangers of courting the Hindu majority in North India by generating communal anxieties, I asked a general secretary of the AICC–I if that really could be the prime minister's intention. He responded, not by denying that this was her aim, but by seeking to justify it as a creative strategy.[52]

It remained the strategy of Congress–I leaders right through the election

[52] Interview with Satyanarayana Rao, Delhi, 18 August 1982.

of 1984. Detailed accounts of the campaign were scarce in the Western press because many reporters at that time were engaged with the ghastly events in Bhopal. Although it may seem difficult to believe that Hindu chauvinism and anti-Sikh sentiments were important elements in the Congress–I election campaign, it was, in fact, the case. For example, at a November rally in Delhi, Rajiv Gandhi refused to prevent the city's Sikh mayor (a member of his own party) from being shouted down and then went on to use the word "*badla*," "revenge," in a speech that followed. He also refused to criticize the Hindu extremist organization, the RSS, which at every previous election had supported the Jan Sangh/BJP, but which swung heavily and in some cases openly behind the Congress–I on this occasion. The prime minister further refused to disavow RSS support, thereby conforming to the precedent set by his mother in mid-1983 in Kerala where the Congress–I received RSS backing[53]—and one of his leading party spokesmen even declined to admit that it was a communal organization.[54]

Sikh opinion was outraged and many Congress–I leaders were privately alarmed when two sitting MPs in Delhi who were said by an independent investigation to have been involved in the anti-Sikh riots of November were kept on the Congress–I ticket and when a third activist, also allegedly involved, was given a ticket that had been denied to a Sikh incumbent. The anti-Sikh theme cropped up in numerous subtle and not-so-subtle remarks in speeches by Congress–I leaders, in posters that appeared in some localities showing Mrs. Gandhi being gunned down by turbaned assassins, and in one of the party's full-page advertisements that appeared nationwide in most English and indigenous language newspapers. The advertisement began with the question "Will the country's border finally be moved to your doorstop?" and, after mentioning "Assam, Punjab . . . ," described the anti-national forces:

> They put a knife through the country and carve
>   out a niche for their cynical, disgruntled
>   ambition disguised as public aspiration.
> They raise a flag and give this niche the name
>   of a nation.
> They sow hatred and grow barbed wire fences,
>   watered with human blood.
> But it's you who step out and bump into the fences
>   and bleed while they cash your vote to buy
>   their ticket to power.

[53] See, for example, *Deccan Herald*, 12 August 1983.
[54] See the sources cited in note 50.

In case the anti-Sikh implications of much of this were not sufficiently clear, the text asked "Why should you feel uncomfortable riding in a taxi driven by a taxi driver from another state?"[55] Because a great many taxis in North India are driven by Sikhs, the message was clear.

It is essential that we understand the logic by which this strategy was reached, because it has major implications for the party system. First of all, both the Congress–I general secretary who tried to justify Hindu chauvinism to me in 1982 and, I believe, Mrs. Gandhi saw the move to the communalist right as an exercise similar to her move toward the Marxist left in and after 1969. It was a means of undermining the parties that stood to the right of the Congress–I—mainly the BJP, but also to a degree the Lok Dal, which had elements within it susceptible to Hindu chauvinist appeals. It was clearly from the right that the main threat to the Congress–I was anticipated.[56]

The move to the right was also probably based on a curious belief by Mrs. Gandhi that only she (and her son) stood between India and serious communal strife. So, still more curiously, she apparently believed that, by catalyzing communalist sentiments, by becoming the main mouthpiece for Hindu communalism, she was protecting India from the dangers of it. She appears to have rationalized this dangerous quest for short-term political advantage by concluding that communalism was safe only in her hands and that by taking it up, she could disarm it as she had leftist sentiment after 1969. I heard echoes of this view in December 1984 from several Muslim intellectuals who were clearly frightened at the anti-Sikh, Hindu chauvinist content of Rajiv Gandhi's election campaign and who were seeking desperately for a benign explanation.

Congress–I leaders also adopted what Rajni Kothari has correctly termed "the rhetoric of all-out confrontation," in which the opposition parties were repeatedly attacked as antinational forces. We should recognize that this intolerant view of the opposition is in a sense a logical outgrowth of the history of Congress. During the struggle for independence, Congress sought and claimed to speak for all Indians, to be, as its name implied, an Indian national coming-together. After 1947, this theme survived as Congress attempted to be what B. D. Graham has called "a rally of the people as a whole."[57] It is thus not altogether surprising that some Congressmen tend to see the party and the nation as identical, or that they tend to see opposition forces as antinational.

It was, however, far from inevitable that Congress leaders should adopt

[55] See, for example, *The Statesman* (Delhi), 15 December 1984.
[56] Pranab Mukherjee's comments in *Times* (London), 29 December 1983.
[57] B. D. Graham, "Congress as a Rally," *South Asian Review* (January 1973), pp. 111–124.

this narrow, intolerant view. Jawaharlal Nehru generally did not, although he sometimes slipped into this idiom when discussing communalist parties, but Indira Gandhi often did, and so, in the 1984 election campaign, did her son. He claimed, for example, that the opposition parties were "receiving assistance from certain foreign powers, which were interested in making India weak" and that conferences of opposition leaders "had sown the seeds of poison" that endangered national unity. He alleged that the Janata party, the Bharatiya Janata party, and the Dalit Mazdoor Kisan party had links to Sikh extremists living in Britain.[58] He offered no evidence to support these charges, and none of them appears to have any substance. Mr. Gandhi also described the chief minister of Andhra Pradesh, N. T. Rama Rao, as a "secessionist," a charge he has subsequently admitted to be false.[59] On a visit to Janata-ruled Karnataka, he implied that the Janata party had assisted those who had murdered Mrs. Gandhi. This was untrue, as were his assertions that the Janata party "was working hard to divide the country" and "shielding extremists,"[60] and that two prominent members of that party were collaborators with Pakistan.[61]

The prime minister also repeated "at every campaign meeting"[62] that the opposition parties had supported the "Anandpur Saheb Resolution."[63] When opposition leaders heatedly denied this, Mr. Gandhi said on 12 December that "the proceedings of the Lok Sabha bore ample testimony to their attitude."[64] On 13 December, the *Indian Express* published the text of the relevant parliamentary debate on page one. Although it showed that the opposition had repudiated the resolution unambiguously, the premier continued making this charge.[65] These tactics dismayed many, including Congressmen and commentators, who had often supported Mrs. Gandhi.[66]

The Congress–I campaign of newspaper advertisements carried this ag-

[58] *Hindustan Times* (Delhi), 13 December 1984 and *Indian Express* (Delhi), 26 December 1984.

[59] *The Hindu* (Madras), 7 December 1984.

[60] *Hindustan Times* (Delhi), 18 December 1984.

[61] *The Statesman* (Delhi), 18 December 1984.

[62] *Times of India* (Delhi), 14 December 1984.

[63] This phrase actually refers to a number of resolutions that are open to varying interpretations, but which are regarded by many as separatist in character. It usually refers to the first, 1973 resolution, the contents of which are a matter of dispute.

[64] *Hindustan Times* (Delhi), 13 December 1984.

[65] *Indian Express* (Delhi), 14 December 1984 and *Hindustan Times* (Delhi), 18 December 1984.

[66] This is based on numerous interviews with such people. See for example, G. K. Reddy's scorching criticism in *The Hindu* (Madras), 9 December 1984.

gressive approach further. One of these sought to persuade voters that opposition rule might produce ghastly consequences. When government lacks firmness, it said,

> Vipers crawl out of their holes, predators prowl the streets
> and seemingly normal citizens take off their masks and
> shuffle in the shadows, waiting for the hour of the gun.
> The hour of acid bulbs, iron bars and daggers . . .
> Your vote can stop your groceries list turning into an arms
> inventory.
> Your vote can make all the difference.
> Between order and chaos.
> Give Order a Hand.[67]

This sort of thing naturally infuriated the opposition, particularly when considered alongside official figures that showed a steady rise in disorder and riot during Mrs. Gandhi's last five years in power[68] and against the findings of two independent enquiries into the slaughter of over 2,400 Sikhs in Delhi after the assassination. These enquiries uncovered evidence of involvement by Congress–I activists, evidence that a police investigation has reportedly found credible.[69] Despite these findings, however, the prime minister has recently refused to launch an official investigation into the riots because "it will raise issues which are really dead."[70]

His confrontational approach was part of a process that carried him well to the right of the BJP, which for some time had itself been moving away from the Hindu chauvinist right toward the center of the political spectrum. His hard-line rhetoric resembled, far more than that of the BJP, RSS claims that the loyalty to India of Communists, Muslims, and others was in doubt.[71] Yet, even as they swung to the right of parties like the BJP, Congress–I leaders continued to denounce opposition parties for their dangerous rightist tendencies.[72]

Readers should not presume that less caustic rhetoric would have been used in the election campaign had Mrs. Gandhi not been murdered. Even before the assassination, Rajiv Gandhi was taking this line, as when he

---

[67] *The Hindu* (Madras), 15 December 1984.

[68] Ibid.

[69] People's Union for Democratic Rights and People's Union for Civil Liberties, *Who Are the Guilty?* New Delhi: privately published, 2d. ed., 1984, and *The Guardian* (London), 30 January 1985.

[70] *India Today*, 15 February 1985. As the book goes to press, Rajiv Gandhi has authorized an official commission headed by Justice Ranganath Mishra.

[71] See, for example, *Deccan Herald*, 12 August 1983.

[72] *Times* (London), 29 December 1984.

"attacked the opposition for supporting and instigating the Assam agitation, joining hands with anti-national forces in Kashmir and Punjab, and trying to sell the country."[73] This is not an isolated example. The main themes of the election campaign had been decided well in advance of the assassination on 31 October. That outrage clearly provided an additional reason for using such scorching rhetoric, for it crystallized in many voters' minds the anxieties about national unity that this kind of language sought to exploit. But the leaders of the Congress–I had been taking a vehemently confrontational line with the opposition for many months, most especially in their attempts during 1983 and 1984 to overturn the opposition-controlled governments of Karnataka, Jammu and Kashmir, Sikkim, and Andhra Pradesh.

Why did Congress–I leaders adopt this confrontational approach? Two different reasons come to mind. First, although it caused a change in relations within the party system, confrontation was also a symptom of changes that had already occurred. By the early 1980s, both the Congress–I and most opposition parties had become so porous that a substantial leakage of personnel out of any of them became a very real possibility. And the more that Congress–I and most opposition parties suffered organizational decay, ideological laxity, and the imposition of personal control by those at the apex, the more they resembled each other. Potential defectors from one to the next therefore felt that they had less distance to travel. By confronting and reviling the opposition parties, Congress–I leaders sought to impede defections to the opposition by erecting barriers between their party and the other parties and by putting distance between Congress–I and the others. In this respect, there is a curious similarity between the confrontational election campaign and the post-election and antidefection law. Both are designed to erect the kind of walls around the ruling party that its organization had had the strength to generate in the 1960s, but which had wasted away when the organization decayed after 1969.

The second reason for the choice of this confrontational approach is that, given the nature of Congress–I rule between 1980 and 1984 and the assumptions that had underpinned it, the Gandhis had few other options. I have already noted that by the time Mrs. Gandhi assumed power in 1980, she had lost confidence in the state as an agency for creative action in society. As a result, next to no serious attempts were made by the authorities during her last premiership to develop carefully designed social programs. There were, therefore, few new legislative achievements between 1980 and 1984 to which Congress–I leaders could point. Indeed,

[73] *Indian Express* (Delhi), 22 October 1984.

their election speeches and the party manifesto made virtually no reference to government programs after 1980. It seemed at times as if some other party had been in power during that period. The only major reference in the manifesto to positive developments after 1980 was to advances on the economic front, where credit tended to go to market forces and not to the government.[74]

The government had sought, in the period after 1980, to direct popular attention to a number of major "spectaculars" in order to justify the existence of a state in which the prime minister had lost confidence. Much was made of the Asian Games, the Commonwealth Heads of Government Conference, Antarctic explorations, and the like. But Congress–I leaders rightly sensed that these were not election winners. They also rightly believed that Mrs. Gandhi would have great difficulty obtaining a majority in the election,[75] and, given the absence of any major legislative achievements and the presence of a highly unreliable party organization, they were driven to present Mrs. Gandhi as a figure of stability amid increasing instability and to continue to court the votes of the Hindu majority across North India by making appeals based on Hindu chauvinism and the notion that India's unity was in jeopardy. If a party adopts that set of themes, it is impelled by the logic of chauvinism and its "India-in-danger" message to raise alarums and to excoriate the opposition as dangerous, antinational destabilizers.

A brief comment is needed here on the manner in which Rajiv Gandhi and his party won the election of 1984. At least five factors appear to have had a significant impact, although, as I have argued elsewhere, we will probably never be able to say with certainty what their relative importance was.[76] First, there was, of course, a sympathy factor after the murder of Mrs. Gandhi, but its impact has probably been overestimated. It was a "factor" rather than a "wave." Another obvious element was the abject failure of most opposition parties, especially the so-called national parties, to provide a credible alternative to the Congress–I. Yet both of these seem to have been less important than three other things. First, Rajiv Gandhi's youth, his freshness, and his apparent lack of a political past helped him to represent himself both as a figure of stability and continuity, on the one hand, and as a figure of renewal and change, on the other. As Rajni Kothari wrote long ago, this was an unbeatable combination.[77] A second cru-

[74] *Indian National Congress (I) Election Manifesto, 1984*, New Delhi: 1984.
[75] This is based on interviews with a large number of Congress-I officials in December 1984.
[76] James Manor, "The Indian General Election of 1984," *Electoral Studies* (August 1985), pp. 149–152.
[77] Rajni Kothari, "Government by Mandate," *Seminar* (January 1972), p. 23.

cial factor was the widespread (and, I believe, erroneous) perception that national unity was in danger. This fear was crystallized in many people's minds by the trauma of the assassination and was relentlessly exploited by the Congress–I. Finally, there was a related Hindu backlash that was encouraged by the prime minister and his party. To point to these factors as decisive is to identify this election as distinct from most of the national and state-level elections since 1972. Those earlier elections tended to be decided on concrete issues and, particularly, on the quality of the incumbent government's performance. The 1984 election was decided at the level of anxieties, images, evocations, and symbols. The result bespoke an aggrieved and fearful assertiveness together with a desperate need for hope and some prospect of renewal in government.

In order to see how things had changed by the end of this phase, let us recall some of the specific observations that Morris-Jones and Kothari made about the party system. In late 1984, India still had a multiparty system that permitted free competition, a system in which one party, bearing the name of Congress, occupied a dominant position in the New Delhi Parliament and in many state assemblies. However, the Congress–I no longer possessed a party organization strong enough to place it in a dominant position outside of the legislatures.

The 1984 election landslide was achieved in spite of serious organizational weaknesses. The Congress–I organization was insubstantial, highly corrupt in many regions, wracked with factions that engaged in severe conflicts, unrepresentative of the broad array of social groups for whom it claimed to speak, and very inefficient at delivering goods and services to them and at arranging bargains between them. It was very short of idealists, intellectuals, and, most essentially, honest, skilled managers. Those it possessed were often excluded from positions of influence. The party was, therefore, in no fit condition to administer governments at the state and national levels in a rational, reliable, effective manner. It was also distinctly short of policies in many spheres (although the new prime minister has begun to change that), and where such policies existed, it lacked the personnel at the district and subdistrict levels to ensure that bureaucrats actually implemented them.

Neither was it true any longer that this was a dominant party system "without a trace of alternation." Most elections at the state and national levels since 1972 have led to alternations (indeed, every Indian state has now had a spell of non-Congress government), as an awakening electorate has made re-election increasingly difficult to achieve. And it is hard to see how the 1984 Lok Sabha result, which was substantially the product of the extraordinary circumstances in which it occurred, can be expected to change that basic tendency in the system.

Opposition parties in the post-1980 period did not have much influence over sections of the Congress–I in the legislatures the latter dominated. There was little "positive communication and interaction between them." This was partly explained by the increasingly confrontational approach that various parties, most notably the Congress–I, adopted toward rival organizations and by the expectation within many opposition parties that they might one day defeat the Congress–I. But it is more adequately explained by the decay that had occurred within many political parties, again, most notably, within the Congress–I. The Congress no longer contained an organization rational enough to enable rightist or leftist factions within it to produce results by applying pressure on party leaders or within the councils of the party. Information seldom flowed freely from one level of the organization up to the next, because the abandonment of intraparty democracy had caused party operatives to tell those at higher levels only what they thought the latter wanted to hear. And even when pressure or information did flow up through the hierarchy, it seldom elicited an adequate or logical response from an organization crippled by harsh factional fighting and, in many areas, galloping normlessness. So, opposition groups saw little point in seeking to strike up good relations with like-minded Congressmen.

The decay within the Congress–I also made it impossible for the party to conduct itself with enough efficiency to manage within itself, as it once had, most of the major conflicts in Indian public life, to interpret the logic of politics at one level to the levels above and below, or to play the central role in integrating India's many and varied regions, subcultures, and social groups. Indeed, many social groups received such inadequate or even harmful responses from Congress–I politicians, or were so dismayed by the normless or criminal behavior of Congressmen in many regions, that they have turned away from the Congress party and, because many opposition parties have also suffered decay, from politics in general.

In these circumstances, Congress–I leaders after 1982 or so sometimes adopted the opposite of their former policy of arranging accommodations between social groups, subcultures, and regions and actually sought to set them against one another. This enabled the ruling party to absorb within itself discontented groups who saw it as the only party capable of providing stability amid chaos—which the Congress–I had itself willfully helped to generate. But these actions and reactions may ultimately cause more problems than either the Congress or the political system can cope with and may, in the long term, present opportunities for rival parties on the extremes of the party system.

There still may have been in this phase considerable validity in Morris-Jones' suggestion, made in the late 1960s, that complexities and ambiguities in Indian society prevent the political system from having to face the kind of serious conflict that societies more prone to polarization and contradiction might generate. It has always been difficult to measure this, for it entails the enumeration of dogs that do not bark. But there is no doubt that a great many more contradictions existed in Indian society in the early 1980s than in the 1960s, contradictions between interest groups (caste, class, communal, regional, and issue-specific), most of which had not crystallized in the 1960s. Some of them had not fully formed even in 1984, but they had acquired enough substance and collective self-consciousness amid the general political awakening to produce conflict that could no longer be defused by bargaining and co-optation.[78] This would have been true even if the ruling party had possessed the means to perform those tasks well, which it did not.

This is not to say that India was on the brink of a social crisis or breakdown. As I have argued at length elsewhere, Indian society is particularly well equipped, in both structure and habits of mind, to insulate itself from damage that might result from decay and anomic forces originating in the political sphere.[79] But it still needs to be recognized that in the 1980s this society threw up conflicts and problems that made it well-nigh impossible to maintain the sort of broad coalition that gave Congress its dominant position in the party system in the 1960s (and which may have given the Congress–I its huge victory in the 1984 election).

During this third phase, between 1977 and 1984, the Congress was a good deal less assiduous than it had been in the period described by Kothari and Morris-Jones in its efforts "to preserve democratic forms, to respect the rule of law, and to avoid undue strife." Neither has it shown "great sensitivity on the question of respect for minorities."[80] Because these were traits that assisted it in defusing and even in reaping benefits from opposition-led agitations, it is possible that recent changes may, over time, reduce its capacity for accommodation and thereby create opportunities for opposition groups.

In their later reassessments of the party system, Kothari and Morris-Jones emphasized two major, interconnected points. The first was the continuing ability of Congress, even after the 1967 election, to play the central role in maintaining and restructuring political consensus in India. The second was the continuing growth of a "market" polity, that is to say, a polity based on bargaining. Most of the important bargaining in that pe-

---

[78] See, for example, R. I. Duncan, "Levels, the Communication of Programmes, and Sectional Strategies in Indian Politics," D. Phil. thesis, University of Sussex, 1977.

[79] James Manor, "Anomie in Indian Politics: Origins and Potential Wider Impact," *Economic and Political Weekly* 18 (May 1983), pp. 725–34.

[80] Kothari, "The Congress 'System' " (n. 2), pp. 1168–1170.

riod still occurred within the Congress, among factions, among representatives of social groups, and between people at different levels and in different regions. But bargaining also occurred between the Congress and the opposition parties.

Much of this sounds unfamiliar in the light of events over the last decade or so. It is certainly possible to say that the 1984 election victory of Rajiv Gandhi represented both the maintenance and the restructuring of political consensus. But we need to ask whether his party is capable of continuing to sustain and renew that consensus week in and week out throughout the government's term in office. This seems unlikely, mainly because by 1984 it was incapable of arranging and maintaining political bargains that are essential to that task.

One feature, though not the central one, of the "market" polity to which Morris-Jones called attention was an increase in defections. This raises a difficult issue that has never been fully examined: to what extent can defections be seen as contributions to the maintenance and restructuring of consensus in Indian politics? I submit that a defection can be seen as such a contribution, provided it is primarily the result of discontent among a legislator's supporters over unacceptable treatment by the party to which he or she originally belonged, and provided the switch to another party was mainly intended to obtain better treatment. Such defections represent rational responses from social or subregional groups to parties' misdeeds or omissions, and they serve to remind parties of the need to maintain consensus.

Many defections in the period that Morris-Jones described were not of that nature, however. Many, indeed, appear to have been undertaken by individual legislators to enhance their position in terms of power, money, or both.[81] Defections of this kind are clearly part of the "market" polity, for bargains of a sort are being made. But such privateering is likely to impede the maintenance and restructuring of consensus, for such defectors are responding to a logic other than that which governs the maintenance of consensus. The defections that became such a prominent feature of Indian politics in the 1980s tended overwhelmingly to be responses to large cash payments by the Congress–I, which, as the ruling party could alone command such vast financial resources. In fairness, however, it should be emphasized that more than a few defectors and near-defectors were turning to Congress–I out of frustration with unresponsive leaders. This was especially true in Andhra Pradesh before August 1984, where N. T. Rama Rao was excessively autocratic.[82]

[81] It is not always easy to identify the motives of defectors. See for example, Kochanek (n. 26), pp. 293 and 447.

[82] This is based on a large number of interviews with legislators and journalists in Hyderabad, 11 and 12 January 1985.

It should be apparent to anyone who glanced at newspaper reports from India between 1982 and 1984 that very serious center-state conflict had developed in cases where opposition parties were in power at the state level. In the post-1967 period, Y. B. Chavan was able to maintain relatively civil relations with opposition-led state governments because the Congress did not adopt a confrontational posture toward the opposition and because it was entirely possible that Congress might join opposition parties in coalitions at the state level. This happened several times during the period. It is not the sort of thing that happened in the 1980s, however, except in Kerala, where extraordinary circumstances applied. The Congress–I was pugnacious toward the opposition, because the personality of its leaders (or at least its former leader) inclined in that direction and because it needed to be standoffish once so little separated the decayed Congress–I from decayed opposition parties.

1984 FORWARD

The final phase in the evolution of India's parties and party system is the period since the eighth general election in the last week of 1984. Our conclusions in this section must be tenuous for, at this writing, the phase is only twelve months old.

In the year since his election victory, which he achieved by reviling and confronting the opposition parties, Rajiv Gandhi has been more accommodating in his dealings with the opposition than his mother ever was. He has also been more conciliatory toward regional movements and parties, some of which he had sought to topple from power at the state level through bribery[83] and maneuvers of dubious constitutionality. This has earned him appreciative comments from the opposition chief ministers of Karnataka and Andhra Pradesh. Moreover, his agreements with leaders of regional movements in Punjab and Assam, and the subsequent elections in those states are among the greatest achievements of his first year in office.

Some doubts still linger, however, about his commitment to accommodation. His abrupt change from an assertive to a conciliatory stance in Assam lost him a great deal of support among those who had been attracted by the former approach. The same thing may also have occurred in Punjab during 1985. Because his turnabout entails a departure from the Hindu chauvinism of recent years and because this will disappoint many voters in other states, he may eventually find the cost of conciliation too great. It is also possible that he will feel able to pursue accommodation only so long as he feels politically secure, that if he begins to feel vulnerable he

[83] See, for example, *Indian Express* (Bombay), 1 January 1984.

may revert to the confrontational stance of 1984. But for the present, the predominant trend is toward a reconstruction of the tolerably good relations with the opposition that characterized the pre-Indira Gandhi years.

Rajiv Gandhi's main preoccupation during his first year in office has been a re-ordering within the formal institutions of state. He has concentrated on changing personnel within both the bureaucracy and ministerial ranks of the central government, though not, to any significant degree, at the state level. He has sought to persuade officials at intermediate levels to take the initiative more often in order to break the log jams that had immobilized much of the central government in his mother's day. He has also rid the prime minister's secretariat of the unqualified personnel who held posts thanks to their fierce loyalty to Indira Gandhi, and he has decentralized power somewhat by curtailing the power of the secretariat.[84] All this may suggest a reordering of affairs within the Congress party. The prime minister appeared to indicate that intention in late 1985 when he shifted key aides from his secretariat to leading party posts, but very little was said or done about the party until the last week of 1985.

Then in Bombay on 28 December, the hundredth anniversary of the Indian National Congress, the prime minister delivered the most scorching critique of the party ever uttered by one of its leaders. He spoke of "cliques . . . enmeshing the living body of the Congress in their net of avarice." He complained of Congress operatives' "self-aggrandisement, their corrupt ways, their linkages with vested interests . . . and their sanctimonious posturings . . . ," and he added that "corruption is not only tolerated . . . but even regarded as a hallmark of leadership."[85]

This attack on the Congress party, which was quite accurate, is likely to produce one of two outcomes. Given the wretched state of the party, Rajiv Gandhi may take drastic action to cleanse Congress, or he may conclude that there is so little hope of restoring a modicum of rationality and probity to the party that no serious effort will be made. If he takes the latter route, he will, in effect, be gambling that he can get along without a party organization. He will be depending on the performance of the formal institutions of state, manned by his ministers and bureaucrats, on his personal appeal, and on innovations such as the liberalization of the economy and the introduction of microtechnology to win him the support of the electorate. In a political system in which parties, particularly the Congress party, have been the main instruments for integrating and governing the nation, for detecting and responding to discontents and pressures from in-

[84] James Manor, "India: Rebuilding amid Awakening and Decay," *Current History*, (March 1986).
[85] *Times of India* (Bombay), 29 December 1985 and *Times* (London), 30 December 1985.

terest groups, for managing social conflict and for cultivating electoral support through the distribution of resources, in such a system, to do without a party organization is to ask for trouble. Even a powerful executive presidency on Gaullist lines—which is an option under consideration—is unlikely to perform adequately the roles formerly played by party organization.

Nevertheless, the evidence from Rajiv Gandhi's first fifteen months in power suggests that he may eventually be compelled to do without a strong Congress organization and even to seek a radical reduction in the importance of parties in the political system. The prime minister appears already to have dallied too long to revive the Congress–I. During the first few months after the murder of his mother, he had and spurned a clear opportunity to make radical changes in the party. That opportunity appears now to have passed and is unlikely to arise again. It was mainly available between the assassination on 31 October 1984 and the state assembly elections in March 1985, when many candidates for national and state legislatures were selected. Why did he let it pass? His hesitation is explained in part by the trauma the assassination produced and the difficult task of taking command of the government and mounting an election campaign. It is also likely that he was somewhat deceived by the misleading appearance of unity and order that his party presented in that period. To understand how it came to give that impression, it is necessary to recall how the extraordinary circumstances that pertained to India during those crucial weeks freed the new prime minister from many of the intraparty factional troubles that would normally have assailed any leader of the Congress–I.

Consider first the speed with which events unfolded in the aftermath of the assassination. The first thirteen days were a time of mourning and uncertainty about what would happen next. It was impossible in that period for faction leaders at the state and national levels within the Congress–I to engage in maneuvers or to lobby the bereaved premier. When the official mourning ceased, it was announced almost immediately that polling in a general election would begin on 24 December, two weeks earlier than most people anticipated. This gave faction leaders fourteen fewer days in which to deploy their forces in the struggle for party tickets.

Candidate selections had to be finalized almost immediately and, given the tragic nature of recent events, it was both unseemly and politically unwise to engage in aggressive, disruptive behavior or to attempt to put pressure on their new leader. Congressmen expected Rajiv Gandhi to lead them to victory, thanks to a sympathy wave, and they were therefore doubly reluctant to risk annoying him. And, because he was something of an unknown quantity to many of them, and it was not at all clear exactly what sort of action might upset him, they were rendered still more cautious. It made more sense in the short run to fall in with whatever decisions the high command might make and then wait for a more promising day to renew the fight with their factional opponents.[86]

Then on 16 December, just as the election campaign was reaching top gear, the government persuaded the election commission to announce that state assembly elections would be held in nine states plus Pondicherry in March or April 1985.[87] The implication clearly was that, if factions within Congress–I whose members had been denied Lok Sabha tickets attempted to sabotage their factional rivals during the election campaign, they would pay a price when the time came to distribute party nominations for the assembly polls. This was a highly effective threat to make, for, with the main locus of factional conflict within the ruling party at the state level, nominations to the state assemblies are of prime concern to potential squabblers. The result was a remarkably low incidence of dissidence among Congressmen who had quarrelled frequently, openly, even violently and, occasionally, murderously among themselves in the years since 1980.

A great many people who were capable of quite normless factional conflict were still present within the Congress–I. Unless substantial numbers of them could be removed or neutralized, destructive factionalism was virtually certain to recur. There is little evidence to indicate that the prime minister and his aides took steps during the election campaign to begin this process. No fewer than 121 sitting Congress–I MPs were denied renomination in 1984 (that is, just under 37 percent of the party's old Lok Sabha delegation), but this did not represent a cleansing of corrupt, criminal, or contentious elements. Potential candidates were mainly assessed on their ability to win by leaders who were remarkably insecure about their prospects, and many people with very unsavory reputations were reselected.[88] Only a very small number of such types were expelled, most notable among them, A. R. Antulay. Selections for the state assembly elections in March 1985 were only marginally less cautious, despite the reassurance of a general election triumph only a few weeks earlier.

After the election, the prime minister took some modest steps to improve the performance of his party, but they have so far had little impact,

---

[86] I am grateful to Iqbal Narain for this information.

[87] *The Statesman* (Delhi), 17 December 1984.

[88] These statistics can be extrapolated from Press Information Bureau, Ministry of Information and Broadcasting, *General Elections 1984: Reference Handbook*, New Delhi: Press Information Bureau, 1984. These comments are also based on numerous interviews with Congress operatives and political analysts in Delhi and five states during December 1984 and January 1985.

although they have served to illustrate how severe the problems are. He has, for example, insisted that top party administrators give him frank reports on political events around the country. This may sound like an obvious request, but for years under Mrs. Gandhi, leading Congressmen told the premier only what they thought she wished to hear. They had seen too many bearers of sad tidings sacked for their candor. Leading party officials now contend that this former practice has been reversed in the national Congress–I headquarters in New Delhi. What has not yet been much affected is the tendency of state-level party units to send rosy reports to New Delhi.[89] Changing that will require major and highly risky structural changes within the Congress–I. It was Mrs. Gandhi's abandonment of intraparty elections in the early 1970s that turned Congress into a party of "yes-men," and it will probably require a democratization of Congress to restore its once formidable information-gathering capacity. There is at this writing much talk of party elections soon. But unless an energetic purge of factious and criminal elements takes place first, elections will simply entrench unreliable groups in power.

Rajiv Gandhi has begun, tentatively in a few of India's numerous political arenas, to replace dubious figures with people of competence and probity. In the state of Rajasthan during 1985, for example, he ousted a chief minister whose reputation for ineffective administration and less than rigorous bookkeeping had alarmed several of the state's leading Congressmen. He replaced him with a former chief minister who had solid accomplishments but whose loyalty had been judged insufficiently fierce by Mrs. Gandhi. The result is a major improvement in the party and the government in Rajasthan.

In several other states, the new premier's appointments of new leaders to provincial units of the party indicate that he, unlike his predecessor, does not perceive strong regional leaders to be threats. (Although this does not yet mean that power within the party has been significantly decentralized.) His problem in many regions, however, is that he cannot find people of skill and integrity who also possess the minimal local following to equip them to take command. In many states, if he were to purge the party's upper echelons of dubious figures, he would have no upper echelons left.

Consider, for example, his decision to name Bansi Lal to a cabinet post, a choice that raised many eyebrows, not least in Congress. On investigation, this move seems to have been made because Rajiv Gandhi needed Bansi Lal as a counterweight to another potent Jat leader from Haryana, the state's chief minister, Bhajan Lal. The latter was expected to resist any accommodation with the Sikhs and the state of Punjab. But why not sim-

---

[89] Interview with A. K. Antony, New Delhi, 6 January 1985.

ply dismiss Bhajan Lal—who after all defected en masse with his state cabinet to the Congress–I in 1980 from the Janata party—and spare himself the odium of having one of the hard men of the Emergency, Bansi Lal, in his government? The answer is that the prime minister can find no one else in the Haryana party who could take over the state and withstand the subversive doings that could be expected from both Bhajan Lal and Bansi Lal. Rajiv Gandhi is trapped by the wretched condition of his party there into perpetuating that very condition. Early elections within the Haryana Congress–I can only reinforce the problem. Similar dilemmas exist in numerous other states.

In several states, the Congress–I is also faced with severe internal divisions that prevent it from taking advantage of useful opportunities. This is true, for example, in West Bengal, where violent clashes within the Congress–I are common—indeed, one even occurred in faraway Bombay where two Bengali factions skirmished at the party's centenary celebrations—and where intraparty murders are not unknown. It is also true in Karnataka, where at least seven splinters prevent the Congress–I from developing any significant coherence.

Perhaps the most damaging such conflict has plagued the Kerala unit of the party. In the wake of the 1984 election, in which the Congress–I and its allies made major gains against the Marxist-led alliance, it was clearly in the party's interest to hold an early state assembly election. By taking advantage of their momentum from the Lok Sabha poll, they might have broken the stalemate with the Marxists that has persisted for many years. The Kerala chief minister was, however, unwilling to fight a state election, because he feared that another faction within the Congress–I, with better connections in New Delhi, might gain most of the nominations for the new assembly and oust him from leadership. His faction's interests were therefore put before those of the party, and the Congress–I let a highly promising opportunity slip away. If Rajiv Gandhi is to free himself of this kind of self-defeating factionalism, drastic action will be necessary.

His blistering critique of the party on the occasion of its centenary may suggest that he is poised to do this, but certain other recent actions indicate that the caution that marked his candidate selections in late 1984 and early 1985 may continue. The appointment of Jagdish Tytler, first to the post of joint secretary of the party, and then to a junior ministerial post is such a selection. Tytler was one of Sanjay Gandhi's more aggressive lieutenants, a man who had numerous criminal charges standing against him when Congress–I returned to power in 1980 and who has openly admitted an assault on a policeman.[90] He is also reliably alleged, along with sev-

---

[90] *New York Times*, 16 January 1985.

eral other Congress–I leaders, of involvement in the anti-Sikh riots in Delhi after the murder of Mrs. Gandhi.[91] Rajiv Gandhi's decision to promote Tytler twice suggests that, far from pursuing a thorough purge of figures associated with the normlessness of former days, he wishes to signify to such people that there are still places for them in the Congress–I. It therefore seems unlikely that the party will soon overcome the ills that the premier himself so vividly depicted in his centenary address. Unless it can overcome these and recover some of its old organizational strength outside the legislatures, it will not be able to remain dominant within the legislatures. In future elections, it will not be able to count on the kind of intense emotionalism that compensated for its organizational weakness at the general election of 1984.

These problems of the Congress–I, and the difficulties that confront anyone seeking to attend to them, have also made the party vulnerable to infiltration by political forces that used to operate within opposition parties. This has, for the time being at least, somewhat altered relations within the party system. It is even possible that it could one day threaten the open, freely competitive character of the political system. I refer here to the entry into the 1984 Congress–I election campaign at grass-roots levels of a huge number of activists from the Hindu extremist group, the RSS.[92] It is impossible to say how many have remained within the ruling party since the election, but even if most have departed, the Congress–I has shown its vulnerability to infiltration, and the possibility of a recurrence is far more likely than it once was.

It is of course true that, when Mrs. Gandhi's Congress moved leftward in the late 1960s, it was able to absorb and disarm leftists who came into it. But the Congress–I of today is a good deal less able to contain the forces of the communal right. RSS activists entered the party in far larger numbers than came over in the late 1960s and early 1970s. They also came into widely scattered arenas across much of India and at low levels, whereas the earlier leftist influx tended to occur at elite levels where they were more manageable. The RSS men, unlike the leftists, appear mainly to have entered in coherent groups large enough to outweigh the strength of the pre-existing Congress–I organization in many parts of northern and central India. Given the decay of the party since the early 1970s, entrants no longer require much manpower or cohesion for this to happen.

It is also possible, to make matters worse, that communalism is more difficult to contain than are leftist sentiments. Jawaharlal Nehru certainly

[91] People's Union (n. 69).

[92] This was clear from numerous interviews, particularly in North India, with BJP and Congress–I activists during December 1984 and from sources cited in note 50.

thought so, mainly because he could see how reforms could remove the main causes of leftist agitations, but he could not see how communalist or caste agitations might be defused. In his day in most parts of India, the agrarian social order weighed very heavily against the development of a mass base by leftist forces. But it is far from certain that society today presents communalists with the sort of natural impediments that greeted (and still greet) leftists. The steady rise of communal violence in recent years[93] suggests that the awakening of the electorate (which entails the crystallization of the collective self-consciousness of many caste and communal groups) amid the decay of institutions may mean that existing social conditions often facilitate rather than retard the advance of communalism. The manipulation of parochial sentiments has always been a dangerous game in South Asia, as the avoidable tragedy of Sri Lanka demonstrates,[94] but in India it has probably not been as dangerous as it now is since the immediate aftermath of partition.

Finally, it is difficult to say these days, as Morris-Jones did after the 1967 election, that the political system had moved away from dependence upon one leader and that recent changes in the Congress and the party system made the stability of the regime seem more assured than ever. The situation today is not without promise. Several opposition parties are now more attuned to the possibility of taking power at the state level and of joining a ruling coalition at the national level. Despite their disastrous showing in the 1984 election, some of them could still forge themselves into a plausible alternative to the ruling party. But Congress–I today is patently dependent on one leader, an inherently unstable situation. There are signs that Rajiv Gandhi recognizes the need to rebuild the party as an institution with genuine corporate substance. But it is far from clear that he possesses the determination to press ahead with the thorough cleansing and restructuring that is required. Even if he does, the task will be fiendishly difficult, given the extent of the popular awakening and the institutional decay of recent years. It is nonetheless important that he should succeed, for there must be serious doubts about the liberal, representative order, or what has increasingly become over the last twenty years "India's democracy," surviving many more shocks unless substantial reinstitutionalization takes place within the ruling party and unless more open and civil relationships can be developed within the party system.

[93] *Times* (London), 18 May 1984.
[94] See, for example, James Manor, ed. *Sri Lanka in Change and Crisis*, London and New York: St. Martin's, 1984, especially the articles by Gananath Obeyesekere and Jonathan Spencer.

THREE

The Military and
Indian Democracy

STEPHEN P. COHEN

p. 128-9

INTRODUCTION

The military dominates politics in almost half the "developing" states of the world, and in most of the others it is not far from power.[1] Until quite recently the armed forces were a major political force in many European nations; in the Leninist states they remain under civilian control, but only because the dominant party—following Lenin's lead—has militarized itself.

India stands as a remarkable exception to this prevalence of military dominance, or influence. Although outsiders and Indians have for years been predicting the imminent "takeover" by the Indian army, it is as far from seizing power today as it was thirty years ago. The Indian army remains an outstanding example of an apolitical, professional force, almost the model of a bureaucratic instrument of state policy. This is all the more remarkable when the Indian experience is compared with that of Pakistan and Bangladesh, states that share not only South Asian culture and geography, but the British military tradition.[2]

The present, compatible relationship between the military and India's democracy did not just happen. Nehru, Patel, and other Indian politicians, as well as their civilian advisers, had a clear idea which elements of the

Key—maintain some awers of British system.

[1] "Developing" is only a slightly less obnoxious term than "Third World." India has a fully developed political system and many economic and social problems. There are richer countries incapable of dealing with problems of lesser magnitude and no poorer countries better able to cope.

[2] There are no objective histories of the Indian military since independence, although there are very good studies of individual wars, units, battles, and problems. For a survey, see V. Longer, *Red Coats to Olive Green*, Bombay: Allied, 1974, by a former government official, and for a survey of current historical writing by a government historian, see Sri Nanadan Prasad, *The Military History of India*, Calcutta: K. P. Bagchi, 1976. My own book, *The Indian Army: Its Contribution to the Development of a Nation*, Berkeley: University of California Press, 1971, examines the development of the professional officer in British India and during the first twenty-four years of independent India.

"British tradition" they wanted to keep and which they wanted to discard. Even so, there were numerous turning points between 1947 and 1985 when events might have taken a different direction: the army was successfully transferred from British to Indian leadership; the officer corps underwent a dramatic change in its social base; and the army suffered and recovered from a severe and humiliating defeat. There have been lesser adjustments as well: all three services have had to run fast merely to keep up with new military technologies; the army has again been asked to perform demanding domestic roles (especially with regard to internal security), and from 1980 onward, India's national security apparatus has had to figure out a way to manage a strategic alliance with a major weapons supplier that is at the same time an occupying power in a neighboring state.

Lesser crises have triggered military intervention in a number of states. India surprises because the military has *not* intervened. A coup is not likely, impending, or inevitable. Nevertheless, one can observe the slow expansion of military influence within the Indian political system, although in some ways that influence is considerably less than one encounters in several industrial democracies, most notably in the United States. One can also observe the militarization of Indian political discourse and the growth of an enormous military-industrial-political complex. And one can also point to the institutional anomaly of caste-based units recruited on a "martial races" basis, the great social distance between officer and *jawan* (soldier)—even though they increasingly come from the same class background—and the presence of trappings left over from the British raj. The most recent challenge to democratic values was the army's expanded role in governing Assam and Punjab, in addition to Mizoram and Nagaland. In 1984 there were at least 40 million Indians living under military rule, if not military law, making India one of the world's largest military-dominated states—while it was simultaneously the world's largest democracy.

These examples suggest several important linkages and the need for a broad definition of the term "democracy." With regard to linkages, it is important to remember that there are innumerable contacts between the military and the broader society that supports and sustains it, and which it is sworn to defend. The armed forces deal with peasants and presidents, with village caste structures and nuclear delivery systems; they manipulate public opinion and they are ultrasensitive to that opinion; they draw their resources from Indian society, and they make important technical and cultural contributions to that society. These are not discrete, watertight activities: military intervention in several of India's neighbors was triggered by a variety of strategic, political, professional, and social causes, not merely the disobedience or ambition of a few generals. Similarly, the term "democracy" refers to both a process and a category.

We must examine the military. The question is not merely whether there will be a coup, changing India from "democracy" to "military dictatorship."[3] Democracy has a participatory dimension, involving elections and change in leadership at local and state levels, not merely the national level (under Indira Gandhi plebiscitory democracy seemed to be evolving). Democracy also has a libertarian dimension: is the ordinary citizen free from police harassment, unlawful search and seizure; are civil rights protected; does one have the right to travel and assemble; and is the press free? Finally, it has, in South Asia, a dual economic dimension. The first can be summed up in Mrs. Gandhi's phrase, "economic democracy," that is, the prospect of a better life. The second is whether citizens have the material means with which to enter the political arena.

We do not regard the present role of the Indian military as anomalous, although it certainly is unique in many ways. It is not an historic accident, but the product of careful planning. It has not been static, but has undergone significant structural and doctrinal change. What remains an open question is whether the pattern of gradual, adaptive change will continue. Recent events suggest it may not and highlight the importance of a fresh look at the Indian military.

· The salience of the military's coercive dominance within India has been recently dramatized with the breakdown of police and paramilitary forces in several states, after a major attempt to insulate the armed forces from civil disorder. When thousands of Sikh soldiers themselves mutinied after the occupation of the Golden Temple, the fragility of the barrier between a unified and a disintegrated India—and the military's vital rôle in maintaining that barrier—was emphasized as never before since 1947.

· India's external security environment remains unsettled. Leaving aside the armed stalemate with China and the recent war scare with Pakistan (which emanated largely from the Indian side), new problems have arisen with Sri Lanka and Bangladesh, and, after eight years, the Soviet Union has increased military activity in that part of South Asia which it occupies.

· Events elsewhere in South Asia suggest vulnerabilities in India's own political culture. Pakistan and Bangladesh underwent extended spells of martial law after 1971. Because India is itself undergoing some of the

---

[3] As many undertrials are killed in some Indian states as in all of South Africa's jails; there is now probably more genuine political freedom in parts of Pakistan than in several Indian states. This does not make South Africa or Pakistan "democracies" or India a "dictatorship," but it suggests caution in applying such undifferentiated labels.

same stresses that led to military rule in both of these states, it is important to note the similarities and differences between them, not only for the sake of understanding India, but because its neighbors look to India as a model.

· Certain recent events have had a direct and dramatic impact upon the military and may have far-reaching consequences. It is hard to say which of these is most significant: the murder of Mrs. Gandhi, the mutiny of Sikh soldiers, the development of a Khalistan movement, direct military rule in the Punjab, and the continuing arms race with Pakistan. A host of minor events and trends has taken its toll as well: the bypassing of paramilitary forces in quelling riots in Bombay, the dramatic increase in retired unemployed servicemen, irregularities in senior promotions, controversy over caste recruitment to the army, and a protracted struggle by all three armed services to improve the quality and quantity of their weapons in order to implement new, offensive military doctrines.

Although this chapter will touch upon most of these events and problems, our central theme and perspective will remain that of the military itself. In the final analysis, it is the restraint of the armed forces that allows civilian control, pluralist politics, and democratic civil liberties to survive, if not thrive, in India. Our central concern is less *how* the military defends the Indian state from internal and external threats than those mechanisms, values, and procedures that have limited its political role, even as it has become socially, economically, and culturally more important.

We are, with one exception, not concerned with the social composition or caste structure of the larger military establishment, as this does not bear directly upon the political and constitutional role of the armed forces. The important exception is the reduced recruitment of Sikhs, a process that became a Sikh grievance and a matter of special concern to some Sikh officers.

Finally, because of India's special qualities, certain comparative insights may be useful. India is a democratic, poor, federal system; it is South Asian, pluralist, and multilingual; it shares in the British imperial and colonial traditions; it is surrounded by powerful and sometimes hostile neighbors, as well as weak and dependent ones; it could easily acquire a nuclear weapons capability and is also, in places, economically and technologically advanced. The role that its military plays is not exactly comparable to *any* other state, but there are important structural, ideological, economic, and strategic points in common with Pakistan, the United States, Bangladesh, China, Israel, and others. Pakistan has a similar army, but different political context; Israel has a similar political system, but a different kind of army; China is similar in size and economic level, but differs in ideology and political structure. We shall be attentive to comparisons throughout this chapter not only for purposes of explication, but because of the special achievements of India's civil-military structure.

THE INDIAN OFFICER CORPS: A GROUP BIOGRAPHY

Because the future political role of the military is ultimately dependent upon the restraint (or intervention) of the officer corps, it is vital that we describe that officer corps. This task is simplified by the fact that the officer corps is itself a formal bureaucracy and thus slow to change. Its members have written extensively about the social, bureaucratic, and even political problems they face. We can also draw inferences about the impact of particular major events or trends, basing our analysis upon known consequences in other military establishments. It is thus possible to treat the Indian military as a kind of extended, historical family, in which succeeding generations undergo somewhat different experiences while sharing certain key familial characteristics. Some of these critical historic events are summarized in Figure 1.

The British Legacy

The present Indian military establishment is led entirely by officers recruited and trained in independent India. The bulk of them entered after 1962–1963, when the army was almost tripled in size. Today the army itself has about 35,000 officers. They share a number of values and beliefs inherited from their British forerunners.[4] Their perspective is all-Indian, and they view affairs in a national or even subcontinental context, rather than from a regional perspective. They also inherit the view that "politics" (in the partisan sense) is to be kept out of the mess. They feel that the army is the only effective force standing between chaos and order; their frequent involvement in "aid to the civil power" operations, whether in the form of disaster relief or riot control regularly drives this lesson home, as it did for their British predecessors. But this involvement has also led to another lesson: India is so vast and disorderly a country that the army would find it difficult to manage it. The British taught, and the Indians learned, that the military must remain above politics, if possible, lest it be torn apart by sectarian differences. Yet this belief provides a motive for intervention when the armed forces come to believe (as they did in Pakistan and Bangladesh) that their own organization is threatened by political rot.

[4] For a detailed survey of the British-trained Indian officers, see Cohen, *The Indian Army* (n. 2), chap. 5, "The Professional Officer in India."

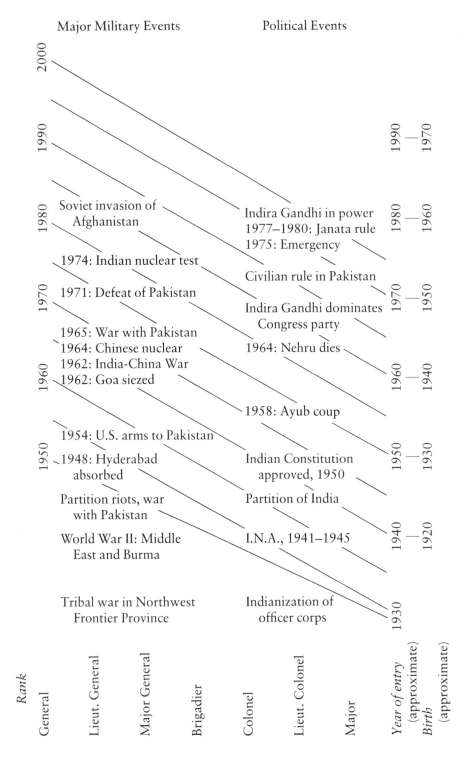

FIGURE 1 Military Generations in India

The Post-War Army

The Indian army managed the transition from colonial instrument to nationalist force with amazing ease. Nehru and Patel, as well as the British, all agreed that any abrupt change in the structure of the army, its ideology, or even its recruitment pattern would lead to political instability. They were assisted in the process of "democratizing" the Indian army by two important facts, first, the serving *Indian* officers were all very young—only a few had reached brigadier rank—and posed no threat to the politicians. Second, the ideologues who wanted to create a truly na- tionalist force could not press their case while the army was barely able to meet its security obligations during partition, in Kashmir, and then in Junagadh and Hyderabad. These internal "liberation" wars confirmed the nationalist, if not yet democratic, pedigree of the Indian armed forces.

Shortly afterward, the officers corps underwent a transformation, changing the class structure of the military. Even though the Punjab continued to dominate the officer corps (today Sikhs still constitute about 20 percent of the officers), the army became less attractive to India's upper classes. Pay fell behind inflation, service conditions were increasingly difficult (especially after 1962), the formal status of the armed forces was sharply reduced, and military policy was subordinated to a foreign policy that placed more emphasis on diplomacy than force.[5]

Bright young Indians from "good" families have stayed away from the military, especially the army, for years. At the elite private schools, the first preference for graduates (after a college education) has become foreign firms and then Indian private firms. In their place have come the sons of noncommissioned officers (NCOs) and junior commissioned officers (JCOs).

This trend has eradicated the elitist character of the officer corps, espe- cially in the army. More precisely, it will be one generation removed from the peasantry, as the largest single category of entrant into the National Defense Academy (NDA) and the Indian Military Academy (IMA) are sons of NCOs and JCOs, who have themselves spent several years of service at other ranks. Very senior officers openly describe the intellectual caliber of leadership material attracted to the armed forces (especially the army) as "intellectually mediocre."[6]

[5] For a survey of changed pay and promotion opportunities see Lt. Gen. (ret.) M. L Chibber, *Leadership in the Indian Army During Eighties and* Nineties, New Delhi: U. S. I. papers, no. 8, n.d. [1980?].

[6] Maj. Gen. K. S. Bajwa, "Military Leadership and the Changing Social Ethos," *U. S. I. of India Journal* (July-September 1978), p. 235. Bajwa urges a "realistic" approach, as the Indian army must work with poor quality officer material.

The decline in the formal status of the Indian army officer has been fully documented in the military's own journals. An analysis by one of India's leading soldier-scholars, the then Brigadier S. K. Sinha, points out that every one of the 3,000 Indian Administrative Service (IAS) officers is bound to become commissioner or collector in twenty years and achieve the statutory status of a major general.[7] Compared with the pyramidal structure of the armed forces, the IAS and police are rectangular in shape. Whereas an army officer will only be guaranteed of reaching lieutenant colonel in twenty-four years, the IAS cadre, one tenth the size of the officer corps, had some fifty appointments (now, in 1986, one hundred) at secretary-level equitable with the army's sole general slot.[8]

A follow-up study noted that the situation had actually worsened after the 1971 war when the chiefs of the three service staffs were placed below the comptroller and auditor general, and lieutenant generals were placed below the chief secretaries of states (even though one might be a corps commander with responsibility for the defense of half a dozen states).[9] Further, because individual states can establish their own warrant of precedence for officers of the rank of brigadier and below, some created "ludicrous anomalies." In Tamil Nadu, Bihar, and Orissa, a brigadier is now ranked above deputy commissioners and IAS officers with less than twenty-five years of service but is below such officers in Rajasthan (in fact, he ranks below an officer with as little as nine years of service), and in Rajasthan, Manipur, Mizoram, and Nagaland, brigadiers are ranked below deputy commissioners.

Similar disparities in pay and pension allowances and in housing conditions have contributed to the decline in status of the military profession in India to the point where the subject has become a regular feature of the professional military literature. Significantly, virtually no such complaints are heard from the navy or air force. Thus the largest service is the one in greatest social decline, and the two armed services that are weakest within the government remain the most popular among the general educated elite of India.

This military is neither elitist nor ideological but is officered by average talent. Officers are increasingly the product of the military culture itself, many having been taught entirely in cantonment schools, raised in the cantonment atmosphere, and obligated entirely to the military for their

---

[7] Brig. S. K. Sinha, "Career Prospects for Officers in Armed Forces," *U. S. I. of India Journal* (July–September 1968), p. 265.

[8] Ibid. See Lt. Gen. M. L. Thapan, "Profession of Arms," *The Statesman* (Calcutta), 14 September 1982, for recent figures.

[9] Lt. Gen. M. L. Thapan, "The Army as a Career," *U. S. I. of India Journal* (July–September 1977).

livelihood and enhanced status from cradle to funeral pyre. The officer is not, however, isolated from his own society. The contemporary officer is keenly aware of the personal and institutional corruption that surrounds him, even among the political leadership of the state. Published reports indicate that this corruption has touched the military directly.[10] In particular, contact with the broader civilian society in the area of recruitment and in purchases of stores and equipment is known for its "opportunity." Young officers who want to make money on the side gravitate to recruiting details, where bribes of several thousand rupees are not uncommon.

There is one important principle involved in this brush with corruption. A man who resists temptation from this direction, who resists pressures from family, caste, or friends to bend the rules, and who tries to uphold the highest professional standards will feel doubly betrayed by the politician who uses him and his men for corrupt goals. He will also regard a threat to his service as a threat to himself, for he is unlikely to have any place to go after resignation. In brief, when the officer corps is both professional *and* drawn from the lower middle class, the military becomes increasingly sensitive to lateral pressures from a materialistic society *and* to pressures from above.

Future Generations

All available evidence indicates that the young officers now in the Indian army—the colonels of the year 2000, and the generals of 2010—are very much like their predecessors.[11] The lure of private industry has reduced the status of all but a few government-related jobs for the average Indian. Very few sons of commissioned officers join the army: according to one study; probably not more than 10 percent; "today there is no such thing as martial tradition. Sons who automatically joined the old man's regiment are now plumping for 'civvy street.' The incentive is gone. The so-called good families no longer consider the armed forces as a last resort for a not very intelligent offspring. Even he goes to a firm."[12]

[10] See the article by Maj. Gen. P. M. Pasricha on military leadership and corruption in *Strategic Analysis*, IDSA, New Delhi, November 1983; Sudhansu Mohanty, "Honesty in the Forces," *The Statesman* (Calcutta), 4 February 1984; press coverage of the Samba spy scandal, the Larkin spy scandal, and the recent court martial proceedings against Maj. Gen. D. S. C. Rai in *India Today*, 30 April 1984.

[11] See, for example, R. P. Gautam, "Causes of Higher Secondary Students Preference for Military Career," *U. S. I. of India Journal* (October-November 1979), p. 380.

[12] Bikram Vohra, "Fair Deal for our Fighting Men," *Illustrated Weekly of India*, 23 June 1974. For a rare feminist critique of the military's recruitment and employment policies, see

This lack of interest in the armed forces by the educated and upper-class families of India is not without parallel in other countries, including Pakistan and the United States. It is probably related to the decline in interest *within* the army in the fighting branches, which had traditionally attracted the best and the brightest. Now there are severe shortfalls in officer volunteers for the infantry and artillery, whereas the service and ordnance corps are oversubscribed.[13]

Does this change in the social composition of the officer corps have political implications? In itself, probably not. Those who fear the Indian army as the last bastion of an elite upper class need not worry. Neither are there likely to be direct political consequences of this shift in social class. The Pakistan army underwent a similar transformation after World War II and remains politically active. The U. S. military also saw its social composition altered after World War I, and transformed after World War II, but remains politically inert. As we shall discuss below, any change in the political role of the Indian armed forces will depend more upon actions of the civilians than of the armed forces and will probably come about through other routes. Nevertheless, military grievances over pay and status are substantial and may be contributing factors to an increased role for the armed forces.

THE COMBAT EXPERIENCES OF THE INDIAN MILITARY

It is important to note the type of armed conflicts that the Indian military has engaged in, because this has some bearing upon its political role. Figure 2 summarizes these conflicts. It shows that the military has been almost continuously active since 1947 at every level from police action to preparation for nuclear war. How has this shaped the relationship between India's armed forces and its democratic structure?

The Partition Riots and Internal Conflict

From 1947 onward the Indian military (especially the army) has been regularly involved in the suppression of communal violence and large-

---

Dr. A. Mahajan, "Women in the Armed Forces: A Case Study of India," a paper presented to the 1980 Inter-University Seminar on Armed Forces and Society (IUS).

[13] Exact figures, based on a leaked army document presented to the Fourth National Pay Commission, are contained in "Asking for More," *India Today*, 31 January 1985. Not only are the figures remarkable, but so is the explicit linkage of a demand for greater pay with the army's heightened internal security role: the document begins with a discussion of Operation Bluestar and the security problems of the Punjab.

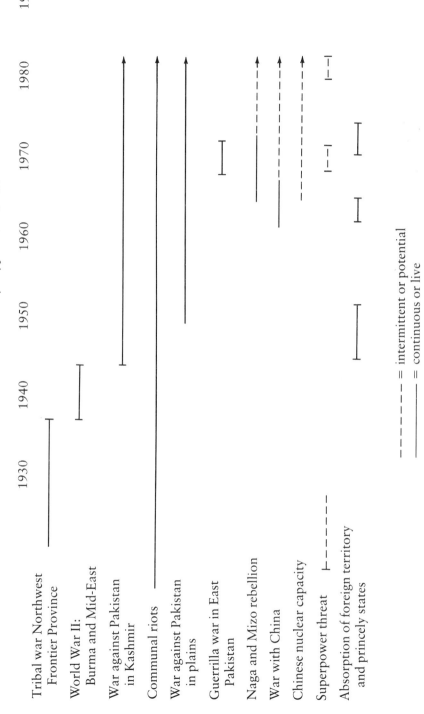

FIGURE 2   Wars of the Indian Military: Type and Duration

scale counterinsurgency action. The military's involvement in these operations is inherently paradoxical. On the one hand, it demonstrates the national character of the armed forces, the contribution the army makes to the unity and integrity of India. Yet, the army hates such operations. No army can train efficiently for conventional war and stand by for riot control: not only does the latter disrupt training cycles and demand different kinds of tactics and doctrine, but it is no longer feasible, after conflict with Pakistan, to have the army quartered in and around India's major cities.

paramilitary forces to serve as buffer.

Therefore, in the 1950s and 1960s a number of important paramilitary forces were created to serve as a buffer between the army and domestic disorder that could not be contained by the increasingly corrupt and incompetent police. At first, these paramilitary forces were welcomed, and some observers thought that India had become coup-proofed. Indeed, during the critical months of the Emergency, Indira Gandhi did not have to call upon the military at all, relying entirely upon state and central intelligence, police, and paramilitary bureaucracies. But this step was taken without adequate attention to the root cause of the problem of domestic

domestic upheaval results in...

disorder, which was the growth of political corruption and the linkage between politicians and the state police forces. Indeed, the police and paramilitary forces were themselves to become one of the chief causes of internal disorder.[14]

The attitude of the Indian military toward the new paramilitary forces was decidedly mixed. On the one hand, there was universal agreement that such forces are necessary to insulate the military from direct involvement with communal, regional, religious, or other civil disorders. On the other hand, the officers are jealous of these forces. Their officers and men receive considerably better pay than the army and often a status and authority that they do not deserve. The military would like to control such forces or be able to place their own officers and men in them on a temporary basis.[15]

[14] A former army officer and current member of parliament has written an incisive post-Bluestar analysis of the assumption of the police function (a state subject) by the union government in Jaswant Singh, "The Security Mix-Up," *Seminar* (Using the Army), no. 308 (April 1985). See also K. P. Misra, "Paramilitary Forces in India," *Armed Forces and Society* (Spring 1980), pp. 371–388. Misra stated that, having established the buffer between the military and society, the system had become coup-proofed. A more cautious military assessment is that of Maj. Gen. S. K. Sinha, "In Aid of the Civil Power," *U. S. I. of India Journal* (June 1974), pp. 115–123. He notes that the Indian military engaged in 476 aid-to-the-civil-power actions between 1961 and 1970.

[15] The Pakistan army does this with the Khyber Rifles and other Frontier Force's Regiment wings; regular army officers are sent on deputation for two or more years, command a larger unit than they would in the regular army, and then return to their home regiment. Stephen P. Cohen, *The Pakistan Army*, Berkeley: University of California Press, 1984.

At its upper levels, "aid to the civil power" blends into full-scale military operations designed to contain regional dissident movements. From the mid-fifties onward, the army was called upon to deal with recalcitrant tribal groups who were seeking autonomy or independence. The army has been continuously deployed in Nagaland and Mizoram in a counterinsurgency role. Some of the counterinsurgency literature it has produced out of the Nagaland experience can stand with the best written on the subject.[16]

The army has accepted close political supervision of its actions in Nagaland and Mizoram and understands the need for restraint. The tribal struggles do not have the potential (as does Punjab or Kashmir) for rapid escalation, and they serve the useful purpose of giving various units combat experience under controlled circumstances. Yet there is a certain chafing with political control. It is exacerbated when the army must work with police officers of lesser experience or with paramilitary forces over which it has limited or no control. In these and related operations the army regards itself as an extension of national policy, containing groups that would leave—or destroy—the Indian state. For many Nagas and Mizos, of course, the army is seen as an imperial occupation force, which from time to time has resorted to extremely brutal tactics. Most Indians are oblivious to the scope and operation of their own military in these states, although the problem has been raised by various international and Indian civil rights groups.[17]

A Communal Riot with Armor

The three wars between India and Pakistan have had a special quality about them. In the words of one Indian general, they are more like "communal riots with armor," than wars between sovereign states. The identities of India (a secular state with a large Muslim minority) and Pakistan (an avowedly religious state) stand as a challenge to each other, and both are extremely sensitive to the domestic politics of the other, especially in communal matters.

The Indian armed forces have built up considerable experience and doctrine from their wars with Pakistan. Until recently, this doctrine was passive and reactive and also reflected a lack of civilian interest in offensive

[16] Two books by Col. Vijay Kumar Anand are of special merit: *Conflict in Nagaland*, Delhi: Chanyaka, 1980, and *Insurgency and Counter-insurgency: A Study of Modern Guerilla Warfare*, Delhi: Deep and Deep, 1981.

[17] For an analysis of army behavior in an Indian state, Nagaland, see Nandita Haksar, "A Case Study," *Seminar* (Using the Army), no. 308 (April 1985).

strategies.[18] Nehru, of course, was wary of the military and tried to keep it as small as possible as long as possible—his reaction to the expansion of Pakistan's armed forces was quite restrained compared with recent subcontinental arms "racing."[19] Shastri and Indira Gandhi were also reluctant to contemplate offensive strategies. Pakistan was too formidable a foe to attack, especially because India had a two-front military problem after 1962 and no civilian (or military) official willing to divert substantial resources from developmental projects to the military.

[margin note: key military didn't get too many resources.]

Thus, India has never faced a situation against its main enemy, Pakistan, in which there was a sharp divergence between civilian and military approaches to strategy. Nor, with one exception, has military action been viewed from an ideological perspective. The exception, and it is only partial, was the invasion of East Pakistan, resulting in the creation of a temporarily democratic Bangladesh. At the time, the army was widely praised as having liberated Bangladeshis from military tyranny and of furthering the cause of democracy. This euphoria was short-lived, and there has been a general recognition that military power is not an effective instrument in creating or even supporting regional democracies, as much as India would prefer its neighbors to have compatible political systems.

Interventions: Chinese and Soviet

India's armed forces have also had to cope with external interventions into South Asia by China and the Soviet Union. Each influenced the military's thinking in important ways.

[margin note: post-62 defeat]

The 1962 war and its aftermath showed that the Indian army was professional enough to reconstruct itself after a shattering military and moral defeat.[20] It had the full support of the political community and

[margin note: log]

---

[18] For three recent statements of IAF, IN, and army thought on first-strike or pre-emptive war and the relationship to deterrence (especially of Pakistan), see "India's Defense Policy and Doctrine for 1980s," the keynote address by CAS Air Chief Marshal Dilbagh Singh, before the Second Annual Session of the National Congress for Defense Studies, Poona University, 7 June 1982; "The Pre-Emptive Naval Strike in Limited Wars," by Cdr. K. R. Menon, I. N., *U. S. I. of India Journal* (January–March 1978), pp. 46–54; and "Deep Thrust," by Lt. Col. J. K. Dutt, *U. S. I. of India Journal* (January–March 1978), pp. 69–74.

[19] For an excellent study of the regional military balance, see Robert G. Wirsing, "The Arms Race in South Asia: Implications for the United States," *Asian Survey* 25, no. 3 (March 1985), pp. 265–291.

[20] I reviewed the literature produced by the 1962 war in "India's China War and After," *Journal of Asian Studies* (August 1971), pp. 847–857. Since then, a number of additional important books have been published, triggered by Lt. Col. J. R. Saigal, *The Unfought War*, Bombay: Allied, 1979, which charges the senior military leadership with incompetence; one of the NEFA divisional commanders has his rejoinder in Nirinjan Prasad, *The Fall of Towang, 1962*, New Delhi: Palit and Palit, 1981.

some American, British, and Soviet assistance, but basically the post-1962 expansion and reform was an internal military achievement. This successful effort did not obscure two vital lessons drawn by most officers.

First the 1962 performance of the officer corps itself ranged from mediocre to incompetent, with a very few brave (and largely posthumous) exceptions. Second, the military as a whole had been betrayed by the politicians, including Nehru and Krishna Menon. This lesson was applied in 1965 when the then chief of army staff (COAS), J. N. Chaudhuri, asked for and was granted operational freedom, a situation exactly opposite that of 1962, when Nehru, Menon, and senior intelligence officers and civil servants controlled the tiniest movement of army units. The 1965 pattern was followed in modified form in 1971. Once permission to attack was given, the army was left entirely on its own in the east until the Pakistan army surrendered. This time the army played a greater role in the peacemaking process and insisted that, for tactical military reasons, some territories taken from Pakistan *not* be returned.

An intervention of current consequence is the Russian occupation of Afghanistan.[21] The military regard this as an unmitigated disaster from two perspectives: it has enabled Pakistan to acquire new weapons, and it has raised an entirely new set of strategic problems. Unlike 1971, when East Pakistan was virtually isolated from all important external contacts, a war with Pakistan would not mean a free ride for the Indian army. The Soviet Union, as a presence in South Asia, is both a potential collaborator and a rival to India for the role of dominant South Asian power.

Nuclear War

Finally, the Indian military has at least a theoretical interest in nuclear war. The subject was included in the army's staff college syllabus as early as the mid-fifties, but only when an Indian weapon became a distinct possibility (by the late sixties) did the army take the bomb seriously.[22] From an army perspective, there is some fear that the budget for conventional weapons would be cut to support a nuclear weapon and its delivery systems. Army officers have also raised the problem of control. Not only are

[21] An analysis of the implications of the Soviet invasion for regional security is in Stephen P. Cohen, "South Asia After Afghanistan," *Problems of Communism* 34 (January–February 1985), pp. 18–31. For a careful study of the issue, see Elie D. Krakowski, "Defining Success in Afghanistan," *Washington Quarterly* 8, n. 2 (Spring 1985), pp. 37–46.

[22] For a sampling of Indian military attitudes toward nuclear weapons, see E. A. Vas, "The Bomb," *U. S. I. of India Journal* (October–December 1967), pp. 309–320, "A Nuclear Policy for India," *U. S. I. of India Journal* (January–March 1969), p. 27, and D. K. Palit, ed., *Nuclear Shadow over India*, New Delhi: U. S. I. of India, 1981.

they concerned that another service might assume the responsibility for nuclear weapons, but that this unequal responsibility would further strain interservice cooperation.

Although one can find critics of an Indian nuclear weapon in the military, most officers subscribe to the "option" strategy, and there has been a movement toward, rather than away from, nuclear acquisition. The military, after wishing that the issue would go away, has positioned itself so that it cannot be accused of pressuring the government to go nuclear, but it will be the first to stake a claim for control over nuclear weapons once the decision is reached.[23]

To summarize, the Indian military has undergone a complete transformation from its earliest status as an imperial auxiliary, lacking any significant modern weapons, to something approximating a balanced military force possessing nearly all modern arms. It has grown from a hundred thousand to a million men, yet it retains both its professional competence and its distance from an active political role. It would seem, however, that the key to the latter is not to be found in the former: during the same period, the Pakistan army also evolved into a modern fighting force while simultaneously placing itself at the center of Pakistani politics. This suggests that we shift our focus from the military's own institutions and experiences to the institutional and social means by which this large and powerful machine is guided.

THE ARMED FORCES AND THE POLICY PROCESS

The Indian armed forces play a remarkably small role in the shaping of security and defense-related policies and virtually no role in the shaping of policies outside this area. Indeed, probably no military of equivalent importance or size has less influence. This situation was not inherited from the British but was assembled, piece by piece, over the years, and is now enshrined in various constitutional and bureaucratic structures. We shall examine these below and then discuss vulnerable points in the following section.

[23] One of the most provocative studies of nuclear weapons by the armed forces was put together by K. Sundarji, then (1981) commander of the army's College of Combat. He later organized the military action in the Golden Temple, was appointed vice chief of the army staff, and became the chief of the army staff in January 1986. Sundarji argues for a tactical nuclear weapons capability now, to be followed by a larger, strategic force in the future. He may be the first army chief to have carefully studied the nuclear issue. See K. Sundarji, ed., *Effects of Nuclear Asymmetry on Conventional Deterrence*, Mhow: College of Combat, 1981.

Formal Structures

When India achieved independence in 1947, a number of structural and constitutional arrangements were instituted that had the net effect of ensuring that decisive military power would remain in the hands of the union government and that within that government the armed forces would be strictly subordinate to civilian political and administrative control.[24]

The initial step, taken when the interim government was formed in September 1947, involved removing the commander in chief of the Indian army from the governor general's executive council. He was replaced by a civilian defense member (Sardar Baldev Singh). A Defense *Member's* Committee was created and had the commander in chief, the defense secretary, and the financial advisor as members. After August 15, 1947, this was transformed into the Defense *Minister's* Committee, and the heads of the air force and the navy joined it. The army commander in chief then became theoretically equal to the heads of the other, much smaller and weaker services (in 1955 the heads of all three services were renamed as chiefs of their respective staffs, further reducing their status).

The Indian constitution of 1950 vests the "supreme command of the defense forces of the union" in the president of India, but the president is obligated to be "regulated by law," and de facto control over the government apparatus was vested in the prime minister. Article 74 (1) of the constitution states that "There shall be a Council of Ministers with the Prime Minister as head to aid and advise the President in the exercise of his functions." Conventions, established over the years, and later constitutional changes, have ensured that "aid and advice" is authoritative, and no president has attempted to exercise independent command over the armed forces.

Indian defense policy has usually been formulated at the highest level by a subcommittee of the cabinet, now the Political Affairs Committee. The chiefs of staff of the armed services are not members but may be invited to sit in on its meetings. They are members of the Defense Minister's Committee and have their own interservice committee, the Chiefs of Staff

---

[24] For surveys of the defense policy process, see Subrahmanyam citations below and A. L. Venkateshwaran, *Defence Organization in India*, New Delhi: Publications Division, Ministry of Information and Broadcasting, Government of India, 1967; P.V.R. Rao, *India's Defense Organization Since Independence*, New Delhi: U. S. I. of India, 1977; P. R. Chari, "Civil Military Relations in India," *Armed Forces and Society* 4, no. 1 (November 1977), pp. 3–28; and Jerrold F. Elkin and W. Andrew Ritezel, "The Debate on Restructuring India's Higher Defense Organization," *Asian Survey* 24, no. 10 (October 1984), pp. 1069–1085. For an excellent survey of the defense budgeting process, see Raju Thomas, *The Defense Of India*, Delhi: MacMillan, 1978.

Committee. This committee is chaired by the service chief with the longest tenure *on the committee*, ensuring that the dominant service, the army, will not automatically chair this committee. "Collectively, the Chiefs of Staff Committee is the highest professional advisor to the government on defense matters."[25]

Although civilian defense officials claim that this complicated system of committees ensures authoritative political guidance to the military and sound military advice to the politicians,[26] many in the military would disagree. They have written that, because of the increase in the ministerial membership of the Cabinet Committee on Political Affairs, the actual participation of the service chiefs at the highest level of decision making has become more diffuse, and there is a tendency not to invite the service chiefs even when defense matters are discussed.[27] Instead, the services have been represented by the defense secretary, further weakening their access to what is, on paper, the final decision-making authority on defense matters.

Bureaucratic and Political Control

The Indian military is not only legally circumscribed but has been bureaucratically and politically contained by the powerful Ministry of Defense. The ministry must approve all service-originated proposals. It determines all policy concerning the location and operation of defense industries, including the choice of weapons that will be produced in these industries, and it is responsible for all public information and policy statements pertaining to defense and security matters. The Ministry of Defense

[25] Chari (n. 24), p. 13.

[26] Venkateshwaran (n. 24), p. 125. However, the most perceptive analyst and critic of the Indian defense policy process (and the weakness of both civilian and military personnel) is K. Subrahmanyam. He was also instrumental in getting the military to undertake operations research in the mid-sixties. See "The Cultural Dimension of Managerial Reform," *Defense Manager [Management]* (October 1974), pp. 10–16. Also, his books contain references to the problem of defense organization in India. See especially *Perspectives in Defense Planning*, New Delhi: Abhinav, 1972, and *Defense and Development*, Calcutta: Minerva, 1973.

[27] The military has now begun attacking the process in earnest. Defense Manager (later titled *Defense Management*) has carried several perceptive articles criticizing the present system as cumbersome, inefficient, and wasteful. For an explicit reference to Venkateshwaran, arguing a "crying need at the moment to decentralize decision-making in the higher echelons," see Brig. V. Nagabhusan, "Management of Defense Effort," *Defense Manager* (October 1974) pp. 20–25. The author, an engineer serving with a corps headquarters, suggests that the service headquarters not only should be the originators and executors of plans but "should also be vested with adequate authority in the spheres of both approval of plans and apportioning of financial resources—within the gambit of approved policies and appropriations." In other words, no civilian bureaucratic interference.

has no *operational* authority, but it decides what is or is not a "policy" matter, and hence fit for ministry or cabinet level review.

The civilian officials of the defense ministry regard themselves as the pivot on which the defense policy process revolves. The ministry's class I cadre remains quite small, considering their responsibilities and influence. Generally, the civilians who fill these positions have only the most rudimentary military or defense background. Because their tenure is only five years, K. Subrahmanyam notes that for their first two or three years they are still acquiring knowledge about an unfamiliar field; they are only in a position to contribute to policy making during the last half of their tenure. Few have had extensive international experience. Typically, they are intensely aware of the internal political and social aspects of defense, not the role of defense policy as an instrument of foreign policy.

These shortcomings of civilian officials, coupled with their enormous veto power over what the generals propose, greatly irritates the military. One retired officer characterized the civilian defense official as "one who can talk about and pronounce judgment upon the knottiest professional problem with nonprofessional competence but professional air."[28] For their part, senior civilian defense officials have noted the caution and timidity of the military, although some have indicated considerable improvement in the quality of senior military leaders in the past ten years.

Over the years varied appointments have been made to the defense portfolio, and these fall into two types. The first have been politically weak but administratively competent individuals, who have "managed" the military and the Ministry of Defense. With one exception, Mrs. Gandhi's appointments were in this category. The exception was Bansi Lal, who reportedly abused his authority and angered the military. After returning to power in 1980, Mrs. Gandhi reverted to her earlier pattern by appointing, first, R. Venkataraman and, then, S. B. Chawan to the defense portfolio.

Earlier, more activist ministers had been appointed by Nehru (Krishna Menon and Y. B. Chawan) and during the Janata period (Jagjivan Ram). Menon and Ram, in particular, involved themselves in recruitment, training, and promotion practices with mixed reactions from the armed services. Rajiv Gandhi at first placed a reliable but powerless figure (P. V. Narasimha Rao) in the defense ministry, but by mid-1985 had assumed the portfolio himself and made a trusted friend and associate (Arun Singh) minister of state defense production—perhaps the de facto defense minister. This step was followed by a rush of decisions concerning foreign weapons purchases and the reorganization of the armed services.

[28] Maharaj K. Chopra, *India: The Search for Power*, Bombay: Lalvani, 1969, pp. 245ff.

The Chiefs' Controversy

The Indian military has accepted, but not enjoyed its ever-lessening influence at the higher levels of the policy process. It is faced with a dilemma: as long as it retains active command over its respective services, civilian officials are reluctant to increase their influence within the central decision-making process. The Indian chiefs have enormous operational authority, especially during wartime, but only advisory power at the center. There they are treated as formal equals, despite the obviously greater operational authority of the army COAS, and kept well away from the ultimate level of decision making.

Naturally, the armed services—especially the army—would like to change this arrangement, and this issue lies at the heart of the long-standing debate over the role of the chiefs. Should there be a *fourth* chief, as in the U. S. and U. K.? If so, who should it be? The suggestion of a fourth chief goes back at least to 1949 and was raised again in the 1960s by General J. N. Chaudhuri and more recently (in 1982) by another COAS, General Krishna Rao.[29]

The army is the natural advocate of an expanded joint chiefs system along the lines of the British chief of defense staff (CDS) system or the U.S. joint chiefs. In virtually every Western country (the army argues), such a system exists for coordinating military operations during wartime and providing coordinated and combined advice to civilians. The Indian system has been notorious for the lack of both. During 1965 and 1971 there was very little interservice coordination (in 1962 the navy and air force were not involved in the fighting in any significant way). P. C. Lal, the then air marshal, claims that Chaudhuri created the problem in 1965 by his unilateral determination of army strategy and failure to consult with the other two services; Lal himself determined what the Indian Air Force (IAF) strategy targeting would be in 1971, apparently without reference to army wishes. Other accounts indicate that the successful combined operations against Karachi were due more to good luck and fortunate timing than integrated military planning.

Somewhat disingenuously, the army advocates of a CDS system claim that the chief need not be from the army, but might be an air force or navy man. Whoever it was would presumably have to leave his own service parochialism behind.

The CDS system is strongly opposed by most navy and air force officers

---

[29] Gen. Krishna Rao's suggestion that there should be a chairman of the JCS was promptly refuted by Indira Gandhi's civilian defense minister, R. Venkataraman. The subject was extensively discussed in the Indian press; see *Indian Express*, 5 June 1982, *Times of India*, 14 July 1982, and Elkin and Ritezel, "Debate" (n. 24).

and a good number of politicians and the civilian bureaucracy. The navy and the IAF naturally feel that they would never get to hold the chairmanship. Further, because the Indian military fights on or near its own borders, a CDS system is unnecessary, for proper coordination could take place within the current system—especially if the army would cooperate.

The political arguments *against* the CDS system are not as openly voiced but in the current situation are powerful and final. First, there is the long-standing civilian suspicion of men in uniform and a deep-seated belief (held by Nehru and, apparently, Mrs. Gandhi) that the military remains a potential trouble spot for Indian democracy. Creating a fourth chief would mean creating a fourth general, or even an officer of field marshal rank, without good cause. More to the point, it runs counter to the divide and rule strategy employed by Nehru, Shastri, and Indira Gandhi, implemented by the civilian bureaucrats and directed against the armed forces—in particular, the army.[30] In India, the navy and the air force present no credible political threat, but the army might. The present arrangement reduces the army chief to no more than equal (and less than equal, when he does not chair the joint chiefs committee). Would changing this system actually improve the quality of military advice (ask those civilians who oppose change) when the military at best are not terribly inventive? Reshuffling the chief's system—they argue—would not improve military decision making, but it might enhance the political power of the military.

An additional word is in order on the *selection* of the chiefs, particularly the COAS. This selection process has two dimensions: the failure of a Sikh to become chief of the army staff (even though the army's officer corps is about 20 percent Sikh) and the apparent manipulation of appointments to ensure that the COAS will be an officer who is politically acceptable to the government. We shall discuss the problem of the Sikhs when looking at the Punjab crisis, although it should be noted that two Sikhs have been chiefs of the air staff.

When considering promotions to the COAS position, the first step is the preparation by the defense ministry bureaucracy of a statement of qualifications and experience of the five regional commanders: northern, southern, eastern, western, and central, plus the vice chief of staff—all lieutenant generals. The six constitute a panel from which the COAS is se-

[30] K. Subrahmanyam, who is less concerned about civilian control than an effective system of decision making and war fighting, is in favor of a chief of the joint chiefs or a chief of the defense staff, but wants a truly multiservice staff to be built up before the appointment and then to be followed by giving the actual command of combat units to this CDS/CJCS system. He sees individual service parochialism and pride as a barrier to good defense management, not as an aid to a "divide and rule" system of civilian control. "Chief of Defense Staff for India," *Defense Manager* (April 1975), pp. 5–8.

lected by a cabinet subcommittee for appointments presided over by the prime minister.

Until recently, the principle of seniority has been followed in promoting the COAS from this group (promotions at earlier levels are made largely by the military itself). There had earlier been great controversy when Lt. Gen. Harbaksh Singh and Lt. Gen. P. S. Bhagat, two outstanding officers, were allowed to retire because they barely lacked seniority.

The first overt violation of the seniority principle came on June 1, 1975, barely a month before the imposition of the Emergency, when Lt. Gen. T. N. Raina was made COAS, jumping over at least one other officer with greater seniority. The second violation occurred in May 1983 with an even more controversial appointment.[31] One of India's most brilliant soldiers, Lt. Gen. S. K. Sinha, was superseded by Lt. Gen. A. S. Vaidya, even though Sinha was vice chief of the army staff and thought to be in line to become the new chief. Vaidya was thought to have seriously compromised himself with public criticism of the ruling Communist party of India– (Marxist) (CPI[M]) government in Tripura and praise for the election alliance between Congress–I and another party. He was attacked in the press by the CPI(M) party leadership as having given "political statements," and the defense public relations service had to issue a statement to the effect that the Indian army "continues to remain apolitical in its best tradition."[32] Sinha responded to his supersession by turning in his resignation. Several newspapers reprinted some of his perceptive writings on the problems of civil-military relations in India. He has since unsuccessfully entered politics and received widespread support from a group of journalists and retired officers who regard him as one of the best officers ever produced by the Indian army.

These two incidents occurred under Mrs. Gandhi, and it is widely believed that she was responsible for the supersessions. Her defenders argued that the principle of seniority was not inviolable, although they had earlier used it to justify the retirement of otherwise very well qualified generals. These episodes fit into the broader pattern of her style of governance, in which appointments were made—and unmade—as a matter of

---

[31] Sinha had taken over as vice chief of the army staff in January 1983, expecting to become chief a year later. Instead, Vaidya's appointment was announced on 31 May 1983. Sinha is the author of two military books and an important study on Indian defense organization, *Higher Defense Organization in India*, New Delhi: U.S.I of India, 1980. The best account of the whole episode is in *India Today*, 31 December 1983. This is reproduced, along with other documentary material, and a brief biography of General Sinha, in a volume issued by Sinha's supporters in Bihar—he was the only Bihari general in the Indian army. See D. P. Singh, *The Supersession: Spotlight on Lt. Gen. S. K. Sinha*, Patna: Parijat, 1984.

[32] Both stories in *The Hindu International Edition*, 8 January 1983.

convenience and later justified. The practice disturbed the military and further divided it by encouraging senior officers to curry favors from the political leadership. The generals could accept a system in which promotion was based on a principle of merit, or one based upon strict seniority, but a system in which promotions are made in order to keep the military divided is likely to have exactly the opposite effect in the long run.

Although the military's formal role in the higher decision-making system has declined over the years, there has been a continuation of military influence at other levels. Under Mrs. Gandhi, retired senior officers were appointed as governors, headed various defense production and research facilities, and served on various public commissions and agencies. In some cases active duty officers have received nonmilitary appointments to such bodies. One recent (1985) chief of the air staff, Air Chief Marshal M. L. Khatre, had been head of the giant manufacturing and research complex Hindustan Aeronautics, Ltd. Quite often, senior officers are appointed to such choice positions immediately upon retirement (Gen. K. V. Krishna Rao was made governor of the militarily sensitive states of Manipur, Nagaland, and Tripura in June 1984).

There is considerable indirect evidence to show that these government-controlled appointments are not given to recalcitrant officers, but to those who have cooperated with the government during their tenure in the military. As the social status of the armed forces continues to decline, it will be easier for the government to use postservice employment as a reward to pliable officers, especially if these officers have no other career or income to fall back on.

This strategy may be effective in the short run, but it does risk embittering those officers who have not "cooperated" and who feel that their colleagues have sold out the profession for personal advancement.

CIVIL-MILITARY RELATIONS: SUBORDINATION OR EQUALITY?

In a reasonably well developed political system such as India's, with a long tradition of civilian dominance over the military, any change in the relationship between the two will be incremental, not dramatic. Despite this, there is a long tradition of alarmist writing about the imminent takeover of the military in India. This has been a popular subject for journalists, who have been predicting the increased intervention of the army for years.[33]

[33] The most influential of these has been Neville Maxwell, who has written that the 1965 war brought the Indian army "into a position of respect and influence within the state par-

Scholarly analyses have usually been more restrained. Their picture of a large, diverse, sprawling military establishment, divided into three services, numerous commands within each service, all directed by political and bureaucratic elites fully aware of the need to maintain civilian authority, legitimacy, and control is essentially accurate.[34] Interestingly, even the journalists have begun to subscribe to this view, and predictions of military takeover have been replaced by relatively balanced analysis. The Indian army is now held up as an exception to the dismal parade of coup and countercoup.[35]

Although I am one of those who have made a strong case for regarding India as an exception to the widespread pattern of military intervention, optimism about the political role of the Indian military is premature, and a number of the barriers to military intervention have been removed or weakened. Others remain, but the circumstances under which they, too, might crumble are not difficult to imagine.

Military intervention in politics will in part be a function of the size of the state and the development of the political system. Large countries are difficult to govern from the center, although if regional institutions are relatively underdeveloped, even a large country may in some ways be *easier* to steer from the center than a small one. Intervention will also be influenced by the prevalent form of civilian control: whether the military is ruled because it is different from civilians or just like them. Armies the size and complexity of India's do not intervene lightly but do so because of overwhelming organizational pressures and political compulsions. Above all, they will intervene to protect their own institutional integrity or to protect or restore a political order that in turn shields them or to remove one that they regard as detrimental to national interests.

The Indian army is a long way from overt intervention, but there have been many signals that some of the barriers to intervention, or to increased military influence, have disappeared. The most important such barrier—the legitimacy, integrity, and competence of the central political system—has badly eroded in the past fifteen years. This erosion includes

allel to that which the Pakistan Army had enjoyed from the beginning," that the deterioration of the Indian polity was creating a "vacuum," and that "military government would solve few if any of India's problems, but unless present trends are reversed continued avoidance of military intervention in the 1970s would be more surprising than intervention itself." *Times* (London), 28 January 1969.

[34] Lloyd I. and Susanne Hoeber Rudolph, "Generals and Politicians in India," *Pacific Affairs* (Spring 1964), pp. 5–19.

[35] See, for example, June Kronholz, "The Big Indian Army is Tough, Respected, Keeps out of Politics," *Wall Street Journal*, 16 September 1981; Mohan Ram, "The Generals Stand Aloof," *Far Eastern Economic Review*, 27 February 1981; and Salamat Ali, "In Step with Tradition," *Far Eastern Economic Review*, 31 May 1984.

the decline of the Congress party (except as a vehicle for Indira Gandhi's personal rule) and the simultaneous failure of opposition parties to demonstrate their ability to govern effectively, fairly, and without serious corruption. For the professional soldier there was not much choice between the capricious Janata government and the willful combination of Bansi Lal and Sanjay Gandhi. Service resentment over political incompetence, especially when that incompetence affects the conduct of war or the readiness of the military to fight a war, runs deep. Some day it may be the force that propels the military into politics. The armed forces, especially the army, are not passive observers of the deterioration and increasing violence and lawlessness of Indian politics. They have begun to play a direct role in the political system through the rear entrance called "aid to the civil power."

From Aid to the Civil to Military-Civilian Partnership?

One of the central myths of the Indian political system is that the Indian military is "apolitical." This is true only insofar as the armed forces do not *rule* India and the decision-making process is dominated by civilians. It is also true that the folklore of the mess says that politics and the military profession do not mix, and that young officers are taught that the Indian military must remain apolitical. However, it is not true in the sense that the military knows nothing about politics, or that it does not act in support of political objectives, or that it does not itself directly govern more and more of India.

Most officers, especially army commanders, are very well informed about domestic politics, let alone broader strategic and foreign policy issues. Every Indian district is in an area command, and many cities are part of, or adjacent to, cantonments or bases. In each of these cases the area commander has, as part of his professional duties, a complete knowledge of local politics. He will be able to recite with precision the factions, interests, and objectives of each local political, religious, or other interest group. In this he is supported by the military's own intelligence services and close liaison with police and civilian bureaucracies.

This knowledge is important should the military be called upon "in aid of the civil power." After independence it was recognized that "aid to the civil" could be damaging to the preparedness of the armed forces. The example of Pakistan (where the army ultimately intervened in central politics after having been repeatedly called out to prop up civilian authority) was also noted. These two considerations led to the creation of a massive structure of paramilitary forces, which were to serve as a buffer between the regular armed forces and the rough and tumble of domestic disorder.

Despite these paramilitary forces, and in a few cases because of them, the direct intervention of the armed forces in state and local matters has steadily increased in the past few years. Most of these interventions have been limited and were quick "in and out" operations. In this sense, the military has acted in support of the political structure, providing ultimate force in situations in which political solutions had failed and in which the police could not cope.

- increase in interventions

The increase in such interventions has been dramatic. During the period from 1951 to 1970, the army was called in to suppress domestic violence on approximately 476 occasions.[36] By contrast, the figures for the eighteen-month period, June 1979 through December 1980, saw sixty-four instances of army assistance to civil authorities. A list of typical army interventions is presented in Table 1. Table 2 lists disturbances in the paramilitary and other security forces themselves.

These data suggest that the police and paramilitary forces within India are themselves a security problem for the army. The literature on the subject indicates deep army concern about the failings of these forces, beginning in 1973, when the Uttar Pradesh Armed Constabulary took up arms against the government in a labor dispute.[37] This concern is justified, because the number and size of these paramilitary forces is increasing faster than their reliability and efficiency.

The army's support of political authority in these aid-to-the-civil operations has led into actual military rule in more than one state. The legal basis for enhanced army responsibility varies, but a number of ordinances, promulgated under the president's emergency powers, are now in place:

· the Armed Forces Special Powers Act (1956, subsequently amended) enables the union government to declare a state or district a "disturbed area." In areas where the declaration comes into force, army and paramilitary commanders are given authority to arrest suspects, conduct searches, and use lethal force without regard to the authority of the district magistrate (who ordinarily supervises aid-to-the-civil operations).

· the National Security Act (1980) authorizes security forces to arrest and detain suspects for up to six months without a warrant. Although there are provisions for judicial review, the intent of the legislation is to give the armed forces a relatively free hand in dealing with agitators, ter-

---

[36] Lt. Gen. S. K. Sinha, *Of Matters Military*, New Delhi: Vision Books, 1980, p. 37. For a discussion of the armed forces expanding aid-to-the-civil-power activities, see Jerrold F. Elkin and W. Andrew Ritezel, "Military Role Expansion in India," forthcoming.

[37] See the useful survey of the police-paramilitary breakdown by the former director of the Border Security Force (BSF) in K. Rustomji, "Dealing with Disorder," *Seminar* (Using the Army), no. 308 (April 1985). The same issue contains an extensive bibliography on internal security matters.

TABLE 1
Indian Army Deployments in Aid-to-Civil, 1973–1984

Year	Where Deployed	Reason	Dates	Approximate Duration
73	Assam	language riots	13 Apr–17 May	1 month
	Lucknow, Uttar Pradesh	police unrest	21 May–13 Jun	3 weeks
	Arunachal Pradesh	tribal violence	13–18 Jun	1 week
	Imphal, Manipur	riots	13–21 Sep	1 week
	Nasik Maharashtra	election violence	23–24 Apr	2 days
74	Baroda, Gujarat	communal unrest	10–14 Jan; 25–26 Feb	1 week
	Ahmedabad, Gujarat	food riots	28 Jan–16 Feb	3 weeks
	Dhanbad and Ranchi, Bihar	communal violence	20 Mar–2 Apr	2 weeks
	Palampur, Himachal Pradesh	?	25–26 Apr	2 days
	Patna, Bihar	student riots	18–26 Mar	1 week
	All India	national rail strike	7–20 May	3 weeks
	West Bengal (4 districts)	riots	27 Aug–5 Sep	2 weeks
75	All Indian port cities	dockers' strike	? Jan	1 week?
	Delhi	communal riots	? Feb	1 week?
	Cooch Behar, West Bengal	rural unrest	9–17 Feb	1 week
76	Prime Minister Gandhi declares a state of national emergency. The army is not called out in aid-to-civil.			
77–79	No reliable information available[a]			
80	Assam	"antiforeigner" stir; election violence	Feb	continuous
	Tripura[b]	tribal violence	7 Jun–14 Nov	6 months
	Meghalaya[b]	tribal insurgency	"frequently"	continuous
	Manipur[b]	student/tribal unrest	17 Apr–17 May	1 month
	Nagaland[b]	tribal violence	23–30 Jul and 15 Nov	continuous
	Uttar Pradesh, Madhya Pradesh, Gujarat, Delhi	communal violence (Moradabad)	Aug–Sep	2 months
	Jammu and Kashmir	?	?	?
	Tamil Nadu	?	?	?
	Bihar	CISF strike	? Oct	1 week?
	Himachal Pradesh	?	?	?
81	Assam	"antiforeigner" stir	continuous	1 year
	Gujarat	antireservation stir	1 Feb–2 May	3 months
82	Assam	"antiforeigner" stir	continuous	1 year
	Arunachal Pradesh	student/tribal unrest	17 Jul–21 Aug	4 weeks
	Goa	communal disturbances	2–7 Nov	5 days

TABLE 1 *(continued)*
Indian Army Deployments in Aid-to-Civil, 1973–1984

Year	Where Deployed	Reason	Dates	Approxima Duration
	Baroda, Gujarat	communal disturbances	28 Oct–5 Nov	2 weeks
	Kerala	communal disturbances	30 Dec–12 Jan 83	4 days
	Maharashtra	Bombay police strike	8 Aug–9 Sep	1 month
	Mizoram[b]	election violence	May and Dec	4 days?
	Nagaland[b]	election violence	? Oct	2 days?
1983	No known army deployments other than counterinsurgency operations in the northeastern states and continuous peacekeeping duties in Assam. Army put on alert in Punjab, Chandigarh, and Haryana.			
1984	Maharashtra (Bombay, Bhiwandi, Thane, and adjoining suburbs)	communal riots	May–Jun	4 weeks
	Punjab, Chandigarh (limited deployments in adjoining areas of Uttar Pradesh, Haryana, Rajasthan, Delhi, and Kashmir)	Sikh terrorist campaign centered in Amritsar; Army mutinies	5 Jun–present	ongoing
	Hyderabad, Andhra Pradesh	Hindu-Muslim riots; political demonstrations	9 Sep–present	ongoing

SOURCE: Compiled from various Indian newspapers and the *Reports* of the government of Indi Ministry of Defense.

[a] Ministry of Defence *Annual Reports* do not mention any army involvement with domes peacekeeping chores during the Janata years in power. The *Reports* only highlight army aid-to-civil in ca of natural disasters.

[b] Regular army troops are stationed and on alert in Maghalaya, Manipur, Mizoram, Nagaland, a Tripura on a continuous basis. The *Reports* ordinarily refer to army operations in these states unde separate heading dealing with "counterinsurgency operations."

rorists, and rioters. Many provisions of this act are identical to those of the Maintenance of Internal Security Act (MISA), which was the legal basis for the Emergency of 1975–1977.

· the Essential Services Maintenance Act allows army troops to replace striking workers in "vital" industries such as oil production and rail transport. The industries are effectively taken over by the army pending settlement of the dispute. Strikers can be subject to arrest under provisions of the National Security Act.

Table 2
Incidents of Unrest within Peacekeeping Forces, 1978–1984

Date	Location	Immediate Cause of Unrest	Resolution
Oct 1978	Tamil Nadu	CRPF strike; state police unwilling to move against strikers	2 battalions of BSF sent in to crush the strike
May 1979	Gujarat	Police strike	Army called in to restore order; strikers fired on; 5,000 arrested
Jun–Oct 1979	Bhubaneswar, Puri, Trivandrum, Cuttack, Neemuch, Thumba, Cochin, Madras, Port Blair, Delhi, Bokaro	Wildcat strikes by CRPF, CISF, and RPF units	Army and BSF dispatched to disarm strikers; 24 CISF strikers and 3 army *jawans* killed at Bokaro; 3 CRPF mutineers killed in Delhi
Oct 1979	Tamil Nadu	Police strike	BSF and CRPF units dispatched; 3,000 policemen detained
Nov 1979	Bombay (Maharashtra)	Abortive police strike	BSF and CRPF personnel quell the Congress-supported strike
Oct 1980	Industrial locations in Bihar and West Bengal	CISF strike leads to clashes with police	Army dispatched to disarm CISF mutineers
Jan–Feb 1981	Gujarat	Police discredited during caste reservation protests	Army sent in to fill police vacuum and restore order
Aug 1982	Bombay (Maharashtra)	Police strike	Army sent in to restore the peace
Jun 1984	Army barracks in Bihar, Maharashtra, Tripura, and Rajasthan	Uncoordinated mutiny by over 1,500 Sikh conscripts in the aftermath of Army actions at the Golden Temple of Amritsar	Loyal army units capture the mutineers; army discipline restored.

SOURCE: Compiled from various Indian newspapers and the *Reports* of the government of India's Ministry of Defense.

· the Unlawful Activities Prevention Act (1967) allows the center to ban subversive organizations. This currently applies to rebellious Sikh organizations in the Punjab and several insurgent groups in the northeast.

· the Terrorist Affected Areas (Special Courts) Ordinance (1984) was designed to help the army root out Sikh terrorists in the Punjab.[38] This provides for secret tribunals to try terrorists and is based upon the presumption of guilt—the accused must prove himself or herself innocent. It also confers special powers upon the security forces.

This stunning array of legislation and ordinance has given the military and paramilitary forces considerable power in many affected areas of Assam, Punjab, Kashmir, and other states. For millions of Indians the effective government has been the local area or subarea commander; in some areas the system has been no more protective of civil liberties than the recent martial law in Pakistan, where civil courts and religious courts function parallel to the martial law system, and appeals from decisions by the latter have been frequent and successful. As an informed Pakistani military writer has noted of the 1982–1983 situation in Assam: "Such a state of affairs is certainly not martial law but it may well contain all its normal concomitants, such as a suspension of civil liberties, imposition of press censorship, search and arrest without warrants and enforcement of curfew order in sensitive and badly affected areas." By itself, such involvement may be necessary and desirable, but the same commentator notes that "the military's repeated deployment in situations of extreme civil disorder could, on the one hand, induce the civil authority to lean more and more upon it, and, on the other, give the military establishment the sugary foretaste of power," as it did in both Pakistan and Bangladesh.[39]

Civilian Control: From Objective to Subjective?

Samuel Huntington suggests that civilian control over the military ultimately takes one of two forms. "Objective" control is exercised by a legitimate civilian elite that respects and encourages the differences between it and the military professionals. The latter are devoted to their profession and maintain a conservative, restricted ethic. By contrast, "subjective" control is brought about through the merger of civilian and military val-

[38] For an analysis, see A. G. Noorani, "The Terrorist Ordinance," *Economic and Political Weekly*, 28 July 1984.

[39] Brig. A. R. Siddiqi (ret.), "Indian Army in Assam: Some Implications," *Dawn* (Lahore), 23 February 1983. Kuldip Nayar has similarly written about the ambiguous role that the Indian army played in the removal of Dr. Farooq Abdullah as chief minister of Kashmir, suggesting that the dependency of the Indian government on the military was more and more resembling Pakistan's earlier experiences. *The Telegraph* (Calcutta), 24 July 1984.

ues: the armed forces are controlled because they *share* dominant civilian values and their distinctiveness is blurred.

India has been undergoing a transition from objective to subjective control for a number of years. At first, the gap between civilian and political elites was very large, and there were important social and class differences between the two. However, the military is now recruited from the same social classes as the political and administrative leadership and is in some ways more representative of the country. Increasingly, the military is called upon to assume tasks it would have rejected thirty years ago. Further, it is also called upon to voice the values and attitudes that are held by politicians; it has been asked to become "committed" in the same way that the civil service has been asked to identify itself with the values and aspirations of Mrs. Gandhi and the Congress party.[40]

At the same time, some politicians, most notably Mrs. Gandhi, have encouraged military-like values and attitudes, a form of civilian militarism.[41] Unlike her father, Mrs. Gandhi cultivated the legend of Subhas Chandra Bose and the secular, neototalitarian, egalitarian, militarism of the Indian national army:

> Although the comparison may not be exact, some of Mrs. Gandhi's appeal would seem to be due to the similarities rather than the differences between herself and Bose. She is certainly a secularist and professes faith in democracy, although perhaps democracy of a special

[40] The question of political influence in the military has been sharply debated in the military, especially since Indira Gandhi came to power. For two contrasting views, see Brig. N. B. Grant, "The Committed Soldier," *U. S. I. of India Journal* (April–June 1974), pp. 134–137; and Brig. J. Nazareth, *U. S. I. of India Journal* (July–September 1972), pp. 228ff. Grant argues that some compromise with Indira Gandhi's call for "deeply involved, deeply committed" civil servants cannot help but be applied to the military. Nazareth takes a much tougher line against "the danger of being infected"; since the armed forces were once before "emasculated by unscrupulous politicians," it could happen again; democratic armies face a greater danger than those in dictatorships for they are under greater political pressures to conform; the triple threat of becoming physically flabby, infected with "the lust for money or personal gain" and "political interference" all confront the Indian army, and only strict adherence to professional standards can preserve the military itself, and in the long run the state it defends.

[41] Although Mrs. Gandhi emphasized the martial virtues of discipline, obedience, and order, especially during the Emergency (1975–1977), she was careful not to involve the armed forces in the Emergency, relying entirely on the police and paramilitary forces. No studies have been made, but my impression is that the military generally supported the Emergency. Their views on that period closely resemble those of the Pakistan army: the trains ran on time, taxi drivers were polite and did not overcharge, and the entire country was more serious, disciplined, obedient—in fact, it was more like the military. Like their Pakistani counterparts, Indian officers want a country as good as the army; they also fear the deterioration of the political and social order, with troublesome consequences for the armed forces.

variety. Her speeches are dominated by references to the need for discipline and order . . . there is no doubt that she believes that internal and external enemies require continual vigilance, militancy, and preparedness. In the face of such enemies, even the enemy poverty, civil liberties are expendable. . . .[42]

This appeal proved to be very popular, and it will be important to see whether any other national politician attempts to exploit the theme of militancy and militarism. It certainly does find resonance in some regions of India, especially those with strong, local, martial traditions.

Similarly, it will be important to see whether the military is again called upon to make statements in support of specific political parties. It only takes a few such statements to have a great impact upon the entire military establishment and the political community, for, if the military gives the impression that it has even implicity thrown its support to one or another political leader, it will be rapidly cultivated by all politicians.

Several astute observers have addressed this development. Romesh Thapar has observed that India's new breed of officer, drawn from the middle classes of the subcontinent, will invariably come to reflect the varied emotions of that subcontinent, "making politics very much a part of the culture of the Indian military establishment, even though the same distance still continues to be maintained between it and the politicians." He places blame for this on the political community and offers several remedies, including the revision of the higher defense decision-making process, clipping the power of the "ill-informed IAS network," and reprofessionalism of the Indian army. Otherwise, "India will find itself with a million-man army that has lost its professionalism, that reflects the worst qualities of Indian life, and that has important parochial service interests to protect."[43]

The military literature is replete with nostalgia for an era when the army kept to its narrow professional concerns, but I know of no senior officer who has resigned his commission on the grounds that the armed forces were being asked to undertake inappropriate tasks. The officers have, perhaps, decided to bend under pressure. As one of India's most literate retired officers has written,

Let's face it, whether the civil servant or the soldier likes it or not, the political system and its ideologies have now become part and parcel of his daily living and the environment in which he works. Wrongly

[42] Stephen P. Cohen, "The Military," in *Indira Gandhi's India*, edited by Henry C. Hart, Boulder: Westview, 1976, p. 210.

[43] Romesh Thapar, *An Indian Future*, New Delhi: Allied, 1981. See also "The Military Establishment," *Economic and Political Weekly* (Bombay), 12 May 1979; and "The Militarization of Indian Politics," *Economic and Political Weekly*, 28 July 1984.

or rightly, they have been allowed to permeate into almost all facets of his professional and cultural life, and he can no longer pretend to remain outside this system and yet be effective as he has managed to do so in the past. . . . [The services] will have to learn to live with the particular ideology and be "committed" to it without appearing to be political.[44]

Brigadier Grant, who has in the past advocated an apolitical and neutral officer corps sadly concedes that "sympathizers" will do better than "neutrals."

If the trend continues, there is reason to be concerned about the future professional integrity of the Indian armed forces, especially the army. There is already a functional differentiation between officers who pursue strictly professional goals and those who take advantage of the increasing opportunities for corruption. Those who seek money and corruption can find it, particularly in the recruiting commands, in the service and supply corps, in the neo-martial law slots in the Punjab and elsewhere, and in any position that brings the officer into contact with civilian contractors and manufacturers. As in Pakistan, part of the Indian army may become entangled in a corrupting civilian society and part will remain true to its professional ethic.

However, increasing corruption within the armed forces is not likely to lessen the chances of a future military intervention. The example of Pakistan indicates that corruption and civilian meddling in internal military promotions and policies can be a contributing factor in the decision to intervene.[45] Indeed, the young Pakistani officer is taught, as is his Indian counterpart, that intervention is undesirable, that the military cannot effectively run the country without ruining itself, that his country is too large and too complex to be run from the center, and that military rule runs against the historic traditions of the armed forces. All this turns out to be irrelevant when the military faces a situation of domestic political breakdown that ultimately (and sometimes, quite rapidly) affects the integrity of the military. For, above all, soldiers in both countries are taught that, although they are the first line of defense against external enemies, they are also the last barrier to internal disarray. When the politicians, the bureaucrats, the police, and the paramilitary have crumbled, only the armed forces stand between national integrity and national dissolution. The armed forces tend, therefore, to regard any incident that affects their

[44] Brig. N. B. Grant (ret.), "Apolitical or Committed?" *Hindustan Times*, 3 September 1984.
[45] Those concerned about the possible Pakistanization of India might consult Stephen P. Cohen, *The Pakistan Army* (n. 15), and Hasan Askari Rizvi, *The Military and Politics in Pakistan*, Lahore: Progressive, 1976.

own internal integrity as of transcendental importance. Pakistan underwent such an experience as a consequence of several ill-fated aid-to-the-civil-power operations in Bengal and Punjab in the 1950s. These convinced the military not only of its own supreme importance but of the threat to its integrity from incompetence. We now turn to the tragic, but comparable events in the Punjab in 1984, which may turn out to be equal in their importance.

THE SIKH PUNJAB CRISIS AND THE ARMY

[handwritten margin note: worst crisis in army]

No single event in modern Indian history has so affected the armed forces as the Sikh/Punjab crisis of 1983–1984. Although the 1962 loss to China was humiliating and revealed serious internal military problems, it led to a purge of incompetents and a major rebuilding effort. The army was stronger after the war than before it. The events of 1984 were quite different. The integrity of the armed forces was shaken at every level, and all three services were affected; the crisis also altered the strategic assumptions upon which the armed forces have based their war plan.

Sikhs and the Indian Military

Sikhs have been a major component of the Indian army for over 130 years, or about five generations. They constituted about 25 percent of the Indian army during World War II and have always been regarded as among the most effective of the army's classes. In the army they comprise two separate regiments. One is the Sikh Regiment, largely made up of Jats; the other is the Sikh Light Infantry, made up of Mazbhis and Ramdasias—Scheduled Castes. One of Mrs. Gandhi's assassins, Beant Singh, was reportedly a Mazbhi Sikh who had been discharged from the army.[46] Sikhs are also found in several other infantry regiments that recruit on a mixed basis. They are present in large numbers in the Army Service Corps, the engineers, artillery, armor, and other specialized branches. They are also found in large numbers in the air force (perhaps a quarter of the IAF pilots are Sikhs), and there are substantial numbers in the Indian navy.[47]

After independence it was decided to freeze the number of "pure" one-class regiments in the Indian army, but this did not substantially limit Sikh

[46] *The Telegraph* (Calcutta), 11 November 1984, and *Washington Post*, 1 November 1984.

[47] The Indian navy and Indian air force do not recruit by class. Some of the army branches, e.g., engineers, recruit on a territorial basis. Thus, Sikhs living in South India can join the Madras Sappers, and Sikhs living anywhere in India can join the IAF and IN.

enrollment, which may have been about 20 percent of the other ranks and perhaps a somewhat greater number of officers. However, because of a policy established in 1953, and further modified in 1963 by the military affairs committee of the cabinet (which stated that no state would have a dominant position in recruitment), there began a concerted effort to make the army more representative and to recruit from those states that had not traditionally provided many soldiers (Tamil Nadu, Bihar, Gujarat, and Andhra Pradesh, among others).[48] In 1974 the Punjab was still providing over 15 percent of the army; it was assigned a quota (2 to 6 percent) commensurate with its population. This figure includes Hindus.

The recruitment issue was taken up by Sikh politicians and comprised one of the demands of the Akali Dal's Anandpur Sahib Resolution in 1973. When the recent president of India, Giani Zail Singh, was chief minister of Punjab (1972–1977), he raised the issue of Sikh recruitment with Mrs. Gandhi (then prime minister) and the union defense minister (Jagjivan Ram). The Akalis and other Sikh politicians demanded that fitness and merit be the sole criteria for recruitment to the armed forces; retired Sikh officers have complained that in order to exclude Sikhs, recruiting officers follow a discriminatory policy toward qualified Sikh candidates.

By 1981 the Punjab was still sending four times its population percentage to the army, which led the then army chief, O. P. Malhotra, to remark that "I don't think that people of these states [referring to Punjab and Haryana, another traditional recruiting ground] have any reason to be dissatisfied."[49] By this time the overall percentage of "traditional," that is, previously recruited classes, had dropped to 40 percent and "all classes" comprised 60 percent of the army. The actual figures are not available.[50] It is not clear where Gurkhas are counted, although their numbers—even though they are not Indian citizens—have increased since the new policy went into effect.

Other regions of India have had exactly the same kind of controversy

---

[48] Cohen, *The Indian Army* (n. 2), pp. 187ff.

[49] *Sainik Samachar*, January 1981, p. 8.

[50] There are different estimates of the number of Sikhs in the Indian armed forces. *The Economist*, 16 June 1984, states that the two Sikh regiments together account for about 16,000 soldiers (roughly equivalent to a full division), but that the total number of Sikhs in the army is about 95,000, implying that there are about 79,000 Sikhs in other infantry regiments and in various other fighting and support arms. Sanjoy Hazarika of the *New York Times* has quoted a "military analyst" that there were about 20,000 Sikhs in the Indian army, or 2 percent of its strength (14 June 1984). This figure must exclude Sikhs outside of their two regiments. No source gives figures for Sikhs in the IAF and IN, but the percentage of pilots must be very high, as all pilots are officers, and there are many more Sikh officers than other ranks in the armed forces—perhaps 20 percent of the total.

over "reservations." The Sikhs, like high caste Hindus, resent the effort to increase Scheduled Caste and Backward Class representation in government services. However, they differ from these groups in that angry Sikhs have the skills and resources to effectively resist government policy with violence, and they have a religious sanction for their claim to a major role in the armed forces.

The issue of derecruitment is very important for practical and ideological reasons. There must be well over 500,000 retired Sikh soldiers living in the Punjab, most of whom would like to place at least one male relative in the army, navy, or air force. Further, Sikhs regard the newly recruited classes as inferior. As an old Sikh recruiting handbook stated, all Sikh traditions are ultimately martial traditions, and the Sikh community is reluctant to yield its special claim to "martial" status.[51] Many Sikhs find the norms of a secular democracy, where all groups are now regarded as "martial,"[52] to be naive and misguided.

Resentment and Mutiny

There is a long history of resentment among Sikhs in the armed forces, especially the army. No Sikh has ever become chief of the army staff, despite the great overrepresentation of Sikhs in the senior ranks of the army. In 1962 six of the Indian army's lieutenant-generals were Sikhs (two of them were to die in a 1963 air crash). Out of twenty-eight major-generals, thirteen were Sikhs, and of seventy-nine brigadiers, there were thirty Sikhs.[53] Sikhs failed to reach the position of COAS in 1969 and 1974 when non-Sikh generals received extensions in their term of service. There is a belief that other groups within the officer corps do not treat Sikh officers with proper respect. For the most part, however, Sikh soldiers have had a brilliant reputation and have had no incentive or inclination to support terrorist, separatist, or other extreme dissident Sikh groups. Indeed, they had been deeply involved in the many antiterrorist and counterinsurgency operations undertaken by the Indian army, especially in the northeast.

Ironically, it was the antiterrorist efforts intended to cope with disturb-

---

[51] "All Sikh traditions, whether national or religious, are martial; in times of political excitement—and to the Sikhs politics and religion are closely allied—the militant spirit reasserts itself." Maj. A. E. Barstow, 2/11th Sikh Regiment, *Sikhs*, Handbooks for the Indian Army, Calcutta: Central Publications Branch, 1928, p. 40. This is one of the recruiting handbooks written for officers commanding particular regiments, in this case, Sikhs.

[52] Cohen, *The Indian Army* (n. 2), p. 190.

[53] These figures are from Dr. Hasan Askari Rizvi, "Sikhs and the Indian Army," *The Muslim* (Islamabad), 29 April 1984.

ances at the Asian Games that precipitated active dissent among retired Sikh officers. Many of them were harassed en route to New Delhi and several then proceeded directly to the Punjab, offering their services to the Akali agitation. Maj. Gen. Jaswant Singh Bhullar has been quoted on this episode:

> We had gone to Delhi and I found that in spite of the fact that we showed them my identity card, we were taken out of the bus at about nine places in Harayana. I told them I was a retired army officer but they did not listen and were very rude and abusive. I felt very humiliated. I have taken part in practically every war and been wounded twice. It was very upsetting to think that I had to prove my patriotism in this country and to think I needed a passport or some document in order to be able to go to Delhi.[54]

Worse was to come. Several thousand Sikh ex-servicemen met in a convention at Amritsar on January 23, 1983. Among them were five retired major generals, and other retired officers of general rank sent their messages of support. The convention provided the leadership for a volunteer force that the Akalis began to organize in March–April 1983. Several senior retired officers joined Jarnail Singh Bhindranwale and helped train his followers.[55] One, Maj. Gen. Shubeg Singh, had earlier organized the Mukhti Bahini and was a recognized expert in insurgency warfare.

By the time Operation Bluestar was launched, most Sikh units had been moved out of the Punjab. They were not informed of the advance on the Golden Temple, and about two thousand Sikhs in a variety of training and active field units mutinied. Although the government attempted to minimize the seriousness of the mutinies, it is known that they included the Sikh Regimental Center, units guarding Santa Cruz airport in Bombay, and combat units in Rajasthan. *Jawans* and officers from these units may have fled to Pakistan.

Many Indians were surprised at the Sikh mutiny, but they should not have been. *All* Indian army regiments bind their members with a religious as well as a civil oath, a practice that the British merely carried over from earlier Hindu, Sikh, and Muslim armies. Sikh soldiers are accompanied into battle by unit priests and the Granth Sahib. The perceived desecration of their religion signaled a call to arms because of their oath, not in contradiction to it.

The situation in the Punjab in 1984–1985 was grave from both the

[54] Tavleen Singh, "Bhindranwale's Generals," *The Telegraph* (Calcutta), 18 June 1984.
[55] Ibid.; and Saijev Gaur, "Akali-Army Connection," *Indian Express* (Bombay), 18 November 1982.

Sikhs' and the army's perspective. Sikhs, including at least 300,000 retired service personnel and their families, were subject to even harsher laws and regulations than those enforced in Nagaland, Mizoram, and elsewhere.[56] Some of the Sikh community have undergone a revolutionary alteration in their self-image, from a "we" that included Hindus, in opposition to Pakistan, to a "we" that excludes Hindus and has rediscovered the many common elements between Sikhism and Islam.[57] This is truly the stuff out of which new nations are made, and the Khalistan movement received support from Sikhs within India as well as outside it. This was support offered by default. Conversations with retired Sikh officers indicate a realistic appraisal of the weaknesses inherent in "Khalistan" but a fatalistic willingness to support the cause in the absence of what they regard as fair terms from the government of India.[58]

As for the Indian army, its occupation of the Punjab is unprecedented and dangerous. There was no possible military solution to the Punjab situation. Yet, the army was called upon to supervise the most intimate and detailed aspects of life in the state. This further embittered the Sikh population in the Punjab and caused the army to regard all Sikhs, including those in the armed forces, as potential terrorists. No aid-to-the-civil-power doctrine can provide effective guidelines for such a situation.[59] No

[56] Their sense of hurt and alienation is vividly present in much of the literature distributed overseas by various Sikh groups and individuals. For a perceptive analysis, see Jaswant Singh, "Punjab: The Challenge Within," *Illustrated Weekly of India*, 24–30 June 1984; and for an eyewitness report of martial law in the Punjab, see Sahnaz Anklesaria, "Fall-out of Army Action: A Field Report," *Economic and Political Weekly*, 28 July 1984.

[57] Pakistanis, who have reason to be pleased at the opportunities presented to them by the disaffection of the Sikhs, are cautious in their support of Khalistan. The similarities between Sikhism and Islam are superficial; although maps of the erstwhile Khalistan do not include any Pakistani territory, historic Sikh kingdoms included much of what is now Pakistani Punjab and the Northwest Frontier Province; finally, "Khalistanis" openly speak of "balancing" Pakistan and India. From a Pakistani perspective, therefore, support for Khalistan not only risked alienating and angering India but—should it be successful—it could worsen Pakistan's strategic position as well as stimulate its own internal dissidents to renewed action.

[58] The 1985 agreement between Rajiv Gandhi and the Akali Dal, followed by a series of political concessions and an election in the Punjab, represent a turning point in the restoration of civil order in the state and reconciliation with the Sikh community. Although violence is likely to continue, it now appears unlikely to spread to Sikh units. The potential political role of retired officers in India is a subject of considerable importance about which little is known (other than they were prominent in the Khalistan and Bhindranwale movements). For an insightful report, see Hugh and Colleen Gantzer, "Alienation of ex-Servicemen," *Indian Express* (Bombay), 27 July 1983, and A. L. Bery, "The Retired Soldier: A Sentimental and Material Alienation," *The Statesman* (Calcutta), 18 October 1983.

[59] A distinguished retired army general, Eric Vas, has published a brief study of the counterinsurgency problem in the Punjab. See "The Faces of Terrorism," *Seminar* (Using the Army), no. 308 (April 1985).

wonder that the army has welcomed the Punjab's gradual return to normalcy through the political process.

Strategic Considerations

One complicating feature of the Punjab crisis has been its strategic location. From India's perspective, there are important objectives in Pakistan's Punjab, although new strategic plans seem to indicate a thrust in Rajasthan and Kashmir, rather than Punjab. However, the major road and rail routes to Kashmir run north through Punjab, and important canals run south to Rajasthan; the army needs the active cooperation of all Punjabis to fight a major war with Pakistan. In 1965 and 1971 that cooperation was freely and generously offered by Sikh farmers, transport owners, and merchants. In 1984–1985 the Indian army could not trust the local population. The army and the various paramilitary units in the Punjab had to cope with numerous acts of sabotage, despite an extended curfew. In the event of a crisis with Pakistan or in Kashmir, such sabotage would severely hamper the movement of troops, supplies, and food.

Finally, the Punjab crisis had one unprecedented impact upon the Indian armed forces. Given the evidence of the mutinies that occurred in June 1984, the temporary alienation of retired Sikh officers, and the close links between Sikhs in and out of the military, one can assume that no Sikh unit was fully trusted, especially in a situation that involved the Punjab itself. The government made unprecedented statements about the attempts to "spread disaffection in the ranks of the armed forces"—the situation may have been worse.[60] The overall integrity of the Indian armed forces, especially the army, may have been badly, if temporarily, weakened. If Sikhs comprise about 12 percent of the army, then the effective fighting strength of the army was probably reduced by at least that figure (more, if non-Sikh units must be deployed so as to contain another mutiny).[61]

[60] See the Press Trust of India story, "Forces Being Denigrated," based on Ministry of Defense "sources" that attack those who would "denigrate" the military in the press, as well as those who have forgotten the sacrifice of the army in the Golden Temple. Presumably, such sources are senior army officers angry at the sympathy given to the 2,000 or so Sikh soldiers who had mutinied. Also see "Leave the Army Alone," editorial, *Times of India* (Bombay), 28 November 1984, which also attacks "lurid" and exaggerated press reports of army brutality.

[61] One writer suggests that the Indian army will have to maintain five divisions exclusively for internal security in the years to come: two in the northeast, two in Punjab, and one in Tamil Nadu. If the Punjab crisis were to worsen, the effective fighting strength of the Indian

This decline in the efficiency and reliability of the Indian armed forces in 1984–1985 was probably greater than the increase in the capabilities of Pakistan's armed forces since 1982; the two combined do not add up to a shift in the strategic balance between India and Pakistan, but it must reduce Indian dominance to mere superiority. This poses no immediate threat to India, for the present Pakistani leadership is not likely to engage in any strategic adventurism, but a further decline in relative Indian capabilities would create new temptations and new problems. A different Pakistani leadership might meddle in Kashmiri or Punjabi politics, safe in the knowledge that India had lost its capacity for escalation dominance; conversely, an insecure India might turn to nuclear weapons to make up for its relative decline in conventional capabilities; finally, a worsening of the Punjab crisis could lead to open guerilla warfare in that state, widespread sabotage, and the breakdown in the integrity of the Indian armed forces if their critical Sikh component should be removed.

CONCLUSION

The Indian armed forces are under strict constitutional constraints and play a very limited role in the central decision-making process, although they have somewhat more operational authority than many of their foreign counterparts. Because of India's insecure regional environment, they must devote a great deal of time to preparation and planning for war (this would seem obvious, but most armies in Latin America and Africa will never have to fight). The Indian armed forces are sending more and more trained individuals into civilian society every year, and their role in the vast military production industry is also growing. The domestic law and order role of the army has dramatically increased in recent years, and there is also a new trend for civilian politicians to praise some of the military virtues while asking the armed forces to commit themselves to specific social and ideological goals.

None of this adds up to a dramatic change in the historically limited political role of the Indian armed forces. There will be no coup in India, there is no chance of a "colonels" or "brigadiers" conspiracy to seize power, although there are some angry and many disillusioned officers, especially among the Sikhs. There may be further terrorism, but the structure of the Indian civil-military system is fundamentally sound, and—for most Indians—the legitimacy of the political system remains high. Our frequent al-

---

army would be reduced by at least two or three Sikh division-equivalents. India would still retain superiority over Pakistan, but the margin would be greatly reduced. G. C. Katoch, "Soldiers as Policemen," *The Statesman* (Calcutta), 18 January 1985.

lusions to Pakistan have indicated that under certain circumstances a professional army committed to democratic politics *can* intervene to reform the system, and many Indian observers are properly concerned that India might now be where Pakistan was in the mid-fifties.[62] However, the military in Pakistan has acted to protect not only its interests but Punjabi interests, whereas no single ethnic group dominates the Indian armed forces. Further, Pakistan was in a more precarious strategic situation than India, and its generals had developed direct foreign ties to military suppliers that enhanced their authority. Finally, the Pakistani political system never put down roots as deep as India's, and the Pakistan army could govern more effectively than civilians. The Indian armed forces have no such foreign ties, and they openly dismiss the idea of seizing power and governing India's more complex and sprawling political system.

In sum, from the perspective of sustaining India's democracy, the Indian armed forces have made a major positive contribution as they have carried out their duties with competent professionalism, and they have made a *negative* contribution in that they have not sought power, or even influence. This historic achievement is not to be taken lightly and certainly deserves more attention and study. However, we have identified a number of vulnerable points in the Indian system and conclude this chapter by noting these points and the ways they might lead to a change in the relationship between India's democracy and its armed forces.

A New Constitution?

The constitutionally determined role of the Indian armed forces is quite narrow and specific. The president remains the commander in chief, and policy direction is provided by the prime minister. One of the strengths of the present constitutional arrangement is that it provides some check on a prime minister tempted to politicize the military. However, there are frequent discussions of a change in this structure, moving toward elements of a French or American system, in which the presidency becomes a more "political" office. In such a system the military would find it even harder to resist efforts to politicize it and to force conformance to a particular political or social ideology. Any significant alteration in the Indian constitution in this direction appears now to be unlikely, but if it were to occur, it would be in response to a sense of peripheral decay and central weakness in India's federal structure.

Somewhat more likely is a gradual, even informal, modification of the

---

[62] Girilal Jain, "Army in Supportive Role," *Times of India* (Bombay); and Romesh Thapar, "Militarization" (n. 43).

Indian federal balance with the military and paramilitary forces as pawns in a subtle struggle for power. This process has been underway for some time, particularly in those Indian states with non-Congress governments. These governments resist the introduction of the regular armed forces or centrally controlled paramilitary units and have instead begun to create their own armed militias.[63] They have the right to do so in order to maintain law and order (a state responsibility), but it has also been argued that this right is not absolute, and that the union government has "overriding" law and order responsibilities.[64] This controversy contains the seeds of intense union-state conflict, up to and including serious violence, and, if pressed to that point, further military involvement in the management of an Indian state.

From Objective to Subjective Civilian Control?

If officers are further encouraged to conform to a dominant political and social ideology, and they do, they will compromise their conservative institutional perspective on national issues and begin to formulate political and social positions of their own. Although this may suit the politicians in the short run, sooner or later it will lead to a divergence based on the corporate interests of the officer corps (at the very best) or a split in the officer corps or the movement of the officer corps in directions more extreme than those now contemplated by the politicians. The acceptable price of civilian control is a military with essentially inward-looking, conservative views. In the past, this ethic was strengthened by the class origins of the officer corps, but now such views must be inculcated. It is tempting to ask the military to serve political ends—increasingly as saviors of law and order—but each such request further politicizes the military by bringing it into too close contact with civilian society and by placing more and more civilian tasks in its hands. And, although force is effective in the short run, it will fail, and the military will then blame its failure on civilians. A controversy has grown up around the purported success or failure of "Operation Bluestar," with the military blaming poor civilian intelligence for their own problems in rooting out Bhindranwale and his supporters. In contrast, the military apparently demanded, and received, a free hand when it was called out in over forty Indian cities to control

---

[63] For a discussion of Tripura's "Special Force Battalion," see *The Statesman* (Calcutta), 12 December 1984.

[64] An excellent discussion of federal aspects of the law and order problem is in several chapters of Abhijit Datta, ed., *Union-State Relations*, New Delhi: Indian Institute of Public Administration, 1984, especially chapters and comments by K. K. Dass, G. C. Singhvi, and Amal Ray.

rioters after Mrs. Gandhi's assassination, and it has been fulsome in praise of its own operations as if to show the rest of India that it really could carry out a domestic military operation with speed and skill.[65] It is true that these events are unprecedented and that disasters of this magnitude may never recur, but the rapid expansion of the army's role after Bluestar and the assassination suggests that the armed forces were on the edge of a new activism.

Changes in the Strategic Environment?

Some states, most notably the United States and Great Britain, historically limited the role of the army by keeping it small or adopting strategies that emphasized the role of the navy. India cannot do this as it must maintain a large standing army within its own borders in a high state of readiness. De Tocqueville and other democratic theorists argued that democracy and a large standing army were incompatible, but India seems to have so far managed both. Is this an historical anomaly, and will changes in the strategic environment, necessitating changes in the size or structure of the armed forces, have an impact on India's democracy?[66]

It is hard to predict the future of India's regional environment, as there are new factors that might lead to both greater and lesser conflict. On the

[65] After Mrs. Gandhi's assassination, Lt. Gen. G. S. Rawat (vice-chief of the army staff) summarized the situation in a press interview: the army played a "vital role" in bringing the situation "totally under control;" it was on a "mission of peace" and had to frustrate all attempts "to undermine the stability and integrity of the country," whether from within or without. The delay of four days in restoring normalcy was explained by the fact that the army had to move units from some considerable distance to occupy all or parts of the states of Himachal Pradesh, Bihar, Uttar Pradesh, Harayana, West Bengal, and Tripura, as well as Delhi and many other cities, *Times of India* (Bombay), 6 November 1984. However, other reports indicate that much of the army was being diverted to the Pakistani frontier for annual maneuvers and that the actual aid-to-the-civil operations in Delhi were incompetently managed. For example, the public was *told* that the army had arrived in Delhi on 1 November, but the army did not show up in force until three days later; nor was a joint army-police command post established, and army officers have complained of inadequate or misleading police and civilian intelligence. See Richard Nations, "Dynasty or Division," *Far Eastern Economic Review*, 15 November 1984, pp. 14–17, and "Who Are the Guilty," *Economic and Political Weekly*, 24 November 1984, a summary of the findings of the Indian People's Union for Democratic Rights and People's Union for Civil Liberties on the causes and consequences of the Delhi riots.

[66] Israel presents an interesting point of comparison. The Israelis are under even greater external pressure than India and—proportionately—maintain a larger military establishment. However, the close connections between the Israeli defense forces and Israeli society have prevented the growth of a separate "military" perspective on security and foreign policy issues: many civilian officials have had extensive military experience. This is not the case in India where few, if any, important politicians have ever served in the military.

one hand the Soviet Union has occupied Afghanistan, perhaps permanently, and there is no indication that they can either win or be defeated. This has led to increased American interest in South Asia, arms for Pakistan, and strains in the Indo-Soviet relationship. The military is probably more distressed at this turn of events than are most civilians, and is more attuned to the long-term strategic consequences of the Soviet occupation. This, and a feeling that civilian strategic incompetence is making things worse, might lead to greater military involvement in strategic decision making.

Simultaneously, however, there has been a move toward regional integration, and possibly arms control, with the rise of SAARC (South Asian Association for Regional Cooperation) and expanded bilateral Indo-Pakistan talks. Should these developments move ahead, the Indian armed forces might find themselves less important to India's overall strategic position and even asked to engage in a form of regional arms control. Some generals would not be averse to this, as they would prefer a smaller but better equipped military establishment; surplus manpower could be absorbed into the paramilitary forces, which in turn could be upgraded. The Indian armed forces would, I believe, unlike many other armies, accept a cut in levels as part of a regional peace settlement. There is a greater risk to Indian democracy from an increase in regional conflict, with its concomitant growth in dependency upon the Soviet Union and the fueling of the military's appetite for weapons and manpower than a step-by-step process of normalization with Pakistan and China.

Expansion of the Aid-to-the-Civil Role?

The expansion of the army's law and order function is perhaps the most dangerous trend of all, from the point of view of military integrity and an expanding military role in politics. The past few years have seen a creeping military role, and in the Punjab, Assam, Mizoram, Nagaland, Manipur, and elsewhere, "martial law" in all but name. The problem has, at last, been addressed by the intelligentsia, and there is no question as to where the remedies lie.[67] The central reform must take place in the police, reform that in turn requires effective political leadership at the state as well as union level. The linkage between the police, criminals, and corrupt politicians is potentially fatal to India's democracy: it only leads to further military intervention. This, in turn, is part of the problem, not part of the solution, and is a sure road to enhanced military involvement in politics.

[67] See the excellent editorial in *India Today*, "Misusing the Army," 15 May 1985, and the articles by Sinha, Rustomji, Thapar, Vas, and Jaswant Singh in *Seminar* (Using the Army), no. 308 (April 1985).

India is well below the threshold at which the military decides that *it* should rule if it is going to be asked to do so by civilians, but every additional aid-to-the-civil operation brings it that much closer. With the repeated breakdown of police and paramilitary forces in dealing with politically contentious disturbances (such as the reservations agitation in Gujarat), the military is now regularly called in for flag marches and to maintain essential services. It is effective in these roles, but it is only a matter of time when it becomes, as in Pakistan, the object of popular hatred. And, when the police and paramilitary forces are themselves in revolt, the army must contend with armed and trained rioters.

Decline in Political Legitimacy?

The armed forces operate at the margin of moral behavior, and their obedience to civilian authority will continue only so long as that authority is regarded as legitimate—and hence legitimizes the behavior of the military. In a developed political system, such as India's, legitimacy is the consequence of effective performance in open and free elections *and* of a degree of competence in matters that directly affect the military. In the case of Nehru and Mrs. Gandhi, there was also a direct, even charismatic, link to the *jawans*, NCOs, and JCOs, over the heads of the officers. No general could compare his own popularity with that of such leaders. However, in the absence of such a charismatic leader, civilian legitimacy must be based on the actions of politically effective and administratively competent ministers who are able to protect the vital interests of the military and the state. Civil servants cannot substitute for them, as they lack any mandate other than "civilian control," a mantra that will not survive genuine military concern.

As for the future, it is apparent that the government of Rajiv Gandhi is trying to reverse a trend in which political legitimacy has been increasingly personalized and thus increasingly vulnerable. It is not yet self-evident that his government will be able to successfully resolve those foreign and domestic problems—most notably, the Punjab crisis and relations with Pakistan—that are least amenable to charismatic appeal but are viewed by the military as vital to their own, and India's, survival. However, the efforts made in this direction over a one-year period are more than encouraging.

The views expressed in this chapter, which was completed before Professor Cohen joined the U.S. State Department, are his own and do not reflect the policies of the United States Government.

FOUR | Ethnicity, Democracy,
and Development in India:
Assam in a General
Perspective

JYOTIRINDRA DAS GUPTA

The persistence of ethnic politics in contemporary developing countries raises a number of important issues concerning the prospects of development in multiethnic settings. Theoretical traditions in development studies offer little help, however, in organizing these issues in an ordered manner. Theories of political modernization have attended to ethnic claims as sources of tension that normally, but not necessarily, impede the processes of strengthening the state or impair the prospects of national integration.[1] These theories are informed by a conventional liberal assumption that ethnic claims are expressions of undevelopment and that a theory of development should imply that emotional solidarities will be displaced by rational formations of collective interest. Radical theories of development leave little room for ethnic factors in their analyses of either underdevelopment or development. There is no entry, for example, for ethnicity in a recently published dictionary of Marxist thought, and the word "ethnicity" does not even find a place in the index of this volume of nearly 600 pages.[2]

Given this general tradition of relegating ethnic factors to a status of transitional irritants in the path of development, it will obviously take some effort to demonstrate the developmental significance of ethnic factors in a country like India. India, however, is not alone in experiencing an

[handwritten margin note: impediment to process of strengthening state, natl. integration]

---

[1] Theories of political modernization and development are discussed in Samuel P. Huntington and Jorge Dominguez, "Political Development" in *Handbook of Political Science*, edited by Fred Greenstein and Nelson Polsby, Reading: Addison-Wesley, 1975, vol. 3, pp. 1–114. Conventional economic theories of development do not treat this issue at all. The recently fashionable political economy orientation in development studies ignores it. A recent edition of Charles K. Wilber, ed., *The Political Economy of Development and Underdevelopment*, New York: Random House, 1984, does not make any reference to ethnic issues in its index.

[2] See Tom Bottomore et al., eds., *A Dictionary of Marxist Thought*, Cambridge, Mass.: Harvard University Press, 1983.

almost dramatic reversal of the earlier theoretical expectations regarding development processes. Instead of classes gradually erasing ethnic lines of solidarity, one increasingly finds a process of ethnic combination overtaking class formation. If this paradox seems overstated, it should at least sensitize us to the growing and not declining role of ethnic mobilization as an organizing principle in the transition periods of multiethnic developing and developed countries. Even the revolutionary regimes are not immune to the problems of ethnic mobilization. The dilemmas of the revolutionary leadership in Yugoslavia and Nicaragua may be less acute than those faced by the Indian reformist leadership but the revolutionary leaders find it no easier to come to terms with ethnic politics. No useful purpose will be served by simply assuming that the processes of development in our time will eventually reproduce the experience of early precursors. Contemporary transition in multiethnic developing countries has to come to terms with the fact that the ethnic coin is hard to melt precisely because it may have a valuable function to perform that may not be readily forthcoming from its rational competition.

ETHNIC IMPACT: ISSUES TO EXPLORE

The purpose of this paper is to elaborate the developmental functions of ethnic formations in the political system of India and to assess the significance of these functions in terms of their positive and negative contributions to economic and political development. After discussing some general issues, the analysis will shift to the more specific case of Assam.

Ethnic action, in this context, is best understood as a form of collective action conveniently using emotional affinity to make claims on the powers that decide who should be the beneficiaries of the development process. These claims can be divided into roughly two categories: quiet claims made within the ruling system and unquiet claims made on the ruling authorities. Ethnic political action, however, is not exhausted by claims expressed on or through the state. It may seek to strengthen its developmental claims by cultivating other ethnic groups in alliances or by aggression on ethnic groups labeled as adversaries. Because the strategies of alliance and aggression are parts of the overall politics of claims, our focus in this paper will be mainly on these claims, their capacity to evoke the desired response and their implications for national economic and political development.

It should also be noted that ethnic claims and ethnic action are not natural expressions of ethnicity. Although we are inclined to treat them as mobilized expressions apparently designed to serve the ethnic collectivity,

ETHNIC
claims serve
mobilizers not
collective

they may, in practice, serve the mobilizers more than the collectivity for which they speak. Ethnicity as a source of identity formation should thus be distinguished from its actual political use of seeking or retaining advantage in its name.[3]

We shall focus our attention on how ethnic claims have impinged on official developmental policies pursued in India during the last four decades; how the nature of the developmental state has served to encourage reactive ethnic action; and how the resulting ethnic politics has affected the processes, products, and outcome of national economic and political development. It is argued below that the very nature of national power and the conduct of the central government in steering the course of economic development have offered a system of incentives for ethnic combination within and outside the ruling authority at the national and regional levels. This implies that ethnic calculations are not exclusively associated with an oppositional mode of politics. Ethnicity, for our purpose, is not to be regarded merely as an exogenous source of nonrational action impinging on the rationality of Indian planned processes of economic development. Planning may simply conceal and rationalize a pattern of ethnic domination that by its nature may evoke opposing forces of resentment and generate demands for access to the club of dominance and advantage.

Development of economic resources enhances opportunities. Enhancement of opportunities usually favors those who have superior resources to make the best of new opportunities. Because most of the developmental initiative and investment in India after independence has come from the central government, if the government has chosen a design of development that selectively dispenses benefits to certain ethnic groups, then excluded groups will naturally feel that ethnic mobilization may yield access to central power and therefore to the desired opportunities. Democratic rules of politics, as professed in India, permit several options for such access. If inclusionary avenues are left open, the ruling party can be permeated to alter the ethnic balance of power within the leadership. If not, the ruling party can be submitted to pressures from outside or can be displaced—at least at the local level—to yield new access.

Inclusionary treatment at the party level, the system level, or even the bureaucratic level, does, however, raise the issue of how gradual expansion of access affects the course of development. Does it create an over-

[3] Fairly useful samplers of relevant literature would be Nathan Glazer and Daniel P. Moynihan, eds., *Ethnicity, Theory and Experience*, Cambridge, Mass.: Harvard University Press, 1975, and Wendell Bell and Walter E. Freeman, eds., *Ethnicity and Nation-Building*, Beverly Hills: Sage, 1974. For our purpose, a more interesting treatment can be found in Donald S. Rothchild and Victor A. Olorunsola, eds., *State Versus Ethnic Claims*, Boulder: Westview, 1983.

load problem? Does it violate the logic of insularity that a technocratic notion of efficient planning adores? Does it put a premium on an ethnic definition of hegemony that may strengthen a discounting of class interests so that whoever wins in the ethnic battle of access, the lower classes will always lose? Our discussion of Indian ethnicity will consider these questions and, at the same time, add one more: Can it be that the ability of the system, including the parties and the central government, to incorporate disadvantaged ethnic groups may not increase the total adverse weight of pressures on distribution and production but may, instead, actually succeed in reducing them by reallocation of resources and by reconstructing the means of access to them? Clearly, a complex political skill will be required to incorporate demands without straining national resources and their effective use for development. If this skill can be put into effect, much of the suspicion of ethnic implications may be unwarranted. On the other hand, if it cannot be put into practice, the prospects of both development and democracy may be bleak indeed.

ETHNIC INCIDENCE ON INDIAN POLITICS

Ethnic affinity in India is expressed in terms of various identifying groupings such as religion, language, region, or caste. The same person may have a number of identities from which to choose, depending on how he wants to use which identity for what immediate purpose. A Hindu speaking one language may cast his lot with a Muslim speaker of the same language and engage in rivalry with other Hindus, just as he may, at another moment, parade his Hinduness against Muslim adversaries. Similarly, within his religion-language group he may assert his superior caste affinity to challenge the mobility aspirations of lower caste groups. Or both upper and lower caste groups may unite against their counterparts in a relatively more prosperous subregion of their region. In this sense, Indians are multiethnic both in terms of plural social division and multiple personal identification. This multiethnicity leads to a perplexing series of cross-closures for bargaining, rivalry, and combination that are quite different from the mutually re-enforcing ethnic ties in, for example, Malaysia or Sri Lanka—to cite two cases where, as in India, ethnicity is a salient issue, but where the impact on democratic development may differ because of the specific patterning of ethnic closures.[4]

The long history of the Indian nationalist movement shows how these

[4] The issue of fluidity, affinity, and combination in India is treated in Jyotirindra Das Gupta, "Ethnicity, Language Demands and Traditional Development in India," in *Ethnicity, Theory and Experience* (n. 3), pp. 466–488.

two levels of ethnic multiplicity have posed problems as well as opportunities for political mobilization. Secular nationalists rejected the legitimacy of religious separation but did not hesitate to use religious affinities to serve the purpose of nationalist mobilization.[5] Muslim nationalism rejected the legitimacy of language-based ethnicity and advocated the case for religious separation. Both these strands of nationalism were remarkable for selective legitimization of ethnicity in politics, and each resulted in partitions of the subcontinent, in 1947 and 1971. But the ambivalence has continued. Indian secularism after independence was mostly articulated by leaders like Nehru, who used the formal instruments of the central government to impress an ideology of secular rationalization. The political expressions of ethnicity were regarded by Nehru as reflections of parochial sentiments unworthy of a modernizing nation seeking to realize developmental objectives. "The most important factor," he said, "the overriding factor, is the unity of India. . . . and even more than previously, our thoughts have gone towards laying a greater stress on the unifying factors."[6] He continued to repeat this sentiment with a sense of torment derived from the increasing demands for a reorganization of the Indian states on linguistic lines. It was his hope that "unifying factors" could be realized in the nation if the country thought more in "economic and developmental terms."[7] When his audience reminded him that his Indian National Congress had pledged linguistic reorganization for about three decades before independence, he conceded that even during those years he was "never very enthusiastic about linguistic provinces."[8] He admitted, however, that his party was enthusiastic about it all those years and that despite the efforts of the top leaders to soft-pedal the issue after independence, the regional leaders of the party continued their enthusiasm.

Leaders like Nehru were aware of their political inheritance. Colonial politics for about half a century had institutionalized ethnic representation in carefully selected installments. Congress nationalism had systematically cultivated support from ethnic groups to strengthen itself. The new state of India was founded at a moment of massive ethnic turmoil. Nehru's own colleagues at the top layer of Congress leadership had a long history of identification with ethnic demands. Rajendra Prasad's report on

[5] The widespread use of religious mobilization for expanding mass support for the Indian National Congress is discussed, for example, in Sumit Sarkar, *Modern India 1885–1947*, Delhi: Macmillan, 1983, pp. 96ff, and 195ff.

[6] *Jawaharlal Nehru's Speeches*, vol. 3, Delhi: Publications Division, Government of India, p. 193.

[7] Ibid., p. 193.

[8] *Jawaharlal Nehru's Speeches, 1949–1953*, vol. 2, Delhi: Publications Division, Government of India, p. 53.

Bihar, endorsed by the Congress in 1938 had already claimed a virtue for the sons of the soil criterion for preference in employment.[9] But Nehru hoped that economic development would dissolve the potency of ethnic politics. He encouraged a public language in Indian politics that celebrated the notion of economic development as a rationalizing instrument that would make affective sentiments redundant.[10]

What this public language of development failed to bring out was the other face of economic development that can frequently reinforce ethnic politics. Indian economic development, as defined by the first generation of leadership after independence, was designed to be led by the national government. This called for a centralized government willing to extract revenues from different parts of the federal system in order to centrally allocate them for appropriate developmental investment.

The constitution of India envisaged a welfare state for India but left it to a complex federal coordination of decisions to arrange the priorities among welfare objectives. As the first prime minister, Nehru initiated a process of economic planning administered by the center, or what may be called the federal government, working in association with the constituent states of the federation. Planning in India, since the early fifties, for the most part refers to centrally controlled allocation of investment funds for what is regarded as worthy programs and projects consistent with developmental priorities. Because these funds are both scarce and largely extracted by the center from taxes imposed on the states, it is quite reasonable to expect that a scramble will ensue for gaining access to power to determine the flow of these funds. This is where ethnic politics gains an edge, particularly because ethnic affinities offer a base of mobilization that can yield a bargaining advantage available to few other organizing principles in the Indian setting.

Four decades of economic development policies in India have considerably enlarged the control of the center over national economic resources. The expansion of the public sector and public control systems expressed in licensing, taxing, pricing, and subsidizing powers have enabled the center to assume unprecedented powers. Democratic representation has ensured that access to this power can be gained by mobilizing the required support. If ethnic affinities have served as a base for such support, they have also entailed that the benefits of power should belong to the respective ethnic groups. These benefits have been counted in terms of new opportunities for income and employment made possible by new invest-

[9] A. I. C. C. Papers, 1938, Nehru Museum Collection, G60, p. 18.

[10] This is the public language that one finds in the Indian media, plan documents, official writings, and intellectual expressions, which includes terms like casteism, communalism, parochialism, provincialism, and obscurantism with, of course, negative connotations.

ment in agriculture, industrial plants, transportation, power generation, education, and welfare services.

When nationally dominant ethnic groups have succeeded, or have been perceived to have succeeded, in channeling flows of income and employment to their chosen areas, other ethnic groups have been provoked to react. Later, when the protesting groups have succeeded in redirecting these flows to their favored areas, problems of subethnic distribution have often arisen. Marathi gains in resources, for example, have tended to generate internal resentment from Vidarbha or Marathwada subregional ethnicity. Again, within each of the latter disaffected groups, lower caste–based ethnic demands have been mobilized against the usually rewarded higher caste groups. Individual multiethnicity, then, has permitted a development of fluid loyalties demonstrating an inbuilt complexity of ethnic politics that is rarely captured by headline stories in the national press. In any event, it is the developmental activity of the center conducted in a democratic setting of political competition that initially reinforced the politics of ethnicity. What Nehru's hope and the planners' public language had expected and what planning in practice has turned out to be can thus be read as two entirely different stories.

THE STATE AND ETHNIC DEMANDS

Ethnic claims in independent India have been expressed at several levels. At the national level, language-based ethnic demands have been directed at the federal policy makers in two forms. One form was concerned with the official language of communication. The controversy between Hindi and non-Hindi movements reflected the deep concern of a broad coalition of ethnic groups that a disproportionate developmental advantage should not be enjoyed by the five Hindi states by virtue of a monopoly status granted to Hindi as the official language of the federal government.[11] This issue was largely settled by a compromise decision. but controversy attending the official language issue demonstrated how the political leadership of all major parties, including the ruling party, could be moved by ethnic issues. It also showed how, at one level, different ethnic groups could successfully combine to realize their common objectives.

The second form included movements for autonomy based on regional language. These were moves to bring together segmental social groups such as castes, tribes, dialectical speech groups, and religious communities

---

[11] See Jyotirindra Das Gupta, *Language Conflict and National Development*, Berkeley: University of California Press, 1970, for a detailed treatment of this issue.

within the relatively wider unity of regional communities defined by linguistic affinity and closure. Tamil, Telugu, Marathi, Gujarati, and Punjabi language sentiments provided the most prominent sources of organized demands on the national state during the early decades following Indian independence. A second level of ethnic demands was directed toward regional political authorities. Minority languages within each state, subregional economic deprivation, lower caste disaffection were some of the issues that questioned the rights of the dominant groups within regional ethnic unities. Whereas the interregional resource allocation issues of development were dramatized at the national level, the actual distributional and welfare implications for the most deprived segments of the population were brought out at the intraregional level.

The central government responded to the regional demands for autonomy during the early fifties with a sense of apprehension and initial hostility to the general principle of linguistic reorganization. By 1952 Nehru was grudgingly conceding individual "justified" cases but emphatically declaring that he was not prepared to reshape India on a linguistic basis. Successive waves of mass movements and the gradual erosion of the support for the Congress party gradually led the national leaders to concede the demand for linguistic states. The creation of the Andhra state in 1953 was followed by Maharashtra's and Gujarat's statehood in 1960 and that of Punjab and Haryana in 1966. It appeared, then, that the ethnic demands for autonomy had been largely satisfied, until the events of the eighties demonstrated otherwise. The interruption of intensity of ethnic demands at the national level can, however, allow us to examine the developmental implications of ethnicity in two parts—the impact of gradual containment of ethnic movements of the first phase and the implications of explosive ethnicity of the second phase.

THE INCLUSIONARY PHASE

How have the linguistically reorganized states fared? When we examine their political and economic performance over the two decades of their statehood, we find that the original fears of the Congress leaders, nationalist intellectuals, and many external observers have proved largely unfounded. Although ethnic movements had challenged Congress dominance in their respective areas, they had not challenged the democratic system of national government. After gaining autonomy, these regions quickly settled down to work out a constructive partnership with the national leadership, the national economic planning system, and the national administrative system. Whether these new states were ruled by the

Congress party or by regional parties made little difference from the point of view of order, administration, or contribution to national unity. Once ethnically induced regional demands were legitimized, the national government secured new supporters, and even new elements of strength. For example, when inducted into power and included within the national political system, the intensity of the aggressive rhetoric of the DMK in Tamil Nadu was gradually tempered into the normal language of the Indian political establishment.

But there was an element of new political mobility associated with the DMK, and later the AIDMK, that cannot be missed. The ascent of these ethnic organizations to power in their region ensured that the days of Brahman dominance in politics were over. In fact, the ability of the ethnic movements, in influencing the formation of linguistic states, to displace formerly entrenched political status groups and to replace them by relatively lower, though not the lowest, status groups was demonstrated in other cases as well. Though the ethnic movement for Maharashtrian autonomy reflected a coalition of all caste groups, it was dominated by middle caste groups. Following the formation of the new state of Maharashtra in 1960, the leadership in power ensured middle caste dominance—sometimes described as the hegemony of the upper segments of the Maratha caste–cluster—and at the same time openly sought to cultivate the relatively lower castes in order to undercut the power of the left opposition.[12] Although this process of deliberate incorporation was limited in its ability to benefit the poorest segments of the population, it did expand the base of participation and access to patronage beyond that possible in regions undisturbed by major ethnic movements. In fact, it may not be a mere chance occurrence that the few states in which the lower status groups have registered discernible social advancements also happen to be the ones where ethnic politics has played a large part.[13]

If governance has not been impaired and the national system has succeeded in incorporating ethnic groups, one may infer that the implications of ethnicity for political development have been at least positive and con-

[12] See Donald B. Rosenthal, " 'Making It' in Maharashtra" in *Contemporary India*, edited by N. R. Inamdar et al., Poona: Continental, 1982, p. 3ff. On the notion of upper Maratha hegemony, see Jayant K. Lele, "Chavan and the Political Integration of Maharashtra," in *Contemporary India*, pp. 29–59 and Lele, "One-Party Dominance in Maharashtra: Resilience and Change," in *State Politics in Contemporary India*, edited by John R. Wood, Boulder: Westview, 1984, p. 177.

[13] See Roderick Church, "The Pattern of State Politics in Indira Gandhi's India," in *State Politics in Contemporary India* (n. 12), pp. 236–237, where he compares reports on seven states and divides them into roughly two groups—inclusive or exclusive with respect to lower castes. Gujarat, Karnataka, and Maharashtra are included in the first category. Bihar and Uttar Pradesh are in the second category.

ceivably better than before. But the question still remains as to what these political gains have meant for economic development. Have these political gains impaired the efficacy of planning or impeded the process of economic development? Perhaps we can begin by using the most favored indicator of economic development used by planners, that is, per capita income.[14] Of the six states resulting from major regional ethnic movements, four have achieved the highest per capita income level in the country. From the sixties to the eighties, Punjab, Haryana, Maharashtra, and Gujarat have consistently remained at the top rank. Andhra Pradesh moved up from a rank position of 9 (among 15 states) in 1950–1951 to 7 in 1971–1972 and retained this position in 1981–1982. Tamil Nadu's rank was 12 in 1950–1951, improved to 5 in 1970–1971, but fell to 10 in 1981–1982. If constant prices (1970–1972) rather than current prices, are used for the 1981–1982 calculation, then both Andhra Pradesh and Tamil Nadu would improve their positions, with the ranking of the top four remaining unchanged. If we take the annual rate of percentage increase in per capita income at constant prices (1970–1971) between 1971–1972 to 1981–1982 as a reasonable indicator of income growth, the highest rank (among 15 states) will go to Punjab, the third position to Maharashtra, a tied fourth to Andhra Pradesh and Haryana, sixth to Gujarat, and seventh to Tamil Nadu, with the respective rates of growth being 2.9, 2.5, 2.0, 1.3, and 1.1. The national average of annual growth rate for all 15 states for this period is 1.3 percent.

If we assume that these popular indicators show that the reorganized states can generally claim a much better record of performance in economic development than the national average of states, the question still remains as to what this means in terms of mass poverty. Again, judging by the proportion of the population that is calculated to be below the Planning Commission's recent estimate of the poverty line, the record of these states is for the most part superior to the national average. The sixth five-year plan's estimate of the percentage of people below the poverty line for the country as a whole was 48.1.[15] Compared to this, the figure for Punjab was 15.1; for Haryana 24.8; Gujarat, 39.0; Andhra Pradesh, 42.2; and Maharashtra, 47.7. Only Tamil Nadu scored below the national average, with four other states of the total fifteen faring still worse.[16]

Many other indicators can be used to measure the economic develop-

[14] The source of data for this section is *Basic Statistics Relating to the Indian Economy*, vol. 2, Bombay: Center for Monitoring Indian Economy, September 1985, table 14.1.

[15] The data on poverty is based on Planning Commission estimates of 65 to 75 rupees per capita per month for rural and urban areas, respectively, and then making a combined poverty line. Ibid., table 14.9.

[16] Ibid., table 9.8.

ment performance of these states, with much the same result. A word about industrialization would be appropriate, however, because Indian planning has always regarded it as the cornerstone of economic development. In 1960, taking the index of per capita value added in the factory sector (India average = 100), Maharashtra had the highest rate of growth (226), which it retained in 1980 although its score slid to 192. Haryana (154 in 1980) and Tamil Nadu (104 in 1960, 145 in 1980) were third and fourth highest, respectively, and Punjab (65 in 1960 and 132 in 1980) was sixth. Andhra Pradesh had a rather low score in 1960 (39) but improved its record by 1980 (62). As one can see from these data, the record of industrial development in these states compares quite well with that of the other states in India. What is even more interesting is that a comparison of 1970 and 1984 figures for central investment in public enterprise in Indian states indicates that national planners recognized this superior performance and increased investment in these states, with, however, the one exception of Tamil Nadu.[17] Apparently, inclusionary strategies could turn yesterday's adversaries into constructive partners for national development.

—economic development and new states.

EXCLUSION AND DESPERATION: THE CASE OF ASSAM

The ethnic explosion of the 1980s in Assam and Punjab may tell us either that there was something very different about the ethnic movements in these two areas or that the inclusionary orientation of the national authorities had by this time exhausted itself. It is interesting that ethnic politics in the eighties has been intensified in both the least advantaged and the most prosperous regions of the Indian subcontinent. We shall concentrate here on the first, Assam, and shall discuss the Punjab problem only for comparative purposes. Unlike previously discussed ethnic situations, the issue in Assam is not the creation of a new state. It is, rather, the control of resources within the state and access to national resources by those who consider themselves authentic Assamese. The question of authenticity offers insights into the problem of what we have called individual multiethnicity. Assam's perceived deprivation has an objective basis in its economic backwardness; the Punjab ethnic movement, on the other hand, brings out the issue of transformation of a regional movement into a movement for autonomy of a religious community. The extensive use of violence and repression that have characterized ethnic politics emerging in

ASSAM DIFFERS

MAIN CONFLICT

PUNJAB

[17] Ibid., table 9.12. The relevant percentage share figures for 1970 and 1984 respectively, are Maharashtra 3.1, 15.2; Andhra Pradesh 2.5, 7.9; Gujarat 2.5, 3.9; Punjab 0.7, 1.7; Haryana 0.2, 0.9; and Tamil Nadu 8.0, 5.5.

both these regions calls attention to the problem of exclusionary strategies pursued by the national political authorities and their impact on national development. The two cases also point out the significance of the Rajiv Gandhi phase of national leadership and its strategies. The 1985 "accords" in Assam and Punjab may produce different consequences, but at least in Assam, following the 1985 election, a stage of resolution has been reached.

NATL. STRATEGIES

The developmental implication of the movement in Assam has been complicated by the fact that there has been no coherence in the agenda proposed by its leaders in recent years. The leaders of the Assamese movement have been less secure within the state as well as within their own community than were their counterparts in the Tamil, Telugu, Marathi, or Gujarati movements. They have failed to adhere to a consistent definition of what constitutes Assamese authenticity, and their targets have shifted from time to time. Worst of all, the movement was intensified at a turning point in Indian national politics when strategies of inclusive incorporation both at the center and at the party level were being drastically replaced by strategies of manipulation and exclusion. Indira Gandhi's statecraft progressively reduced the scope of negotiation in favor of administratively manipulated solutions. The insecurity of the movement and the lack of responsiveness at the center after 1980 cumulatively contributed to a desperation that claimed a massive human price.

NATL. POLITICAL STRATEGY CHANGED

Assam's population was close to 19 million by 1980. The proportion of Assamese language speakers in Assam was 59 percent, and when other major Indian languages, officially called "scheduled languages," are added, the figure rises to 86 percent. Sixty-three other languages are spoken by the rest of the population. Even the marginal majority of the Assamese speakers in the state of Assam is complicated by the fact that it includes a substantial number of speakers who are either Muslim immigrants or their descendants from Bangladesh.[18] Those who regard themselves as the original and authentic members of the Assamese speech community alternate between grudgingly recognizing the newcomers as authentic Assamese people and violently rejecting them as illegal intruders on their soil. The political cohesion of the community thus remains uncertain and this uncertainty adversely affects the bargaining strength of the Assamese ethnic movement.

BARGAINING STRENGTH OF MOVEMENT

---

[18] The mean decennial growth rate of population in Assam has been higher than the national average: the rates for Assam are as follows (with the national average in parentheses): 1921–1931, 17.6 (10.5); 1931–1941, 17.9 (13.3); and 1941–1951, 17.4 (12.5). For a survey, see Niranjan Dhar, "Social Tension in Assam: An Impact of Immigration (1872–1951)" in J. B. Bhattacharjee, *Social Tension in North-East India*, Calcutta: Research India, 1982, pp. 9–23.

Ethnic politics in Assam mainly calls attention to a set of deeply perceived disadvantages of the Assamese speech community. Within Assam, it raises the issue of Assamese fears of losing their rightful place in the structure of wealth and power. Within the country as a whole, it reflects the Assamese concern for a fair share of the developmental resources generated in the state and in the nation. In short, the Assamese movement thrives on feelings of neglect, injustice, and inadequate opportunity to develop. The movement seeks to control Assam's resources and to make sure that the management of these resources remains with Assam's own personnel. In addition, it wants to establish a negotiated term of partnership for sharing the resources of the nation. It recognizes that Assam is one of the poorest states of the country and that this poverty calls for a special attention from the national authority. This recognition of dependence on the central government for assistance to reverse the disadvantage within the state and to ensure better access to national resources makes it difficult for the movement to engage in an enduring confrontation with the center.

What complicates the ethnic politics of Assam is the state of insecurity of the Assamese people involved in the movement. Assam's boundaries have frequently changed, first, as a result of colonial administrative designs and, after independence, as a result of new domains of autonomy carved out and granted to various hill areas by the federal authority.[19] The present boundaries, in effect since 1972, make the state much smaller and at the same time endow it with relatively less heterogeneity than before. The Assamese movement's major base lies in the Brahmaputra valley, where most of the Assamese people live, but even there they constitute only about 61 percent of the population.[20] Their numbers include Muslim immigrants who are, as pointed out earlier, sometimes excluded depending on the Assamese movement's direction. Besides boundary and identity issues, Assamese insecurity is also fueled by the demographic and economic fact that urban life in Assam is dominated by the "Bahiragata," outsiders speaking languages of the neighboring states.

In fact, Assam's economic situation and internal control of resources clearly indicate a form of injustice that would make the people of any

[19] British colonial control of Assam from 1826 gradually expanded by incorporating new areas, including it in the province of Bengal, separating it from Bengal in 1874, redesigning it as a part of a separate Muslim Bengali province in 1905, and then reconstituting it in 1912. In 1947, it lost the district of Sylhet to Pakistan, and since then the formation of units like Nagaland, Meghalaya, Arunachal, and Mizoram has substantially altered the map of the state. For an account of these processes, see Myron Weiner, *Sons of the Soil, Migration and Ethnic Conflict in India*, Princeton: Princeton University Press, 1978, pp. 84ff.

[20] According to the 1961 census, 73.2 percent spoke Assamese in this valley. A. K. Das reports that this was reduced to 60.9 percent in 1971. See his *Assam's Agony*, New Delhi: Lancers, 1982, p. 53.

comparable state feel a profound sense of insecurity and of alienation from the center. Assam's per capita annual average income of 110 U. S. dollars in 1981–1982 compares disfavorably with all the major states of India except six.[21] Ten Indian states enjoy higher levels, and the richest state has a per capita income two and a half times better. Between 1961 and 1971, the population in Assam grew by 35 percent compared to the national average of 24.8 percent. According to the 1981 census, Assam's literacy rate was lower than the national average, and its ratio of urban/rural population is less than half the national figure. The largest part of the urban population comprises non-Assamese speakers. By 1980 Assam produced less than 2 percent of the nation's food grains, and its share of per capita bank deposits was 161 rupees compared to the national average of 483 rupees.[22] In sharp contrast to the state's relative poverty, Assam is a rich source of oil, tea, coal, and plywood. These cash commodities do not, however, necessarily enrich the state. In fact, the leaders of the Assamese movement complain that these are precisely the resources, in addition to land, that have invited outsiders to practice internal colonialism in Assam.

The leaders of the Assamese movement point out that, although Assam supplies 60 percent of India's crude oil production, it receives from the central authority less than 3 percent of its value in the form of royalties. One refinery located outside the state earns three times this royalty and is allowed a refining capacity twice that permitted Assam.[23] Assam is a major center of tea production in India, producing about 55 percent of the country's supply of tea. The ownership of the tea gardens and the profit from the tea sales are, however, mainly controlled by outsiders. Only a small part of the tea produced is sold through auction in Assam. Eighty-five percent is sold through Calcutta, in West Bengal, and London auctions. In fact, Assam's share of royalties for tea amounts to less than half that which West Bengal receives. Assam supplies about 60 percent of India's plywood, but only a very small part of the return from the product is retained by the state—a disproportionately large share goes to the center in the form of taxes.

The leaders of the Assamese movement indignantly point out that Assam's uneven share in the process of national economic development and its consequently persisting underdevelopment are due to the intrusion of outsiders and the unresponsiveness of the central authority. In spite of

ASSAM'S claim

---

[21] This is calculated on the basis of current prices. Conversion to U. S. dollars is according to the exchange rate in early 1985. Most of the data in this section are from *Statistical Outline of India, 1984*, Bombay: Tata Services, 1984.

[22] Ibid.

[23] For detailed evidence on this and other data in this section, see Mahesh Joshi, *Assam: The Indian Conflict*, New Delhi: Prachi, 1981.

being the largest supplier of valuable commodities such as oil, tea, and plywood, the budgetary position of Assam has consistently indicated net deficits in revenue. During 1981–1982, for example, Assam still remained a deficit state when most of the major states of India maintained a revenue surplus.[24] Assam's performance in raising her revenue has been significantly poorer than that of most states. Assam's own tax revenue as a percent of total revenues in 1970–1971 stood at 27.3 compared to the national average of Indian states at 44.3. Total revenues include a state's share of national tax, its own nontax revenue, and a central grant of the federal government.[25]

By 1971–1972, Assam's per capita tax revenue was 22.3 rupees; its per capita total tax revenue, including the national share, was 37.5 rupees, and the national grant was also 37.5 rupees. The corresponding figures for the home state of the prime minister of India were 17.7, 35.3, and 7.2. These figures for Uttar Pradesh fail to suggest any deliberate motive of the national leadership to deprive Assam of a fair share of central grants. In fact, among the major states of India, the magnitude of grants from the central authority to Assam has been close to the highest level. These grants, however, tell only part of the story of sharing.

That the level of the grant and other assistance from the federal government could be much higher is, of course, another question. What disturbs the members of the Assamese movement more is the fact that the nature of administration in Assam has not left significant levels of control with the sons of the soil. Within the state administration, the Assamese speaking personnel are outnumbered by "outsiders," who supply 62 percent of the state service. Assamese personnel in central services located in the state, such as railroad, postal, and nationalized banking services, constitute only 10 percent of the total employees. The educated, middle-class Assamese leadership considers this imbalance as evidence of encroachment. What is involved, according to them, is more than a matter of losing employment opportunity in the public sector. What they resent more intensely is the loss of control over their own administration.

It is interesting to note that historically the leadership of the Assamese movement has not succeeded in using the state government, which is composed of Assamese politicians, to make a united vehicle representing As-

[24] Assam's revenue deficit amounted to 180 million rupees in 1981–1982. The corresponding deficits in 1980–1981 and 1979–1980 were 669 and 401 million rupees respectively. This can be compared with the revenue surplus in the same years registered in the two other equally underdeveloped states of India, i.e., Bihar and Orissa. *Statistical Outline of India* (n. 21).

[25] The revenue distribution data are from Ram Niranjan Tripathy, *Federal Finance and Economic Development in India*, New Delhi: Sterling, 1982, pp. 106 and 131.

samese interests. Ever since 1972, when the movement significantly stepped up its pace and desperation, it has been mainly led by students, professionals, and literary people. Precarious coalitions of prominent politicians eagerly seeking support of vote groups drawn from different classes, ethnic and religious groups have ruled the state until 1985 with appropriate linkage with the ruling parties at the national level. In recent years, particularly after the failure of the Janata party coalition, prolonged presidential rule was made possible primarily by the political cleavage among the Assamese political leaders.[26]

The failure of organized and institutional leadership within a structure of democratic representation has encouraged the rise of interest associations such as the All Assam Students' Union (AASU), which has led, since July 1978, the movement to demand expulsion of foreigners from Assam. Eleven different groups came together to form the All Assam Gana Sangram Parishad (AAGSP), or the Assam popular movement front. One particularly interesting partner in this movement is a group that represents respected writers in Assamese literature organized as the Assam Sahitya Sabha (ASS). The major issues of the movement articulated in recent years have been concerned with a) the alleged intrusion of "foreigners," mainly from neighboring Bangladesh; b) the prevention of Bengali domination, and c) the prevention of national and outsiders' exploitation of Assam.[27] The most explosive issue engaging the major public attention of the movement has concerned the issue of foreigners. The AASU and the AAGSP have engaged in extensive mass mobilization strategies and, occasionally, desperately violent tactics to expel the "foreigners" and to put the already settled ones in a place that the movement considers as proper. In 1983 alone, the movement against foreigners led to extensive violence that cost several thousand human lives.

The state of Bangladesh, which gained independence on grounds of ethnic self-determination, is supposed to be the source of illegal immigrants settling in Assam. In fact, this is not a new problem. Neither is resentment against immigrants from east Bengal in any way new. As early as 1926 an organization called the Assam Protection Association was formed to prevent Muslim immigration from east Bengal. What is new is the vastly increased scale of the agitation and its success in gaining mass support from the Brahmaputra valley. The original fear was expressed in terms of the Assamese Hindus' sense of eventual erosion of their majority. The present fear is not publicly expressed as a Hindu anxiety; rather the emphasis is

---

[26] For details of the rise, fall, and abdication of parties in recent years in Assam, see T. S. Murty, *Assam, The Difficult Years*, New Delhi: Himalayan, 1983.

[27] See A. K. Das, *Assam's Agony* (n. 20), p. 7.

on the impending loss of territorial control of the Assamese in general as a result of being outnumbered by Bengali and Nepali foreign immigrants. The main targets, however, are the Bengali Muslim immigrant groups who have entered the area in different phases, that is, before and after the formation of the new state of Bangladesh.

The present form and direction of the movement reflect a number of complications that appear to undermine the movement's effectiveness. First, Bengali Muslim immigrants have poured in for decades, going back to pre-independence days, and many of them are considered "proper" Assamese by the strict standards of the Assamese language movement leaders. Second, Assamese Congress leaders have used the immigrants' support as a crucial vote bank for their electoral and mobilizational success. Third, the differential recognition accorded to Bengali Muslim immigrants has been a product of the changing requirements of political success of the electoral leadership of the state and the movement leadership. Because both these leaderships claim the loyalty of the Assamese population, their divergence on the issue of the Assameseness of the immigrants simply confuses the Assamese people. Fourth, because all the major political parties of Assam need Muslim support and because the Muslim leadership in religious and political organizations feels threatened when a substantial number of Muslims are made targets of organized agitation, the Muslim people feel it necessary to bargain separately with the major political parties in Assam and with the national political parties. This process obviously weakens the secular claim of the Assamese movement to represent a coherent community and gradually identifies the movement with the ethnic interests of the Assamese Hindus.

Finally, the more desperate the Assamese movement is to throw out the recent immigrants or to restrict their political rights, the more it may encourage its adversaries to organize a common cause among the settled Bengali Hindus and Assamese Muslim ethnic groups in the hill areas and immigrants from other areas of India. The combined voice of all these groups speaking to a divided Assamese leadership could make a political impact that might receive a positive hearing from the national political leadership. It is in this confrontation that the basic structural weakness of the Assamese autonomy movement lies.

Ethnic politics as pursued by the Assamese movement has also revealed a lack of coherence regarding the selection of adversaries. During the fifties and sixties, its focus was on the urgent need for Assamization of the state official language, the state services, and the general levers of political and economic control. From 1948 to 1977, the targets of attack were mainly the settled Bengali population and, secondarily, other ethnic groups who dominated the private enterprise and the labor market in the organized sector.[28] The issues were predominantly connected with affirming the rights of the educated Assamese to control resources. From the late 1970s, the major target of attack was identified as Muslim immigrants grabbing lands and thus tilting the ethnic ratio against the Assamese people. Before this phase, the movement leaders found it hard to mobilize the peasantry and particularly the peasants and tribal peasants of the hill areas. In fact, most of the hill areas had broken away and formed separate states by the seventies, as we have already noted.

The prominence of the land issue since the late seventies may enable the movement to deepen its mass base. But the same process of deepening may also contribute to the formation of new political cleavages to the eventual detriment of the movement. The pattern of extensive mass violence witnessed in 1983 during the movement to detect and deport Bengali Muslim nationals of Bangladesh origin indicated a tragic confusion of adversary identification and targets of annihilation. The movement to detect and deport foreigners had gained momentum in 1979 when an official move began to correct the list of voters. From 6.3 million voters in 1972, the figure increased to 7.2 million in 1977, 7.9 million in 1978, and 8.6 million in 1979.[29] The abnormal rise in the number of voters was accompanied by an 80 percent rise in Assamese speakers in the two decades ending in 1971. For the movement leaders this was ominous. They suspected that the "foreigners" were using the cover of Assamese language as a ruse that they could easily drop when convenient, redeclaring themselves Bengali speaking. That, of course, would make the Assamese people a minority in their own land.

It is this loss-of-land-complex that is supported by using a figure of 7.8 million as the number of illegal immigrants in Assam. But the problem was more complicated than a single case of an ethnic leadership expressing anxiety about its impending loss. Along with that concern was a fear that these immigrants, who were mostly poor peasants, might radicalize the peasantry in Assam and thereby jeopardize the individual possessions of the Assamese property owners. One agitation leader frankly expressed the fear that the political loyalty of the immigrants was shifting from its traditional support for the ruling party toward the leftist parties, including the Communist party of India–(Marxist).[30] He feared that the "entire Brahmaputra valley, once an oasis of nationalism in this desert of insur-

---

[28] For an analysis of shifting targets, see T. Bhattacharjee, "Tension in North-East," in *Social Tension in North-East India* (n. 18), pp. 123–135.

[29] This is based on a report in *India Today*, 28 February 1983, intntl. ed., p. 18.

[30] Again, the Bengali association of India's leading communist movement represented by the Communist party of India (Marxist) adds complexity to this issue, particularly because this party has been the ruling party in the neighboring state of West Bengal in recent years.

gency, is surrounded by Marxist expansionists and Bengali cultural expansionists."[31] Official estimates in Assam use a figure of illegal immigration that is less than a third of that used by the movement.

The desperation of the movement to correct electoral rolls and to expel the unwanted immigrants was aided considerably by the rigidity of the dominant political party at the national level of government and in Assam. The Congress–I party intended to use the increasing minority resentment of the Assamese movement in its favor and went ahead with the February election in 1983. The movement, attempting to foil the election, resorted to widespread agitation leading to an unprecedented wave of violence and destruction. What has been called the Nellie Massacre of February 18, 1983 indicates the magnitude of the tragedy. In one day, close to fourteen hundred men, women, and children were killed. It was an act of a mob comprised of about 12,000 people. This was a sample of the price paid for an imposed election conducted without revising the rolls. Although the acts of violence mostly affected the immigrants, they also involved many other victims, not excluding Assamese plains people who were included as the targets of hill peasants' violence. The aftermath of the massacre saw a deep division between the Hindu and Muslim sections of the Assamese leadership.[32] Multiple dimensions of social cleavage in Assamese society became more rigid in political and organizational expressions. Issues of linguistic and religious dominance, so long separated in Assam, now came to a head. The Assamese autonomy movement could have been stronger if the religious issues of dominance had been strategically contained. Similarly, the restoration of land-rights questions brought out not merely the issue of immigrants' intrusion but also the issue of the dominance of the Assamese plains peoples in the hill peoples' domain.

Assamese language politics clearly brings out the dilemma of an educated elite that seeks to use ethnic mobilization to enhance its share in local and national developmental resources. This involves sharing political and administrative control, revenues generated in the state, employment, and other opportunities. In the process of seeking these rights, the ethnic movement uses a number of threats against its local and national adversaries, but it rarely uses secessionist demands. Normally, the techniques of struggle employed by the movement have included both persuasive and

[31] *India Today*, 28 February 1983, intntl. ed., p. 15. This is from a statement of H. K. Bhattacharya, who formerly was a senior police official and who, incidentally, was in charge of the first official detection operation for correcting electoral rolls in 1979.

[32] See, for example, a report on the infighting in the AASU leadership in *India Today*, 15 May 1983, intntl, ed., p. 18. This issue also contains a detailed documentary report on the Nellie Massacre by Arun Shourie, pp. 28–37.

coercive means. Before the tragic events of 1983, the leaders were averse to negotiation. But their negotiating strength has been considrably weakened by divisions in the Assamese leadership, their shifting sense of adversaries, and, of course, by the diplomacy of the national leadership, which sought to divide the Assamese movement to consolidate its own power in the state. The advantage held by the national leadership lies in the fact that Assam's bargaining power at the center is highly limited. Deep-seated mutual suspicion between the plains and hill populations in Assam has made it easier for the national leadership to follow a strategy of differential affection. Political and religious divisions within the plains people supplying the Assamese leadership further facilitate the strategy of defusing by dividing the social base of support for the movement's leaders. When these leaders opt for violence in sheer desperation, they lose the control of the movement to the detriment of their own interest.

The ethnic movement in Assam cannot be said to be intrinsically disruptive of the nation. The national leaders could have avoided the 1983 tragedy by not forcing an unwanted election. National investment for generating development and employment in Assam has been much less generous than in other states. When one examines the percentage of financial assistance sanctioned by national public sector financial institutions, it becomes apparent that the center can do considerably more than it has in recent years. By 1978, Assam was sanctioned only 1.6 percent of this type of assistance compared with 15.7 percent in Maharashtra and 10 percent in Uttar Pradesh.[33] The distribution of central government employees according to state, taking into account employees receiving below 800 rupees per month, indicates that Assam's share amounted to only 2.8 percent in 1975, whereas Uttar Pradesh enjoyed a share of 16.1 percent.[34] Assam's educated population might suffer from less insecurity if a little more sensitivity regarding resource allocation, employment creation, and political negotiation could be demonstrated by the central authority. Clearly, initiative in this regard is likely to be a more productive strategy than frightfully diversionary gambles such as the imposition of unwanted elections.

The Assamese movement, on the other hand, can benefit from a greater sense of realism than it has historically demonstrated. If it genuinely wants to represent the Muslim population, it has to realize that a more realistic assessment of the illegal immigration issue will be a necessary condition for success.

[33] See K. R. G. Nair, ed., *Regional Disparities in India*, New Delhi: Agricole, 1981, pp. 98–99.
[34] Ibid., p. 55.

The use of massive violence by ethnic movements does not necessarily help them to cover their internal contradictions, although such violence shifts attention to the targets for a while. In Assam, after 1983, a temporary respite helped the newly elected government under Hiteswar Saikia to benefit from Muslim suspicion of the AASU-AAGSP leadership. As the Muslim student leaders' resentment of the dominant Hindu leaders hardened, the Saikia leadership used another element of internal contradiction of the movement. Saikia's Ahom background helped him to play the Ahom sentiment of the upper districts against the Brahman and Kayastha dominated lower Assam regions. If religious and regional sentiments have divided the ethnic movement in the immediate aftermath of violence in 1983, the feelings of the hill states peoples around Assam did not provide much comfort for the movement's leadership. As the chairman of the North-East Regional Congress–I, Hiteswar Saikia sought to use its platform to isolate the movement's leadership.[35] At best, however, these were all temporary efforts to prepare the ground for the more constructive solution called for by the situation. The Assam accord of August 12, 1985 brought about by the new national leadership of Rajiv Gandhi indicated a shift toward a revised national policy favoring a process of accommodation to arrive at a constructive solution. At the same time, the accord was facilitated by increasing moderation on the part of the movement's leadership. For the national leadership, a negotiated peace in Assam was important for gaining better political control over the northeastern cluster of states as a whole. The prize was worth a few concessions to the movement leaders especially because the national leadership was confident that the post-accord election would strengthen Congress rule in Assam. Even if the Congress were to lose the election, its replacement could be expected to lend support to the national system. This revised calculation of national strategy, marking a departure from the previous exclusionary strategy, was welcomed by movement leaders because it promised access to formal power in the state and a legitimate place in the national system of power and resources.

The Assam accord shows how little the national leadership needs to concede to secure crucial gains for the national system, if only it can settle for a distinction between short-run manipulation and long-run gains. According to the new agreement, January 1, 1966 would serve as a base year for detecting "foreigners." Although this appears to be an improvement over the previously offered base line of 1967, in practice the 1967 electoral rolls had been agreed to be the basic document for identifying for-

[35] See S. Guha, "Hiteswar Saikia," in *The Telegraph* (Calcutta), 10 February 1985.

eigners.[36] In addition, some general measures to protect the ethnic identity of the Assamese people were agreed upon although no specific steps were indicated. It was further agreed that some cases of disciplinary or punishing action against the participants in previous movements would be reconsidered. In sum, the concessions were more symbolic than substantial, but the movement retrieved some of its prestige and the accord served both the agreeing parties equally.

With the announcement of a new election, various components of the movement hurriedly got together to form a regional party called Asom Gana Parishad (AGP). AASU leader Prafulla Mahanta took a leading part in converting the movement into a political party. The AGP won 64 of 126 seats in the December 16, 1985 election, with the Congress–I trailing behind with 25 seats. Mahanta at thirty-two thus became the youngest chief minister in Indian history. He lost no time in declaring that AGP's victory implies a victory of "regionalism with a nationalist outlook."[37]

Constructive Implications and Their Limits

It would be unfair to assume that the AGP leaders have suddenly discovered the virtues of nationalism after gaining power. Ethnic regionalism and secular nationalism are not necessarily competing values. As our preceding discussion has indicated, from the very early phase of Indian independence, the leaders of the central government have consistently underestimated the national concerns and aspirations of ethnic movements. It was easy for leaders at the center to doubt the national credentials of the ethnic movements from the secure heights of the central government. From the Andhra movement of the early fifties to the Assam movement in the eighties, however, ethnic politics has demonstrated that regional movements can add depth to nationalism. When ethnic leaders are allowed to share power, they generally act according to the rules of the regime and quickly seek to build linkages with other regional leaders as well as with national leaders. By 1985 six major states of the Indian federation have come under non-Congress rule. Four of them are led by persons who are products of ethnic movements. How these four states will share national power, participate in national planning, and implement development policies will largely depend on the quality of incorporation that the national democratic and federal processes can offer.

The initiative can be said to lie with the central government precisely because of the magnitude and the centralized nature of its control over the

---

[36] *India Today*, 15 September 1985, intntl. ed., p. 27.
[37] *India Today*, 15 January 1986, intntl. ed., p. 10.

coercive apparatus, economic resources, strategic administration, and mass communication. It can generate ethnic dissent by displaying selective affection for a preferred set of ethnic groups from which it derives strategic political support. It can strengthen ethnic disaffection by putting ethnic movements into untenable positions, as it did in Assam in 1983, or it can, with little sacrifice, generate collaboration as it chose to do in 1985. It can also "communalize" a simple set of regional demands, as it did in Punjab, when, instead of treating the Akali Dal demands on their merit, the national state authorities gave them a secessionist label because they had been put forward by an ethnic organization.[38] The central government sought, furthermore, to undermine the influence of the Akali leadership, which had ruled in Punjab when the original charter of demands were drawn in 1978 but had lost the elections in 1980. The Akalis had done virtually nothing to press these issues while in power,[39] but their loss of the elections raised the bargaining value of their demands. The exclusionary mood of the national leadership in the 1980s left little room for negotiation. In Assam, at about the same time, a divide and rule strategy was used to weaken the support base of the ethnic leadership. Akali Dal in Punjab was subjected to similar treatment. The ethnic base of the Akali leadership was more cohesive, however, than that in Assam and had the benefit of organized religion–based networks of people and money. The attempts to divide the Akalis failed to work and led to a phase of mutual reinforcement of repression and violence on an ascending scale. When the new national leadership of 1985 tried a policy of accord and electoral opportunity to share power, the Akali response was positive. Although the Akali Dal won the election, its capacity to undo the systemic damage accumulating over five years was limited. Exclusionary manipulation is not difficult to practice for a state that has a decisive control of coercive and communicational apparatus, but the consequent trail of political damage is much harder to repair.

-key

The earlier inclusionary phase of the sixties belied the prediction of some intellectuals that ethnic "disarray" in India joined with "developmental frustrations" would create "convulsion" leading to either "totalitarianism" or "partial communist control" in India.[40] A notion of the

[38] See D. Gupta, "The Communalizing of Punjab, 1980–1985" in *Economic and Political Weekly*, 13 July 1985, pp. 1185–1190.

[39] This charter of demands is known as the Anandpur Sahib Resolution of 1978 of the Akali Dal. It begins with the statement that "India is a federal . . . entity . . . Indian constitutional infra-structure should be given a real federal shape. . . ." See the text in Government of India, *White Paper on the Punjab Agitation*, New Delhi, 10 July 1984, p. 72.

[40] Selig Harrison, *India: The Most Dangerous Decades*, Delhi: Oxford University Press, 1960, pp. 338–339.

modern developmental state being battered and overwhelmed with parochial pressures to the extent of frustrating both the development of economic resources and the democratic institutions did not materialize. The
"dangerous decades" became, instead, constructive decades. Where pru-
dent incorporative strategies were employed, ethnic political forces
learned to use formal power for productive development and helped in-
duct new elements of political and social mobility. Although access and
mobility do not necessarily decrease inequality, they can make it more tolerable.[41] When ethnicity was used to compete politically for economic re-   TRANSFORMED
sources, its political success in acquiring power transformed itself from
unquiet pressure exerted from outside the system to quiet pressure inserted into the national planning system.

Did this mean a loss of the insularity that some claim is necessary for
the effective conduct of rational planning? If insularity refers to the freedom of policy makers to pursue rational planning unaffected by nonrational pressure, it is hard to see how the quiet pressures generated by ethnic leaders from within the system would differ from the quiet pressures
generated within the monopoly Congress system of earlier years. In any
case, even a high-handed and ethnically homogeneous South Korean developmental authoritarian system is not free from such pressures.[42] The
idea of insular planning itself may not be as much of a virtue as is claimed
in the developmental literature with an explicit or implied managerial perspective.

However, democratic incorporation of ethnic groups, even at its best
moments in recent Indian history, does raise issues that reveal some of its
limitations. The major beneficiaries of expanded access made possible by
the induction of ethnic movements into the national system of planned development are usually drawn from the middle layers of those ethnic

---

[41] The issues of access and mobility raise the importance of distinguishing between the
static and the dynamic pictures of inequality at a given time. Witness, as a reminder, a comment from H. W. Singer: "If there is a fairly rapid turnover between those occupying the
different rungs of the income ladder, a given degree of inequality would be more tolerable
. . . than if the opposite is the case . . . ," "Reflections on Sociological Aspects of the Economic
Growth Based on the Work of Bert Hoselitz" in *Essays on Economic Development and Cultural Change in Honor of Bert Hoselitz, Economic Development and Cultural Change*, vol.
25, edited by Manning Nash, Supplement, Chicago: University of Chicago Press, 1977, p. 9.

[42] A case like South Korea, an example that casts a spell among many scholars of development, indicates that regional pressures have been conspicuous even in this ethnically homogeneous and politically authoritarian country. These pressures are more open during elections, remaining concealed on other occasions. The impact of regionalism on the elections of
1963 and 1967, particularly the regionalist factors in Park Chung Hee's election, is analyzed
in Chong Lim Kim, ed., *Political Participation in Korea*, Santa Barbara: Cleo Books, 1980,
p. 67.

groups. As we have noted above, this raises the issue of what the lowest status groups or class groups can do to widen the range of beneficiaries. Intraregional ethnic conflict is one course that they can use, and have increasingly used, for gaining their rights.[43] This may assume the form of popular movements based on class, caste or deprived areas.

Besides the problem of limited beneficiary selection, there is also the problem of reliance on patronage to serve the expanded clientele even within the middle layers of the society. Patronage in such situations normally takes the form of subsidy and relaxation of the rules of economic extraction. How will these forms affect capital accumulation and productive efficiency in the future if this incorporative style is continued? To concede the present virtues of democratic incorporation of ethnic politics is, then, not to deny the significance of the future implications of these questions.

---

[43] See, for example, A. Mudholkar and R. Vora, "Regionalism in Maharashtra" in *Regionalism: Developmental Tensions in India*, edited by A. Majeed, New Delhi: Cosmo, 1984, pp. 89–114. See also Jayant Lele, *Elite Pluralism and Class Rule: Political Development in Maharashtra, India*, Toronto: University of Toronto Press, 1981, pp. 141–194.

FIVE

The Punjab Crisis and the Unity of India

PAUL R. BRASS

INTRODUCTION

In the early years after independence in India, as in other countries of Asia and Africa, it was common to view the maintenance of national unity, peace, and internal order as among the central, if not the central, political problems. There was also a shared view among the leaders of the new states that national unity could best be maintained by a process of national integration that involved the development of new loyalties to a centralizing, modernizing state. That view was shared also by virtually all Western scholars who wrote about these questions in the 1950s and 1960s.

natl. unity was needed.

In *Language, Religion, and Politics in North India*, written in the late 1960s and early 1970s and published in 1974,[1] I argued against the shared view. My position was that India was not and could not be a nation-state, but was instead a developing multi-national state. The argument was based upon a distinction between political integration of diverse peoples through politics, policies, procedures, and institutions and national inte-

I am grateful to Joyce Pettigrew for her critiques of two earlier versions of this manuscript. I am afraid I may not have satisfied her on all matters. A lively exchange with Baldev Raj Nayar also helped me to sharpen my thinking, though we disagree even more substantially. A very heated exchange in Delhi with Rashpal Malhotra and his colleagues from the Centre for Research in Rural and Industrial Development in Chandigarh caused me to rectify some imbalances in my treatment of Mrs. Gandhi's policies and decisions and of the opposed points of view on some matters. I doubt, however, that we are yet in agreement. I appreciate also the comments of Kenneth Jones, Atul Kohli, Christopher Shackle, Bhagwan D. Dua, and Mark Tully and have revised the manuscript in several places as a result of some of their comments. With regard to this essay, however, more than most, it is necessary to emphasize that I am solely responsible for the accuracy of the statements, for the interpretation, and for the opinions expressed.

Elizabeth Mann helped me to prepare the original manuscript for submission.
[1] Paul R. Brass, *Language, Religion, and Politics in North India*, New York: Cambridge University Press, 1974.

gration through assimilation of diverse peoples to a common national culture. My view was that Indian policy makers had themselves made such a distinction in practice, if not in principle at the central level, though not in the states, and had consequently developed workable means of maintaining political unity in the world's most culturally diverse country. The center had been following pluralist policies in relation to the various linguistic, religious, and other minorities in the country. The conflicts between language and religious groups that were so common in India in the 1950s and 1960s had their origins in local and regional conditions and were influenced by specific patterns of inter-group political and economic competition and state government policies. Such conflicts often became intense, politically destabilizing, and sometimes violent. Moreover, state governments, in contrast to the central government, often pursued assimilative and discriminatory policies in relation to minority groups within their jurisdictions.

DIFFERENCE state ves & center

In the face of the turmoils that arose in the 1950s and 1960s in nearly all the regions of India, I argued that the central government had not acted in a vacillating and indecisive way that led to the intensification of such conflicts, which was the common view. On the contrary, my view was that the central government had developed a set of consistent rules that were not all written down or consciously pursued, but that guided its actions in all these different situations. Those four rules, stated concisely, were that no demand for political recognition of a religious group would be considered, that explicitly secessionist movements would not be tolerated and would be suppressed by force whenever necessary, that no capricious concessions would be made to the political demands of any linguistic, regional, or other culturally defined group, and that no political concessions to cultural groups in conflict would be made unless they had demonstrable support from both sides in the conflict.

-4 guidelines for Indian po govt. policy

-rules provided a broad context

These rules provided a broad context for specific policies pursued by the government of India which made it possible for lasting, agreed solutions to be reached on some highly controversial cultural issues. The two great successes in this regard were the adoption of a multilingual policy at the center and the completion of the long process of linguistic reorganization of states. These policies also facilitated the consolidation of a process of dual nationalism, the comfortable accommodation of most Indians to a recognition of themselves as members of two nations: a Sikh, Bengali, or Tamil nation at one level of identity and an Indian nation at another. Since Sikhs, Bengalis, Tamils, and most other regional nationalities either never or, because of the policies settled upon during the 1950s and 1960s, no longer came into conflict with each other, there was no reason why such a duality of loyalties could not be maintained indefinitely.

Although the Government of India did preside successfully over the satisfactory resolution of complex and difficult linguistic, religious, and other minority conflicts, several others were left unresolved, of which some became worse, and one "new" (but really old) problem cropped up. The problems left unresolved concerned the status of minorities in the linguistically reorganized states, Hindu-Muslim relations, migrant-native conflicts in some parts of the country, and the conclusion of the reorganization of the Punjab.

The new problem that is really a very old problem that has arisen in the last fifteen years concerns the movement for increased regional autonomy in several of the Indian states, including Punjab. Although the contemporary salience of this issue dates to the 1973 Anandpur Sahib Resolution of the Akali Dal in the Punjab, it cannot fail to remind Indian leaders and historians of India of the controversies that arose in the subcontinent in the 1930s and 1940s concerning center-provincial relations in an independent India. Many historians are also likely to point out that issues of center-provincial relations go back to the Mughals and even earlier in Indian history. Moreover, in contemporary times, the demand for regional autonomy preceded the secession of Bangladesh from Pakistan.

It appeared, in fact, in 1982–1984 that the old problem of Indian unity was approaching a new period of crisis concerning these old and new unresolved problems. The flash-points were, of course, Assam and Punjab primarily, but there were indications of problems to come in Kashmir as well. The conflict between the Congress at the center and the Telugu Desam in Andhra is also, I believe, relevant in this context. Finally, of course, Hindu-Muslim riots are always there and a severe one occurred in Bombay in 1984.

What I propose to take up in this paper is whether this combination of unresolved problems in contemporary Indian politics in fact constitutes a new critical test of Indian unity. The issue will be approached by asking whether the old methods of handling separatist, communalist, and regional problems broke down during the Punjab crisis in the 1980s or whether the old rules are in place and need only specific policies to be devised to resolve the contemporary crises. I propose to look in detail at the Punjab in the early 1960s and in the 1980s to compare the way Sikh political demands were handled by the central government in these two periods. I will also consider whether or not the recent accommodation between the government of India and the Akali Dal constitutes a return to the old rules that might produce a permanent or, at least, a reasonably long-term satisfactory resolution of the recent crisis. In this way, it will be possible to reassess the relationships in contemporary India among sepa-

ratist tendencies, political integration, and national integration as they
have revealed themselves specifically in the recent Punjab crisis.[2]

The Changed Context of Center-State Relations

Fundamental changes in center-state relations and in the general process by which power is aggregated in India occurred during Mrs. Gandhi's
tenure as prime minister. Those changes occurred because, for the first
time since the struggle for power at the center in 1950–1951 was decided
decisively for a generation in favor of both the Congress as the dominant
party in the Indian political system and Pandit Nehru as its leader, the
dominant position of the Congress and the authority of its new leader,
Mrs. Gandhi, were challenged after 1965. Moreover, the struggle for
power at the center this time was much more prolonged both within the
party and in the relations between Congress and opposition parties.

The major turning-points in this prolonged struggle for power that have
been widely commented upon were the 1967 elections, in which the Congress lost power in half the Indian states and had to depend on support
from other parties to retain a comfortable majority in Parliament as well,
and the 1969 split in the Congress occasioned by the presidential election

[2] My focus in this paper, therefore, is deliberately restricted to the political context of Punjab politics and center-state relations to the neglect of the socioeconomic background to the
Punjab crisis of the 1980s. The explanations to be offered below, therefore, for the disastrous
course of events in Punjab between 1980 and 1984 are proximate rather than remote explanations. By remote explanations, I mean those that would draw our attention to changes in
class relations in the Punjab during the past two decades arising out of the Green Revolution
and other economic developments in the province or to increases in university enrollments
and in the numbers of the idle educated classes at a time when military recruitment of Sikhs
that previously had offered desirable careers for many educated youth in the Punjab had declined.

It is possible, however, that the remote causes of Punjab events in the 1980s may be of
equal or greater importance than the proximate causes in the sense that, without them, the
situation would never have reached such drastic proportions. In other words, it may be that
the decisive differences between the 1980s and the 1960s lie in the changed socioeconomic
context rather than in the changed political context. To deal adequately with changes in both
contexts, however, would require a book not a chapter. My own view is that there are sufficient differences in the political context between the 1960s and 1980s to warrant specific
attention to the changed political context as a causal factor, but that changes in the socio-
economic context provided additional stimulus and a recruiting basis for terrorist violence
among Sikh youth in Punjab.

For some explanations that emphasize the socioeconomic context, see especially, Sucha
Singh Gill and K. C. Singhal, "The Punjab Problem: Its Historical Roots," *Economic and
Political Weekly* [hereafter referred to as *E&PW*], 7 April 1984, pp. 603–608, and Prakash
Tandon, "Another Angle," *Seminar* 294 (February 1984), pp. 35–37.

of that year. In 1971–1972, after the massive electoral victories of the Congress under Mrs. Gandhi's leadership at the center and in the states, it appeared that the struggle had ended decisively once again in favor of the Congress as the dominant party and Mrs. Gandhi as its unchallenged leader. However, in the process of consolidating her power, Mrs. Gandhi took several actions that led to important transformations in the character of center-state relations. These included a decisive intervention in U. P. politics in September 1970, the delinking of parliamentary from legislative assembly elections in 1971, and the establishment of a new pattern of selection of chief ministers for most of the Congress-ruled states by Mrs. Gandhi herself in consultation with or relying on the advice of her personal advisers in New Delhi.

When the Congress lost power in half the Indian states after the 1967 elections, including in the Punjab, it became increasingly evident that the Congress as a party and Mrs. Gandhi as its unchallenged leader could not retain their dominance unless stability, Congress dominance, and the dominance of persons loyal to Mrs. Gandhi were established in most of the Indian states. A decisive moment that, I believe, began a major transformation in the character of center-state relations occurred in September 1970 when the BKD of Chaudhuri Charan Singh failed to deliver the three votes that Mrs. Gandhi needed, and expected, to pass the Twenty-Fourth Constitutional Amendment Bill in the Rajya Sabha, abolishing the privy purses of the princes. In retaliation, the Congress, which had been in a coalition government with the BKD under Charan Singh in U. P., withdrew from the U. P. government and brought it down. The significance of this moment is that, for the first time in the history of post-Independence India, the fate of the central government and the fate of a state government became interlinked. The Congress could not remain in power at the center, let alone pass desired legislation, without controlling U. P. But the lesson that the Congress leadership learned from this experience extended far beyond relations between Delhi and Lucknow to encompass the whole pattern of center-state relations in India.

It was not that Mrs. Gandhi learned for the first time what her father surely knew very well, namely, that one must control the states if one is to control Delhi. It was, rather, that the old boundaries between central and state politics had been decisively broken and that state politics no longer mattered in their own right. The old pattern of the center intervening as an impartial arbiter to resolve conflicts in a state political arena that was largely autonomous was replaced by one in which the center became a partial intervener in state political arenas to select chief ministers whose principal qualification would be their personal loyalty to Mrs. Gandhi. The process, which was later applied by the Janata government as well, did not, however, free the center from dependence on the states. Instead, it became increasingly dependent for its own stability on controlling the states and state chief ministers in turn became increasingly dependent on the favor of the center. Center-state politics became increasingly inter-linked and interdependent and the autonomy of state politics disap-peared.[3]

Moreover, the whole process of aggregating power in India was re-versed. During the 1950s and 1960s, no one seriously thought of replac-ing Pandit Nehru as prime minister and Congress rule in Delhi seemed un-shakable. Ambitious politicians who wanted substantial power and control of government resources had to build their influence from the dis-tricts to the state level. District and state politics were largely autono-mous, but the center intervened whenever it felt it necessary to do so to ensure that the ability of the Congress to control the state and win elec-tions was not threatened.

From the mid-1960s onwards, however, most roads to extra-local and even to much local power and resources have had to pass through Delhi. Ambitious politicians in both the districts and the states had to please the party leadership at the center to gain power and resources in the states. The center, for its part, had to be always watchful to ensure that reliable persons were in power in the state capitals and even in the districts and that useful and reliable MPs were elected to parliament.

In order to maintain power at the center, Mrs. Gandhi and the Congress felt obliged to centralize power, nationalize issues, and intervene increas-ingly in state and even district politics. Centralization of power occurred in the nomination process for selecting party candidates to contest elec-tions, in the direct selection of chief ministers by the prime minister and her advisers, in the direct distribution of patronage from the central gov-ernment to district politicians, bypassing the state government, and in the ruthless application of President's Rule at the whim of the central govern-ment. Nationalization of issues was facilitated by the delinking of parlia-mentary from legislative assembly elections, by the increasing use of slo-gans and symbols to appeal to broad categories of voters such as the poor and the minorities, by the dramatization and distortion of local issues in-volving violence, and by other means that placed a high premium on dem-agogic skills. Intervention in state politics became increasingly necessary despite these tendencies, however, because they both undercut the very bases of stable politics in the states, namely, autonomous leadership and

[3] See Paul R. Brass "Pluralism, Regionalism, and Decentralizing Tendencies in Contem-porary Indian Politics," in *The States of South Asia: Problems of National Integration*, ed-ited by A. J. Wilson and Dennis Dalton, London: C. Hurst, 1982, pp. 246–255.

strong local party organization. Finally, because of the very absence of autonomous state leadership and strong local party organizations, the interventions of the center increasingly became misguided, misinformed, and even desperate.

The Congress also faced a new challenge in the 1970s that it had not faced before, namely, the use of agitational tactics by opposition leaders to bring down Congress-dominated state governments and to threaten the central government as well. Two major agitations in 1974 led to the fall of a state government in Gujarat and the near-collapse of the Bihar government in the same year.[4] The following year, in June 1975, when a successful election petition threatened Mrs. Gandhi with the loss of her seat in Parliament and hence the prime ministership as well, she clearly feared also that a mass, nationwide opposition agitation was in the offing that would make it impossible for her to survive politically. The Emergency regime from 1975 to 1977 was imposed in order to prevent that eventuality.

The Emergency, the massive defeat of the Congress after its withdrawal and the holding of parliamentary elections in January 1977, and the harassment of Mrs. Gandhi and her son, Sanjay, by the Janata regime between 1977 and 1980 added two further dimensions to the new context of center-state relations. One was the realization that, to maintain power at the center, one could not ignore state politics and one could certainly not permit state politicians to act autonomously even when massive and apparently secure majorities seemed to offer a respite in the perpetual struggle to retain power at the center. Second, the events between 1973 and 1980 brought a new ruthlessness into inter-party and inter-personal leadership rivalries in Indian politics from the center down to the local level. When Mrs. Gandhi returned to power, opposition politicians had to be alert to the possibility that an attempt might be made to impose a new Emergency regime. Mrs. Gandhi in turn clearly harbored deep personal resentments over the treatment meted out to her and her son by opposition politicians between 1977 and 1980. At the state and local level also, especially in the north, politics were becoming increasingly ruthless and violent, the police were becoming more and more corrupt, criminalized, and lawless, and hooligans and ruffians were inducted into the Congress by Sanjay Gandhi personally.[5] Not only in Punjab, therefore, but every-

[4] John R. Wood, "Extra-Parliamentary Opposition in India: An Analysis of Populist Agitations in Gujarat and Bihar," *Pacific Affairs* 48, no. 3 (Fall 1975), 313–334.

[5] On the increasing importance of violence and the threat, manipulation, and control of violence at the local level in North India, see my "National Power and Local Politics in India: A Twenty-Year Perspective," in Paul R. Brass, *Caste, Faction, and Party in Indian Politics*, Vol. I: *Faction and Party*, New Delhi: Chanakya Publications, 1984, pp. 196 and 210–220.

where in north India, most important politicians travelled with guns or bodyguards or both.

Punjab is not a critical state from the point of view of parliamentary seats in the new context of center-state relations. It has a critical importance in other respects, however. First of all, events in Punjab are linked to events in Haryana, which was formerly a part of the old Punjab province, and are thereby connected to events in the rest of North India. The course of Hindu-Sikh relations in Punjab, for example, may affect the attitudes and voting behavior of Hindus in north India and, thereby, the ultimate fate of the contest for power in Delhi. Second, agitational politics are endemic in Punjab, used by the leading non-Congress party there, the Akali Dal, to mobilize support when it is out of power. It is especially significant to note in this context that the *only* sustained agitational movement against the Emergency regime was carried out by the Akali Dal during those years. Third, as the home of a minority religious group in a border state, Punjab has always been of special concern to the government in Delhi. In the past, those concerns centered on the dangers of Pakistani involvement in and exploitation of potential secessionist feelings in Punjab, especially in the event of war. More recently, however, as demands for regional autonomy have been made by non-Congress parties in other peripheral, border, and non-Hindi-speaking states, such as West Bengal, Tamil Nadu, Andhra, Kashmir, and Assam, the center has felt obliged since the Anandpur Sahib Resolution of 1973 demanding regional autonomy for Punjab to be sensitive to the implications of such a demand for the whole pattern of center-state relations in the Indian union.

CENTER-STATE RELATIONS AND SEPARATIST POLITICS IN PUNJAB IN THE 1960s

The course of Sikh politics in the Punjab and the relations among the Akali Dal, the state Congress, and the central Congress leadership in the years between 1960–1961 and 1966 illustrate clearly the application of the four rules as well as the general character of center-state relations during the period of Nehru's dominance in the Indian political system. In 1960–1961, a major turning-point occurred in the history of Sikh politics and in the movement to gain control of a territory in which the Sikhs would be the dominant people and the Akali Dal the dominant party. Two of the leading figures in the Sikh movement, Master Tara Singh and Sant Fateh Singh, attempted alternately to coerce the government of India to concede the Akali demands by going on fasts-unto-death, on the one hand, and to settle the dispute through negotiations with Pandit Nehru, on the other hand. The two leaders, though sharing the same objective of creating a Sikh-majority state in the Punjab, presented the demands somewhat differently. Sant Fateh Singh insisted that the Sikh political demand for a Punjabi Suba was not a religious communal demand for a Sikh majority state, but simply a linguistic demand, no different from others conceded to numerous linguistic groups in India, for the creation of a Punjabi-speaking province within the Indian union. Master Tara Singh, however, had always been associated with the idea that the Sikhs were entitled to determine their own future in 1947, but had been deprived of it by the Congress. He also never hesitated to declare that the Punjabi Suba he envisioned was to be a Sikh-majority province.

The Congress leadership, with Nehru at the center and Pratap Singh Kairon in Chandigarh acting in a united and coordinated way, refused to make any concessions to Master Tara Singh, whom they considered a communalist and potential secessionist politician. Moreover, according to an account by Pettigrew,[6] the Congress leaders went further and set out by outright bribery, use of liaison persons, and duplicity to divide the Akali Dal, discredit Master Tara Singh and replace him with Sant Fateh Singh. It chose to discredit and displace the more extremist, communalist, potentially secessionist leader and replace him with a no-less militant, but non-communalist, non-secessionist leader. Ultimately, when both Nehru and Kairon had passed from the scene and Sant Fateh Singh was firmly in place as leader of the Akali Dal, the Congress under Lal Bahadur Shastri and then finally under Mrs. Gandhi moved to settle the dispute by agreeing in 1966 to create a Punjabi Suba defined as a Punjabi-speaking state. By its handling of the agitations and negotiations, however, the government of India had made it clear that it would not consider demands made on the basis of religious communal identity by leaders whom it considered had secessionist inclinations.[7]

[6] Joyce Pettigrew, "A Description of the Discrepancy between Sikh Political Ideals and Sikh Political Practice," in *Ideology and Interest: The Dialectics of Politics*, edited by Myron J. Aronoff, Political Anthropology Yearbook I, New Brunswick, NJ: Transaction Books, 1980, pp. 151–192.

[7] This is not to say, however, that the mere change in the rhetoric used to formulate the Punjabi Suba demand explains its acceptance by the government of India. The latter may have had as much to do with the Indian government's desire to recognize the critical military role played by Sikh forces in the armed services and the strategic importance of a stable Punjab in general in the aftermath of the 1965 Indo–Pakistan War, on the one hand, and the fact that, with the death of Pratap Singh Kairon in 1964, there was no Congress leader in the Punjab strong enough to stand up to the Akalis, on the other hand. The change in rhetoric was a precondition for acceptance of the demand, which required other conditions for its success. I am indebted to Bhagwan D. Dua whose comments in a personal communication stimulated this clarification.

Several aspects of center-state relations in this period also should be noted here. First, the center was reluctant to take an action that could be seen as favoring one side over another in a regional conflict. The center was unwilling to divide the old Punjab province as long as both the Punjabi-speaking Hindus and the Hindi-speaking Hindus in Haryana were opposed. Only when the Haryana Hindu politicians agreed to accept the reorganization of the state and the creation of a Punjabi Suba was the Akali demand conceded. Second, the central and state Congress leadership took united and concerted action throughout every phase of the crises and negotiations. Third, the principal stage throughout the Punjabi Suba crisis was the state capital of Chandigarh and the principal actor was Pratap Singh Kairon. Nehru and the central Congress leaders played supporting, not directing roles. All the hatreds of the discontented politicians in both the Congress and the Akali Dal were directed against Kairon while the central leadership adopted a pose of benevolent willingness to facilitate compromise solutions.

THE CONTEXT OF PARTY POLITICS IN THE PUNJAB

Inter-Party Relations

Since Independence, and most especially since the creation of the Punjabi Suba, a persistent dualism has characterized party politics and inter-party relations in the Punjab in which the Congress and the Akali Dal have been the principal contenders for power. That dualism, however, has been qualified in several important respects. It has been, first of all, unbalanced because the Congress has been generally the far stronger of the two parties. Second, the imbalance between the two main forces has required the weaker opponent, the Akali Dal, to seek inter-party alliances in order to defeat the Congress and win power in the province. The Akalis' principal alliance partner since 1967 has been the Jan Sangh/Bharatiya Janata Party (BJP). Third, because the alliance with the Jan Sangh/BJP makes the Akali Dal a genuine threat to the Congress' ability to win and maintain power in the Punjab, the Congress has always included in its political tactics to defeat the Akali Dal efforts to divide it. The Congress has thus promoted defections and splits within Akali ranks in order to weaken its prospects for gaining an electoral victory or to bring down an Akali-led government on those occasions when the Akali Dal has defeated the Congress in legislative assembly elections.

Between 1967 and 1972, two Akali–Jan Sangh coalition governments were formed and both were brought down by factional quarrels within the Akali Dal. The fall of the first coalition was engineered directly by the

Congress. In the case of the second, the Congress threw its support, ineffectually as it turned out, to the Gurnam Singh group that was toppled by the dominant group in the Akali Dal. Thus, the dualism between the Congress and the Akali Dal is qualified both by the necessity for inter-party alliances with a third party (and with other parties as well) and by inter-party communication and penetration across the divide between the two main contenders. Not only has the Congress penetrated the Akali Dal by dividing it and giving support to dissident factions within it, but often it also has recruited its own leaders from Akali ranks, including such prominent persons as Pratap Singh Kairon, Swaran Singh, Giani Zail Singh, and many others. In the past, the Akali Dal has also twice entered the Congress in a body, between 1947 and 1951, and again in 1957. Each time, the Akali Dal lost some of its members to the Congress when its leadership decided to withdraw and revert to an opposition role. In the period of unstable coalition politics between 1967 and 1971, there was a two-way flow of defections from the Akali Dal to the Congress and vice-versa.

It should be obvious from this description of the basic features of inter-party competition and collaboration in the Punjab that, until recently, party divisions did not reflect or promote a polarization between Hindus and Sikhs in the Punjab. Although Sikhs are a majority in the province and the Akali Dal is overwhelmingly a Sikh party, the Akali Dal is also a minority party. The Congress, as a majority party, has drawn support from both Hindus and Sikhs. The Akali Dal, in order to match the Congress, has had to seek political alliances with the Hindu-based Jan Sangh/BJP. Party politics, therefore, have normally tended to moderate Hindu-Sikh political polarization and to work against the entrenchment of communal divisions.

EFFECT

Two factors noted above, however, were at work in the 1970s and 1980s to alter this basic pattern. One was the increased interdependence after 1971 of central and state politics and the necessity for the Congress to control most of the states in the Indian union, and particularly the north Indian states, to maintain itself in power at the center. The second was the increased ruthlessness of inter-party conflict in the country after the Emergency, manifested most strikingly in the induction into the Congress by Sanjay Gandhi of young men who did not follow the conventional rules of political behavior and of outright *goondas* (toughs), hooligans, and criminals.

Factors merge 1980

In the Punjab, these two factors merged in preparation for and after the 1980 elections. The 1977 parliamentary and legislative assembly elections in Punjab had made the Akali Dal appear a much more formidable rival than ever before. Previously, the Akali Dal had only once, in 1969, won more seats in the legislature than the Congress, and then only because of its alliance with the Jan Sangh and other parties, which made possible its better showing than the Congress despite a much smaller percentage of popular votes. In the 1977 parliamentary elections, however, the Akali Dal polled a higher percentage of votes than the Congress and won all nine Lok Sabha seats. In the legislative assembly elections that followed, the Akali Dal polled a slightly smaller share of votes than the Congress but won, in alliance with Janata and the Communist party of India–(Marxist) (CPI[M]), 58 seats compared to only 17 for the Congress. The previous electoral dominance of the Congress in Punjab, therefore, seemed less secure. Moreover, the former tactics used by the Congress when it was in opposition—of engineering defections from the Akali Dal to bring down the government—could not be effectual when the Congress was reduced to such a minority status in the legislature.

The strengthened position of the Akali Dal and the much weakened position of the Congress required, therefore, a different set of political tactics from before, namely, an attack on the support base of the Akali Dal in core areas and among core groups: the rural Jat Sikh peasantry under the political influence of the Akali Dal and under the religious influence of the Sants and preachers in the gurdwaras and missionary organizations in the Sikh-majority districts of the province. Sant Jarnail Singh Bhindranwale was used for that purpose and was supported by the Congress, most particularly by Sanjay Gandhi and Giani Zail Singh from 1977, after the massive defeat of the Congress, onwards.[8] The involvement of Sanjay Gandhi in the recruitment of Bhindranwale also meant that criminal actions, manipulation of the police and the judiciary, and the use of violence were considered acceptable tactics by Congressmen, by the police, and by its allies to defeat and discredit the Akali Dal.

Bhindranwale proved not to be especially effective in weakening the Akali Dal by conventional political means. Although his men contested against the Akali Dal candidates in the 1979 elections to the Shiromani Gurdwara Prabandhak Committee (SGPC), the body which manages all the Sikh shrines in Punjab and provides the main resources for the Akali Dal itself, they won only four seats. Nor did his support for a few Congress candidates have a significant effect in the 1980 general elections in Punjab.

However, Bhindranwale's violent confrontation methods did prove

[8] The involvement of Sanjay Gandhi and Giani Zail Singh in the building up of Bhindranwale was widely reported in some sections of the press in India and among opposition parties. The most recent support for this analysis comes from Mark Tully and Satish Jacob, *Amritsar: Mrs. Gandhi's Last Battle*, London: Jonathan Cape, 1985, pp. 57–62. See the section below on Bhindranwale and the Sikh community for further details on the rise and significance of Bhindranwale.

useful to the Congress at first. The Akali Dal leaders in the Akali-Janata government were divided and embarrassed by a violent clash between militant Sikhs and the heterodox Nirankari sect in April, 1978, in which Bhindranwale played a prominent role. The Tohra-Talwandi faction in the Akali Dal used the Sikh-Nirankari clash against the dominant Badal-Longowal faction, which it accused of not acting firmly enough against the Nirankaris. The factional divisions within the Akali Dal in turn contributed to its defeat and the victory of the Congress in the 1980 elections.

When the Darbara Singh government came to power in Punjab in 1980, the time was ripe to put an end to Bhindranwale's activities, which, if they were not themselves murderous, included praise for those who killed Nirankaris.[9] Bhindranwale, however, was too useful in factional conflicts *both* in the Akali Dal and the Congress to be dealt with easily, though he had by no means yet become the pivotal figure in Punjab politics. Giani Zail Singh continued to find Bhindranwale a useful ally, now for two purposes: to use as a foil against his factional rival in the Congress, Darbara Singh, and simultaneously to keep the Akali Dal on the defensive. So, when Darbara Singh tried to arrest Bhindranwale for the murder of Lala Jagat Narain in 1981, Giani Zail Singh protected him.[10] From the viewpoint of Gurcharan Singh Tohra, the president of the SGPC and leader of one faction in the Akali Dal, Bhindranwale was useful as an ally in his struggles with the Longowal-Badal faction. Consequently, Tohra permitted Bhindranwale to move into the Golden Temple complex with his men

[9] Tully & Jacob (n. 8), pp. 65–66.

[10] The position of Congress leaders close to Mrs. Gandhi on this matter of arresting Bhindranwale was stated by one of them in the following way: "The point is you have all kinds of people floating around. You don't go about grabbing them and putting them in jail. . . . Bhindranwale was one of the Sants. Now, how do you proceed against a Sant until he does something? And if he is a Sant, if he is a saint, then you give him a longer rope, if at all. So, how does anyone expect us to go and grab Bhindranwale and put him in a jail? . . . For instance, Zail Singh was Home Minister here. Now, they [critics of the government] say you should have put him behind bars in Delhi [after the murder of Lala Jagat Narain]. He's on his way to Punjab. It is for the state government of Punjab to grab him or do whatever it is, whatever they want to do if he has done anything wrong, if he has really been guilty of something. It's not in transit that you do this. This is just hindsight. You avoid bloodshed, you avoid going into a temple, you avoid laying your hands on a person who is a saint, who has his own school . . . in the hierarchy of sants. . . . So how can you simply grab him and put him behind bars?" Interview in New Delhi, August 22, 1986.

One response to these comments is that the government of India, using various preventive detention laws, often puts people behind bars to prevent violence or even lesser alleged threats to civil order. Bhindranwale was placed in a special category, even though there were obviously grounds for his arrest and trial, let alone detention. The account of whose responsibility it was to arrest him, the government of India or the Punjab government, supports very strongly one of the main themes of this chapter, namely, that the central and state governments did not act in unison as they did under Nehru and Kairon.

and his arms. From September 1981 on, therefore, after his arrest and release in connection with the murder of Lala Jagat Narain, Bhindranwale
alternated between the sanctuary of the Golden Temple and, when he
wished to roam about, the protection of the home minister, which kept
him safe until terrorists began murdering innocent Hindus in the Punjab.
After a particularly vicious set of murders of innocent Hindus in September–October 1983, Mrs. Gandhi finally imposed President's Rule on the
Punjab and sent one of her most trusted police officers to Punjab to take
firm action against all suspected terrorists, including Bhindranwale, who
now took sanctuary in the Akal Takht within the Golden Temple complex
itself.[11]

For its part, the Akali Dal, ousted from power by the Congress and
placed on the defensive by Bhindranwale and other leaders and groups
suspected of terrorist activities, who were placing themselves in the forefront as defenders of Sikh interests against the Congress, the central government, and the Hindu community, opted for the adoption of aggressive
but non-violent confrontational tactics in pursuit of Sikh and Punjabi regional interests. It was in this context that the Anandpur Sahib Resolution
of 1973 was reactivated and placed in the forefront of Akali demands.
For, if the Akali Dal could achieve significant political concessions
through a direct, but non-violent challenge to the Congress, it would
strengthen its position in relation to non-Akali Sikh militants in the Punjab. And, if center-state relations were readjusted in such a way as to reduce significantly the ability of the center to intervene in state politics,
then the Akali Dal and other similarly placed regional parties in India
would be strengthened and the regional Congress parties weakened.

Akali Factions in the 1960s and 1980s

Superficially, there would seem to be no substantial differences in the
internal dynamics of Akali politics in the 1960s and 1980s. Rather, there
would appear to be an uninterrupted tradition of internal factional conflict stretching back to the 1920s, to the earliest days of the Akali Dal, up
to the present. Before the 1960s, there were always at least two groups in
the Akali Dal, who struggled for control both over the party organization
itself and over the SGPC, which provided the bulk of the resources for the
Akali Dal. It was always the case, moreover, that no group could retain
dominant leadership of the Akali Dal without controlling also the SGPC.
Consequently, there was a compulsion to exert dual control of these two

[11] Up to this point, Bhindranwale and his men had been taking refuge in the hostel complex adjacent to the Golden Temple, but not in the areas of the Golden Temple complex considered sacrosanct.

bodies by a single leadership, which was certainly the case in Master Tara Singh's heyday and then again under Sant Fateh Singh, when the latter wrested control of both bodies from the Master.

In the 1960s, or rather, from 1967, when the Akali Dal became a governing party in Punjab, a third source of factional power within the Akali Dal became available, namely, control over the chief ministership and the government of the state. Such control clearly offered enormous patronage power to whichever faction became dominant in government, but it was also inherently unstable in contrast to the resources of the SGPC, which were always available to the group in control. Consequently, control over the SGPC has remained the key to dominance in the Akali Dal up to the present. Until Sant Fateh Singh's death in 1972, his dual control over the Akali Dal and the SGPC made it possible for his faction to remain dominant in relation to the ministerial groups in control of government and even to replace a recalcitrant chief minister such as Gurnam Singh in 1970.[12]

3rd source of Factional Power

After the death of Sant Fateh Singh, no single leader was able to unify the Akali Dal or even to gain decisive dominance in both the party organization and the SGPC. Instead, a three-way split developed in which the leaders of each wing sought the support of the others for their own purposes. Tohra, as SGPC chief, sought the support of the other groups to retain both the presidentship of the SGPC and a seat in the Rajya Sabha. Jagdev Singh Talwandi, as president of the Akali Dal, sought the support of Tohra in his struggles with Prakash Singh Badal, who controlled the ministerial wing of the party. In 1980, the Badal group successfully supported Sant Harchand Singh Longowal for president of the Akali Dal. The two then formed an alliance with Tohra to isolate Talwandi, who left the Akali Dal (Sant) to form a rival Akali Dal.

By the early 1980s, therefore, it appeared once again that a single group now controlled the Akali Dal and the SGPC. In fact, however, there were two distinct differences in the Akali Dal between the situation in the 1980s and that in the 1960s. One was that there was in fact no dominant group in the Akali Dal, but three groups forming alliances of mutual convenience: the group of Tohra (SGPC), of Longowal (Akali Dal), and of Badal (ministerial). Second, the terms of the factional quarrel were fundamentally changed *within* the Akali Dal by Congress actions outside it and by the rise of Bhindranwale.

2 different things of 60s - 80s

In the 1960s, there were three principal resources in Akali factional struggles: the SGPC, government patronage, and agitational leadership in

---

[12] Dalip Singh, *Dynamics of Punjab Politics*, New Delhi: Macmillan India, 1981, pp. 104–107.

struggles against the Congress. Sant Fateh Singh, as leader of the Akali Dal, established his dominance in the party organization through his agitational skills and his ability to lead the Sikh community in its struggles *against* the Congress on, first, the Punjabi Suba issue, and second, the status of the city of Chandigarh. He was careful to let no one usurp his symbolic role as principal defender of Sikh interests as he himself had usurped the role of Master Tara Singh. That position in turn gave him the support necessary to gain control of the resources of the SGPC. Dual control of the Akali Dal and SGPC then made it possible for him to control the ministerial wing of the party.

The rise of Bhindranwale and other extremist and terrorist groups and leaders[13] made it impossible in the 1980s for any single leader within the Akali Dal to repeat the feat of Sant Fateh Singh, though Longowal tried very hard to do so through the revival of the Anandpur Sahib Resolution and through his various *roko* (stop or block) movements and the *Dharamyudha Morcha* in the period between 1981 and 1984. The shift in Congress tactics also made the repetition of Sant Fateh Singh's feat impossible. The Congress in the 1960s had, after all, materially helped Sant Fateh Singh to establish his dominance first by supporting him against Master Tara Singh, then by conceding his principal demand for Punjabi Suba. In sharp contrast in the 1980s, the Congress refused to accede to the major political and economic demands of Longowal and thus to contribute once again to the establishment of a moderate leadership group in firm control of the Akali Dal. Since the government also was not only not able to control Bhindranwale, but had helped to launch him, the Akali leaders were forced to compete with an extremist, non-Akali leader to maintain agitational and symbolic leadership of the Sikh community. In turn, factional groups inside the Akali Dal which, in the 1960s, might have defected to the Congress or otherwise sought Congress support in their internal struggles with each other, now sought to use Bhindranwale and his demands, slogans, and *goondas* against each other. In particular, Tohra found his

[handwritten margin note: EXTREMISM IS SOUGHT BY AKALIS]

[13] Bhindranwale, of course, was never convicted in a court of law of murder or of supporting terrorist activities. However, the term "extremist" may be applied to him and his followers in the way he defined it, namely, Sikhs who have taken Amrit, who keep weapons, who obey any orders "given by the Panth," "who seek justice for the martyrs," especially for those who suffered at the hands of police officials whose names and locations were given during his public addresses at the Golden Temple. It is difficult to imagine a clearer form of incitement to violent, revengeful, murderous activities than this combination in the circumstances of the time. Citations and references are from Sant Jarnail Singh Bhindranwale's Address to the Sikh Congregation [November 1983], translated from the original in Punjabi by Ranbir Singh Sandhu, Columbus, Ohio: Sikh Religious and Educational Trust, 1985. For a different view, see Joyce Pettigrew, "Take Not Arms Against Thy Sovereign," *South Asia Research* (November 1984).

Sant in Bhindranwale to counter the alliance of Badal with Sant Longowal. In effect, therefore, the Congress itself through its drive to weaken its principal opponent in Punjab politics and through its initial support for Bhindranwale and its refusal to control his activities, terminated the old pattern of alternation between inter-party conflict and inter-party, inter-communal penetration. The Congress also forced the moderate Akali Dal leaders into a competition with the extremist Bhindranwale and thus into an inevitably escalating confrontation with the central government.

In the 1960s, Pandit Nehru and the central government made it clear to the Akalis that they would not bow to any pressure for creation of a Sikh-majority state defined in relation to religion. They, therefore, compelled the Akalis to moderate their principal demands to one consistent with the structure of the Indian federal system, which encompassed linguistic but not religious states. In contrast, in the 1980s, the central government supported, or at least failed to control, the most extreme proponents of Sikh hegemony, Hindu-Sikh confrontation, and explicit or implicit supporters of Khalistan while refusing to accede to the moderate, legitimately presented demands of the Akali Dal in pursuit of regionally defined interests and a reconsideration of the structure of center-state relations. Consequently, the Akali Dal's demands in its various agitations had to be framed with one eye on Bhindranwale. In practical terms, this meant that the Akali Dal had now and then to add to its long-established list of regional, political and economic demands other demands of a specifically religious nature and demands to free Bhindranwale when he was arrested (since he was certain anyway to be freed by a government clearly not serious about restraining him). It was also compelled to use language that emphasized the nationhood and sovereignty of the Sikh people in presenting its demands, which the central government in turn used to argue that the Akalis too were supporters of Khalistan. It will be shown below, moreover, that when the government of India did make concessions, again in utter contrast to its position in the 1960s, it conceded the religious demands of the Akalis and not their political and economic demands.

Congress and Congress Factions in the 1960s and 1980s

There were several critical differences in the character, functioning, leadership, and recruitment strategies of the Congress in the 1960s and 1980s as well that help to explain the containment of communal demands and conflicts in the earlier period and the fact that they went completely out of control in the 1980s. First, in the 1960s, as already noted, the Congress was dominated by a single leader and a single faction, with the solid backing of the central government. The situation that prevailed in the

Punjab Congress and in relations between the state and national leadership of the Congress in those days conformed to the ideal pattern that Nehru favored: strong state leadership pursuing the secular, economic goals of planned development in close cooperation with the central government. A similar pattern existed in state politics and center-state relations in West Bengal under B. C. Roy, for example, and in several other states from time to time.

Nehru hated and fought against factionalization in state politics and politicians who were not committed to his goals of economic planning and development. He preferred "bossism" in state politics for the sake of stability and electoral predominance and leaders who spoke the language of secularism and economic development. He detested politicians who did not at least pay lip service to socialism, planning, and industrialization as the methods and goals of Indian policy and who spoke instead a language of Hindu or minority communalism, casteism, linguism, and provincialism. Although Kairon was himself a former Akali politician, he conformed to Nehru's image of the ideal state boss politician when he established his dominance in the Punjab Congress. Under his leadership, minority communalism was controlled, the economic basis was laid in agriculture for the Green Revolution that began after his death and for the boom in small-scale industry in Ludhiana and Jullundur that provided off-farm employment for those displaced from the land.

After Kairon's and Nehru's deaths, Punjabi Suba was conceded, the Congress was factionalized, and the party was faced with much stronger opposition from its main rival, the Akali Dal, in the smaller Punjab state. After 1971, when Mrs. Gandhi reconsolidated Congress power in the country and, perforce, in the Punjab as well, she did so on an entirely new basis and with the support of a different type of leadership and Congress organization in the states of the union. She preferred sycophants to bosses and a factionalized Congress led by persons selected by her or her clique of advisors in Delhi. Like Nehru, she too preferred leaders who spoke the language of socialism, development planning, and industrialization. However, since the persons she selected were generally unable to or were not permitted to establish dominant groups of their own in state politics, they could not be effective and could not guarantee stability and electoral dominance. The lack was made up by the personal appeal of Mrs. Gandhi herself to large categories of voters, by the liberal use of money to buy and control politicians and, particularly after the Emergency, by the "lumpenization"[14] and criminalization of the Congress organization at the local level.

[14] Pritam Singh, "Punjab: Lessons of Panchayat Elections," *E&PW*, 22 October 1983, 1822–1823.

From among the various Congress faction leaders who were contesting for dominance in the Punjab Congress after the death of Pratap Singh Kairon, Mrs. Gandhi selected Giani Zail Singh to be chief minister after the Congress achieved its huge electoral victories in Punjab, as elsewhere in the country, in 1971 and 1972. Although Zail Singh was a major contender in the factional politics of the Punjab Congress in those days and not a mere puppet of the center, it is generally acknowledged that the "rapport" he established with Mrs. Gandhi[15]—which his detractors have characterized as outright sycophancy—was the decisive factor in his selection as chief minister.

Zail Singh's tenure as chief minister is notable for the following features. Although the Green Revolution continued its progress and government provided support for tubewells, rural electrification, and rural link roads to facilitate transport of the agricultural surplus to markets, the ministry also emphasized, in conformity with Mrs. Gandhi's policies, programs in support of the scheduled castes and backward classes. Some of these programs, such as lowering land ceilings, antagonized the more prosperous rural Jat Sikh farmers. Although Zail Singh attempted to compete with the Akali Dal by appealing to the religious sentiments of rural Sikhs through such gestures as leading the great march in celebration of the completion of Guru Gobind Singh Marg, linking all the important religious sites of the Punjab, and other similar acts, the ministry as a whole was identified more with the interests of Harijans, Mazhabi (lower caste) Sikhs, and the poor and smaller farmers than with the middle and upper segments of the Jat Sikh peasantry. Zail Singh himself was, aside from Giani Gurmukh Singh Musafir, who had a brief tenure as chief minister in 1966–1967, the first non-Jat Sikh chief minister in Punjab. He had no base among rural Jat Sikhs and was engaged in continuous factional rivalry with his own Jat Sikh ministers during his tenure as chief minister.[16] The 20-point program implemented during the Emergency also was aimed more at the poor, the landless, and the marginal farmers than at the middle Jat Sikh peasantry, who were effectively mobilized by the Akali Dal in a *morcha* that was sustained successfully throughout most of the Emergency period.

The most notable feature of the Zail Singh period, however, from the point of view of Punjab politics is what was not done. No effort was made whatsoever to undercut the Akali Dal by resolving, in a way acceptable to Punjabi regional interests, the major outstanding issues left unresolved at the creation of the Punjabi Suba in 1966, namely, the disposition of the

[15] Dalip Singh (n. 12), p. 221.
[16] Ibid., pp. 75–76 and 87.

city of Chandigarh, of the Hindu Punjabi-speaking tahsils of Abohar and Fazilka, and of the distribution of Ravi-Beas river waters.

During Mrs. Gandhi's darkest hours in the Janata period from 1977 to 1980, both Giani Zail Singh and his chief rival for power in Punjab Congress politics, Sardar Darbara Singh, demonstrated their steadfast loyalty to Mrs. Gandhi. Both remained with her when the Congress split in Punjab, as elsewhere in the country, in 1978. Both were relatively evenly balanced in their support among Punjab Congress legislators elected in the Congress victory of 1980. Consequently, Mrs. Gandhi, who rewarded those who had remained personally loyal to her during the Janata period, rewarded both men: Giani Zail Singh was made home minister in the government of India and Darbara Singh the chief minister of Punjab.

Zail Singh, however, could not countenance the selection of Darbara Singh as Punjab chief minister, for he would certainly use his position to eliminate Zail Singh's supporters from power in the Punjab. Consequently, Giani Zail Singh used his personal influence with Mrs. Gandhi and his powers as home minister to undercut Darbara Singh throughout his tenure as chief minister. In this conflict with Darbara Singh, Bhindranwale again proved useful. He and other extremist elements had been found useful for embarrassing the Akali Dal–Janata government during the Sikh-Nirankari confrontations. He could now be used for the dual purpose of continuing to undermine the Akali Dal and to demonstrate the inability of Darbara Singh to govern Punjab effectively. For her part, Mrs. Gandhi, in sharp contrast to the relationship established by her father with Pratap Singh Kairon, allowed Zail Singh to continue to meddle in Punjab politics, consulted him for advice in handling the disintegrating political situation in Punjab, and failed to provide full backing to Darbara Singh's efforts to root out the terrorists by arresting Bhindranwale and other extremist leaders and clearing them out of the Golden Temple complex before they had taken sanctuary in the Akal Takht itself and had fortified the entire complex.[17]

The difference between Mrs. Gandhi's handling of the Punjab situation in the Congress in the 1980s and her father's in the 1960s is of a piece with the change in center-state relations in this period that Mrs. Gandhi herself brought about. Nehru often brought powerful and influential politicians, including ex–chief ministers, into his central cabinet from the states. He did not usually do so, however, as a device for solving factional conflicts in a state. Moreover, once at the center, such persons were expected either to use their provincial influence over their followers to maintain stability in their home states or they were expected to remain aloof from state-level

[17] For details on the above, see Tully and Jacob (n. 8), pp. 66–70, and below.

conflicts so that they could be used as impartial arbiters to resolve crisis situations among contending state-level groups. The idea that a central minister would be used or even allowed to function in a manner that would undermine the stability of a province was entirely foreign to Nehru's method, except on the rare occasions when Nehru himself deliberately set out to remove a chief minister whose policies or methods he disliked. Mrs. Gandhi, however, preferred weak chief ministers dependent on her, direct control from Delhi, and provincial instability, which she found useful in maintaining central control and ensuring the loyalty of all groups, whose leaders might be made or broken at her whim. Mrs. Gandhi's methods proved entirely unsuited to the escalating situation in Punjab which required decisive action and united leadership in Delhi and Chandigarh.

BHINDRANWALE AND THE SIKH COMMUNITY

Sant Jarnail Singh Bhindranwale has emerged as the central figure in discussions and analysis of the violent confrontations and terrorist actions that occurred with increasing frequency in the period from 1981 to June 1984, when he died during the Indian army's storming of the Golden Temple. Bhindranwale's actual role in the increasing violence of those days, his own purposes, and the extent and sources of his support in the Sikh community remain highly controversial matters. Many observers consider that Bhindranwale was the actual source of the worst terrorist actions in the 1981–1984 period and some also feel that he was in favor of Khalistan secretly, if not openly. Among such persons, Bhindranwale's vocation as a preacher is either not considered relevant to the political issues or is treated as a separate and secondary matter. Bhindranwale is considered by these observers to be merely one among many itinerant preachers of the Punjab, who happened to be picked up by prominent Congress leaders of the Punjab and brought into politics in order to divide the Akali Dal and, thereby, ensure the persistence of Congress rule in and political control over the province. Once brought into politics, however, and built up in this way, he developed his own line, his own methods, and increasing support that, according to this view, made him an independent political force, feared by all politicians in the Punjab, who ultimately reached such a pass that they were willing to take no action that Bhindranwale might oppose and became incapable of participating effectively in a political process gone completely out of control and dominated by violence.[18]

[18] This is a composite view of Bhindranwale, various elements of which can be found in

An alternative view emphasizes Bhindranwale's role and background as a preacher, treats his political activities as incidental thereto, and blames the violence primarily on other groups in the Punjab, including extremist political groups, religious sects, and the police.[19] In one account, Bhindranwale was an authentic saint, with a "charismatic appeal," who was giving "religious expression" to "broadbased rural discontent and anger" over the recent history of alleged discrimination against Sikhs in the Punjab, including police harassment and violence, in response to the Akali political movements. To volunteers who came to see Bhindranwale before courting arrest in Akali political campaigns, "he gave a purely religious message."[20] In another view, his primary political role was as a "scapegoat"[21] used by the Congress government to displace all the blame for its own disastrous policies in the Punjab that were the true source of its recent disorders.

The bulk of scholarly and journalistic writing on Bhindranwale favors the first view, though there are some elements of truth in the second. What is most important, however, is to assess his significance in relation to the perceptions of the Sikhs of themselves as a community and Bhindranwale's place in the Sikh sense of communal identity. It is known that Bhindranwale was, in fact, an itinerant preacher who, in 1977, at the age of 30, was chosen to become the head of a Sikh mission known as the Dam Dami Taksal. He was chosen in preference to the son of the previous head, Amrik Singh,[22] who nevertheless remained close to him in his religious and then, in his political activities, until they were both slaughtered inside the Golden Temple. He is best described in origins as a Sikh preacher, who saw his mission in part as spreading Sikhism to non-Sikhs, to Sikh-Hindu groups such as Sahajdharis and Nirankaris, and to the untouchables in the Punjab, whose uncertain religious identity as Sikhs or Hindus and politi-

---

Khushwant Singh, "Genesis of the Hindu-Sikh Divide," in *The Punjab Story*, edited by Amarjit Kaur et al., New Delhi: Roli Books, 1984, pp. 9–11; Avtar Singh Malhotra, *Save Punjab, Save India*, New Delhi: Communist Party of India [CPI], 1984, pp. 11, 12, 19; *E&PW*, 8 October 1983, p. 1725, 29 October 1983, p. 1858, 24 March 1984, p. 482, 2–9 June 1984, p. 865, 30 June 1984, p. 965, 14 July 1984, p. 1076; Gill & Singhal (n. 2), p. 607; Kuldip Nayar and Khushwant Singh, *Tragedy of Punjab: Operation Bluestar & After*, New Delhi: Vision Books, 1984, pp. 30ff; Tully and Jacob (n. 8), chs. 4 and 5.

[19] The Sikh English-language weekly newspaper, the *Spokesman*, generally subscribed to several aspects of this alternative view. See, for example, the issues of 10 January 1983 and 14 January 1985.

[20] Pettigrew, "Take Not Arms" (n. 13).

[21] Letter of Ranjit Singh Sandhu (a Sikh living in America), 25 April 1985.

[22] See Pettigrew, "Take Not Arms" (n. 13); Tully and Jacob (n. 8), pp. 52–54; and Nayar and Singh, (n. 18) pp. 24–25.

cal identity as Congress or Akali supporters has for decades been a major source of religious and political controversy in the Punjab.

Bhindranwale was also a "revivalist," that is, a "religious puritan" who followed strictly and literally what he perceived to be the basic tenets of the Sikh faith transmitted by the Gurus, enshrined in the Guru Granth Sahib, and embedded in the rituals and outward markers of the Keshdhari Sikhs. Sikh students and "rural Sikh youth" were the special targets of the mission of Bhindranwale and his closest companion, Amrik Singh, who became head of the All India Sikh Students Federation (AISSF). In their mission to the Sikh youth of Punjab, their design was certainly to get the young men of Punjab to take Amrit, to wear the outward signs and carry the markers of Keshdhari Sikhs, and to avoid the corrupting secular and Marxist ideologies to which they were otherwise susceptible in the Punjab, where the left was traditionally dominant among students.[23]

In these respects, Bhindranwale was hardly a new phenomenon in the Punjab, which has been the scene of countless local and regional revivalist movements among Hindus, Sikhs, and Muslims during the past century. If there is anything new in this, it is not the doctrine or the message, but the use of contemporary methods of transmission, notably the distribution of taped messages to the faithful, a practice lately used widely around the world from Rajneeshpuram to Iran. Such a movement among the Sikhs in the Punjab inevitably has political implications, for one of its principal goals is to create solidarity and uniformity among practicing Sikhs, to turn non-Keshdhari Sikhs, low caste Sikhs, and students attracted by secular ideologies into practicing Sikhs, and to wean both these categories of practicing and non-Keshdhari Sikhs from competing practices and ideologies, religious and political, which might dilute their identity as Keshdhari Sikhs or prevent them from embracing it fully.

Soon after his assumption of the headship, Bhindranwale's "mission" brought him and his followers into a violent confrontation at Amritsar on April 13, 1978, with the Nirankaris, a Sikh-Hindu group considered heretical by Keshdharis because of their "worship of gurus other than the ten recognised by [Orthodox] Sikhs."[24] At the confrontation in Amritsar, 13 people were killed from Bhindranwale's group and from another militant missionary group known as the Akhand Kirtani Jatha. From this point on, a bloody vendetta was launched among the followers of these three groups, during which the Nirankaris were paid back for the debacle of

[23] Pritam Singh, "Akali Agitation: Growing Separatist Trend," E&PW, 4 February 1984, p. 196; Pritam Singh, "Punjab: AIR and Doordarshan Coverage of Punjab after Army Action," E&PW, 8 September 1984, 1571; Spokesman, 10 January 1983.

[24] Khushwant Singh, A History of the Sikhs, Vol. 2, Princeton: Princeton University Press, 1966, p. 125.

April 13 by the killing of 40 of their leading persons, including their head, Gurbachan Singh. Although it appears that the principal anti-Nirankari terrorist group was an organization called the "Babbar Khalsa," led by the widow of Fauja Singh who, as head of the Akhand Kirtani Jatha, was killed in the April 13 massacre, Bhindranwale and his followers were widely blamed for the killings, possibly because he more openly expressed his satisfaction at the results than because he was responsible for them. In any case, from April 13 onward, Punjab became the scene of warfare among heavily armed terrorist groups bent on exterminating each other for the glory and purity of the Sikh faith. At first, it should be stressed, this conflict was confined to Sikhs, it was primarily Sikhs who were killed, and the issues concerned the solidarity of the Sikh community and the purity of the faith of those who claimed to be Sikhs.[25]

Although the issues concerned the solidarity of the Sikh community, the purity of its faith, and hence the separate identity of the Sikhs as a community distinct from Hindus, the conflict with the Nirankaris made evident once again the persistence of doctrinal and social divisions among those who claim to be Sikhs and the persistent fear among many Sikhs that the boundaries between them and Hindus are not sufficiently sharp to prevent their ultimate assimilation into and absorption by Hindus. The doctrinal differences between Nirankari and Orthodox Sikhs were complemented also by social differences. The Nirankaris came primarily from urban trading castes and "continue to marry within their castes regardless of the change in their religious beliefs,"[26] whereas Bhindranwale and his followers, in contrast, came primarily from the numerically much more important Jat Sikh farmers of rural Punjab.

Congress Support for Bhindranwale

Congress leaders initially saw this sectarian conflict among Sikhs, which arose independently of party political calculations, as an opportunity to divide the Akali Dal and to weaken its control over the SGPC, a tactic which Congress leaders have followed repeatedly without success for decades. The Congress also intervened in the Delhi Gurdwara Prabandhak Committee (DGPC), where the Akali Dal has never had the same control as in the SGPC, in support of its opponents. Congress leaders and the state administration and judicial system began to act in ways that implied support for Bhindranwale. Bhindranwale and his followers were released from prison and cleared of charges for the murders of the Niran-

[25] Khushwant Singh, "Genesis of the Hindu-Sikh Divide" (n. 18), pp. 9–10; Gill and Singhal (n. 2), p. 602; Malhotra (n. 18), pp. 5–7.
[26] Khushwant Singh, *History* (n. 24), p. 123.

karis in April 1978. Congress (I) leaders, including Giani Zail Singh's and Sanjay Gandhi's emissaries, supported Bhindranwale and his followers in the 1979 elections to the SGPC in which, however, they won only 4 seats out of 106. The Congress also aided in the formation of the Dal Khalsa. Bhindranwale and his men allegedly reciprocated by supporting the Congress in the 1980 Punjab general elections.[27]

Congress efforts to divide the Akali Dal and to draw rural Sikh support away from it continued after the party's return to power in Punjab and intensified when the Akali Dal resorted to agitational tactics to achieve longstanding Akali demands pertaining to Chandigarh, disputed territories between Punjab and Haryana, division of river waters, and other demands contained in the Anandpur Sahib Resolution of 1973. Moreover, throughout the increasingly bitter and violent confrontations between the government and the Akali Dal, and among the extremist and terrorist groups, and despite their spillover into the broader population, leading to deaths of innocent people and Hindu-Sikh clashes in the towns of Punjab and Haryana, the government was unable or unwilling to reach a political accommodation with the moderate Akalis on the outstanding issues. It will be argued below that the failure of the government to reach such an accommodation was partly because the Congress priority given to political control, including division of the opposition to achieve it, remained till the end of Mrs. Gandhi's life the guiding principle of the party's political strategy to which the goal of a final settlement of the issues in dispute in the Punjab remained secondary. The extent to which this strategy remained primary was indicated by the remarks of Rajiv Gandhi only weeks before Bhindranwale and his men were slaughtered by the Indian army in which he referred to Bhindranwale as "a religious leader" and declared his belief that the latter was not responsible for the terrorism and "extremist politics" prevailing in Punjab.[28]

[Congress policy]

It is possible that the involvement of the Congress and the government in Bhindranwale's rise has been exaggerated in the above account. In fact, it seems to me that Bhindranwale's goals and those of the Congress were ultimately incompatible, though they may have coincided temporarily. As already indicated above, Bhindranwale was operating within the hallowed Sikh ideal of Panthic unity, identity, and solidarity against all ele-

[27] Arun Kumar, "Punjab: Wages of Past Sins," *E&PW*, 14 July 1984, p. 1076. According to Tully and Jacob (n. 8), p. 61, Bhindranwale "campaigned actively for the Congress in three constituencies." It should be kept in mind that Bhindranwale was not yet a major political force in the Punjab. Involvement in three out of 117 legislative assembly constituencies does not constitute a major intervention on Bhindranwale's part.

[28] *E&PW*, 8 October 1983, p. 1725; Gill and Singhal (n. 2), p. 607; *E&PW*, 2–9 June 1984, p. 865; Malhotra (n. 18), p. 12; *E&PW*, 30 June 1984, p. 965.

ments who would divide the Sikhs in their religious practices or in their political goals. The Congress was playing the opposite game, using whatever political divisions among the Sikhs it could to gain and maintain advantage over its main political rival, the Akali Dal.[29] Since their goals were fundamentally incompatible, it was inevitable that they would ultimately clash directly.

It was, however, only when Sikh terrorists began to kill Hindus, and when Hindu-Sikh communal clashes began to occur that the Congress political strategy began to change. The Congress had lost any influence it might have had over Bhindranwale and other extremist Sikh groups, the Akali Dal remained committed to an agitational strategy until the Congress conceded its demands, and the Congress hold over the Punjab Hindus now appeared threatened by the government's inability to protect innocent Hindu bystanders from random massacres. Most important, the government's inability to control the situation in Punjab, following upon its mishandling of the Assam situation in 1983, gave the opposition a stick that it appeared might be powerful enough to bring down the Congress in the imminent parliamentary elections.

The Congress, therefore, began to use the government machinery to attempt to crack down on the terrorist groups. The AISSF was banned in March 1984.[30] However, the police were by now hopelessly divided themselves along communal lines and also feared direct confrontations with the extremist and terrorist groups. It is otherwise difficult to explain the fact that 150 companies of constabulary forces posted around the Punjab, including 90 around the Golden Temple itself, "failed to check the massive induction of arms into the Golden Temple or the apparently free

---

[29] One leading Congressman close to Mrs. Gandhi and the Punjab situation, denied that Bhindranwale was a Congress creation, insisting that he came up on his own with his own ambition, but admitted that local Congressmen may have decided to support or ally with him. However, he justified the general practice of dividing one's rivals and its application to Bhindranwale in the following words: "Now, if I have somebody who is my own opponent in another party and if I find that that party has two factions, one is a more powerful faction who is fighting me and whom I'm fighting and there is another faction, what do I do? Do I ask them to unite? What is politics? Is it not dividing . . . opponents and uniting friends? What are they [opposition party leaders] talking about? Are they not doing the same thing among Congressmen? . . . There is always this effort to drive a wedge." Personal interview in New Delhi, August 22, 1986.

The Congressman's response here is certainly a valid description of Indian—perhaps all—political behavior. However, it raises two questions. One concerns the suitability of the allies chosen for the purposes of dividing the opposition. Bhindranwale clearly did not serve Congress' purposes as well as did Sant Fateh Singh against Master Tara Singh in the 1960s. The second question is at what point statesmanship enters into situations such as that in the Punjab and responsible leaders decide that routine politics no longer apply.

[30] E&PW, 24 March 1984, p. 482.

movement of people suspected to be terrorists."[31] A serious crackdown would also have meant entering the gurdwaras, which were being captured by the AISSF on behalf of Bhindranwale and used as storehouses for arms and sanctuaries for terrorists. Government action in such circumstances, therefore, did nothing but increase the general level of terrorist violence and implicate the police more deeply in it themselves. False encounters, used so effectively to destroy the Naxalites in West Bengal in the 1970s and somewhat less effectively against dacoits and others in U. P. in the 1980s, were now used by the police in Punjab to kill suspected Sikh terrorists. Congressmen in Haryana, allegedly supported by Chief Minister Bhajan Lal, also "organised mob violence" against Sikhs in the towns of Haryana.[32]

Thus, as in the past, the government of India responded to lawlessness and violence with violence and lawlessness. What had begun as an internecine sectarian conflict among Sikhs, and then had become intertwined with the struggle for political control among competing groups within the Punjab in which the central government backed one side, now became a direct confrontation between the extremist, terrorist Sikh groups in the Punjab, on the one hand, and the central government, on the other hand. In this new confrontation, the Punjab Congress was no force at all and the Akali Dal became helpless. The Akali leaders would not condemn Bhindranwale, who continued to speak in the language of Panthic unity and solidarity, and it could not permit Bhindranwale to emerge as the only prominent Sikh personality willing to confront the central government in defense, now not only of the political demands of the Sikhs, but also of the lives and honor of Sikh youth.

Bhindranwale, Sikh Unity, and Akali Factions

One of the striking features of the dynamics of Sikh politics is the remarkable degree of internal political fragmentation that occurs under the cover of the ideal goal of communal solidarity. Any amount of internal political factionalism appears to be tolerable, but no faction will survive whose leaders are maneuvered into a position of perceived betrayal of legitimate Sikh political demands. Moreover, no leader who is seen to be sincerely pursuing Sikh political goals can be criticized in public. Consequently, the frequent charges made in the press that the moderate Akali leaders were cowards because they did not condemn Bhindranwale and

[31] E&PW, 2–9 June 1984, p. 865.
[32] Malhotra (n. 18), p. 17.

other militant and terrorist groups and their actions in Punjab, while they make good rhetoric, are politically naive and meaningless.

The more Bhindranwale became the center of public and media attention and the more his actions and speeches placed him in the role of defending the Panth against an unjust central government and its police, the less the so-called moderate Akalis could criticize him and the more, in fact, they had to come closer to him in public perception. Thus, SGPC President Tohra, who had other reasons as well for supporting Bhindranwale, in December 1983 praised him for having "revolutionised" Sikhism.[33] The minority Akali Dal led by Talwandi also moved towards Bhindranwale in March 1984, to gain advantage in its struggle with the dominant Akali Dal led by Longowal. As for the Longowal forces themselves, while differences between them and Bhindranwale's forces allegedly became murderous in 1984, efforts were continuously made "to patch up differences" and to make a show of Panthic solidarity in public.[34]

In fact, however, the main effort of the Longowal Akali Dal was devoted to maintaining its political leadership of the Sikh community by pressing the longstanding Akali demands in non-violent agitational movements. Thus, in the midst of the terrorist violence extending its grip over Punjab, the Akali Dal launched in September 1981, its *Dharamyudha Morcha*, with a comprehensive list of 45 demands encompassing every major and minor grievance of the Sikh community, including several of the "religious" demands of the Bhindranwale group.[35] The moderate Akali leadership, therefore, was caught between the intransigence of the center, the terrorist violence practiced, incited, or condoned by the Bhindranwale-AISSF forces, and the demands of opposition parties and the media for them to condemn "the violent activities of the Bhindranwale group and to distance itself from them."[36] They took the bold, if not the brave, risky, but the only politically feasible course open to them of pursuing vigorously non-violent agitational movements, including road and rail stoppages, constitution-burning, and other symbolic devices. It was for the center to respond if it wished to preserve the longstanding, competitive, non-violent relationship between the Punjab Congress and the moderate Akali Dal by making the maximal concessions. Instead, the center chose procrastination and countered violence with violence.

[33] *Spokesman*, 2 January 1984.
[34] *E&PW*, 28 April 1984, pp. 694–695 and Malhotra (n. 18), p. 12.
[35] This *Dharamyudha Morcha* went on fitfully and intermittently over the next two years, interspersed with periods of negotiations between the Akalis and the central government when *morcha* activities were halted.
[36] *E&PW*, 28 April 1984.

The failure of the Akali Dal to weaken the intransigence of the central government, the failure of its movements to achieve any significant concessions, meant inevitably its own decreasing credibility and the increasing transfer of political initiative in the Sikh community to Bhindranwale. The next *Dharamyudha Morcha*, therefore, in 1984, was launched by Bhindranwale around a demand for release of two of his arrested "confidants."[37] The Longowal Akali Dal this time had to join the *morcha* declared by Bhindranwale, but still managed to turn it into a broader political movement by linking it with the demand for acceptance of the Anandpur Sahib Resolution. Throughout, therefore, whether attempting to take the initiative or following Bhindranwale's lead, the moderate Akali leadership placed political demands in the forefront, demands which belong to the conventional discourse of Punjab politics. The center's response was again intransigent, including the declaration that the Anandpur Sahib Resolution was secessionist and could not, therefore, even be considered.

Bhindranwale, the Akali Dal, the Sikh Community, and the Problem of Achieving a Political Majority in the Punjab

Until the rise of Bhindranwale, the political struggle in the Punjab between the Congress and the Akali Dal revolved around a few sociocultural realities that set the terms of the struggle and determined its outcome. These were the following:[38] the dominance of the Akali Dal among rural Jat Sikh farmers; the broad-based support of the Congress among Hindus, rural Scheduled Castes, and even some Sikhs; the confinement of the Communist Party of India (CPI) to rural Jat Sikh and Scheduled Caste support in some pockets of Punjab; and the confinement of the Jan Sangh/BJP to caste Hindu, particularly urban Hindu support. The most unambiguous features of the party struggle in relation to social, cultural, and religious groups in the Punjab since Independence have been the dominance of the Akalis among rural Jat Sikhs and the strong, but limited base

---

[37] Gill and Singhal (n. 2), p. 608.

[38] For details on the support bases of political parties in Punjab, see Paul R. Brass, "Ethnic Cleavages in the Punjab Party System, 1952–1972," in *Studies in Electoral Politics in the Indian States*, Vol. 4: *Party Systems and Cleavages*, edited by Myron Weiner & John O. Field, Delhi: Manohar Book Service, 1975, ch. 1; M. S. Dhami, "Caste, Class and Politics in the Rural Punjab: A Study of Two Villages in Sangrur District," in *Political Dynamics of Punjab*, edited by Paul Wallace & Surendra Chopra, Amritsar: Guru Nanak Dev University, 1981, pp. 292–317; Pramond Kumar, et al., *Punjab Crisis: Context and Trends*, Chandigarh: Centre for Research in Rural and Industrial Development, 1984, pp. 63–72; and Dalip Singh (n. 12), pp. 252–260.

[margin note: congress other supporters in PUNJAB]

of the Jan Sangh among urban Hindus. The Congress, though always the strongest force in the Punjab, has also always depended upon an uncertain coalition of Hindus, Sikhs, and Scheduled Castes. The Akalis, the second strongest force, but the most narrowly based party in the Punjab, have always required an alliance with the Jan Sangh to achieve a political majority in the state. In this struggle, as in the historic conflict over religious allegiances in the Punjab as well, the large population of Scheduled Castes is a critical "floating" element. It is here that the revivalist movement of Bhindranwale and the political struggle for votes and a governing majority in the Punjab link up.

A Scheduled Caste population confirmed in or converted to Sikhism is a great danger to the Congress political base in the Punjab and a potential asset to the Akali Dal that could expand its voting base into one potentially larger than that of Congress. In this respect, therefore, Bhindranwale and his followers posed a threat to the long-term political balance in Punjab. If he were to draw some Jat Sikh support away from the Akali Dal and gather support as well among rural Scheduled Castes, an alliance with him would benefit the Congress enormously and weaken the Akali Dal significantly. On the other hand, if he could develop his influence among rural Scheduled Castes to draw them away from the Congress politically, then the political majority of the Congress in the Punjab would be endangered. The link-up between Sikh revivalism and the political struggle became clear in the 1983 panchayat elections when the Akali Dal and the Bhindranwale forces both sought to draw Scheduled Caste support away from the Congress, while the Congress struggled to maintain its base among the Scheduled Castes in preparation for the next round of parliamentary and legislative assembly elections.[39]

[margin note: 1983 key]

During his brief heyday, it was never certain how much support Bhindranwale in fact had. The only clear test of his rural influence, in the 1979 SGPC elections, came before his elevation to the center of Punjab politics. Panchayat elections never provide conclusive evidence of rural support one way or another since local factors are primary and alliances with outside party political forces are *ad hoc* and ephemeral. Bhindranwale in death and martyrdom, however, may have succeeded in altering the political balance in the Punjab in just the ways most feared by the Congress. In the 1985 legislative assembly elections, it appears that the vast majority of Sikhs, rural and urban, Jat Sikh and lower caste, supported the Akali Dal, which won a large majority of 73 out of 117 seats.[40]

[39] Pritam Singh, "Lessons" (n. 14).

[40] See *esp.* the article by Janardan Thakur in *The Times of India Sunday Review*, 13 October 1985. It is probable that the Akali Dal also won the votes of many Hindus who saw a greater possibility of peace in the Punjab under an Akali than under a Congress government.

Much has been made of whether or not Bhindranwale was loved by the Sikh masses, whether or not he is now perceived as a martyr and has thus become in death a more dangerous political foe even than he was in life, whether or not the Sikh peasantry and army mutineers were rushing to fight alongside Bhindranwale in June 1984, and the like.[41] In fact, too much attention has been given to Bhindranwale personally and too little to his symbolic relationship to the Sikh community. I believe it does not matter to most Sikhs precisely what Bhindranwale did and what methods he used. He was seen as a sincere defender of Sikh values, Panthic unity, and communal identity. He was probably not himself as central a figure in the minds and hearts of the Sikh masses as he was made to be by the press. He may very well become forever enshrined among the long list of Sikh martyrs who gave their lives in an heroic struggle with external enemies against hopeless odds, for the sake of the Panth. But, the Sikh peasants who attempted to rush to Amritsar and the Sikh soldiers who mutinied, in the worst such affair faced by the Indian government since 1857, were rushing to defend the greatest symbol of their faith and solidarity as a community and not in support of either Bhindranwale or any of his presumed political goals. Through their own involvement in and mismanagement of the crisis created by Bhindranwale in the Punjab, the Congress has created the very conditions it hoped to use Bhindranwale to prevent: an alteration in the political balance in the Punjab produced by a greatly increased solidarity of the Jat Sikhs and a movement of the Scheduled Caste, so-called Mazhabi Sikhs, to the Akali Dal in the 1985 elections in the Punjab.

Bhindranwale and Khalistan

If the Congress elevated Bhindranwale far beyond his likely fate unaided, the Congress, the government, and the press, even more created the great Khalistan scare and Bhindranwale's association with that idea. The only outspoken proponents of the Khalistan idea were Sikh expatriates living abroad and a few extremists in the Punjab itself. As for Dr. Jagjit Singh Chauhan of the Dal Khalsa, he was an opportunist politician, who moved from party to party in the unstable coalition politics of 1967–1969. He was supported by the Congress in a contest for the speakership of the Punjab legislative assembly in March 1967. In November 1967, along with 16 other independents and defectors, he was used by the Congress to bring down the first Akali Dal government in the Punjab.[42] That

---

[41] See, for example, Khushwant Singh, "Genesis" (n. 18), p. 11; Kumar, "Punjab" (n. 27), p. 1077; and Pritam Singh, "Lessons" (n. 14), p. 1570.

[42] Dalip Singh (n. 12), p. 96 and personal interview in Chandigarh on 27 May 1967.

this man of no political weight in or out of Punjab could have become the center of the great Khalistan scare to the extent of damaging Indo-British and Indo-U.S. relations testifies to two things only: the miraculous powers of the press even in a developing country where the media are less dominant in public opinion manufacture than they are in the West and the fears and insecurities of some government of India leaders, who came to believe that the unity of the country was endangered by expatriate politicians in alliance with foreign governments and intelligence agencies.

It is not certain that Bhindranwale himself was bent upon achieving a separate, sovereign Khalistan in the Punjab.[43] On the other hand, it is certain that the separateness and sovereignty of the Sikh people were integral to his beliefs and that those beliefs are widely shared among Sikhs in and out of Punjab. Such Sikhs demand an acknowledgment that they are a separate people, religion, and nation with the ultimate right, as of any sovereign people, to determine their own future and their relations with other peoples. Acknowledgment of that "right" does not, however, necessarily imply a separate sovereign state. Some Sikhs would argue that the right has been exercised since Independence through political accommodation within the Indian union, but Akali political leaders and rural religious personalities such as Bhindranwale are extraordinarily sensitive to any perceived infringement on the ultimate sovereignty, equality, and separateness of the Sikh people.

It is often noted, and correctly so, that the Sikh perception that they are discriminated against in India is, if not false, a distortion of the actual position of the Sikhs as a whole in comparison with other groups, especially other minority groups. Sikh farmers are, on the whole, the most prosperous in the country, Sikh entrepreneurs have become wealthy not only in the Punjab, but in major cities and towns across north India, and Sikhs are still heavily represented in the Indian armed forces far beyond their proportion in the population of the country. Yet, Sikh perceptions of discrimination are not without foundation. It continues to rankle that Punjabi Suba was the last linguistic state to be conceded in India, and only after two decades of agitation; that Punjabi-speaking Hindus lied about their mother tongue to prevent it; and that the provincial capital, Chandigarh, has till now still not been formally handed over to Punjab and the other outstanding issues remaining from the decision to trifurcate the old Punjab province have yet to be satisfactorily resolved. It is also obvious that

---

[43] In a translation of a taped address given by Bhindranwale at the Golden Temple, thought to have been given in November 1983, Bhindranwale is quoted as having said: "We are not in favor of Khalistan nor are we against it. . . . If the center gives us Khalistan, this time we shall not say no. We shall not repeat the mistake of 1947." Sant Jarnail Singh Bhindranwale's Address to the Sikh Congregation.

the government of India has been following a determined policy to reduce the Sikh proportion in the army to one closer to the actual proportion to the Sikh population of the country. It also rankles that demands made in other parts of the country, whether it be for a linguistic state or for regional autonomy, are treated differently when made in Punjab, as more of an immediate threat to the unity of the country and as posing a secessionist danger. The Akali political position is that, as a sovereign people, the Sikhs chose to join with India in 1947 in the belief that their separate political status would be recognized, but that they were instead betrayed, tricked, and manipulated so that they have had constantly to fight even to have their separate identity acknowledged. Many Sikhs also feel that they have given far more than their proportionate share of blood for the country during the nationalist movement and in foreign wars, but still their loyalty is questioned and they are not trusted.

In this context, therefore, the Khalistan demand is more significant as a reflection of government of India fears than of any reality in the form of a broadly supported demand arising from the Sikh community, the Akali Dal, or Bhindranwale. It is perceived by the most important political forces in the Punjab, associated with the Akali Dal, as a slander arising out of the deep prejudices among Indian political leaders and Hindus generally against the Akalis and the Sikhs as a community.[44]

CENTER-STATE RELATIONS AND SEPARATIST POLITICS IN THE PUNJAB IN THE 1980s

There are similarities and continuities as well as differences and discontinuities in Sikh politics, Congress policies, and center-state relations between the 1960s and 1980s. In fact, a case can be made that all the old rules were followed in the 1980s and that Congress strategy and tactics were not substantially different in the 1980s from the 1960s. I believe the differences are, in fact, critical and that they explain the utterly disastrous and extremely violent course of events in the 1980s. However, in order to provide a balanced perspective, I will consider first the similarities and continuities.

Similarities and Continuities

On the face of it, the Congress government at the center has demonstrated once again by the sternest possible measures that it will not toler-

---

[44] *Spokesman*, 14 January 1985.

ate secessionist movements anywhere in the country, including especially the Punjab. It has castigated the Khalistan demand and its leaders and has protested to the U.S. and British governments their alleged support and tolerance of the Khalistan leaders and movement. The White Paper justifying the invasion of the Golden Temple precincts on June 6, 1984, asserted that the action was undertaken to eliminate terrorist and secessionist groups who were using it as a base for their activities.[45] During the action itself, the alleged secessionist leaders, Sant Jarnail Singh Bhindranwale and Bhai Amrik Singh, were killed while the moderate Akali Dal leaders were spared. And, until his dramatic reversal of policy in July 1985, Rajiv Gandhi had refused to negotiate with even the moderate Akali Dal leaders until they disavowed the Anandpur Sahib Resolution, which he considered separatist, and stopped using "secessionist language."[46]

recognition of a religious community has also been reasserted by the government of India in relation to recent events in the Punjab. *The White Paper on the Punjab Agitation* claims that "the authenticated version" of the Anandpur Sahib Resolution, "issued in November 1982," called for "the constitution of 'a single administrative unit where the interests of Sikhs and Sikhism are specially protected.'" Such a provision, if present (and there are several "authenticated" versions of this resolution), would provide further justification for the government of India's insistence that the Anandpur Sahib Resolution could not "be accepted as a basis for discussion."[47] The government of India also has resisted the Akali Dal demand in the Anandpur Sahib resolutions for granting of "holy city" status to Amritsar as "not in consonance with the secular nature of our Constitution."[48]

The principle of refusing to grant concessions to ethnic groups capriciously is not especially relevant to Sikh demands of the 1980s since the main demands of the Anandpur Sahib Resolution clearly have the support of a major political party and a significant section of the Sikh population. On the other hand, if we consider the demand for a restructuring of center-state relations as a "new" political demand in India (leaving aside the previously noted fact that it is a very old demand), then the government of India has been applying this rule in relation to this demand. It responded initially by rejecting the Anandpur Sahib Resolution outright as inconsistent with the "concept of the unity and integrity of the nation," but also

[45] Government of India, "White Paper on the Punjab Agitation: A Summary," in Kaur (n. 18), pp. 184–199 [hereafter referred to as WP].

[46] *Overseas Hindustan Times*, 2 March 1985.

[47] WP (n. 45), p. 188.

[48] Ibid., p. 186.

by acknowledging, through the appointment of the Sarkaria Commission, the more widespread existence in the country of a demand for restructuring center-state relations. Then in July 1985, as part of the accord between Rajiv Gandhi and Longowal, the government of India agreed to refer the Anandpur Sahib Resolution to the Sarkaria Commission. It is possible that the Sarkaria Commission may be the counterpart in the 1980s of the States Reorganisation Commission appointed in the 1950s and that it will, like its predecessor, initiate a prolonged period of readjustment in the political balance between the center and the states. Such periodical readjustments, of course, are inevitable in the history of large and complex federal republics, as every American should know.

The fourth rule that even broad-based ethnic group demands will not be accepted unless they have support on both sides of a conflict has been very much upheld throughout the history of post-Independence Punjab politics, in which Haryana remains a significant actor, up to the present. In fact, this principle has been a major stumbling block to the settlement of the most important outstanding issues between Punjab and Haryana since 1966, which include the status of the city of Chandigarh, the transfer to Haryana or the retention in the Punjab of some disputed rural areas near the borders of the two provinces, and the allocation of Ravi-Beas river waters.

Differences and Discontinuities: The Failure to Reach
a Political Settlement in Punjab

A brief review of the substance and course of the negotiations between the central government and the Akali Dal leaders between 1980 and 1984 will bring out clearly the differences between Mrs. Gandhi's approach and those of her father and her son. It needs to be noted, first of all, that it was not until September 1981, that Bhindranwale emerged as a central figure in Punjab politics. Until that time, he and his activities had been largely a diversion from conventional politics in the Punjab, which centered as always around the struggle for power between the Congress and the Akali Dal. Moreover, until September 1981, the wrath of Bhindranwale and his followers was directed mostly at Nirankaris and at other Sikhs; it was primarily an internal affair among Sikhs and Nirankaris that concerned issues of religious belief and practice. Bhindranwale and his followers had not presented a coherent political program of their own. Their principal demands to government until then had been one articulated by the AISSF in May 1981 for the banning of cigarettes in the area surrounding the Golden Temple and the declaration of Amritsar as a "holy city."

Until September 1981, therefore, the struggle between the Congress and the Akali Dal was within the bounds of conventional politics, which included the launching of agitations or *morchas* led by the Akali Dal in pursuit of its demands against the state and central governments. On July 26, 1981, the Akalis announced their intention to launch a major *morcha* under the leadership of Longowal in pursuit of a list of 45 demands, which contained a combination of religious, political, economic, and social grievances. Some were trivial, some merely expressed resentment over past wrongs, some were vaguely worded, and the major outstanding issues concerning Chandigarh, the status of Punjabi-speaking areas left out of Punjabi Suba, and the river waters dispute were consolidated in only one of the 45 points.[49] Such a diffuse list of grievances and demands could only have mixed purposes: to provide a basis for political mobilization to maintain the enthusiasm of the workers in a party out of power, to strengthen the agitational leadership of Longowal within the party, and to provide a list of demands long enough to insure agreement on some of them that would avoid loss of face on the part of either the Akalis or the government.

Akali demands

The entire situation changed dramatically, however, in September 1981, with the murder of the Hindu newspaper owner, Lala Jagat Narain, the implication of Bhindranwale in the murder, his arrest on the orders of the chief minister of Punjab, and his release on the orders of the home minister of the government of India. This grand "arrest-and-release drama,"[50] followed by a dramatic increase in incidents of terrorist violence in which innocent Hindus were killed, brought Bhindranwale to center stage in Punjab politics. With Bhindranwale and the terrorists now playing leading roles, the pressure on both the central government and the Akali Dal for a face-saving conclusion of the Akali Dal *morcha* increased significantly.

It has been charged that the central government responded with procrastination, partial concessions on minor issues, and refusal to concede the major Akali demands.[51] There were three major series of protracted negotiations between the central government and the Akalis between September 1982 (a year after the murder of Lala Jagat Narain) and June 1983. On all three occasions, it has been reported that agreement was reached between negotiators on both sides on the major outstanding issues, but that the agreements were finally scuttled on all three occasions

[49] The 45 points are contained in Nayar and Singh (n. 18), pp. 138–139.

[50] *E&PW*, 2–9 June 1984, p. 865.

[51] See particularly the issues of the *Spokesman* from September 1982 through June 1983, which reflect moderate Akali attitudes towards the progress of the negotiations and blame the central government for their failure.

by reversals of position by Mrs. Gandhi herself.[52] These reversals allegedly were made in response to protests from Congress chief ministers in Haryana and Rajasthan who argued that they would have difficulty in explaining to the people of their states the granting of Chandigarh to Punjab without any concession of territory to Haryana and the loss of river waters to Punjab that were also needed in Haryana and Rajasthan.[53] The official position of spokesmen of the government of India involved in these negotiations, however, is that government could not negotiate on the basis of the Anandpur Sahib Resolution, parts of which negated the unity of India and that the Akali negotiators could never get the Akali Dal itself to accept any agreement.[54] It remains in dispute, therefore, whether or not Akali disunity or government of India intransigence on the Anandpur Sahib Resolution stood in the way of resolving the principal issues concerning Chandigarh, the status of Abohar-Fazilka and of the Punjabi-speaking areas left out of Punjabi Suba, and the distribution of Ravi-Beas waters. All three of these issues were regional, secular matters having nothing to do with secessionism or separatism.

Another noteworthy feature of the negotiations is that the only agreement announced by the government during these three years concerned some minor religious issues: banning of cigarette sales near the Golden Temple, relay of Gurbani broadcasts from the Golden Temple abroad, amendment of Article 25 of the Constitution to make clear that the Sikhs were not Hindus, and recognition of the Personal Law of the Sikhs. Agreement on these issues was announced unilaterally by Mrs. Gandhi in a Delhi gurdwara. Mrs. Gandhi's supporters consider this move a generous gesture on her part, while others argue that her unilateral announcement failed to help the moderate Akalis who could not claim even these concessions as a victory.[55] It has also been noted that the gurdwara at which Mrs. Gandhi made her announcement was controlled by her allies among the Sikhs, who were opponents of the Akali Dal (Sant).[56] Moreover, in the view of her critics, Mrs. Gandhi refused to reach agreement concerning regional, secular political and economic demands while conceding reli-

---

[52] On these negotiations, see, among other sources, Nayar and Singh (n. 18), pp. 60–63; Harkishan Singh Surjeet, *Developments in Punjab*, New Delhi: CPM, 1984, pp. 3–6; Avtar Singh Malhotra, *The Punjab Crisis and the Way Out*, New Delhi: CPI, 1984, pp. 18–21; Tully and Jacob (n. 8), ch. 6; and, for a government view, *The Situation in Punjab*, Statement of Home Minister in Parliament on 28 February 1984, New Delhi: Government of India, Ministry of Information and Broadcasting, 1984.

[53] Tully & Jacob (n. 8), pp. 78–79.

[54] Personal interview in New Delhi, August 22, 1986.

[55] Tully & Jacob (n. 8), pp. 90–91.

[56] Malhotra (n. 18), p. 5.

gion-based demands in a pattern opposite to the stance taken by her
father.

The prolongation of the talks and negotiations between the government
and the Akalis without any significant agreement placed the Akali leaders
in an impossible situation between the government and Bhindranwale. If
they accepted an unsatisfactory agreement, they would be condemned by
Bhindranwale and his ally in the Akali leadership, Tohra. Consequently,
their only recourse was to return to agitational politics after each breakdown in negotiations. In the meantime, the government's failure to act
against Bhindranwale made the moderate Akali position increasingly vulnerable and made it increasingly difficult also for them to come to an
agreement without taking Bhindranwale into account. Consequently, the
Akalis would add to their list of grievances and demands some that arose
out of Bhindranwale's confrontations with the police: concerning police
repression, false encounters by police with killing of Sikhs alleged to be
terrorists, release of alleged terrorists, and the like.

The stance taken by the central government in negotiations with the
Akalis between 1981 and 1984 stands in sharp contrast to the negotiations between Nehru and later Lal Bahadur Shastri, on the one hand, and
Sant Fateh Singh, on the other hand. Longowal, like Sant Fateh Singh before him, but much more so, needed a political settlement that would save
his face against Bhindranwale and that would secure his leadership in the
Akali Dal against Tohra. It was in the long term interest of the government
as well to bring about such a result if it wished to preserve a secular non-
violent political process in the Punjab. Mrs. Gandhi, however, never felt
that she could make political concessions that would undermine the position of the Congress in the vast north Indian Hindi-speaking regions of
the country. It was not simply a case of concern that a settlement favorable
to the Akali Dal would help that party in the Punjab and harm the Congress in the neighboring states of Haryana and Rajasthan, but that the
Hindu reaction in the latter two states would spread to the huge states of
U. P., Bihar, and Madhya Pradesh, where widespread discontent over
concessions to the Sikh minority could threaten the Congress with the loss
of the next parliamentary elections.

Mrs. Gandhi's policies differed sharply from those of her father and her
immediate predecessor Lal Bahadur Shastri as well. Nehru refused to concede a Sikh majority state to a movement led by a man he considered an
extremist, a secessionist, and a fraud. Lal Bahadur Shastri laid the basis
for the concession of Punjab Suba to an Akali leadership helped to power
by Congress policies. Mrs. Gandhi implemented the reorganization of the
Punjab and the creation of Punjabi Suba, which brought peace to the Punjab for 15 years, but she then failed to take advantage of the peaceful at-

mosphere and her own predominant power in the country to settle the outstanding issues.

The failure to complete the Punjabi Suba settlement was one objective basis for the often-repeated claims of the Akalis that the Sikhs were discriminated against in India. Before the Punjabi Suba was conceded, Punjabi-speaking Hindus had conspired to deny their mother tongue in order to prevent the concession of a Punjabi Suba as a Punjabi-speaking state. When a Punjabi-speaking state was at last conceded, the central government then refused to transfer to the new state its capital, initially created out of a Punjabi-speaking area, unless two tahsils of Punjab containing numerous Punjabi-speaking villages were simultaneously transferred to Haryana. In effect, therefore, the central government first appeared to be denying to Punjabi-speaking Sikhs the right to have a linguistic state of their own on the grounds that it was a cover for a Sikh-majority state and then, having conceded the demand, wished to take away some of the rural Hindu Punjabi-speaking areas which would, in effect, reinforce the Sikh-majority character of the Punjabi Suba. The Akalis also argued that the central government was favoring the states of Haryana and Rajasthan in the solution of the third major unresolved issue, namely, the disposition of Ravi-Beas river waters by allowing them to take a substantial share of the waters from rivers that flow only through the Punjab. To accommodate the Akalis on this issue, however, the central government would have had to withdraw waters already flowing to these states and halt construction on a major canal project. Such actions would naturally arouse the anger of the affected population and their legislative representatives, with the potential loss of both states in the next election in consequence.[57]

It was generally known to all parties involved on all sides in the dispute from the beginning that Chandigarh was the principal issue. Moreover, all political parties in Punjab, including the Jan Sangh/BJP, were in favor of retaining Chandigarh as the state capital. Its symbolic importance to the people of Punjab was well-known. Mrs. Gandhi's original decision in January 1970, to award Chandigarh to Punjab was consistent with the linguistic character of the original site, was politically sound, and recognized the symbolic importance of Chandigarh to Punjab. Unfortunately, that decision, which was to be implemented in five years, was never implemented. Worse, implementation of the decision was later linked to the disposition of the more controversial and dubious decision to transfer the Abohar-Fazilka belt to Haryana, which was both unprecedented in involving a corridor to link these interior areas with Haryana and appeared

[57] It is not necessary for purposes of this paper to go into the details of this issue. See (n. 52), for some references on this, as well as other issues in dispute.

discriminatory in awarding some Punjabi-speaking areas to Haryana. It needs to be noted here also, however, that the Akalis themselves failed to demand the separation of the Chandigarh and Abohar-Fazilka issues when they were in power from 1977 to 1980 in coalition with the Janata party, which was in power at the center. Moreover, it needs also to be acknowledged that Haryana has a claim to Chandigarh as well since it is presently a bilingual, Hindu-majority city.

By itself, leaving aside the question of Chandigarh, the Abohar-Fazilka question raises issues of principle that would be difficult to resolve under any circumstances. This belt is a mixed Hindi- and Punjabi-speaking area inhabited mostly by Hindus. In the 1961 census, which provided the basis for demarcating Hindi- and Punjabi-speaking areas, many Hindus whose mother tongue was Punjabi falsely declared their mother tongue to be Hindi, in these areas and elsewhere in the pre-1966 Punjab province. The result was that the Punjabi Suba was not, in fact, demarcated strictly on a linguistic basis in the first place.

 The issue of principle raised by this situation is whether or not objective or subjective criteria should be used to demarcate linguistic boundaries. Mrs. Gandhi, however, never even considered the issue in those terms. Until the very end of her life, in two speeches before Parliament justifying the army assault on the Golden Temple and blaming the Akalis for the failure to reach a political accommodation on these issues, Mrs. Gandhi made it clear that her decision on Abohar-Fazilka was entirely political in the narrowest sense of the term. She said that Chandigarh "could not go (to Punjab) unless Haryana got something in its place."[58] Moreover, "if Abohar and Fazilka were also to go to Punjab, then Haryana had to be compensated not just in money for their new capital, but with some territory."[59] Repeatedly, Mrs. Gandhi gave as her *only* criterion for this trade-off the prediction "that there would have been trouble in Haryana"[60] if Haryana did not get some territory in exchange for Chandigarh. Naturally, the answer to such a politically motivated response was another politically inspired one. The Akalis countered that Haryana had been dominated mostly by Congressmen personally loyal to Mrs. Gandhi who, as her stooges, would do whatever she wished.

In fact, however, there was a much larger political issue behind this political trade-off, namely, the sentiment of many Hindi-speaking Hindus in

[58] Indira Gandhi, *Punjab and National Unity*, Speeches of the Prime Minister during the discussions on the White Paper on Punjab in the Lok Sabha on 25 July 1984 and in the Rajya Sabha on 24 July 1984, New Delhi: Government of India, Ministry of Information and Broadcasting, 1984, p. 8.

[59] Ibid, p. 28.

[60] Ibid, pp. 9 and 29.

the vast northern and central regions of the country without whose political support the Congress could not prevail in a general election. The principal opposition party in Haryana, the Lok Dal, was the leading opposition party in north India. The other important non-Congress party in Haryana and the rest of the northern and central region was the Jan Sangh/BJP, whose primary ideological stand centered around symbols of militant Hindu nationalism and whose strength, like that of the Lok Dal, was centered in the Hindi-speaking regions. Both these parties were prepared to exploit any political settlement that appeared to give in to the Akalis at the expense of Hindi-speaking Hindus in Haryana.

Moreover, despite the overwhelming majorities that Mrs. Gandhi obtained several times during her political heyday and despite her exercise of authoritarian rule for two years during the Emergency, there was never a time when Mrs. Gandhi felt politically safe enough to take a decision that would have appeared to favor Punjab. The initial decision to award Chandigarh to Punjab was taken in 1970, when Mrs. Gandhi and the Congress were extremely vulnerable. The time was only a year after the Congress split and before the 1971 and 1972 elections in which Mrs. Gandhi was returned with a massive majority in Parliament and in most of the states, including Punjab and Haryana. The year 1972 was a time when Mrs. Gandhi might have acted decisively to settle all outstanding Punjab issues, but she did not.[61]

During the Emergency, from 1975 to 1977, the Akalis were the only major political force in India brave enough to sustain agitations against the government. Mrs. Gandhi could hardly reward them for their defiance of her regime then.[62] After her and the Congress' victory in 1980 was an-

[61] Dua argues that Mrs. Gandhi's initial decision on Chandigarh was motivated completely by political considerations and was tied into her broader struggle in the country as a whole to consolidate her power and defeat the state party leaders in the Congress (O). For this purpose, she needed the support of Akali MPs in Parliament who might otherwise have joined forces with the Congress (O). After her massive victory in the 1971 elections, Dua argues, she no longer needed the support of the Akali MPs and, therefore, had no further incentive to implement the award. Bhagwan D. Dua, "India: A Study in the Pathology of a Federal System," *Journal of Commonwealth & Comparative Politics*, November 1981, pp. 269–270 and personal communication.

[62] Some Sikhs believe that Mrs. Gandhi's alleged unwillingness to satisfy the demands of the Akali Dal in the 1980s related to her annoyance over the Akali agitation against the Emergency. See, for example, *Spokesman*, 1 September 1986, p. 6. In this connection, it is sometimes also noted that it was Longowal who led the agitation against the Emergency regime. Such an interpretation of Mrs. Gandhi's motivations, though consistent with her actions in other matters in rewarding those who were loyal to her and punishing those who opposed her during and after the Emergency, would suggest a pettiness on her part in the face of a grave crisis that goes beyond the argument of this paper concerning her political actions.

other occasion for decisive action but, as has been shown, an entirely different game was being played. When the situation went completely out of control in the Punjab, the 1984–1985 elections were in the offing and, once again, the time was wrong for a decision that would antagonize the Hindi-speaking Hindus in north and central India.

In the end, in a curious paradox, it was Mrs. Gandhi's rigid stand in the Punjab, including the assault on the Golden Temple, followed by her assassination, that released an enormous wave of Hindi-Hindu nationalism that swept her son and the Congress back to power in 1984 and 1985 and made politically possible the concession to the Akalis that Mrs. Gandhi had never been willing to make. Rajiv Gandhi and the Congress first exploited to the maximum this Hindu nationalism by stealing both the old Jan Sangh slogan of One United India and more than half of the old Jan Sangh voting base in north and central India[63] and then, with an unprecedentedly large and secure majority in Parliament and in most states, conceded everything to the Akalis that Mrs. Gandhi had refused. In the Rajiv Gandhi–Longowal Accord of July 1985, the central government agreed to hand over Chandigarh to Punjab on January 26, 1986, to appoint a commission to determine the Hindi-speaking areas to be transferred to Haryana, to refer the river waters dispute to a judicial tribunal, and to refer the Anandpur Sahib Resolution to the Sarkaria Commission on Center-State Relations.

CONCLUSION

There are several possible explanations for the tragic failure of the central government under Mrs. Gandhi's leadership and the moderate Akali leaders to resolve the Punjab issues. One is that the problems themselves are intractable because all solutions give zero-sum results: Punjab's gain is Haryana's and/or Rajasthan's loss. This argument cannot, however, be sustained, for trade-offs have always been available. Funds can be provided to Haryana for another capital, canals can be built from other rivers to supply some of the needs of Haryana and Rajasthan, and consistent principles can be applied concerning the transfer of disputed territory. It is not, therefore, that solutions to the problems were not available. There were many possible solutions.

The failure to select a package to resolve the issues and to adhere to the chosen solutions was rather a consequence of the unwillingness of either

[63] See the "Postscript: the 1984 Parliamentary Elections in Uttar Pradesh," in Paul R. Brass, *Caste, Faction and Party in Indian Politics*, Vol II: *Election Studies*, New Delhi: Chanakya Publications, 1985.

Mrs. Gandhi or the moderate Akali leaders to adopt a solution that did not provide them with a political advantage or that threatened political damage. Moreover, both sides lost precious time when compromise solutions might have been reached and the political damage limited: the central government between 1972 and 1977, the Akalis when they themselves were in power in Punjab from 1978 to 1980. The Akalis had less time in power, however, than the Congress and it is doubtful that the Janata government in Delhi, with its Jan Sangh and Lok Dal components would have accepted a solution that conformed to Akali wishes. Moreover, because the implementation of a solution of the outstanding issues depended upon the initiative of the central government since its initial decision to create the Punjabi Suba in 1966, greater attention needs to be paid to the failure of the central government to move resolutely to resolve the issue.

One explanation, consistent with Tully and Jacob's analysis, would emphasize Mrs. Gandhi's alleged indecisiveness.[64] On this reckoning, Mrs. Gandhi, who clearly did show the ability to act decisively on many occasions, did so, however, only when pushed to the wall. This explanation, however, will not do to explain the *type* of response Mrs. Gandhi ultimately resorted to when forced finally to act. Why could it *not* have been political accommodation with the Akalis instead of an army assault on the Golden Temple?

The answer is too obvious and places her actions within both the changed (by her) context of center-state relations and the political bases of her own decision-making. Mrs. Gandhi altered the Indian political system in the 1970s in such a way that her power at the center depended on two things: 1) her ability to control most of the Indian states, which, however, remained always problematic because of the absence of strong state leaders; and 2) her ability to sway large categories of voters by creating a "wave" on an emotive issue or set of issues. A wrong move on an issue such as Chandigarh and Abohar-Fazilka could have lost power for her in two states: in Punjab to an Akali Dal waxing victorious over her concessions and in Haryana to the Lok Dal, exploiting negative reactions to her concessions. More important, such a wrong move might have then precipitated a "wave" in the wrong direction and her loss of power in Delhi and the country as a whole.

The second part of the answer is that Mrs. Gandhi failed to articulate the issues in terms of principle and to attempt thereby to contain their negative political consequences. She presented the issues herself largely in terms of political gains and losses and the need to make political trade-offs between one state and another, while insisting she was only protecting na-

[64] Tully and Jacob (n. 8), pp. 13–14.

tional unity and the interests of parties other than herself and while blaming the deterioration of the Punjab situation upon the malevolent influence of "foreign" hands, rather than her own government's failures.

reasons for India's problems

The principal argument of this essay has been that relentless centralization and ruthless, unprincipled intervention by the center in state politics have been the primary causes of the troubles in the Punjab and elsewhere in India since Mrs. Gandhi's rise to power. Rajiv Gandhi came to power in 1985 on a wave of Hindu militant nationalist sentiment that supports centralization, national unity, and intolerance towards aggressive minority demands. He soon moved away from that sentiment in search of political solutions in Punjab and Assam and displayed a willingness to give up power in these small states for the sake of restoring peace and normalcy.

good ideas but no implementation

The Rajiv-Longowal accord also has provided a basis for a settlement consistent with the traditional rules followed by the central government in dealing with minority demands in the 1960s. At this writing, however, that accord has still not been implemented. The commission appointed to adjudicate the Abohar-Fazilka dispute failed to reach a decision on the areas to be transferred to Chandigarh. Another commission called for Punjab to transfer 70,000 acres of land to Haryana in exchange for Chandigarh, which the Punjab government has refused. The central government failed to hand Chandigarh over to Punjab on the appointed date of January 26, 1986 without a general agreement. The Akalis on their part have failed to work unitedly to demand implementation of the accord. The major responsibility for failing to implement this accord, however,

Prime Minister is to blame

rests with the prime minister, who alone could have made the decisions on the conflicting claims, restrain Congressmen in Haryana, and accept the political damage while the Congress' majority in the country was secure and time remained to repair the damage. It is regrettable, therefore, that the political will to implement the Punjab accord has once again been lacking and that the opportunity to enforce a just solution while the Congress held an unshakable position of political dominance in the country for five years is being allowed to slip by.

The more general point of this essay, insofar as the future unity of India is concerned is that, though the Punjab constitutes a special case, it also has highlighted a major structural problem in the Indian political system that requires a broader political solution. That structural problem arises from the tensions produced by the centralizing drives of the Indian state in a society where, as I have argued elsewhere, the predominant long-term social, economic, and political tendencies are towards pluralism, regionalism, and decentralization.[65] Mrs. Gandhi fought those tendencies by

[65] See Brass, "Pluralism" (n. 3).

centralizing power and decision-making in Delhi, nationalizing issues, and intervening incessantly in the politics of every state. A more stable political solution will require just the opposite: willingness to accommodate regional political demands, to grant greater powers to the states, and to share power in Delhi itself. Rajiv Gandhi may postpone facing the deeper structural problems because he has an unprecedented governing majority in Delhi and in the country as a whole. That majority will, however, certainly begin to disintegrate before long. When it begins to disintegrate, the same issue will then face him as faced his mother: allow it to happen and lose power or resort to new centralizing measures to prevent it. The content of the issues that are likely to arise at that point cannot be predicted, but it is certain that the choice will again be faced.

SIX

Dominant Proprietary Classes and India's Democracy

PRANAB BARDHAN

Democracy in its present form, like the cinema, is a relatively recent Western import to India. Although initially meant primarily for elite consumption, both have, in a short span of time, struck roots in the hearts and minds of the Indian masses. In the process, both have been reshaped and refurbished by unmistakably indigenous styles, images, and modes of operation. While both are usually noisy, shallow, and gaudy, and often provide unintended cases of the theatre of the absurd, both have, at times, reached unscaled heights. Just as Indian filmmaking has produced many examples of artistic excellence, Indian democracy has led to historically exceptional achievements. Never before has such a large, diverse, and desperately poor population been held together in a commonly accepted basic framework of democratic rights for as long as four decades.

The postindependence adoption of a democratic structure is largely attributable no doubt to the liberal values of the professional elite leading the freedom struggle. But a high-minded adoption of democratic structure does not guarantee its regular maintenance. The mortality rate of infant political democracies in developing countries has been high. In particular in India, a country where the ideal of equal access of all to some basic political rights clearly conflicts with what may have been history's most elaborate and well-entrenched ideological system of legitimizing social inequality, one would think that the tendency for the body politic to reject the foreign transplant would be rather strong. Moreover, faced with such massive and excruciating poverty, people are apt to be impatient with the slow processes of democracy and to find arguments for alternative systems compelling. In this context, the continuing survival in India of democracy, ramshackle and battered but still full of life and resilience, is an interesting puzzle.

Without minimizing the importance of a certain liberal tradition in the Indian political culture and legal system of the last one hundred years and a degree of continuing commitment on the part of India's political leaders, I would suggest that a possible clue to the puzzle lies in the complex heterogeneity of India's socio-economic interest groups. In terms of ethnic and regional diversity, India is clearly an extreme case. But even in terms of organized economic interest groups, India contains a relatively large plurality. Of the dominant proprietary classes[1]—industrial capitalists, rich farmers, and white-collar workers and professionals—none individually is substantially more powerful than the others, in some contrast to the class alignment in most advanced capitalist countries, where the dominant class is more homogeneous. No doubt a part of this contrast is attributable to the historically weak development of capitalism in India. The industrial capitalist class has not yet been strong enough to undermine the economic importance of the class of rich farmers or to absorb them into giant capitalist agro-business enterprises; neither has it succeeded in colonizing the bureaucracy and molding it to suit largely capitalist goals. In addition, the diversity of Indian society militates against the emergence of a single dominant class whose writ can be enforced throughout the country. Outside these dominant proprietary classes there are also sections of unionized industrial workers, traders, and small propertied groups that are quite vocal in lobbying for their separate economic interests.

In the political science literature on Europe socio-economic heterogeneity is often regarded as a factor working *against* democracy. Theorists of democracy in the tradition of John Stuart Mill or Harold Laski have shown that deep social and economic cleavages may endanger democracy. Marx and Engels earlier traced the roots of the absolutist regimes of Europe to the matched power of contending social classes boosting the autonomous power of the state. As Engels wrote in 1884 in *The Origin of the Family, Private Property and the State*, "Exceptional periods, however, occur when the warring classes are so nearly equal in forces that the state power, as apparent mediator, acquires for the moment a certain independence in relation to both. This applies to the absolute monarchy of the 17th and 18th centuries, which balanced the nobility and the bourgeoisie against one another."[2] In *The German Ideology* Marx and Engels offered a similar explanation of the persistence of absolutism in the Germany of their time.[3]

---

[1] For a brief description of these classes (including why I choose to call the professionals a proprietary class) and an analysis of the nature and consequences of conflicts among them in the context of Indian political economy, see Pranab Bardhan, *The Political Economy of Development in India*, Oxford: Blackwell, 1984.

[2] Frederick Engels, *The Origin of the Family, Private Property and the State*, New York: International, 1972, p. 231.

[3] Karl Marx and Frederick Engels, *The German Ideology: Part One*, New York: International, 1970, p. 80.

Although the autonomous power of the state can clearly increase if none of the classes constraining state action dominates the others, and although social cleavages make compromise difficult and multiply the stresses and strains on the polity, the Indian experience suggests that the very nature of class balance and heterogeneity may make the proprietary classes somewhat more interested in the maintenance of democratic processes. In a country where the elements in the dominant (though tacit) coalition are diverse, each sufficiently strong to exert pressures and pulls in different directions, political democracy may have a slightly better chance than elsewhere, particularly in view of the procedural usefulness of democracy as an impersonal (or least arbitrary) rule of negotiation, demand articulation, and bargaining within the coalition, and as a device for one partner to keep the other partners at the bargaining table within some moderate bounds. Even in European history, divisions within the dominant proprietary classes played an important role in the rise of democracy. In France, Louis Napoleon shrewdly used the restoration of universal male suffrage to play the landed classes against the urban; he even reportedly advised the Prussian government in 1861 to introduce universal suffrage because "in this system the conservative rural population can vote down the liberals in the cities."[4] In mid-nineteenth-century Britain, competition between the landed class and industrial capital led to significant extensions of franchise for the working class. In a related context, Marx cites the English proverb, "when thieves fall out, honest men come by their own."

In India strategic alliances with numerically large lower classes or ethnic groups have been quite frequent: The ruling party has often successfully used electoral alliances of well-off urban classes with poor tribals and lowest castes from rural areas against rival parties with support bases among rich and middle income farmers. Populist rhetoric has been a useful weapon in clipping the wings of an overgreedy bargaining partner in the dominant coalition; profuse tears of commiseration with the masses shed on the floor of Parliament and elsewhere have drowned a rival's extravagant claims. If the industrialists at any time overstep in their bargaining, sure enough there will be an uproar in Parliament about "the anti-people conspiracy of the monopoly capitalists"; similar invectives against the "kulaks" or, somewhat less frequently, the "parasitic *babu* class," will also be aired on appropriate occasions. The competitive politics of democracy thus serves to keep rival partners in the coalition on the defensive.

[4] See Matthew S. Anderson, *The Ascendancy of Europe, 1815–1914*, London: Longman, 1972, p. 115.

More significantly, Indian democracy, particularly under the Congress system until the early seventies, has provided a subtle and resilient mechanism for conflict management and transactional negotiation among the internally divided and regionally diverse proprietary classes. The democratic "machine" of Indian politics,[5] with its well-defined network of distribution of spoils in exchange for support, its highly decentralized organization responsive to pressure from important interest groups at different levels in the political system, its institutionalized procedures of transaction lending it a degree of legitimacy as well as moderation, and its ability to absorb dissent and to co-opt leaders of the subordinate classes, has impressed many a political scientist. This machine is vastly more complex and diversified and very much larger in scale than not only the classical machine model of political clientelism, best illustrated by the Daley machine in Chicago, but also the Christian Democratic machine in Italy.[6] This complex organization in India was an outgrowth of the multiclass alliance network that Gandhi forged to fight the British. As Congress came to power, it developed, beginning with the levels of municipal and provincial administration in the 1920s and 1930s, into an elaborate structure of patronage distribution in a multiclass coalition in independent India. The cause of democracy in India certainly owes a lot to the liberal professional elite at the helm of the freedom struggle, but its general persistence and the form it has taken has much to do with the political exigencies of bargaining within its heterogeneous dominant coalition. In the nineteenth-century history of liberal movements in Eastern and Southern Europe, one usually notes a long historical gap between the onset of what has been called "the liberalism of the intellectuals" and the later liberalism of the manufacturers; in India, with a much shorter gap, the proprietary classes have adapted the liberalism of the intellectuals to their own primary needs. If these classes remain seriously interested in the maintenance of democratic processes, if only for the sake of their own bargaining procedures, it will be difficult for the state to supplant them directly, except at times of military crises (real or contrived). We shall indicate later how over the last ten to fifteen years sizable cracks and strains have developed

---

[5] For a similar description of the Congress system, see James Manor, "The Dynamics of Political Integration and Disintegration," in *The States of South Asia: Problems of National Integration*, edited by A. Jeyaratnum Wilson and Dennis Dalton, London: C. Hurst, 1982, pp. 99ff.

[6] See Luigi Graziano, "A Conceptual Framework for the Study of Clientelistic Behavior," *European Journal of Political Research*, no. 2 (1976), pp. 149–174, and Shmuel N. Eisenstadt and Rene Lemarchand, eds., *Political Clientelism, Patronage and Development*, Beverly Hills: Sage, 1981.

in the framework of the machine politics that has served the members of the dominant coalition so well for many years.

The politics of buying support with patronage and of accommodating the conflicting demands of a large and heterogeneous coalition of interests has had serious adverse implications for the pace and pattern of economic growth in India. Massive doses of public investment in basic industries and infrastructural facilities, such as coal, transport, power, and irrigation, are crucial at the early stages of industrial and agricultural transformation. Increasingly, however, the bulk of public resources are being frittered away in nondevelopment expenditures and political and administrative mismanagement of public capital. When diverse elements of the loose and uneasy coalition of the dominant proprietary classes pull in different directions and when none of them is individually strong enough to dominate the process of resource allocation, one predictable outcome is the proliferation of subsidies and grants to placate all of them, with the consequent reduction in available surplus for public capital formation. Huge subsidies from the government budget are required every year to maintain high support prices for farm products, while the vocal urban consumers (as well as the industrialists whose wage costs will go up otherwise) have to be pacified with lower issue prices of grains at the public distribution points. Government subsidies are necessary as well to maintain low prices of fertilizers, irrigation water, power, and diesel for rich farmers; to supply all kinds of underpriced public sector produced materials and services for rich industrialists; and to provide substantial subsidies to export interests. The total amount classified as subsidies in the expenditure of all administrative departments of central and state governments is estimated to have exceeded 40 billion rupees in 1983–1984, compared to less than 1 billion rupees in 1960–1961. These subsidies do not include persistent losses in government-owned irrigation works, state electricity boards, road transport corporations, and other public enterprises. Neither do they include the vast amounts of subsidies implicit in the overmanning at different levels of public bureaucracy, supporting a whole army of salaried parasites. In recent years the gross domestic product (at 1970–1971 prices) from the public sector in banking, insurance, public administration, and defence taken together exceeded the total contribution to the gross domestic product from all of registered manufacturing, both in the private and public sectors, even though at the beginning of the seventies the latter was substantially above the former.

Subsidized credit by public lending agencies, which has seen a phenomenal expansion during the last decade, has become a political boondoggle. Lending targets are sometimes set by partisan political priorities rather than considerations of maximum social return. Some of the worst loan

scandals involving the nationalized banks originated essentially in the politicization of public banking, including the packing of bank boards of di-
rectors with people affiliated to the ruling party. In the rural sector there
is a dismal record of repayment of loans given to rich farmers by commercial banks and cooperative credit societies. Influential farmers in several
parts of the country have made nonrepayment of loans from public financial institutions a major plank (along with nonpayment of irrigation
charges and betterment levies) in the agitations they have led. There have
also been reports that in some areas large farmers obtaining subsidized institutional credit have recycled the credit given them into their local
moneylending operations rather than using it for productive investment.
Concessional financing to the industrial sector has often been used in
nursing "sick" private companies. Lame-duck private companies often try
hard (and pull strings) to get themselves placed on the sick list. In some
states such industrial "sickness" has reached epidemic proportions.

The Indian public economy has thus become an elaborate network of *Public*
patronage and subsidies. The heterogeneous proprietary classes fight and *Economy*
bargain for their share in the spoils of the system and often strike compro- *CLASS*
mises in the form of "log-rolling" in the usual fashion of pressure-group
politics. The political deal between the contending industrial and agricultural classes in Bismarck's Germany has often been described as the "marriage of iron and rye"; similar arrangements in Southern Europe under the
trasformismo systems of the last quarter of the nineteenth century have
been described as the marriage of cloth and wheat. The dowries of such
arranged marriages can be high. In any case, with three major proprietary
classes involved, as there are in India, the arrangement is more like a *me-
nage a trois* than a marriage, and accordingly somewhat more complicated.

The Indian style of politics is deceptively consensual, but over the years
the process of intense bargaining and hard-fought-for apportionment of
benefits among the different partners of the dominant coalition has come
out more in the open, and political activity has acquired a more unseemly
image in the public mind. And, as in all large complicated bargaining
counters, there has emerged a group specializing as brokers, who act as
agents for various bargaining interest groups and who, of course, take a
cut for themselves for services rendered. These are gangs led by a large
number of MLAs and MPs, political middlemen who over the years have
specialized in the profession of brokerage services. The fees they charge
and part of the favors they get for their clients are usually not accounted
for in the official statistical bookkeeping, an omission contributing to the
thriving underworld of what is called "black money." As elections have
become more expensive and as professional expertise in brokerage has in-

creased, these fees skimmed off the surplus of the economy have multiplied.

Political democracy has also encouraged greater pressure for state subsidies from a growing number of groups beyond the confines of the dominant coalition. Sections of unionized workers, small traders, and other small propertied interests, taking advantage of their larger numbers, are increasingly vocal in demanding, through electoral politics, a larger share of the pie. Regional and sectarian pressures for increased claims to federal money have also increased. From time to time a significant number of crumbs must be thrown to these groups clamoring just outside the gates of the dominant coalition. Equally expensive is the process of manning and securing those gates, and of controlling the crowds if they appear too threatening. The cost of the consequently expanded police and paramilitary forces has risen enormously, particularly over the last two decades. Placating the heterogeneous elements of the dominant coalition, guarding the fortress, and alternately coaxing and coercing the intermediate groups banging at the gates all contribute to the mounting nondevelopment expenditures in the budget and leave for the state a dwindling share of revenues for reinvestment in public capital formation.

If patronage and subsidies threaten to silt up the channels of surplus mobilization and public investment, one wonders why the proprietary classes, who have much to gain from economic growth, do not pull together in their long-run collective interest and cooperate in dredging the silted channels. Their failure to do so is, in my judgment, largely attributable to the difficulty of taking collective action in large and heterogeneous coalitions, a difficulty emphasized by Mancur Olson and others in a somewhat different context.[7] The problem has aspects of a classic "prisoners' dilemma" game. For any single partner in such coalitions, the risks and sacrifices of what may turn out to be one-sided dismantling of carefully cultivated patronage structures may be too costly. The inevitably crowded agenda and the weight of the pre-existing list of complex understandings in large lobbying coalitions make any negotiation on changing the basic game rules excruciatingly slow. Incentives for plodding along the well-worn grooves of short-run rent-seeking are, on the other hand, too strong. These general problems are, of course, far more acute in a country of India's size and bewildering crisscross of interest alignments within the dominant coalition.

The pervading atmosphere of the politics of patronage is also reflected in the high capital-output ratio and low capacity utilization in the public

---

[7] Mancur Olson, *The Rise and Decline of Nations: Economic Growth, Stagflation and Social Rigidities*, New Haven: Yale University Press, 1982.

sector, even in cases of substantial public investment. Part of this failure is no doubt due to genuine technical reasons or to pure managerial inefficiency or lethargy induced by monopoly positions in a sheltered domestic market. But many cases of mismanagement and labor tension may ultimately be traced to the nature of the political regime. Senior appointments in the public sector are sometimes made more on the basis of political patronage than on merit, often leading to low morale in the technocratic ranks of the enterprises. Headships of public sector units, particularly under the state governments, are indiscriminately used as political sinecures, and efficient managers who fail to satisfy the minister's political clients are often arbitrarily transferred. Expensive projects are hastily initiated on grounds of political expediency or regional favoritism, without proper design and preliminary spade work. The result is long delays and cost escalations. In addition, the deliberate promotion of trade unions affiliated to the ruling political party has often led to damaging union rivalries and irresponsible "economism." Overstaffing, "featherbedding," fake payrolls, absenteeism in regular hours, working only for "overtime" payments, and other irregularities are condoned, if not actively encouraged, by trade unions and their political bosses, who cite flagrant cases of corruption, political patronage, and cronyism at the top in many public enterprises. Irresponsibilities at the managerial, technical, and worker levels thus feed on each other, creating a general atmosphere of demoralization and parasitism on the state. Plundering of public sector produced goods by agents of influential politicians in collaboration with public enterprise staff, private contractors, and the criminal underworld is also far too common. Thus, a regime of clientelist machine politics, fostered by a flabby and heterogeneous dominant coalition preoccupied with an anarchical grabbing of public resources, has choked off efficient management and utilization of capital in the public sector.

Democracy has also put ideas in the heads of the lower classes, creating proliferating demands that threaten to catch up with the operators of the machine. With sluggish economic growth, these outside pressures leave little room for the coalition to maneuver and little scope for their selective co-optation tactics. The capitalist democracies of Western Europe and North America never faced this problem in comparable intensity, except, perhaps, during the depression in the thirties. This is partly on account of the technological dynamism and expansive capacity of capitalism in Western Europe and North America, but also largely because the industrial revolution in all these countries (at least its first round) was completed before large-scale democratic demands became pressing.

The fiscal and managerial crises that are associated with the pattern of slow economic growth in India have in turn generated a kind of political legitimation crisis.[8] As tensions and frustrations with the old patronage distribution network build up, the legitimacy of the political machine declines, the hegemonic hold of the dominant proprietary classes over the subordinate classes starts slipping away even while their economic grip remains strong, and some partners in the dominant coalition start looking for other, more secure ways of conflict resolution, for more centralized forms of arbitration. By the middle seventies Indira Gandhi, who over the years had shown remarkable skills of political aggregation in a fragmented, continental polity, was too eager to provide leadership in this centralized arbitration process. Deeply suspicious of the aspirations of any of the "bosses" regularly thrown up by machine politics, she used the considerable cunning and state resources at her command to significantly cripple the machine, thus centralizing the whole process of inflows and outflows of spoils and patronage. The once impressive decentralized organization of the Congress party lay in great disarray; the principle of popular representation at different organizational levels of the party was already abandoned; nominated or co-opted political operators came to control much of the political machinery. The electorate, however, having tasted the fruits of democracy, assertively refused to give up its basic democratic rights. Parts of the press and the judiciary, and a growing number of nonparty grassroots organizations, have also shown remarkable vitality and resistance, but the decay of the crucial institutional structure of the party remains.

At this time (end of 1985) it is still too early to assess the effectiveness of the major changes in policy that have been announced with great fanfare by Rajiv Gandhi's new regime. Although much of the time and energy of the new government has understandably been spent in fire-fighting operations, particularly in Punjab and Assam, and in trying to restore normal political processes in those states, a concerted attempt is being made on the economic front to reorient the industrial economy away from zero-sum rent-seeking toward faster growth and technological upgrading. Policies have been initiated to simplify and scale down the system of direct taxation and industrial regulations and to liberalize imports of goods and technology. The aim seems to be to break the economic stalemate in the coalition of upper classes, curbing the power of the meddlesome bureaucracy and increasing the production incentives and tax reliefs for the industrial capitalist class. Predictably, not all sections of the business community support these policy changes: producers (unlike users) of import-competing intermediate products resent import liberalization; medium-

---

[8] The context differs somewhat from that spelled out by James O'Conner in *The Fiscal Crisis of the State*, New York: St. Martin's, 1973.

sized firms are wary of the effects of the expansion of monopoly houses in view of the virtual abandonment of antimonopoly laws; the handloom and the powerloom sector in the country's large textile industry is apprehensive of the relaxation of regulations on the mill sector; and so on. In the class of professionals, although the bureaucrats will resist encroachments on their license-dispensing leverage with supplicant businessmen and on their other sources of corrupt income, the growing managerial and technocratic elite will expect to benefit from the increasing policy emphasis on technological improvement and professionalization of management. The large reduction of tax rates on salaries has been welcomed by all sections of this class. The agrarian lobby, which has not yet reaped commensurate benefits in the new dispensation, is likely to be increasingly suspicious of the alleged urban bias of the new leadership. The unionized working class is also likely to be increasingly vocal and disruptive as it feels the pinch of higher prices brought on by increased excises, administered prices of public sector products, and deficit financing (to make up for revenue losses from tax relief for the corporate sector and the salaried class). Dissatisfaction will be particularly serious in a crop year less good than the last one. In view of all this it is not yet clear that the new leadership will succeed in mustering enough political support to carry through its economic program in the coming years. Even if it succeeds in gaining support, the new economic policy is not likely to make a dent in the problem of unemployment, and, as the mass of urban unemployed youth grows alarmingly large, restive, and lumpenized, it will pose a direct threat to the democratic functioning of the polity.

In the last year many have been impressed by the democratic commitment of the new leadership and by its less high-handed and confrontational style of politics in marked contrast to that of the preceding regime. But the process of personalization and centralization of power, along with the state-centered nature of civic life and the growing use of state violence, continues unabated. Although party organizational elections have been announced for next year, and youth and efficiency are supposedly at a premium in the selection of party leaders at different levels, the whole show is still stage-managed from above (now reportedly with the help of computers). The much vaunted managerial skills of the whiz kids and "boxwallahs" at the top are not enough to repair and revive the old transactional network of a pluralist polity, to restore the institutional modes of compromise and co-optation at the intermediate and local power centers of this vast polyglot country.

Excessive centralization, political, administrative, and financial, has become a source of corrosive tensions in the federal structure in relation to the states. Within the dominant coalition, big business, urban professionals, and the bureaucracy (both civilian and military) will be, in their own interest, committed to a strong center, but this commitment is not so obvious for the agricultural interests. The latter, regionally diffused and fragmented but increasingly vocal, will be interested in expanding the power of the state governments, which for them it is easier to corner. Attempts by the center over the last few years to rule the state governments with handpicked ciphers have backfired, often resulting in intensified faction fights, intrigues, and instability. Without the integrating institution of an effective party organization and without decentralized forms of conflict management, regional frustrations build up, their outbursts often taking the forms of sectarian violence and political anomie, which undermine the very basis of national unity that centralization is supposed to achieve.

Neither has the government succeeded so far in using the centralization of power to insulate the management of the vast public sector (including public lending) from the ravages of patronage politics particularly evident at the state level. At the national level, the top leadership enjoys a degree of autonomy as it presides and arbitrates over a plurality of contending interest groups,[9] deriving special legitimacy in elections that over the last decade and a half have increasingly taken the form of votes of national confidence (or lack of it) for a particular leader and referendums on large regime-type questions. Such autonomy gives the national leadership some leeway in the political insulation of the public economy. But at the state level such autonomy is largely missing and pork-barrel politics predominates, a situation unlikely to improve in the near future, for the ruling party is in many states insecure and in others, out of power. Yet the state and local governments alone control more than half the public sector industrial productive capital in the country and manage the provision of key inputs such as power and irrigation water. Because public investment and management of public capital remain crucial for economic growth, this lack of autonomy at the state and local levels will act as a binding political constraint on economic performance in spite of the new economic policy. If the rate of economic growth does not significantly rise, the tensions among the clamoring groups, both inside and outside the dominant coalition, are bound to rise, and the much admired resilience of the Indian democratic system will be tested again and again over the coming years.

[9] As opportunities to take cuts from deals in foreign trade and agreements with multinational corporations increase, the dependence on domestic capital for contributions to the party funds may diminish, and the autonomy of the national leadership from domestic class interests may rise.

SEVEN

Middle Classes and Castes in India's Politics: Prospects for Political Accommodation

FRANCINE R. FRANKEL

The term "middle classes" in the historical context of modern Europe suggests the emergence of an economic hierarchy detached from inherited wealth and status and based on achievements in business, education, and the professions. The middle classes in India, as B. B. Misra points out, did not emerge naturally in the aftermath of an industrial revolution that weakened the traditional social order.[1] Unlike the merchant capitalists of England, who raised their first successful challenge to ecclesiastical control over education as early as the fourteenth century, Hindu merchants of *bania* status remained insufficiently powerful over the next 400 years to use wealth in order to alter their inferior social position relative to the priestly and literate Brahmans. Largely uneducated, they were constrained in their economic activities by avaricious local officials in a position to confiscate their profits or their property.

The Indian middle classes not only appeared on the historical stage "late" but they were artificially created under British rule, primarily by the educational policy introduced for meeting the administrative requirements of the Raj. Predictably, these origins ensured that the ranks of the middle classes were disproportionately filled by members of the civil services and professions. Equally important, educational achievements interacted with caste status to mark the Indian middle classes as a hybrid social formation that was not encompassed by its position in an economic hierarchy. Initially, the educated classes were drawn primarily from among Brahmans and other upper castes having a literate tradition, thereby introducing social background alongside income and education as the constit-

middle class:
- social background
- income
- education

[1] Bankey B. Misra, *The Indian Middle Classes, Their Growth in Modern Times*, New York: Oxford, 1961, see chaps. 1 and 2.

uent characteristic of the Indian middle classes. The strong correlation between upper caste rank, English education, and the professional classes was recognized in the distinction, drawn from the early twentieth century, between the Forward Castes and the Backward Classes.

British rule, by providing security of property within the framework of free trade, also belatedly spurred the emergence, from the second half of the eighteenth century, of a new commercial class that took to English education. However, other policies pursued by the Raj to preserve the main fields of investment for English capital ensured that the commercial, financial, and industrial classes remained relatively weak. Moreover, the Indian business classes were also dominated by particular communities, initially by Parsis and Gujaratis, and subsequently, by the Marwaris.

Finally, during the colonial period, the term "middle class" referred to more than the educated professional and business classes. Misra includes in this category the landed middle classes. This landed interest comprised proprietors and holders of proprietary undertenures in small estates, both absentee landlords living in cities and towns, and resident proprietors cultivating with the help of tenants. In general, these landholders also had social origins from among the upper castes.

It is hardly an exaggeration to say that Indian politics, until the time of independence, was an exercise in accommodation of the middle classes, the overwhelming majority of whom were drawn from Brahman and other Forward Castes. The pressure to expand English education, recruit Indians into the Indian Administrative Service, and introduce representative institutions of government came from these classes, especially in Bengal, where subdivision of small estates made it imperative for the sons of the landed middle class to seek their livelihood through education. Simultaneously, the educated middle classes dominated the Indian National Congress, which, in advocating the development of Indian industry, drew support from the business classes. Once these groups grew disillusioned with the pace of political reform, they joined forces in support of Mahatma Gandhi's leadership of a "mass-based" nationalist party. In practice, the Congress party recruited workers at the villages from small zamindars and landowners who could support sons engaged in full-time political work out of family earnings. As the suffrage was extended in the 1930s, the landed middle class, enjoying the advantage of numbers, asserted its control over the leadership of the Indian National Congress at the provincial level.

The Indian middle classes were less the product of upward, than of horizontal, mobility. The traditional merchant and trading classes, whose control over industrial assets sharply increased during the last decades of British rule, superseded their caste status by converting great wealth into an acceptable basis of social honor in urban areas. Apart from these classes, however, which remained a small section of the middle classes, the greatest gains from the new educational and economic opportunities went to the Brahmans and members of other literate castes who left the villages to become the dominant groups in the professions and administrative services. When we recall that, before 1950, approximately 15 percent of the adult population could exercise the vote, either on the basis of education or property, it is clear that the political coalition forged between the educated professionals, the emerging commercial and industrial classes, and the landed middle class did not strike roots much beneath the level of elites in towns and villages, elites drawn predominately from among the upper or Forward Castes.

The main concern of this chapter is to analyze the prospects of political accommodation under the new conditions created by universal suffrage over the last thirty-five years. During this period, the middle classes and Forward Castes have been progressively challenged by the much larger layer beneath them. This layer of the "middle" or "intermediate" castes, which overlaps with a large section of the lower middle classes, is drawn substantially from among educationally and socially disadvantaged Sudra subcastes referred to in the 1950 constitution as "Other Backward Classes." Their entry into politics represents a formidable challenge to the politics of accommodation on two grounds. The first is that the number of public offices and the amount of government patronage must be in- creased at a much more rapid rate than in the past to match the growing numbers from underprivileged groups aspiring to a share of economic gain and political power. The second is that this process of accommoda- tion, in order to remain acceptable to the "dominant coalition,"[2] which by the 1980s included a new class of rich farmers and a much stronger industrial capitalist class, must succeed without overturning the overall structure of inequality on which the privileged position of the middle classes and the Forward Castes has rested since the colonial period.

It is not possible in this chapter to deal with the varying patterns of conflict between the Forward Castes and Backward Classes over all the diverse regions of India[3] although, in my view, this conflict is the major un-

[2] Pranab Bardhan, *The Political Economy of Development in India*, Oxford: Basil Blackwell, 1984. Bardhan asserts that by the 1980s the dominant proprietary classes consisted of the industrial capitalist class, the rich farmers, and the professionals, including white-collar workers. See chap. 6.

[3] Regional patterns of caste-class relationships are studied as part of an international research project to be published in two volumes by Francine Frankel and M.S.A. Rao, eds., "Caste, Class, Ethnicity and Dominance: Patterns of Politico-Economic Change in Modern India."

derlying cause of the breakdown, in several states, of the "Congress system" and the subsequent political decay exposed in growing corruption and criminalization of politics, on the one hand, and the resort to populism, on the other.

My purpose in this chapter is to selectively examine how dynamic interactions between caste and class, conceptualized not only as structures but as processes undergoing transformation in response to changes introduced in the economic and political systems, alter dominance in society and power of the state to affect prospects for political accommodation.[4] I do this by concentrating on two important regions distinguished by their sharp differences in initial conditions: the Indo-Aryan "heartland" of Bihar and Uttar Pradesh, and that part of South India confined to the major area of the old Madras Presidency now constituted as Tamil Nadu, with some references to the Andhra Pradesh districts.

The analysis is constructed around a broad question that has two parts: Why, in the states of Tamil Nadu and neighboring Andhra Pradesh have the claims of Other Backward Classes to reservations in educational institutions and the administrative services, as well as for a growing share of political power, so far been accommodated peacefully within the democratic process? Why, by contrast, in Bihar and parts of Uttar Pradesh, has the entry of the Backward Classes into politics caused a polarization between them and the Forward Castes that has led to social and political violence?

The Regional Context: The South

It is more difficult to identify the members of the middle castes, and especially that section corresponding to the twentieth-century category of the Backward Classes than to define the composition of the middle classes. According to Brahmanical Hinduism, all the subcastes of the Sudra *varna* belong to the menial and service classes and can be described as "middle" castes. They constitute a social layer intermediate between the three "twice-born" *varnas* of Brahmans, Kshatriyas, and Vaishyas, dignified by their respective occupations as priests, warriors, and traders and agriculturalists, and those *avarna* groups, or Untouchables, permanently assigned to polluting work. Among the *varnas*, Sudras are the most numerous, accounting for a majority of Hindus in all regions.

This ideal type of hierarchical caste and class social order probably

[4] This analytical framework was developed by M.S.A. Rao for the project cited above and is entitled: "Caste, Class, Ethnicity and Dominance: Some Conceptual Issues in the Study of Patterns of Politico-Economic Change in Modern India," mimeo.

never existed in its pure form. At the same time, Brahmanism as an ideology became sufficiently influential in all parts of India that Brahmans always enjoyed the highest ritual status, while Untouchables everywhere were precluded from sharing in any religious privileges. Evidence from several regions suggests that, when the origin of the king and/or the dominant landowning groups was of Sudra status, these groups either imported Brahman priests or contrived to become their patrons through lavish endowments and gifts to the temples as means of legitimizing their privileges.

This pattern of caste and class interaction was characteristic of the Tamil areas until the advent of British rule. So long as Brahmanical ideology held sway, there seems to have been little alternative, given the caste configuration of the region. Virtually no indigenous Kshatriya or Vaishya groups were present. The "twice-born" castes were represented almost entirely by Brahmans, and even their numbers were small. In the river valley districts and coastal area where the Tamil culture was most highly developed, the concentration of Brahmans reached 6 percent (compared to an average of 3 percent for the Madras Presidency as a whole).[5] Brahmans were large landowners only in Thanjavur district. Overall, they represented a modest proportion of 15 to 20 percent (by 1918) of the population having wealth either in the towns or rural areas.[6]

This caste and class configuration helps account for the peculiar features of Tamil society. On the one hand, Brahman priests played a "secondary and socially dependent" role in economic and political life.[7] On the other, they enjoyed the highest privileged status associated with their functions in the performance of ritual worship. A close relationship of interdependence existed in the river valley districts between Brahmans and the dominant landed castes of Vellalas, despite their status as Sudras. Brahmans customarily involved the Vellalas in the management of the temples and thereby legitimized their de facto elite status. At the same time, the generous patronage bestowed on Brahmans by the large landowning families provided the basis of their material well being.

This mutuality in relations between Brahmans and Vellalas, suggesting a sharing of privileged status, had repercussions for the entire social hierarchy at the middle levels. This is exemplified particularly in the urban South Indian temple religion, which remained intact on the eve of the

---

[5] David A. Washbrook, "Caste, Class and Dominance in Tamil Nadu: Non-Brahmanism, Dravidianism and Tamil Nationalism," chapter prepared for volumes on "Caste, Class Ethnicity and Dominance" (n. 3), mimeo., p. 25.

[6] C. J. Baker, *The Politics of South India, 1920–1937*, Cambridge: Cambridge University Press, 1976, pp. 90 and 95.

[7] Washbrook, (n. 5), p. 11.

nineteenth century. The notion that services performed for the gods, such as donations of land, money, or produce for temple festivals, conferred honor and status, injected a fluidity into the local social hierarchy. These traditions eased the way for rising non-Brahman mercantile families and local *jatis* who acquired control over land to effectively claim relatively higher privileged status. Along with this prospect for upward status mobility, was a tendency toward geographic and occupational mobility. "Local *jatis* had their eyes fixed firmly on the main chance—be this, in varying contexts and at various times, agriculture or trade or manufacturing or, later, education. The barriers which caste posed to occupational mobility were low and . . . were regularly jumped."[8]

Rights in land and other economic resources were also widely, albeit unevenly, distributed through structures of joint ownership. Even when the British introduced individual property rights under *ryotwari* tenure and undercut customary rights to a share in land and grain, the initial prosperity accompanying the introduction of commercial agriculture obscured the decline of corporatist privileges. By the time of the Great Depression, when the agricultural economy was plunged into crisis, rights in land had become very widely distributed, mainly through subdivision of holdings.

The search for the Other Backward Classes in the South is complicated by this regional pattern of caste-class relations. Not all Sudra subcastes can be included in the Backward Classes. The striking example of the Vellalas makes this clear. Leading families were literate in Tamil, especially in the devotional literature that was part of the *bhakti* Saiva Siddhanta tradition. By the beginning of the twentieth century, many Vellalas, like the Tamil Brahmans, had sold their lands, moved to the towns, taken up English education, and entered the professions. The Vellalas were unquestionably members of the Forward Castes.

A variant of this pattern can be found in the neighboring Telegu area of the Andhra districts. Within Andhra, Brahmans constituted 3 percent of the population, with Kshatriyas accounting for another 1.2 percent. The Brahmans, however, made up sizable percentages of the population in the most fertile districts (up to 20 percent) as late as 1921,[9] and a large number also were zamindars. As a group, however, they were reluctant to work on their lands even after the introduction of irrigation in the mid-

[8] Ibid., p. 26.

[9] G. Ram Reddy, "Politics of Accommodation: The Case of Andhra Pradesh," table no. 5a, draft paper presented to the Conference on "Status, Class and Dominance: Patterns of Politico-Economic Change in Modern India," University of Pennsylvania, 3–11 May 1984, mimeo.

nineteenth century made commercial farming profitable. Like their counterparts among Tamil Brahmans, many sold their lands, took up residence in the towns, dominated university education, and entered the modern professions. The result was similar to that in the Tamil region. "The old regime of status was replaced by a regime of competition."[10] The major beneficiaries were the most numerous peasant castes of Sudra rank—the Reddis and Kammas—who gradually formed a middle class. By the beginning of the twentieth century, they had also begun to acquire an English education and were considered part of the Forward Castes.

The emergence of the Forward Castes in the early twentieth century from among the ranks of the middle class Sudra peasantry blunted the process of caste and class polarization that might have developed around a sharp *varna* division. Moreover, economic differentiation within castes elevated only a relatively small elite, to whom poorer caste-fellows then turned for assistance. Corporate caste entities, therefore, remained the most important collectivity for expressing material interests, even when, and perhaps especially when, economic differentiation was well underway.

The argument that, under these conditions, inequalities between Forward Castes and Backward Classes need not lead to a social polarization can be illustrated by the interaction between the non-Brahman movement led by Vellala elites in the 1910s and 1920s and the mobilization of Backward Hindus in the 1930s and 1940s, movements that led, after independence, to reservations in educational institutions and government posts for more than 50 percent of the population.

The history of the non-Brahman movement has been amply documented, and it is necessary to emphasize only a few points here. The great expansion in educational opportunities and employment in government service starting from the turn of the century produced a crisis in relations between Vellalas (and other locally dominant castes) and the Brahmans, who had shared hegemony over traditional society. The conflict arose primarily in urban areas where many former landowning families settled in order to pursue English education and enter the professions.

A number of changes in the legal system introduced by the British had already assaulted the traditional status of non-Brahman elites. British property laws, which made temples public corporations, invested them with full ownership rights over lands donated for their support, and set up elected management committees in consultation with collectors, made it virtually impossible for non-Brahman groups to assert their claims to

<hr />

[10] Ibid.

higher status by demanding participation in temple management in return for "gifts" and other benefactions. Additional features of Anglo-Indian law based on misguided attempts to impose the rigid Brahmanical hierarchy on Tamil society led to the categorization of all non-Brahmans as members of the Sudra *varna* for purposes of settling disputes over management rights in temples, enforcing social reform policies, and even carrying out enumeration in the decennial censuses.

All of this would not have been so disruptive of the actual interdependence between Brahmans and the dominant proprietary castes if the major arena for standing in society had not shifted to the towns, where the most important avenue to advancement was English education. Scholars have shown the extent to which Brahmans were in the best position to take advantage of these new opportunities. In the Madras Presidency, where Brahmans accounted for approximately 3 percent of the population and enjoyed a male literacy rate of over 28 percent (in 1921), they achieved an overwhelming predominance in the emerging middle class. Brahmans provided 67.5 percent of the graduates from Madras University (1918) and held 55 percent, 82.5 percent and 72.6 percent of the posts open to Indians among deputy collectors, sub-judges and district munsiffs (1912).[11]

The emergence of this "modern" educated middle class from the ranks of a priestly caste claiming the highest status in traditional Sanskritic culture ironically encouraged many Brahmans to reassert the claim of birth as the basis of a higher relative position in urban society. Brahmans who had previously played a secondary role to non-Brahman landed castes in the village suddenly attempted to assert their status superiority in the towns. Their efforts to impose an unofficial pattern of social segregation are still remembered as the emergence of a "very big caste calamity in those days."[12] Brahman and non-Brahman students ate in separate messes at colleges run under Congress auspices; Brahmans alone were allowed to enter the watershed in government offices to supply drinking water to non-Brahman staff; Brahman travelers had their own clearly labeled "Brahmans only" dining and retiring rooms at railway stations; Brahmans established and frequented "Brahman Coffee Shops"; and in the temples, Brahmans alone were allowed to enter the inner sanctum of the presiding deity.

The Vellalas, as the foremost patrons and erstwhile partners of the

[11] Eugene Irschick, *Politics and Social Conflict in South India: The Non-Brahman Movement and Tamil Separatism 1916–1929*, Berkeley: University of California Press, 1969, p. 10.

[12] Interview, K. Rajaram, Speaker, Tamil Nadu Legislative Assembly and long-time personal assistant to E. V. Ramaswami Naicker, Madras, 6 February 1985.

Brahmans, experienced the greatest relative deprivation as a result of these practices.[13] They were, moreover, best positioned, as the proportionately greater caste community producing in absolute numbers almost as many literate males in English as did the Brahmans, to assume intellectual and political leadership in rejecting Brahman claims to superiority based on Sanskritic culture. They used the pages of the English language newspaper, *Justice*, to propagate the views of European scholars that the term "Sudra" had no meaning in Tamil society, which had not originally been organized according to Vedic principles of *varnashrama dharma* imposed by Aryan Brahmans.

The South Indian Liberal Federation, or the Justice party, founded in 1916, although spearheaded by Vellala elites, made demands in the name of all non-Brahmans to a larger proportion of positions in every department of government and at all grades of services. These demands were granted by the government of the Madras Presidency within only five years, in 1921. Such speed suggests that the British regarded the non-Brahman movement as a possible counterweight against the agitation for home rule supported by the Indian National Congress and identified with Brahman leadership in disproportionate numbers.

The fact, however, appears to be that elite non-Brahmans used the Justice party primarily to win concessions from government in order to restore their own competitive status vis-a-vis the Brahmans in the new urban middle classes. Once the position of non-Brahmans was secured by the reservations policy, the Justice party, which dominated the Madras Presidency until 1936, permitted its members to enter the Indian National Congress (as early as 1927). By the late 1930s, almost all of the Forward non-Brahmans constituting the limited electorate had gone over to the Congress party, which in 1937 formed the government under the leadership of a Brahman, C. Rajagopalachari.

Nevertheless, claims made by the Justice party to proportionate representation in the name of all non-Brahmans created a new political category including all low-caste Hindus and minorities. The fact that the Justice party did not live up to its promises, but actually filled most reserved seats for non-Brahmans from among the Forward Castes was a major factor in its loss of support among the disadvantaged sections of Hindu society.

Most important, the non-Brahman movement helped to increase political consciousness among castes of Sudra rank whose social, educational, and economic level did not permit them to take advantage of the reserva-

[13] This theme is developed by Marguerite Ross Barnett, *The Politics of Cultural Nationalism in South India*, Princeton: Princeton University Press, 1976, p. 25.

tions schemes. The formation, in 1934, of the Madras Provincial Backward Classes League, made the first distinction between "forward" non-Brahman communities, who received the lion's share of benefits, and the strata above the Untouchables, who needed to secure separate preferential treatment. Galanater refers to the list, presented in 1944, by the Backward Classes League, to the Madras Government, identifying more than 50 percent of the total population of the Madras Presidency as members of the non-Brahman category of Backward Classes.[14] The response of the Madras government , in 1947, was to provide separate reservations for the "Backward Hindus," the first official recognition of this political category composed of a congeries of lower Sudra subcastes making a separate claim to their share of privileged rights.

The social mobilization of the "Backward Hindus" was perhaps the most important unintended legacy of the non-Brahman movement. This process was greatly accelerated by the formation of the Self-Respect League in 1925, under the leadership of E. V. Ramaswami Naicker. "EVR" made use of rhetoric similar in many respects to that already employed by elite Vellala leaders of the Justice party against the Brahmans and all forms of caste privilege to stress the original equality of all Hindus in Tamil society.

The self-respect movement was the first breach in the wall of political privilege constructed on the foundation of forward caste status and middle class affluence, not only in South India, but in the country as a whole. At his most radical, EVR (a poorly educated, but well-to-do Naidu from a merchant family) attacked the Vedic scriptures, the caste system, and the very concept of God. He developed self-respect marriages involving an exchange of garlands at Hindu weddings to eliminate the need for Brahman priests, led agitations to remove affronts to non-Brahman dignity by painting over "Brahman Only" signs at public places, held feasts for all communities, including Untouchables and Muslims, and took part in satyagrahas for temple entry by Untouchables.

Admittedly, EVR was contradictory and inconsistent in his commitment to create a casteless society that unequivocally accepted the equality of Untouchables. His followers among Backward Hindus resisted all ideas of a thoroughgoing social reform that would have destroyed their traditional status superiority over untouchable groups. Nonetheless, the Backward non-Brahmans were first organized as a political force in Tamil Nadu in response to the self-respect movement.

The movement had its greatest impact in the towns, among students

[14] Marc Galanter, *Competing Equalities, Law and the Backward Classes in India*, Berkeley: University of California Press, 1984, pp. 158–159.

and the new urban lower middle classes. These groups legally were among the beneficiaries of reservations, but they could not compete with Vellalas and other Forward Castes who had long established advantages of higher education and professional employment to reach the top rungs of the occupational ladder. At the same time, EVR's impact at the villages was not negligible. His natural constituency in the countryside was the Backward non-Brahman subcastes above the untouchable strata, having nearly no education, and only a meager livelihood as small landholders and laborers. EVR spent a good deal of time moving about the rural areas and delivering his message to the lower sections of society. Traveling in a van, he was received as an honored teacher, discoursing two to three hours at a time about religion, social reforms, and the need to create a "human" society.

By the late 1930s, the Backward non-Brahmans in Madras had become a powerful political force. They played an important role in the June 1938 agitation protesting the Congress ministry's introduction in the schools of compulsory Hindi, which as a Sanskritic language symbolized the social domination of Aryan Brahmans over Tamil society. The urban lower middle classes also responded enthusiastically to the demand made at the same time for a separate Dravida Nadu. By 1944, when EVR merged the Self-Respect League with the rump of the Justice party to form the Dravida Kazhagam, his closest lieutenant, C. N. Annadurai, was already thinking of ways to mobilize Backward non-Brahmans and the lower middle classes to form the social base of a new political party in opposition to the Congress.

At independence the Forward non-Brahmans who dominated the Indian National Congress and succeeded to power at the state could no longer legitimize their position by sharing in the status of Brahmans. On the contrary, in Tamil Nadu, the exodus of Brahman families from the villages to the towns, and from the towns to other parts of India quickened. Subsequently, the privileges of the dominant agricultural castes and the urban middle classes rested only on the material resources at their command and the ingenuity they could muster in disguising the structural bases of large-scale economic deprivation. As Washbrook suggests, they were helped in their efforts by the pattern of political mobilization among the Backward Classes themselves. The constituents of this amorphous category entered politics on the basis of localized corporate or caste entities that aspired to share in the privileges of the dominant groups without wanting to displace them and while measuring their achievements against the subordinate position of the Untouchables, or Scheduled Castes. Such patterns, which later emerged in Andhra Pradesh in the face of even more glaring inequalities, provided the social support for the politics of accommodation, first practiced through controlled patronage, and indiscriminate populism, once larger and larger numbers of persons from the lower castes and lower middle classes became politicized.

THE REGIONAL CONTEXT: BIHAR AND UTTAR PRADESH

The caste and class structure of the Indo-Aryan heartland of Uttar Pradesh and Bihar provides a sharp contrast to that of the South. It is in this region that the Brahmanical caste hierarchy is most fully articulated. The three "twice-born" *varnas* are represented by area-wide subcastes of Brahman, Kshatriya, and Vaishya rank; and the very small Kayastha subcaste, technically of Sudra status, is accorded elite standing because of their literate tradition and long-standing employment as teachers and scribes. Altogether, these "twice-born" and Kayastha castes account for about 14 percent of the population in Bihar and 20 percent in Uttar Pradesh. Indeed, in Uttar Pradesh, the Brahmans alone make up more than 9 percent of the entire Brahman category in India.

This type of *varna* configuration, in which "twice-born" subcastes enjoy relatively large numbers and wide geographical spread, led to a very different pattern of caste-class interaction in the North than in the South. In Uttar Pradesh, in the eastern and central districts, Brahman, Thakur, and Bhumihar zamindars controlled the major share of the land from the time of Akbar, with other landholders drawn primarily from among high status (Ashraf) Muslim groups. Only in the western districts of the upper Doab and Rohilkhand were "twice-born" castes weakened from the middle of the nineteenth century by the challenge of Jats and Gujars, who, in addition to Muslims, expanded their holdings.

The coincidence between high ritual rank and control over land was even closer in neighboring Bihar. The Brahmanical social order was present in its purest form in North Bihar where (Maithil) Brahmans enjoyed substantial numbers, controlled most of the land, founded local dynasties, and acted as generous patrons of Sanskrit learning and fine arts. Although priestly status did not coincide with control over land in other areas of Bihar, substantial landholders were drawn from among other "twice-born" castes, such as Bhumihar Brahmans and Rajputs, along with Ashraf Muslims.

This pattern of overlapping caste status and economic position in the largest part of Uttar Pradesh and in Bihar was reinforced through the land revenue settlements made by the British from the late eighteenth to the middle of the nineteenth century. In the United Provinces, where the British initially made settlements with village zamindars but subsequently favored larger proprietors and *talukdars*, the tenurial pattern varied between one based on small owner cultivators, particularly in the western districts, and large absentee landlords, in Avadh and the eastern region. Nevertheless, at independence, despite the large number of estates lost by default, the rapid turnover in zamindars, and the subdivision and fragmentation of holdings in the densely populated eastern districts, only about 8 percent of all agricultural households owned virtually all the cultivated land. Among them, Thakurs (Rajputs) and Brahmans owned 57 percent of the cultivated area. The intermediate castes owned another 32 percent, the Muslims, 11 percent, and the Untouchables a tiny fraction of 1 percent.[15]

At the same time, the contrast between the western districts on the one hand, and the central and eastern areas on the other, had grown more marked. The Thakur landlords, who owned nearly 50 percent of the cultivated land in most districts of Avadh and eastern U. P., accepted the Brahmanical status culture. They considered it beneath their dignity to engage in direct cultivation, leased out their lands to tenants often from backward castes, and employed field laborers from among low castes and Untouchables on terms that were equivalent to bonded labor.

In the western districts, where moneylenders and bankers belonging to the Brahman and Bania castes gained land (at the expense of Thakurs and Muslims), more fluidity was injected into the social structure. Partly, landlordism had always been less pervasive in the absence of excess agriculturalists seeking land to lease. Even the Brahmans, along with nonelite castes like the Jats, took up cultivation of their own holdings. After the expansion of irrigation and the rise of prices in the early part of the century, a significant agrarian middle class emerged. In this region, owner cultivators accounted for approximately 36 percent of zamindars and operated holdings of five to twenty-five acres, extending over 18 percent of the land.[16]

In Bihar, the introduction of the Permanent Settlement at the end of the eighteenth century had a more uniform effect in widening the social and economic gulf between a small minority of large landlords and the bulk of the cultivating classes. Full ownership rights over 90 percent of the cultivable land were conferred on perhaps 4 percent of the population, drawn mainly from among Bhumihar Brahmans, with smaller representations from among Kayasthas, Rajputs, Brahmans, and Muslims. The only important exceptions to this pattern, which formed a pale counterpart to the

---

[15] Baljit Singh and Shridhar Misra, *A Study of Land Reforms in Uttar Pradesh*, Calcutta: Oxford, 1964, pp. 24–27.

[16] Ibid., p. 215.

western districts of U. P., were Saharsa in North Bihar, and Patna in South Bihar, where settlements were made with small zamindars of Sudra rank from among Ahirs and Kurmis respectively. In all other districts, except in tribal areas, the major cultivating castes were Ahirs, Kurmis, and Koeris. Similarly, the bulk of landless laborers and ploughmen were members of the untouchable communities, such as Musahars, Dusadhs, and Bhuiyas.

Unlike the South, where the *varna* distinction between "twice-born" and Sudra castes was blurred by the interdependence of Brahmans and dominant landed castes of "middle" rank, the *varna* barrier in the North constituted a virtually insurmountable obstacle to sharing social privileges, whether of status, education, occupation, income, or power.

Upper caste zamindars in both U. P. and Bihar shrewdly manipulated the *varna* division between "twice-born" and Sudra tenants to subordinate common class interests to divisive caste privileges. Tenants of high and low castes were called by different generic names, lived in separate sections of the village, and were often granted different terms of tenure. Rajputs and Bhumihars, in particular, sometimes received land at fixed rents in perpetuity, while high caste tenants normally were assessed at lower rents than tenants of Sudra rank. Ahir and Kurmi cultivators were not only subjected to caste discrimination, they were also the first to feel the burden of arbitrary rent enhancements, illegal exactions, forced labor, and evictions.[17]

The Brahmanical belief system, moreover, also structured social relations among subcastes of middle rank. Denied any possibility of sharing in privileged status, they attempted to raise their ritual rank within the caste hierarchy through the process of sanskritization. The Ahirs, in the early years of the century, formed a caste association spanning both provinces to assert a Yadava identity based on descent from the mythological Yadu dynasty of Lord Krishna.[18] Similarly, the Kurmis aspired to recognition as Kurmi Kshatriyas by tracing a fantastical lineage from the God Indra.[19] Such claims were never recognized by members of the "twice-born" castes. More important from the point of view of power relations, the Sudra subcastes, by competing against each other to win upper caste

[17] For a description of discriminatory treatment against low caste tenants in Bihar, see George A. Grierson, *Bihar Peasant Life*, Delhi: Cosmo, 1885, reprint ed., 1975, pp. 198–199, 317, 319, 324–326; and for the United Provinces, see citations in Zoya Hasan, "Class, Caste Hegemony: Patterns of Domination and Dynamics in Uttar Pradesh," chapter prepared for volumes on "Caste, Class, Ethnicity and Dominance" (n. 3), mimeo., pp. 19–20.

[18] M. S. A. Rao, *Social Movements and Social Transformation: A Study of Two Backward Classes Movements*, Delhi: Macmillan, 1978, chaps. 4 and 5.

[19] See K. K. Verma, *The Changing Role of Caste Associations: A Study of Kurmi Sabhas*, Patna: A. N. Sinha Institute of Social Studies, 1980.

status, dissipated their major asset, that of superior numbers, in resisting oppression by the "twice-born" castes. Locked in a struggle for relative superiority within the ritual hierarchy, they could not establish horizontal links uniting cognate caste groups against the "twice-born" to make political demands on government such as those advanced in the South for reservations in the name of all the Backward Classes.

Similarly, low caste tenants, who faced much greater economic disadvantages than those of higher castes, were unable to generate leadership from among their own ranks to mount agitations for implementation of British laws conferring occupancy rights and lower rents on statutory tenants. They were therefore placed in the anomalous position of relying on the leadership of the Indian National Congress to enforce their rights against the very castes and classes on whom the Congress relied for political support.

Although the towns and cities of the United Provinces produced an extraordinary generation of nationalist leaders from among the English-educated professional classes, the overwhelming majority of leaders were drawn from the Brahman and Kayastha castes. More important, the Congress Socialist party, which emerged within the parent organization by 1934, could not overcome the political reality that the party as a whole relied for support in the towns on the new moneyed class of Banias engaged in banking, trade, and small industries allied to the spread of commercial agriculture; and in the countryside, on small zamindars of locally dominant castes, especially the Brahmans and Thakurs. Although Kurmi tenants had provided the backbone of the Kisan Sabha started by the socialists in the 1930s, and Kurmi and Yadava tenants accounted for many of the volunteers during the no-rent campaigns taken up as part of the civil disobedience movements in 1930 and 1932, their interests were abandoned once conservative elements in the U. P. Congress committee won a showdown with the socialists.

The Congress ministry's 1938 tenancy reforms, which granted hereditary rights to statutory tenants, elevated the position mainly of cultivators in the western districts, whose occupancy rights had long been secure. In areas like Avadh and the eastern districts, the legislation intensified the conflict between low caste tenants and upper caste landlords who feared they would lose control of their lands (beyond the area of fifty acres allotted for home farms) to tenants demonstrating documentary proof of occupancy rights.

The situation was worse in Bihar. In that state, the Congress party was led by a miniscule urban elite composed almost entirely of Kayastha and Brahman professionals, many with close links to the countryside through small zamindars of the Bhumihar, Rajput, and Brahman upper castes. The

Bihar leadership of Congress refused to sanction a no-rent campaign as part of the noncooperation movements in 1930 and 1932, despite the dramatic deterioration of the condition of tenant cultivators during the depression. When Congress socialists, in 1934, nevertheless supported the Bihar provincial Kisan Sabha, which led struggles in several districts to restore dispossessed tenants on their lands, the movement was led mainly by Bhumihars and Brahmans, and its followers came from among the larger occupancy tenants who were also Brahmans and Bhumihars.[20] As the struggles intensified, and low caste cultivators were organized against upper caste landlords (especially in the bloody three-year conflict in Monghyrx district between 1936 and 1939),[21] the state party leadership banned all Congressmen from attending or helping to organize Kisan Sabha meetings. The Congress ministry's 1937 Bihar Tenacy Act served the interests of the zamindars as far as possible. Occupancy tenants were given the right to transfer holdings and to reduced rents, but the legislation did not provide any enforcement mechanisms for guaranteeing rent receipts as proof of occupancy.

At independence, both in U. P. and in Bihar, caste, class, and power were closely intertwined. The *varna* division defined the boundary between the Forward Castes and Backward Classes, with the exception of the Kayasthas statewide, and the nonelite Jats in the western districts. The few individuals among the Yadavas and Kurmis who managed to get an English education mostly came from the small middle class of zamindars within their communities, were employed at lower levels of the civil service or in service industries, and could not by themselves affect the social standing of their caste groups. They were, moreover, of no importance in the membership of the Congress party leadership, which was dominated by upper castes.[22]

Simply to raise the question of reservations for Other Backward Classes under these conditions was to risk polarizing the entire society simultaneously along status, class, and power lines. This much appears to have been appreciated by both the educated sections of the Backward Classes and the Forward Castes. Almost immediately after independence, militant lower caste leaders founded the Bihar Sate Backward Classes Federation and joined with activists from cognate castes in Uttar Pradesh to lobby for a constitutional provision giving special facilities to the Backward Classes.

[20] Walter Hauser, "The Bihar Provincial Kisan Sabha, 1929–1942, A Study of an Indian Peasant Movement." Ph.D. dissertation, The University of Chicago, September 1961, p. 77.
[21] Rakesh Gupta, *Bihar Peasantry and the Kisan Sabha (1936–47)*, New Delhi: Peoples, 1982, pp. 50 and 182.
[22] Ramashray Roy, "Caste and Political Recruitment in Bihar," in *Caste in Indian Politics*, edited by Rajni Kothari, New Delhi: Orient Longman, 1970, pp. 242–243.

No one of the twenty-one most important figures in the Constituent Assembly came from among the Sudra castes,[23] and there was little enthusiasm for reservations beyond those originally provided for the Scheduled Castes and Scheduled Tribes. Nevertheless, the decision by the Supreme Court to strike down reservations for non-Brahmans in Madras under the equal rights provisions of the constitution provided the national leadership with an embarassing political problem. This was solved by the First Amendment (16 May 1951), which inserted Article 15(4), establishing the constitutionality of state legislation providing reservations in educational institutions and government posts to "backward classes of citizens."

The Backward Classes Commission, appointed by the government of India in 1953, provided a "ray of hope" to educated sections of the backward communities. Whatever their caste or party, they had begun to realize their shared problem, that the government services that conferred social prestige and political power were manned by the upper castes, particularly the Kayasthas, and also the Brahmans in Bihar, and the Brahmans, followed by the Kayasthas, Banias, and Rajputs in Uttar Pradesh.

Beyond this, publication in 1955 of the Backward Classes Commission *Report*, which recommended reservations of 25 percent to 33⅓ percent for class I and class II government posts, and reservations of 70 percent in various professional schools, became for many of the educated younger generation a major factor in raising political consciousness. They rejected the "old fantasy" of emulating Brahmans and Kshatriyas in order to achieve "twice-born" status as irrelevant to group aspirations for social equality. Many turned their attention to the new possibilities inherent in universal suffrage and the proposals for reservations to achieve social mobility outside the caste system by capturing state power. Very quickly, they shifted their reference group from the upper castes to that of the Backward Classes.[24] In Bihar, where the Bihar State Backward Castes Federation was especially active, a Backward Classes Welfare Committee with membership crosscutting subcaste and party lines was formed in the 1952 legis-

[23] Granville Austin, *The Indian Constitution, Cornerstone of a Nation*, Oxford: Clarendon, 1966, appendix III, pp. 337–346.

[24] As M.S.A. Rao argued, the claims by Yadavas, first to Kshatriya status and then to Backward Class status, are not necessarily contradictory because both are forms of attack on the privileges of upper castes. "By claiming the Kshatriya status Yadavas are attacking the ritual superiority of the twice-born castes and by claiming backward caste reservations they are restricting the entry of the upper castes and dislodging them from the monopolistic positions in the fields of technical and professional educational government jobs." See M.S.A. Rao, "Some Subjective Orientations in Understanding Indian Social Reality." Paper presented at the Symposium on Philosophical Theory and Social Reality, Nehru Memorial Museum and Library, New Delhi, 18–22 January 1982.

lative assembly to support the cause of the Backward Classes on the floor of the House.

There was, however, no equivalent enthusiasm among the senior leadership of the Congress party for implementation of the commission's recommendations. Prime Minister Nehru himself shared the view of the English-educated middle classes that it would be preferable to extend help to backward individuals rather than to groups or classes and only reluctantly recognized the "existing fact" that inequalities were part of "our social structure—we may call them by any name you like, the caste system or religious divisions."[25] Others found the caste criterion repugnant to the secular principles of an egalitarian and democratic society, believing that reservations would be inimical to creating an efficient bureaucracy recruited on the basis of merit. Uppermost in the minds of many of the upper caste elites who urged that economic criteria be used to define social backwardness were fears like those expressed by the chairman of the Backward Classes Commission, who rejected the recommendations of his own *Report*. In a covering letter, Kalelkar explained that he had become convinced that "a few dominant individuals from amongst the backward communities" were trying to divide society into antagonistic "Advanced" and "Backward" groups. Their goal was to organize all the Backward Classes against the advanced communities and aggrandize themselves on the strength of numbers "to capture power and rule over the whole country."[26]

The commission's report, which was placed before both Houses of Parliament in September 1956 created such an uproar that it was immediately tabled and not taken up for discussion until October 1964. Majority sentiment was that economic backwardness should replace caste as the criterion for reservations. It was decided that the central government should not take any action to implement reservations in the All-India Services and that the entire matter of reservations should be left to the states to deal with as they saw fit. The result was that the state governments of Bihar and Uttar Pradesh completely ignored the Backward Classes Commission's recommendations. Until the late 1970s, they had adopted only marginal concessions for the Other Backward Classes to help pay fees or other costs for the very small numbers of students enrolled in postgraduate courses. When the demand for implementation of caste-related reservations finally proved impossible to ignore, after the 1977 elections, resentment between Forwards and Backwards over the issue was so bitter that

[25] India, "The Parliamentary Debates: Part II, Proceedings other than Questions and Answers," *Official Report*, 29 May 1951, p. 9615

[26] Backward Classes Commission (K. Kalelkar, Chairman), *Report*, Delhi: 1955, vol. I, pp. xiv-xv.

it led to street fighting and electoral violence all over Bihar and massed demonstrations of strength between Forwards and Backwards in eastern Uttar Pradesh.

POLITICAL ACCOMMODATION AFTER INDEPENDENCE: TAMIL NADU AND ANDHRA PRADESH

The most dramatic political change occurred in Tamil Nadu in 1967 when the Dravida Munnetra Kazagham (DMK), led by C. Annadurai, delivered to the Congress a decisive defeat from which it never recovered. The advent of the DMK marked the first entry into state politics of the Backward non-Brahmans as a dominant group.

The distinctive features of the DMK were found in its ideology, which emphasized Tamil cultural nationalism, social reform, including the removal of caste distinctions, and the economic improvement of the lower classes who constituted the majority of the Tamil community. Equally important, the party leadership made a painstaking organizational effort to build up a mass base at the grass roots. Shortly after the DMK was formed, members were recruited in the villages and, after paying dues of 4 annas a year, sent membership cards. A "branch" was constituted in any village where twenty-five persons joined together. These branches formed the foundation for a system of indirect elections similar to those then held in the Congress party for taluk, district, and municipality committees, with the general council electing members of the executive. In 1959, a lower tier was added below the taluk level to coincide with the newly established Union Panchayat Raj institutions.

As data collected in 1968 by Marguerite Barnett shows, well-to-do landlords and more religiously inclined upper castes tended to stay with the Congress party.[27] The DMK, by contrast, drew its recruits predominantly from the lower middle class agriculturalists and artisans. Almost half the DMK leaders at the local level were farmers, and those engaged in low-ranking service occupations, small shopowners, and even laborers were represented in larger numbers than the white-collar middle classes. The most striking difference between the DMK and the Congress party was the complete absence of Brahmans, both at the state and local level, and the fact that 43 percent of the DMK local leadership came from Backward non-Brahman castes, in addition to which service castes provided another 4.5 percent and ex-Untouchables, over 8 percent.

The early success of the DMK should be understood not only as a func-

[27] Barnett (n. 13), pp. 188–195.

tion of its radical Dravidian ideology and charismatic leadership, but of the favorable structural conditions in the Tamil countryside. The Congress party, which was identified in the urban areas with Brahmans and Forward non-Brahman middle classes, could not win over the radical lower middle classes despite attempts to Dravidianize its leadership. At the same time, this absence of popular support in the towns would not have been decisive if the Congress had succeeded, as it did in other states, in building a powerful party machine in the countryside based on patronage networks controlled by leading members of the dominant agricultural classes. The distinctive feature of rural Tamil Nadu was the absence of state-wide (or even regional) Forward non-Brahman castes on whom to rely in constructing vote banks. The most influential and largest of the locally dominant castes, the Vellalas, accounted for only 6 percent of the population statewide, and many of them had already migrated to the cities to pursue professional careers. Other locally influential landed castes typically accounted for less than 2 to 3 percent of the total population, occupied different rungs of the status ladder from one area to the next, and lacked the concentrated economic power of their counterparts in neighboring states, such as Andhra Pradesh. It was this relative weakness of the larger landowners as a cohesive social group that allowed the DMK to outflank them in the villages and to mobilize the small farmers, most of whom belonged to the Backward Classes.

Interestingly, the entry into Madras politics of the Backward non-Brahmans did not present any crisis of democratic incorporation either in the form of a confrontation between Brahmans and non-Brahmans, or between the large landowners from elite cultivating castes and the small farmers of lower rank. It is no doubt significant that at the level of the state-wide leadership, Forward non-Brahmans (particularly Vellalas, Chettiars, and Mudaliars) continued to make up the largest proportion of the general council of the DMK in the late 1960s. Although many of these party leaders were committed to the "rational" ideology of the party, which continued EVR's tradition in matters affecting interdining with all castes and even in rejecting the practice of untouchability, they were not in favor of basic agrarian reforms such as land redistribution, which would have ended their economic domination over village society. The leadership therefore concentrated in the early years on issues related to Tamil nationalism (especially as this was symbolized in resistance to Hindi) in order to invoke community sentiments transcending class divisions. The ease with which they succeeded in this approach can be related to the absence of *varna* barriers between the more well-to-do and weaker sections of Tamil society, which made an appeal to core values of shared privilege (against the North) credible.

The "deradicalization" of DMK ideology has been amply documented. The state leadership gradually shifted its emphasis in Tamil nationalism from that of race, which would have emphasized downward alliances with the Adi-Dravidas, or former Untouchables, to that of language, which permitted an accommodation upward to include Tamil Brahmans. The party also dropped its demand for a separate Tamil state once the central government made it a crime, after the 1962 Chinese invasion, to preach secession.

Most striking, neither the DMK nor the splinter party that became its successor from 1977, the All India Dravida Munnetra Kazagham (AIDMK), made any effort to carry out economic reforms that could ameliorate the skewed distribution of income. This is all the more remarkable in contemporary Tamil Nadu where 63 percent of the population subsist below the poverty line. At the villages the most important economic division occurs between marginal landowners, on the one hand, and those with semimedium, medium, and large holdings, on the other. In 1980–1981, the first group accounted for 69 percent of operational holdings, all under one hectare in size, amounting to 25 percent of the area. The second group, representing the top 15 percent with operational holdings between two to ten hectares and above, controlled almost 53 percent of the area.[28] The prospect is that income disparities will grow worse. Larger landowners have purchased pumpsets in record numbers, adopted the Green Revolution technology, and are substantially increasing their earnings through double cropping and diversification of business enterprises.

Similarly, in the cities, the class hierarchy has become much more pronounced in differentiating between the affluent upper middle classes and the struggling lower income groups. Brahmans and members of other Forward Castes have taken the lead in building up the modern business and commercial sector, ranging from banking, light manufacturing industries, storage and distribution, and the movie industry, to newspapers and hotels, while still dominating the specialized professions. This class lives in a world apart from the peddlers, petty traders, owners of small workshops, lesser professionals, schoolteachers, shopkeepers, and lower level government servants kept at the fringes of the modern sector.

The DMKs have substituted for reform an extremely successful set of populist policies that have prevented polarization around caste or class lines while "scarcely alter(ing) the distribution of wealth and significant

[28] India, Ministry of Agriculture and Rural Development, Department of Cooperation (Agricultural Census Division), "All India Estimates of Provisional Number of Operational Holdings and Area Operated, 1980–81," Agricultural Census Bulletin, no. 21, tables 13, 14, mimeo.

opportunity in Tamil society, which still strongly favors the narrow elites constituted in the later colonial period."[29]

Two policies, reservations and social welfare, have simultaneously aroused and satisfied popular aspirations. Tamil Nadu, which pioneered in providing reservations to Backward Classes in education and the government services, had by the 1980s pushed up the proportion of reserved seats in college admissions and government employment to almost 70 percent. Moreover, the formula adopted to identify the Backward Classes eligible for reservations appealed to the old idea that all sections of society could share in the privileges exercised by those in power. The first step involved was to establish lists of caste groups that historically were socially backward (that is, drawn from among Sudra rank); along with this were added certain other criteria such as education and employment in government posts to see if the groups as a whole remained backward. Finally, an income criterion was introduced to prevent the most affluent sections of the caste from profiting by claiming the privileges of "backwardness."[30] Because there is no sharp *varna* division between the Forward Castes and Backward Classes, moreover, eligibility itself was subject to political bargaining, with the same caste groups being dropped and added as lists were drawn up by successive governments.

At the same time, burgeoning social welfare programs, ranging from massive urban housing developments for the lower middle classes, to rural programs for building village roads, constructing school buildings, providing drinking water, installing one electric light connection in every hut, and, most popular, the free midday meal scheme for eight million school children has given substance to the government image of generosity and its claim to caring for the poor.

The net result is that the DMKs have become acceptable to elite caste and class interests, which support the parties although they remain outside formal political office, while the new entrants from the Backward Classes are easily co-opted by the ruling parties. All of this, when added to the charismatic personalities that have headed the DMK and the AIDMK, has successfully defused the class issue.

A brief look at politics in the neighboring state of Andhra Pradesh reveals certain similarities in the use of appeals to an overarching cultural nationalism while implementing reservations and antipoverty programs to defuse the potential for caste and class conflict. In Andhra Pradesh, regional differences between the Andhra region of the Madras province, and

[29] Washbrook (n. 5), p. 74.

[30] At least this is the process followed in theory. Practices are usually adapted to accommodate influential groups who resist any diminution in their privileges, and also the virtual impossibility of verifying information supplied on family income.

Telangana as the heartland of Hyderabad under the Nizam, diluted sentiments of Telegu cultural nationalism. Moreover, the immediate beneficiaries of the non-Brahman movement, especially in the towns, were the English-educated sections of the predominant landed castes, the Reddys and the Kammas. After the formation of a united Andhra in 1956, the Reddys emerged as the largest single caste statewide, but the Kammas, who were concentrated in the most prosperous irrigated areas of the coastal districts, remained formidable rivals for political power. As more wealth began to flow to larger farmers after the Green Revolution, and the industrial sector rapidly diversified from one dominated by agro-industries, to engineering, chemicals, textiles, and electrical enterprises, the Kammas led the Forward Castes in competing with industrialists from outside Andhra Pradesh to raise their share of ownership in major and medium industries.[31]

Until the late 1960s factional rivalries generally centered on personalities who commanded support from both major caste groups. These conflicts were either settled inside the Congress party or, where the protagonists had a different regional base, through agitations that appealed to regional sentiments that were used to advance the power inside the party of the disaffected group.

It was only when the party leadership loyal to Sanjeeva Reddy deserted Mrs. Gandhi after the Congress party split in 1969 that she directed the Andhra chief minister to shift the base of social support for the party from the dominant agricultural castes to the Backward Classes and weaker sections. After 1971, the state government adopted a wide range of antipoverty policies aimed at benefitting small and marginal farmers from the more backward castes. During the Emergency, moreover, the Congress government was able to implement some aspects of the Twenty Point Program of particular benefit to agricultural laborers, especially Harijans (Untouchables). The Janata party could not dislodge the Congress from power even in 1977, because the backward castes and Harijans had identified Mrs. Gandhi with the poor.

Moreover, from 1980, the Congress government greatly expanded the scope of reservations that were first introduced in 1966, even extending reserved places for backward castes in panchayat raj institutions. By 1978, in the legislative assembly, the Backward Classes accounted for 41 percent of Congress seats, and Scheduled Castes and Scheduled Tribes for another 17 percent. This shift was also noticeable in the composition of Congress cabinets, in which the percentage share of Backward Classes had

[31] Reddy (n. 9), table 8.

reached 29 percent by 1982 (whereas the Kammas and Reddys together accounted for about 25 percent).[32]

Just as in Tamil Nadu, however, the political accommodation of the Backward Classes in the government, and also in the administrative services, did not improve their economic position in society. Land reform measures, which had initially been part of the antipoverty programs, had to be quickly abandoned after a separatist agitation was launched by the upper castes in the affluent Andhra region. By 1981, almost 52 percent of all holdings in the state fell within the "marginal" category of below two-and-a-half acres;[33] the percentage of persons engaged in cultivation had fallen below those employed as agricultural laborers, and the percentage of persons below the poverty line on the most spartan criterion of Rs.55 per month ranged at the district level, with few exceptions, from more than 30 percent to 80 percent, with the incidence of poverty well above 40 percent in seventeen out of twenty-one districts.[34]

Seen from this perspective, the emergence of the Telegu Desam in 1983 did not represent a significant shift in the pattern already established by the Congress party. The Congress had been discredited mainly because of its constant intervention in the politics of the state and because of pervasive corruption and the inability to implement its own social welfare programs. The Telegu Desam merely appropriated most of the Congress program, adding to it a dimension of "Telegu pride" that diverted attention from the caste and class disparities while introducing more costly populist schemes such as rice at Rs.2 per measure, and subsidized prices for saris and dhotis.

This type of populist mobilization, which does not replace the Forward Castes as the major economic classes active in agriculture and in the growing industrial sector, politicizes a sizable section of the backward castes and poorer classes and may yet strain democratic stability by stretching available resources beyond their absorptive capacity. Dominant castes and classes who feel the government may go too far in accommodating the weaker sections still have enough power to mount extraparliamentary agitations or to pursue their interests through corruption. Similarly, in the absence of the ability to implement significant economic and social reforms as the condition for incorporating the backward castes and weaker sections as a whole into a grass-roots party organization, the "representatives" of these groups have to be constantly bought off against the danger of defection. This type of situation sets the stage for alternative groups,

[32] Ibid., tables 11 and 12.
[33] "All Indian Estimates of Provisional Number of Operational Holdings and Area Operated, 1980–81," (n. 28), tables 13 and 14.
[34] Reddy (n. 9), table 1.

especially regional parties, to bid for the support of the disillusioned lower castes and classes with more inflated promises to fulfill the neglected needs of the "Tamil" or "Telegu" people. Generally speaking, this pattern of competitive populist politics has emerged in the South.

POLITICAL CONFLICT AFTER INDEPENDENCE: BIHAR AND UTTAR PRADESH

The introduction of universal suffrage under the particular caste configurations of the Indo-Aryan heartland offered unprecedented opportunities for the low castes to assert a claim to power. In Bihar, the Yadavas were the single largest caste category in all districts outside the tribal areas. They accounted for 11 percent of the state population, only somewhat less than that of all the "twice-born" castes combined. Their numbers reached up to 25 to 35 percent of the electorate in some constituencies. Almost overnight, the local units of the Congress party began to admit Yadavas, to give them some representation on the Pradesh Congress Committee, and to allot a modest number of seats to them for the state legislative assembly. By 1957, upper Sudras (Yadavas, Kurmis, and Koeris), accounted for about 22 percent of the members of the ruling Congress Legislature party. They were, moreover, a growing minority of the Bihar Pradesh Executive Committee, constituting 20 percent of the membership in 1955.[35]

In Uttar Pradesh, the Congress party leadership, which had been dominated by the urban middle classes, and by Brahmans, Banias, and Kayasthas during the nationalist movement, was under less pressure to accommodate the lower castes. In the countryside, the Brahmans and Thakurs were spread throughout most of the state and together commanded more than 16 percent of the population. The Yadavas, at 8.7 percent in numbers, stood second to the Brahmans in size. Moreover, the Backward Classes were unevenly concentrated in the central districts of the former Avadh region and in the eastern areas adjacent to Bihar. They did not have a decisive numerical advantage against the upper castes in very many constituencies, especially because the Bhumihars were an important landholding group in the eastern districts.

The politically ambitious among the upper Sudra castes had a more difficult problem in asserting their claim to a share of political power in Uttar Pradesh than their counterparts had in Bihar. Indeed, the dominant upper caste leadership was adamant about maintaining an "upper classes coali-

[35] Ramashray Roy (n. 22), p. 243.

tion in the Congress which will ensure its influence in rural areas."[36] With the vote banks they commanded among the Scheduled Castes (a group that made up 12 percent of the population), and the Muslims, (accounting for another 15 percent), they were well positioned to carry out their design.

Even in Uttar Pradesh, however, the advent of electoral politics created new opportunities for the Backward Classes to assert their claims against the Forward Castes. In particular, 30.3 percent and 27.3 percent of MLAs in the Praja Socialist party and the Socialist party, respectively, came from the Backward Classes in 1962.[37] By that time, moreover, the Socialist party, under the leadership of Rammanohar Lohia had briefly merged with the Bihar Backward Classes Federation (in 1957) and agreed to support the federation's demand for implementation of the 1955 Backward Classes Commission's recommendations on reservations. At the third national conference of the Socialist party in 1959, Lohia's supporters passed a resolution committing the party to secure 60 percent of leadership posts in political parties, government services, business, and armed forces for Sudras, Harijans, Scheduled Tribes, religious minorities, and women. At the fifth national conference in April 1961, the Socialist party resolved that 60 percent of its candidates in the coming general elections should be from among these groups. By the end of the 1960s, the party had established a sizable following among small peasant proprietors of the Yadava, Kurmi, and Lodh castes, especially in the central and eastern districts.

The most important opportunity for Backward Class politicians to establish an independent base of political power in both states came about as a result of intraparty conflict among the dominant upper castes. In Bihar, interelite rivalries between Bhumihar and Rajput-led "subcoalitions" became so bitter by the early 1960s, that the Congress chief minister was forced to turn to leaders of the upper Backwards, who commanded a substantial group following. Krishna Ballabh Sahay, a Kayastha, who could not rely on his small urban-based caste group to hold the balance, cut back the representation of Forward Castes in his Cabinet to 40 percent and increased the share of the upper Backwards to 20 percent. Subsequently, the Yadavas emerged as an important group in their own right within the Congress party.

In Uttar Pradesh, rivalries within the ruling coalition of Banias, Rajputs, and Brahmans did not create similar opportunities for the Backward Classes. Nevertheless, in the western districts, Charan Singh, who

[36] Letter by Sampurnanand, cited by Zoya Hasan (n. 17), p. 86.

[37] Angela Burger, *Opposition in a Dominant Party System: A Study of the Jan Sangh, the Praja Socialist Party and the Socialist Party in Uttar Pradesh, India*, Berkeley: University of California, 1969, p. 54.

emerged as the unrivaled leader of the prosperous Jat peasantry, "was the first to recognize the political potential of channelizing the discontent of the backward castes, most of whom worked as cultivators."[38] As early as 1947, he had proposed reservations in the public services for "sons of cultivators," and in 1956, he defied the party leadership in chairing a statewide Conference of the Backward Classes.

The second phase of political mobilization, which saw upper Sudras aspire to an independent role beyond providing political support to upper caste leaders in return for patronage, coincided with the crisis that overtook the Congress party by the mid-1960s.

On the eve of the fourth general elections, strains on the patronage system manned by state party bosses were apparent from the bitter internal disputes that erupted over allocation of party tickets at the states and the large-scale defections in some areas that splintered the organization around the regional, factional, and caste grouping at its core. In Bihar, leaders of the Socialist party, who had opposed as retrograde the shift from class to caste issues implied by the national party's commitment to reservations, set aside their ideological scruples when they saw an opportunity of defeating the Congress. They leavened promises of agrarian reform with pledges to implement reservations as a means of strengthening their social base among the Backward Classes.

Although differences between the Forward Castes and the Backward Classes did not become the major political issue of the 1967 campaign, it was the first election that produced a popular leader of the Backward Classes. Karpoori Thakur, a Socialist and a member of the low ranking Nai (barber) caste spearheaded his campaign with the slogan:

> Socialist ne bandhi ganth
> Pichara Pave Saumee Sath
>
> Socialists have given their pledge
> The Downtrodden get 60 percent

One of the major defeats suffered by the Congress party in eight states in 1967 occurred in Bihar. The party's popular vote declined from over 41 percent in 1962 to 33 percent five years later, and its seats dropped in number from 185 to 128. The Socialist party, by contrast, recorded the biggest gain of any group, increasing its vote from little over 5 percent in 1962 to more than 17 percent in 1967, and its seats from seven to sixty-eight, making it the single largest non-Congress party. Congress losses in Uttar Pradesh were not as dramatic. Its percentage of votes polled at 32

---

[38] Zoya Hasan (n. 17), p. 85.

percent compared with 36 percent in 1962; but this decline was sufficient to deny the Congress a majority of seats in the legislative assembly.

The defeat of the Congress party organization in the two largest states of India set the stage for a chaotic competition for power between rival politicians, factions, and parties who recognized the need to rally support from the numerous lower castes and lower middle classes. Obscured in the crisis of political instability that overtook Bihar from 1967 to 1971 was the new bargaining power of the upper Backwards, especially the Yadavas, in getting a larger share of ministerial posts in the name of all exploited groups. Indeed, whereas Yadava representation in the legislative assembly had previously trailed behind that of each of the "twice-born" castes, in 1967 they emerged as the second largest caste group after the Rajputs. Within a few months, however, a complex set of circumstances arose that created an opportunity for the Backward Classes Federation to collude with top Congress leaders wanting to topple the Socialist-led Samyukta Vidhayak Dal (United Legislators' party) and to bring down the government in return for installing the first person from the Backward Classes (a Yadava) as chief minister.[39]

A somewhat analogous situation emerged in Uttar Pradesh. Although the Congress party initially succeeded in forming a government with the support of Independents, it was toppled after only three weeks. Charan Singh, convinced that he had been denied the post of chief minister because the "twice-born" castes would not tolerate a Jat as leader, led seventeen of his followers outside the party. He subsequently became the chief minister of the successor coalition government and the first member of a nonelite caste to hold the highest political office in the state.

In both Bihar and Uttar Pradesh, when new elections were held in February 1969, the struggle for power in the countryside expanded beyond the narrow circle of "twice-born" castes. In Bihar, Yadavas and Kurmis counted heavily on their own superior numbers. In addition, for the first time all groups used *goondas*, or armed hoodlums, to engage in "booth-capturing" in some polling booths of South Bihar. Even so, no party obtained a majority. Efforts by Kayastha, Rajput, and Bhumihar Congress party bosses to restore Forward Caste rule under a Congress-led multiparty coalition were resisted by Backward Class MLAs who defeated the ministry in the assembly after only four months. President's Rule was

---

[39] The circumstances surrounding this episode are described in Francine R. Frankel, "Caste, Land and Dominance in Bihar: Breakdown of the Brahmanical Social Order," draft paper presented to the Conference on "Status, Class and Dominance: Patterns of Politico-Economic Change in Modern India," University of Pennsylvania, 3–11 May 1984, mimeo., pp. 91–93.

reimposed after another unsuccessful experiment in ministry-making ended in July 1969.

In Uttar Pradesh, the challenge to the near monopoly of political leadership by upper caste landowning families in the villages, and Bania merchants and traders in the towns, was mounted in a more systematic manner. The Bharatiya Kranti Dal (BKD) formed by Charan Singh found its strongest popular support among the more prosperous middle class peasantry of the Upper Doab districts that had made the greatest gains from the Green Revolution. Not only did they favor larger state investments and subsidies for agriculture than the Bania faction in the Congress was prepared to approve, but the Jats, in particular, who were not officially listed as Backward, resented their weak position both in the public service and the ruling party. Charan Singh followed a natural strategy in seeking to expand the social base of the BKD by appealing to the marginal farmers and low castes who were predominant in the central and eastern districts. The new party fielded candidates in almost all constituencies of the state, criticized the Congress for biased administration in favor of urban capitalists, and introduced house-to-house canvassing at the villages to reach the poorer sections. Most striking, over 60 percent of the BKD's candidates had no previous experience in electoral politics, and 200 of the 402 contestants belonged to the backward and middle communities, of which only nine were Jats. Although the new government was formed by the Congress, which came within two seats of a majority, the most significant feature of the election was the success of the BKD in becoming the second largest party in the state.[40]

The emergence in Bihar and U. P. of the Backward Classes as a new political category capable of mounting a serious challenge to the preeminence of the Forward Castes rested on more than the introduction of universal suffrage. In both states, zamindari abolition played a major facilitating role.

In Bihar, the 1950 Zamindari Abolition Act, despite all its limitations, including the prolonged process of implementation (until 1963), significantly reduced the concentration of landownership in the largest size groups of fifty acres or more. Hardest hit were absentee landlords, among them the upper strata of Kayasthas, Banias, and Muslims, who were resident in urban areas and could not claim any substantial portion of their former estates as *khas* lands, or home farms. A number of ex-zamindars resident in the villages also were left with reduced estates, which narrowed

---

[40] Francine R. Frankel, "Problems of Correlating Electoral and Economic Variables: An Analysis of Voting Behavior and Agrarian Modernization in Uttar Pradesh," in *Electoral Politics in the Indian States*, edited by Myron Weiner and John Osgood Field, vol. 3, *The Impact of Modernization*, Delhi: Manohar, 1977.

their economic advantage over the most substantial occupancy tenants. Petty zamindars, particularly in South Bihar, who could not leave the villages to take up more lucrative occupations in the professions or commerce became "practically ordinary cultivators."[41]

The greatest beneficiaries of this economic change were cultivators in the upper two deciles of landholders: the size-classes between fifteen and fifty acres increased the area under their control by 9 percent.[42] According to one estimate about 10 percent of the total cultivated area ultimately passed from the control of the largest landlords into the hands of this intermediate size group, as the result both of zamindari abolition and the ability of the larger cultivators to redeem their holdings from usufructuary mortgages forced upon them by debts during the depression.[43] The bulk of those who benefited were drawn from among Bhumihar and Rajput caste groups, as the largest occupancy tenants before zamindari abolition, although the number of landowning households at lower size levels among the upper Sudras also slightly increased.

No less important, in some districts the ex-zamindars suffered "a great slump in what was considered a social prestige apart from the decline in financial resources."[44] After zamindari abolition, the lower castes were no longer so deferential in their behavior to castes of "twice-born" status. Under the new conditions, when occupancy tenants enjoyed virtually the same rights in their holdings as ex-intermediaries, and paid rent to the state instead of "tribute" to the landlords, the "twice-born" castes found it difficult to assert the subordination of economic position to ritual status. They had to acknowledge a new situation in which landed Sudra castes gained in social prestige as well as relative economic power. In villages, moreover, where the Yadavas or Kurmis enjoyed numerical superiority, the introduction of universal suffrage, including elections to village panchayats, made it possible for candidates from these lower castes to displace traditional Brahman and Thakur leaders.

In Uttar Pradesh, where the implementation of zamindari abolition was more thorough and less prolonged, the Thakurs lost heavily throughout the state, along with Bania, Kayastha, and Muslim zamindars, especially in the eastern districts. Brahman zamindars also sustained significant reductions in their holdings, but their position as a landowning group actually improved, for many among their numbers had been occupancy ten-

[41] Bihar, Revenue Department, Bihar District Gazetteers, *Patna*, Patna, 1970, p. 112.

[42] F. Thomasson Jannuzi, *Agrarian Crisis in India, The Case of Bihar*, New Delhi: Sangam, 1974, p. 186.

[43] Pradhan H. Prasad, "Caste and Class in Bihar," *Economic and Political Weekly*, February 1979, p. 483.

[44] Bihar, Revenue Department, Bihar District Gazeteers, *Shahabad*, Patna, 1966, p. 200.

ants prior to zamindari abolition. In the western districts, the number of owner-cultivators increased among the Jats, Ahirs (Yadavas), and Gujars, "who then became the backbone of commercial agriculture in the state, especially after the Green Revolution."[45]

As to Bihar, it is doubtful that zamindari abolition significantly augmented the area under control of the intermediate castes. Nevertheless, by reducing the relative economic gap between landowners of the Forward Castes and the Backward Classes, and ultimately forcing even Thakur landowners in the eastern districts to take up commercial agriculture, it struck at the Brahmanical life-style of the "twice-born" castes and wounded their social status.

As a result of the whole complex of changes that simultaneously undermined the ideological legitimacy, social prestige, economic strength, and monopoly political power of the Forward Castes, the demand for reservations in educational institutions and government posts raised by the Backward Classes in the late 1970s was perceived as a signal for an all-out struggle for power. An aggravating factor was that Bihar and Uttar Pradesh, (along with Orissa), were the most industrially backward states in the country. The towns offered few economic opportunities for the educated sections of the upper castes, except those in the enlarged civil services, which they still monopolized by virtue of their dominance in higher education. Similarly, entry into these positions was perceived by the Backward Classes as the only avenue for overcoming the caste disabilities that prevented them from reaching the top positions that alone could establish their equal dignity and power in society.

In Bihar, the 1969 split in the Congress party had first buoyed the hopes of the Backward Classes and later, left them embittered. Among the Forward Castes, only the Brahmans had stood solidly behind Prime Minister Indira Gandhi when senior Bhumihar and Rajput faction leaders joined the rival group. When in February 1970, Mrs. Gandhi's Congress (R) was given the opportunity to form a government, Daroga Prasad Rai Yadav was chosen chief minister. One of his first actions was to appoint a Backward Classes Commission to make reservations in educational institutions and government services for members of the Other Backward Classes. Even when the Daroga Rai ministry was toppled by another SVD coalition, the leader of the Congress Legislature party was also a Yadava.

All of this changed once Mrs. Gandhi's Congress (R) won an absolute majority of seats in 1972 (albeit with 32 percent of the vote). By this time, some Bhumihars and Rajputs started to return to the "real" Congress. Moreover, the Brahmans set out to circumvent the Backwards by building

45 Zoya Hasan (n. 17), p. 47.

up the representation of the Forwards in the Cabinet at the same time as they increased the proportion of more pliant Muslims, Scheduled Castes, and Scheduled Tribes.[46] By 1974, moreover, Charan Singh had launched the Bharatiya Lok Dal (BLD) in an alliance with seven opposition parties, including the successor to the Socialist party, the Samyukta Socialist party (SSP). In Uttar Pradesh the merger of the BKD and the SSP, whose major support base was the small farmers and lower castes in the central and eastern districts, provided Charan Singh with a wider constituency among the Backward Classes across the state.

The brief period of the national Emergency between June 1975 and March 1977 further alienated the upper Backwards. In Bihar, the Brahman prime minister, Jagannath Mishra, opposed the introduction of reservations recommended in February 1976 by the state's Backward Classes Commission. He also alarmed the Forward Castes by aggressive implementation of legislation on land ceilings, minimum agricultural wages, debt exemptions, and distribution of housesites, all of which mainly benefited Harijans and landless laborers.

The January 1977 elections to the Lok Sabha and the June 1977 elections to the state legislative assemblies therefore saw an unusual alignment in Bihar. Bhumihars and Rajputs, as well as Yadvas, supported the hastily organized Janata party that included the BLD, SSP and Jan Sangh. The Congress base shrunk mainly to its Brahman-Scheduled Caste axis. Booth-capturing was practiced on a large scale in about eighty constituencies to prevent Harijans from casting their votes for Mrs. Gandhi. The Janata in Bihar won an unprecedented 68 percent of the vote for the Lok Sabha, and a two-thirds majority of seats in the legislative assemblies of seven states, including Bihar and Uttar Pradesh.

The abrupt victory of Janata saw the unexpected emergence of the Backward Classes as an important force in the northern states. As home minister and head of the BLD, Charan Singh gained the right to select the chief ministers of three states, Bihar, Uttar Pradesh, and Haryana. It was this intervention from the center that was the proximate cause of the renewed conflict between the Backward Classes and Forward Castes.

In Bihar, the Forward Castes were unreconciled to Charan Singh's selection of Karpoori Thakur as chief minister. They were outraged at the composition of Thakur's ministry, which for the time gave the Backward

---

[46] Harry W. Blair, "Rising Kulaks and Backward Classes in Bihar," *Economic and Political Weekly*, 12 January 1980, p. 69. Two Congress ministries were formed, one in 1972, and the second in 1973. In both, the upper Backwards were kept at 23 percent while the Forwards secured the largest share of posts at 38 percent. Muslims, Scheduled Castes, and Scheduled Tribe MLAs, augmented in 1973 by a few lower Backwards, made up the remainder.

Classes the preeminent position, and their caste feelings were ignited by Thakur's announcement of a reservations policy in Bihar of 25 percent for the Other Backward Classes. Large-scale street fighting and destruction of public property by Forward Caste youth who rejected even a watered down version of the reservations policy polarized Backwards and Forwards in towns and villages throughout the state.

The most committed socialists among the leaders of the upper Backwards, like Karpoori Thakur, recognized that reservations affecting about 2,000 jobs a year could never solve the economic problems of the impoverished majority. Nevertheless, they saw in the reservations issue the potentiality for breaking down the Brahminical ideology of caste superiority that prevented the Backward Classes from commanding respect in society and the poor from consolidating their ranks, thereby keeping the majority powerless. The ultimate purpose of the Backward Classes movement, from this perspective, was the organization of the poor in a double assault on the caste system and the class structure.

The factional rivalry between the BLD and the upper caste Jan Sangh, as the other major constituent of the Janata party, prevented Karpoori Thakur from proceeding with such ambitious plans. His government was toppled in April 1979, after which a successor (Janata) government restored the Forwards to their strongest position in the state government since 1967. At the center, the Janata government lost its majority, in July 1979, after Charan Singh and his followers defected to form a rival group. Charan Singh, who briefly became prime minister as head of a tenuous coalition, lost majority support within four weeks and presided over a caretaker government until elections in January 1980.

The general elections that restored Mrs. Gandhi's political fortunes by raising her to power at the center also saw her new Congress–I party rebound in Bihar, where it won 36 percent of the vote. By contrast, Charan Singh's Lok Dal party, led by Karpoori Thakur, polled less than 17 percent. The results revealed a number of miscalculations by those leaders of the Backward Classes who believed it possible to use the reservations issue for raising political consciousness among all backward communities to mobilize the poor. On the contrary, precisely because group consciousness still operated primarily at the caste level, the Lok Dal's identification with reservations policy was effectively manipulated by the Congress–I to isolate the party. Karpoori Thakur was accused of promoting a "casteist approach" in order to strengthen the Yadavas and Kurmis, said to be nursing ambitions of becoming the "new Brahmans."

Another problem appeared at the time of the June 1980 elections to the state legislative assembly. By this time, the Lok Dal could not be sure of retaining intact its strongest support base among the Yadavas. Some leaders, concerned about political survival, joined the Congress–I. Moreover, a splinter Lok Dal (Raj Narain) set up its own Backward Caste candidates in several constituencies. Beyond this, the Janata party split again into the predominantly upper caste Bharatiya Janata party and the Janata–Jayaprakash Narayan, which appealed to the backward communities and Harijans.

For all of these reasons, the social polarization between the Forward Castes and upper Backwards, which fragmented almost all political parties, did not result in a political polarization between a party of the upper castes and a party of the Backward Classes. On the contrary, all political parties, including the Congress–I, tried to placate the Yadavas. Backward Classes candidates, running on rival party tickets, split the Backward Classes vote among them. The net result was that the Lok Dal's strength declined somewhat to less than 16 percent. By contrast, the Congress managed to win one-third of the vote and a majority of seats. Once again, the upper castes, benefiting from the divisions of the backward communities, reasserted their political power. The new Congress–I government, installed in June 1980 was headed by Jagannath Mishra.

In Uttar Pradesh the polarization between Forward Castes and Backward Classes was less pronounced, partly because the major challenge to the ruling Congress–I had been carried by a Jat leadership, which was also identified with the agrarian middle classes. Nevertheless, a similar pattern emerged in the late 1970s. After Charan Singh's nominee, Ram Naresh Yadav, announced in August 1977 a more modest reservations policy providing 15 percent of government posts for the Backward Classes, riots broke out in the eastern districts. The chief minister, who was toppled from power, was also succeeded by a more moderate Janata ministry. Meanwhile, the Congress–I made determined efforts to win back the Rajputs. During the 1980 elections, the Congress–I, following a strategy similar to the one in Bihar, built up a majority coalition to outflank the Yadavas and other Backward Classes by constructing a Brahman and Thakur alignment with the Scheduled Castes. Their task was made easier by the fragmentation of Sudra subcastes, receptivity of some Backward Class leaders to offers of party tickets that could guarantee a share of power, and the difficulty experienced by the Lok Dal in carrying out political mobilization among Backward Classes, Muslims, and Scheduled Castes with only the most meager funds.

Yet, the position in the early 1980s only appeared similar to that at the beginning of the 1970s. The Forwards gained power once again, but the caste ideology that historically legitimated their dominance had been grievously damaged. The upper castes clung precariously to power through the increasing use of corruption and coercion. Indeed, all political parties recruited their own criminal gangs, which played an indispensable role at election time, providing a crude substitute for the upper caste mobilizers who had lost their moral authority.

CONCLUSION

Any assessment of the prospects of political accommodation of the "middle" castes and classes in Indian politics must start by recognizing that the most relevant category is actually composed of the historically disadvantaged communities of the Backward Classes. The emerging competition for power between the more numerous, and in some areas increasingly affluent, subcastes among the Backward Classes, on the one hand, and the leading sections of the Forward Castes, on the other, is bound to bring new pressure on India's resilient democracy.

So far, potentially the most radical challenge to the Forward Castes by the Backward Classes have been mounted in the presumably stagnant North, whereas new groups in the South have been accommodated through politics without threatening the existing social structure. As the foregoing analysis shows, what was at stake in the South was the limited sharing of power at the state level. This sharing did not disturb the overall structure of economic inequality or disrupt established patterns of superordinate-subordinate social relations. By comparison, what is at issue in Uttar Pradesh and Bihar is the age-old privileged position of the upper castes on all fronts: in social status, economic strength, educational advantages, high-prestige occupations, and political power.

Nor is this a phenomenon likely to remain confined to the Indo-Aryan heartland. On this point, it is suggestive to read the 1980 *Report* of the Backward Classes Commission (known as the Mandal Commission). The *Report* classified 52 percent of the population as backward with respect to educational level and recruitment in government services. It used as its major criterion in defining socially and educationally backward classes the "low social position in the traditional caste hierarchy of Hindu society."[47] Significantly, it includes Muslims and members of other minority religions in this category for the first time. The majority of the commission recommended that 27 percent of all posts under the central government should be reserved for members of the Other Backward Classes (apart from reservations for Other Backward Classes in the state administrative

[47] Backward Classes Commission (B. P. Mandal, Chairman), *Report*, New Delhi: 1980, part 1, vols. 1 and 2, p. 1.

services).[48] Interestingly, the commission did not argue that reservation of a few thousand jobs for OBC candidates would elevate the condition of 52 percent of the population. At the same time, high stakes were said to ride on implementation of these recommendations.

The reasoning behind the Mandal Commission's proposals has wide support among educated sections of the Backward Classes. Because the All-India Administrative Services have been looked upon as the symbols of social prestige and political power, the "psychological spin-off" of the appointment of a Backward Class candidate as a collector or superintendent of police is said to be "tremendous." Even if the material benefits flow to one individual or to members of his family, "the entire community of that Backward Class candidate feels socially elevated."[49] More important, this transformation of social consciousness is considered the necessary first step in a more far-reaching process of social change. Whereas historically the higher castes, constituting less than 20 percent of the population, "subjected the rest to all manner of injustice," the scheme of reservation is intended to pave the way for a "new class" of beneficiaries of opportunities for social and educational advancement transforming the political system into an instrument of majority rule.

The recommendations of the Mandal Commission have yet to be taken up for consideration by the ruling Congress–I. The *Report,* moreover, is certain to meet determined opposition, perhaps including violent protest, if the Lok Sabha seriously considers its provisions. Already, in the states, such as Madhya Pradesh and Gujarat, where reservations for Backward Classes were raised sharply in professional colleges, major agitation paralyzed the government's ability to implement its policies.

The first step toward a political challenge to the position of the Forward Castes from the Backward Classes has already been taken at the national level. Just as the Justice party merged with the Self-Respect League to bring forth the Dravida Kazagham as the forerunner of the DMK, the party that brought the low castes and lower middle classes to power in Tamil Nadu, a similar experiment is being tried in the northern states. On the eve of the 1984 Lok Sabha elections, the Lok Dal rechristened itself the Dalit Mazdoor Kisan party. The DMKP's election manifesto promised to implement the recommendations of the Mandal Commission's *Report.*

[48] The commission pointed out that, according to the proportion of OBCs in the population, 52 percent of all posts under the central government should be reserved for them. However, they conceded that such a provision would go against Supreme Court judgments, which held that the total quantum of reservations, including those for the Scheduled Castes and Scheduled Tribes amounting to 22.5 percent, should be below 50 percent. Accordingly, the commission recommended reservations for OBCs at 27 percent. Ibid., p. 58.

[49] Ibid., p. 57.

This deliberate evocation of the DMK was an attempt to create an all-India constituency from among the lower castes and lower middle classes as the social base of a national opposition party or a coalition of regional parties at the center.

The outcome of the 1985 elections in the states, in which the DMKP improved its 1980 performance and emerged as the single largest opposition party in Uttar Pradesh, winning eighty-four seats, and held its own in Bihar with more than forty seats, suggests that the creation of a new pan-India category of Backward Classes may not indefinitely remain in the realm of political imagination. If a charismatic leader emerged who could appeal simultaneously to the status aspirations of the lower castes and the political ambitions of the more affluent among them, who are already educating the first generation to claim the growing privileges of the Indian middle classes, a formidable political base for a challenge to the dominant upper castes and classes could be constructed. The entry of Backward Classes into Indian politics, if they ever came close to mobilizing their more than 50 percent of the population would go far beyond what is normally considered under the rubric of political accommodation. It would involve such far-ranging changes in the distribution of power in the state and status in society that it might more aptly be characterized as the first round of a direct assault on the entire structure of privilege first put in place during the colonial period.

EIGHT

Grass-Roots Mobilization
in Indian Politics

GHANSHYAM SHAH

India is an exception among the Third World countries in that it has opted for and maintained a parliamentary system since independence. Regular elections based on adult franchise have been held during the last three and a half decades. Democracy is more, however, than routine elections at regular intervals or the balance of power among the legislative, executive, and judicial branches of government. It is a political instrument intended to build a participatory, egalitarian, and just social order, in which popular sovereignty rests with the people, and by which common men and women participate in decision-making processes to improve their socioeconomic condition and enhance their lives. The parliamentary system aims at eradicating all kinds of oppression and exploitation. It strives (or should strive) to create, maintain, and enhance conditions that protect and develop fundamental human rights, the social, cultural, and political rights enshrined in the United Nations Universal Declaration of Human Rights of 1948 and in the Directive Principles of the Indian constitution. The fathers of the Indian Constitution envisaged that a democratic political system would bring about social and economic revolutionary changes in the country. In the Constituent Assembly, Pandit Nehru said, "The first task of this Assembly is to free India through a new constitution, to feed the starving people, and to clothe the naked masses, and to give every Indian the fullest opportunity to develop himself according to his capacity."[1]

The present institutional arrangements of the political system theoretically provide scope for the expression of popular demands and grievances. These arrangements are not, however, adequate, and popular aspirations

I am grateful to Atul Kohli and Ronald Herring for useful comments and to M. R. Mac for providing valuable reference material. I thank the Centre for Education and Documentation, Bombay, for providing documentation on fishermen's movements. I also thank Harish Jariwala for typing several drafts of this paper.

[1] Quoted by Granville Austin, *The Indian Constitution: Cornerstone of A Nation*, Bombay: Oxford University Press, 1972, p. 26.

and demands are often expressed through the extraconstitutional methods of protest and mass mobilization. Direct action by the masses—particularly the oppressed section of society—is as vital to the practice of democracy as voting on election day. It is a form of political participation that helps to bend the power structure in favor of the vast majority, a majority that must not be excluded from effective political participation if the system is to survive.

India is one of the largest countries in the world, encompassing an area of 3.3 million square kilometers and supporting a population of 684 million. It is a multiethnic state, divided into twenty-three federal and nine union territories and claims 1,652 mother tongues. There are also several regional and sectarian divisions among the Indians. The Hindus, the largest religious group, comprising 83 percent of the population, are divided into several endogamous localized groups called *jatis*. In the hierarchy that characterizes the caste system, a very small number of *jatis* occupy a high social position with many *jatis* near the bottom of the social scale. Fourteen percent of the country's population occupy the lowest rank in the caste structure and have, for centuries, been treated as unclean. These Untouchables are themselves divided into various hierarchically arranged *jatis*. There are, in addition, a large number of low castes, known as backward castes, and more than seven hundred tribes, known as the Scheduled Tribes.

Seventy-seven percent of India's population live in rural areas, with agriculture as their major source of livelihood. Land distribution in India is skewed. As many as 55 percent of the cultivators are small, marginal farmers owning five acres of land or less. Together they own only 11 percent of the total cultivated land. In contrast, 57 percent of the cultivated land is owned by 13 percent of the farmers. Most of the small, marginal farmers lack even a pair of bullocks or any other necessary agricultural implements. They have no capital with which to buy improved varieties of seeds, fertilizers, and insecticides, and they are compelled to sell their produce, little if any of which is surplus, in the market to buy other commodities for their day-to-day requirements. Overall market forces are not favorable to them. They rely mainly on family labor, although occasionally they must hire labor. Some of their family members also work as agricultural laborers on others' farms.

In addition to land-owning small farmers, 27 percent of rural workers are landless agricultural laborers. Despite the growth in agricultural production, thanks to the Green Revolution, the economic condition of agricultural laborers and small, marginal farmers has been deteriorating during the last three decades. A large number of them live below the poverty line. There are, moreover, people living on the coasts and in the forests who depend on fishing and forest produce for their livelihood. The majority of these earn only meager incomes and, in addition, occupy a low social status. Thus, small and marginal farmers, landless farm laborers, forest laborers, and fishermen constitute India's rural poor.

The rural poor belong to various social, linguistic, and religious groups. A large number of them are also socially and culturally oppressed and exploited by landlords, rich farmers, and the state machinery. In terms of caste and community they belong to backward castes, Scheduled Castes and Scheduled Tribes. But caste/community and class are not coterminous. The backward castes, Scheduled Castes and Scheduled Tribes are not equally poor in all regions. Moreover, castes and tribes are not homogeneous with respect to the distribution of resources. A few of the households belonging to the backward castes, Scheduled Castes, and Scheduled Tribes are relatively well off—owning more than twenty-five acres of land with infrastructural facilities. Although they are not poor, like a vast majority of their caste/tribe brethren, they share a common inferior social status that is a binding force between the two. Economic differentiations and social homogeneity among caste and tribe members affect the nature of political mobilization.

The rural poor constitute three-fourths of the Indian population. A majority of them—between 50 and 60 percent—exercise their voting rights in elections with the hope that the elected government will enact and enforce laws to improve their social and economic conditions. At the same time they resort to collective direct action to express their aspirations and grievances. They protest against injustice and occasionally revolt against the government and the dominant local classes that exploit and oppress them. Their agitations are both localized and widespread, spontaneous and sporadic and organized. Social scientists in general and political scientists in particular have neglected the grass-roots mobilization of the deprived sections of Indian society. Studies on mobilization largely deal with electoral participation. Because only very scanty data are available for grass-roots political mobilization in the postindependence period, it is very difficult to map out the different types of direct action and political mobilizations that have taken place during this period in India. This chapter is an exploratory effort to analyze the nature of grass-roots political mobilization—particularly direct collective action of the oppressed sections of rural society and its impact on the existing institutional arrangements of the political system.

Electoral and direct action in a multiethnic society like India is centered on ethnic as well as economic issues. Because the overwhelming majority of India's poor also belong to traditionally low status groups, their mobilization around economic issues most often raises ethnic problems, or at least invokes ethnic identity and idiom. Although ethnic and economic issues are intertwined, they can be separated for the purpose of analysis. The following discussions are meant to highlight the main thrust of any particular struggle.

Ethnic Mobilization

The term "ethnic" is vague and elusive. I use it as a common denominator for different social groups based on racial, regional, linguistic, or religious identity. Broadly speaking, an ethnic group shares a common culture—language, religion, social customs, and values—and a common historical heritage—real or legendary. At the conscious or subconscious level, the members of these groups feel that their culture is different from the cultures of other groups, and this feeling of difference sustains or develops among them a sentiment of solidarity. Ethnic identity invokes a sense of "we-ness," primarily based on primordial ties, against "them"— a sense that is often, although not always, a driving force for collective political action. In India the number of ethnic groups is very large. It is beyond the scope of this chapter to examine the political mobilization of all these groups. We shall confine ourselves to only a few of the important oppressed groups. They are the Backward Classes, Untouchables, or Scheduled Castes, and the tribes, or Scheduled Tribes.

Backward Classes

The Kaka Kalelkar Commission, appointed by the government of India, identified more than three thousand castes or communities as "Other Backward Classes" (OBC) in 1956. They are "other" than the Scheduled Castes and Scheduled Tribes. Recently, the Mandal Commission (1980) calculated that 52 percent of the population—including non-Hindus—are members of "Other Backward Classes." Both the commissions used social, educational, and economic criteria for identifying "backwardness."[2]

[2] The Kaka Kalelkar Commission adopted the following criteria for considering backwardness: "(1) Low social position in the traditional caste hierarchy of Hindu society; (2) lack of general educational advancement among the major section of a caste or community; (3) inadequate or no representation in Government service; (4) inadequate representation in the field of trade, commerce and industry." *Report of the Backward Classes Commission*, vol. 1, Delhi: Government of India Press, 1955. The Mandal Commission adopted the following indicators for determining social and educational backwardness: "A. Social (i) Caste/ Classes considered as socially backward by others. (ii) Castes/Classes which mainly depend on manual labour for their livelihood. (iii) Castes/Classes where at least 25 percent females and 10 percent males above the state average get married at an age below 17 years in rural

According to the Mandal Commission, "socially and educationally backward classes are economically backward also." The commission has identified more than thirty-five hundred castes as "Other Backward Classes." Numerical size and geographical concentration of these castes vary, with some very small and scattered, and others large and concentrated. Some of them were active in politics even before independence, some have become active in recent years, and many whose numbers are small have remained unorganized and politically inactive as caste groups. The Kolis in Gujarat, the Yadavs, the Koiris, and the Kurmis in Bihar, the Kuruba and the Beela in Karnataka, the Nadars in Tamil Nadu, and the Izhavas in Kerala are some of the important backward castes that have been mobilized in politics.

Not all the backward castes enjoy equal social status in the caste hierarchy or equal economic position. The Izhavas of Kerala were treated as Untouchables until recently, as were the Nadars of Tamil Nadu. The Kolis of Gujarat also belong to lower backward castes, although they are not Untouchables, whereas the Yadavas of Bihar belong to upper backward castes. Relatively, a larger number of middle and rich peasants are found among the Yadavas than among the Kolis. We shall deal with the Kolis of Gujarat to illustrate the nature of political mobilization among the lower backward castes.

The Kolis constitute about 24 percent of the population of Gujarat and are spread throughout the state. They are known variously as Chunvaliya, Khant, Patanvadiya, Talabada, Thakore, Dharala, Gulam, Pagi, and Kotwal. There are several local groups whose social relations are confined to a few villages, and they have no associations with persons residing in other areas and having a similar group name. "Koli" is a generic term used for a group of cultivators. A majority of them in present-day Gujarat are small or marginal farmers and agricultural laborers.

Their status in the caste hierarchy is ambiguous. They are known as "half-caste," because some of the Kolis are socially related to the Rajputs,

areas and at least 10 percent females and 5 percent males do so in urban areas. B. Educational (iv) Castes/Classes where the number of children in the age group of 5–15 years who never attended school is at least 25 percent above the state average. (v) Castes/Classes where the rate of student drop-out in the age group of 5–15 years is at least 25 percent above the state average. (vi) Castes/Classes amongst whom the proportion of matriculates is at least 25 percent below the state average. C. Economic (vii) Castes/Classes where the average value of family assets is at least 25 percent below the state average. (viii) Castes/Classes where the number of families living in Kuccha houses is at least 25 percent above the state average. (ix) Castes/Classes where the source of drinking water is beyond half a kilometer for more than 50 percent of the households. (x) Castes/Classes where the number of households having taken consumption loan is at least 25 percent above the state average," *Report of the Backward Classes Commission*, vols. 1 and 2, Delhi: Government of India, 1981.

and others are close to the Bhils, an aboriginal tribe. The upper castes use the term "Koli" in a derogatory sense.[3] No historical study before the eighteenth century has so far been available that can explain the relation between the Kolis and caste Hindus. However, on the basis of studies carried out in the nineteenth century, we can speculate that the Kolis had been conquered by caste Hindu rulers and pushed into the hilly eastern region or compelled to work as agricultural laborers. The Kolis did not, however, accept their inferior position without protest. During the seventeenth century, the Moghul and Maratha rulers and their henchmen treated the Kolis as "outcastes" of society, confounding them all under the disgraceful and reproachful name "Mewasi" (robber).[4] The Kolis often retaliated against the insulting treatment they received from the upper caste Hindus, their protests varying from direct armed confrontation to the plundering of villages and pilfering of crops from the farms of Patidars, a landowning middle caste. The British government branded some of the Koli social groups as "criminals." Koli agricultural laborers have occasionally demanded higher wages and gone on strikes. In 1916, for example, the leading Kolis of Kheda district resolved to boycott their landlords. "Heavy penalties were threatened for anyone who broke this resolution. The movement spread rapidly, soon covering 240 villages in the northern part of Kheda. Outside laborers were brought in to break the strike, the British pledged their full support to the landlords."[5] Some of the Koli leaders were won over by the landlords, which caused internal dissensions. The struggle petered out.

A small section of the Kolis who improved their economic condition during the early 1910s followed a process of sanskritization, claiming Kshatriya status. Their claim was confined to submitting a memorandum to the census commissioners asking for classification as "Kshatriyas." Because their numbers were very small and localized and their overall economic condition weak in comparison to that of the dominant upper castes, they could not win over the Rajputs and other upper castes. On the eve of independence, however, their aspirations were exploited by some Rajput leaders of central Gujarat to enlarge their political base to fight the Patidars, who had then come to dominate Gujarat politics. Some of the landlords and rulers of the small native states belonging to Rajput castes

---

[3] Gujarati standard dictionary, *Vinit Jodani Kosh*, Ahmedabad, Gujarat Vidyapith, 1954, explains the designation "Koli" as "non-Aryan, or a man of lower caste." In colloquial use by upper castes, the word "Koli" is synonymous with "plunderer."

[4] See A. M. Shah, "Political System in Eighteenth Century Gujarat," *Enquiry* 1 (Spring 1964).

[5] David Hardiman, *Peasant Nationalists of Gujarat Kheda District 1917–1934*, Delhi: Oxford University Press, 1981, p. 50.

feared they would lose not only their political authority but also their ownership of land in the changed political condition. Constituting only 4 percent of the population, they realized the need for a larger numerical support in the democratic polity. They therefore formed the caste organization called Gujarat Kshatriya Sabha and recruited Kolis to broaden their base. Caste pride and sentiment were invoked through various ways among the Rajputs and the Kolis. In 1947, the Rajput leaders organized the *padyatra* that is, pilgrimage on foot, in central and north Gujarat in the traditional style and with gusto. The first team of *padyatris* consisted of twenty-two Rajputs, a symbol of Rana Pratap's army of twenty-two thousand braves. They wore the traditional Rajput uniform of saffron-colored turbans, close trousers, loose shirts, and swords and began their tour after the recital of Sanskrit *slokas* (stanzas) and worship of the sword, a symbol of power. The *padyatris* were welcomed in the villages by the local Kshatriyas—Kolis and Rajputs—with *kumkum* and *gulal* (red powder) in a traditional ceremony. The leaders of the team addressed meetings of the Kshatriyas in which they invoked the past glory of the Kshatriyas and lamented their present weakness and degraded condition. They advised them to rise and unite, and told them that otherwise they would be wiped out. "Let us remove weakness," one leader said," let us get rid of wickedness and let us remember our Kshatriya dharma; if we do so, it will not take time to acquire the position in the power structure that is our due."[6]

The Gujarat Kshatriya Sabha started a journal in 1948 with the object of developing self-consciousness among the Kshatriyas and encouraging them in writing to take their "rightful place" in politics. In order to create a sense of brotherhood among the various strata of the Kshatriyas, they were advised to greet each other whenever they met with the slogan "Jay Somnath" (Victory to Lord Somnath). Worship of "shakti," the sword, was popularized through various caste conferences and articles in the caste journal. Kshatriyas were told that bearing the sword was their birthright. Traditional festivals of the Rajputs were revived among the Kolis. The grievances of the Rajputs and Kolis of central Gujarat against the landowning Patidar caste were expressed by the sabha through various resolutions and meetings.[7] The influence of the Kshatriya Sabha was confined to central and north Gujarat. The Kolis of south Gujarat were relatively well off and did not suffer the humiliations of the Kolis in central Gujarat. Moreover, the Patidars were not a major landowning caste in

[6] *Rajput Bandhu* (Gujarati) 2 (8 December 1949).

[7] For details, see Ghanshyam Shah, *Caste Association and Political Process in Gujarat*, Bombay: Popular, 1975.

south Gujarat. Because they had different historical experiences with the Rajputs and Patidars than had the Kolis of central Gujarat, the Kolis of Saurashtra did not join the Kshatriya Sabha. For them, the Rajputs were not their allies, for they had been subjugated by them; and the Patidars were not their adversaries, for both together suffered the tyranny of the Rajputs. Hence the leaders of the sabha who were Rajputs were not acceptable to them, and the sabha's war against the Patidars did not appeal to them. Thus, although the Gujarat Kshatriya Sabha claimed to be an organization covering the whole of Gujarat, its influence was limited to central and north Gujarat.

A few leaders of the Gujarat Kshatriya Sabha thought of launching a Kshatriya party in 1948–1949, but soon realized that it would be impossible. In 1952, the sabha bargained with the Congress party, demanding party tickets for the leaders of the sabha, which declared its support for the Congress and mobilized the Kshatriyas to vote for the Congress. Justifying its decision, the sabha argued that "the economic problems of Kshatriyas are decided in accordance with policy decisions at the national level. This can only be done through a national organisation like the Congress."[8] However, a split among the leaders of the Kshatriya Sabha, with some of them supporting the Congress and some supporting opposition parties in the 1957 elections, led the Kshatriya leaders to make efforts to develop a common "political ideology" among the Kshatriyas. In 1957, the caste journal *Kshatriya Bandhu* reported, "we have seen during the last General Elections that the organisational strength for social work that we had built through the Gujarat Kshatriya Sabha was shattered owing to internal political differences. . . . In times like this, organisations which lack unity of thought cannot survive. This is clear. Hence for the sake of the organisation it is imperative that all Kshatriyas should adopt a single political ideology."[9] Although all the Kshatriya leaders even from central Gujarat did not join any one political party in subsequent elections, the organization and large numerical strength of the sabha did succeed in putting pressure on several parties in various parts of the state to give tickets to quite a number of Koli candidates in the elections. An attempt was then made to arouse caste sentiments to secure votes for the caste candidates. The Koli voters did not, however, respond positively to the caste appeal when the caste candidates did not belong to the party of their preference. The Congress–I has scored over other parties with regard to Koli candidates in the late seventies and early eighties. The strength of the Kolis increased from 10 percent in 1962 to 21 percent in 1981 in the state assem-

[8] Ibid., p. 103.
[9] Ibid., p. 115.

bly and a Koli Kshatriya from central Gujarat became the chief minister. The Congress Kolis have formed a faction within the party to keep out other factions in the struggle for power, and Koli politicians from Saurashtra and south Gujarat have grudgingly accepted the hegemony of the Kshatriya Sabha because of the organizational and manipulative skill of the sabha's leaders.

Initially, the mobilization of the Kolis led, as had the actions of many other backward castes, to a confrontation with the dominant castes. Soon after independence, the tenant and agricultural laborer Kolis whose land had been usurped by the Patidar peasants took back their land from the landlords. They believed that all the "outsiders" would leave their area, as the British had, returning the land to the "natives." Their struggle was curbed by the new government. This and subsequent confrontations between Koli agricultural laborers and the landed Patidars did not receive organized support from the Kshatriya Sabha. At the most, caste organizations passed resolutions condemning the acts of the Patidars and demanding inquiries. The leaders of the sabha visited the areas and did some relief work among the affected Kolis, and the organization made a show of its strength through meetings and public statements. It adopted the existing institutional mechanism for expressing grievances, and it confined its political activities to electoral engineering.

As dissatisfaction among the poor mounted in the seventies, various state governments granted reservations for backward castes in government jobs and educational institutions. A vast majority of the lower backward castes, however, do not possess even the minimum assets that are the prerequisites to take advantage of the reservations. Hence, the benefits have gone to the upper backward castes and certain higher backward castes like the Yadavas in Bihar. The upper strata of the backward castes are upwardly mobile and only too willing to be co-opted by the upper castes. The gap between the upper strata and the vast poor majority of the backward castes in economic level as well as life style has been widened. The poor support the members of their upper strata as caste brothers against the members of the upper castes in electoral politics, but they hesitate to make common cause with them against the high castes in their struggle on the issue of reservations. This is evident from the recent antireservation agitations in Gujarat in 1981 and 1985 that were led by the middle class of the upper and middle castes. The leaders of the backward castes in Gujarat could not mobilize the vast mass of the poor of their castes for direct collective action against the upper castes to defend the reservation. They lost the battle in Gujarat with respect to the reservation issue. In Bihar, on the other hand, a section of the Yadavas and the Kurmis who had improved their economic condition and become rich peasants took up arms against the agricultural laborers and tenants belonging to lower castes and Scheduled Castes.[10]

Scheduled Castes

The Scheduled Castes, known as "Ati-Sudras," suffer from the stigma of untouchability. Their touch, and sometimes even their shadow, is considered to be polluting to caste Hindus. They are also known as "Harijans," children of God, a term coined by Mahatma Gandhi. According to the 1981 census, there are 104 million persons belonging to Scheduled Castes. They are scattered throughout the country, with 84 percent of them living in rural areas. Most of them are landless agricultural laborers or small, marginal farmers scattered among many villages. They are also cobblers, tanners, weavers, and scavengers. A small stratum of the Scheduled Castes, however, is relatively better off, owning more than five acres of land with at least some infrastructural facilities. In the urban areas, a few of them have engaged in trade and have improved their economic condition.

The Scheduled Castes lag behind the general population in the sphere of education. Their rate of literacy is 21 percent, as against 36 percent for the country as a whole. The gap between the general population and the Scheduled Castes is particularly sharp in high school and college education.

Like many backward castes in the nineteenth and first half of the twentieth century, some of the Scheduled Castes, particularly those that had improved their economic conditions somewhat, such as the Mahars of Maharashtra, and the Jatavas of Uttar Pradesh, attempted to rise in the caste hierarchy through the process of sanskritization. They invented legends about their being Kshatriyas and adopted the sanskritic rituals and norms of the upper castes. They became vegetarians, donned sacred threads, and celebrated upper caste Hindu festivals. Some of the Scheduled Castes of Maharashtra and Kerala organized struggles during the thirties and forties to obtain temple entry. They failed to gain entry, however, and a large section of the Scheduled Castes gave up the struggle as futile and left the Hindu religion. In 1956, about three million Harijans embraced Buddhism.

Along with their struggle against social and religious disabilities, Scheduled Caste members demanded access to secular organizations. Mahars and Izhavas submitted several petitions to the government requesting the

[10] Pradip Kumar Bose, "Mobility and Conflict: Social Roots of Caste Violence in Bihar," in *Caste, Caste-Conflict and Reservation*, Centre for Social Studies, Delhi: Ajanta, 1985.

granting of reservations for positions in government and educational facilities for Scheduled Caste boys and girls. In the early 1930s, a large number of Scheduled Caste leaders rallied around the issue of separate Scheduled Caste electorates, although they gave up their demands when Gandhi began a fast unto death against them.

Dr. B. R. Ambedkar, the leader of the Scheduled Castes, formed the Independent Labour party (ILP) in 1937 with a broader base than the Scheduled Castes alone. Although it was dominated by the Mahars, the ILP claimed to be the party of the laboring class. It made an impressive show in the 1937 Bombay Legislative Assembly elections, when fifteen of its seventeen candidates won their seats. It made a poor show in the 1952 elections, when caste Hindus made up the majority of voters in every constituency. "Again and again, the Scheduled Castes Federation got out the Mahar vote in large numbers; again and again its candidates were defeated by the votes of the caste Hindu majority."[11] In 1957, the Republican party was formed on the model of the earlier ILP. In the 1962 elections, the party contested sixty-eight parliamentary seats and won three, all in Uttar Pradesh. It contested 301 assembly seats and won eleven, three in Maharashtra and eight in UP. In the subsequent elections, it made a poor show, and in time, the party split into factions. The Scheduled Castes as a group have very little opportunity to win the battle in electoral politics because they are a minority in the constituencies. Moreover, their leaders have been co-opted by different parties in an effort to gain the support of Scheduled Caste voters.

The Scheduled Castes offered *satyagrahas* demanding separate electorates before the state legislatures at Poona, Nagpur, Lucknow, and Kanpur in 1946. They also organized a *morcha* in 1965 to the Council House, Bombay, "against the single member constituency." Thus, Scheduled Castes, like other castes, organized themselves to achieve social progress and to protest against oppression by landlords, police, and other government officers. A number of scattered and spontaneous agitations were launched by the Scheduled Castes during the postindependence period, demanding higher wages, distribution of land, and the cessation of atrocities inflicted by landlords. For instance, two massive land *satyagrahas* were offered in Maharashtra in 1954 demanding distribution of wasteland to the landless Harijans. There were in addition, a number of Scheduled Caste sponsored land grab movements in Maharashtra, U.P., and Bihar in the mid-sixties. Confrontations between Scheduled Caste agricultural laborers and upper landowning classes have been frequent in

[11] Lelah Dushkin, "Scheduled Caste Politics," in *The Untouchables in Contemporary India*, edited by Michael Mahar, Tucson: The University of Arizona Press, 1972, p. 198.

U.P., Bihar, Andhra, Tamil Nadu, and Maharashtra. Various demands have been put forward during the last decade that include issues related to identity, economic injustice suffered, and due recognition of the contribution made by Dr. Ambedkar, the Scheduled Caste leader, as a framer of the constitution of India. These demands include 1) a portrait of Dr. Ambedkar as "Father of the Indian Constitution" to be put on the walls of the central hall of the Parliament; 2) a change of the name of Marathawada University to "Dr. Ambedkar University"; 3) the creation of Dalistan for the safety and security of Dalits; 4) the giving of the nation's land to the tillers; 5) the awarding of idle and wasteland to landless laborers; 6) an adequate distribution of grains and control over rising prices; 7) improvement of the situation of slum dwellers; 8) full implementation of the Minimum Wages Act of 1948; 9) an extension of Scheduled Caste privileges to Scheduled Caste members who have embraced Buddhism; 10) the cessation of the harassment of the depressed classes; and 11) full justice under the Untouchability Offences Act.[12]

With the change in market structure in the postindependence period and the rise in education among small sections of Harijans, small entrepreneurs and a white-collar middle class have emerged among the Scheduled Castes. These have become militant and call the Scheduled Castes the "Dalits," that is, a poor and exploited class. Imitating the Black Panthers of America, they have formed the Dalit Panthers, a militant organization of Scheduled Castes. Dalit poets of Maharashtra, Gujarat, and Karnataka have developed Dalit literature, a revolt against the mainstream literature, which has purportedly failed to depict the problems and agonies of the oppressed. The increasing number of atrocities against the Scheduled Castes find their echo in Dalit literature, "which contained intimations of revolt." A number of Dalit journals have appeared for ventilating the grievances of the Untouchables.

Like the elite of the backward castes, the elite of the Scheduled Castes have been won over and co-opted by the Congress and other parties for electoral politics. The central and state governments have launched welfare programs for the benefit of the Scheduled Castes. These programs and policies have not, however, improved the condition of the small, marginal farmers and agricultural laborers. Untouchability in one form or another still persists, although it is less prevalent in urban areas, and atrocities against Harijans have increased. In 1978 the number of atrocities was 15,053, nearly double the 8,860 reported in 1974.[13] In some cases, the

[12] See Eleanor Zelliot, "Learning the Use of Political Means: The Mahars of Maharashtra," in Caste in Indian Politics, edited by Rajni Kothari, Delhi: Orient Longman, 1970, pp. 29–69.

[13] Dilip Hiro, The Untouchables of India, London: Minority Rights Group, 1982.

Harijans have fought back. They retaliated in Bombay city in 1972, Marathawada in 1979, and Gujarat in 1981 and 1985, although they suffered more casualties than did the caste Hindus.[14] They increasingly join hands with other sections of the rural poor to protect their interests and resist the oppression to which they have been subjected.

Scheduled Tribes

According to the 1981 census, 51 million persons, or 7 percent of the total population, are members of Scheduled Tribes, known also as Adivasis. They can be divided into two categories: frontier tribes and non-frontier tribes. The frontier tribes are those that inhabit the northeast frontier states—Arunachal Pradesh, Assam, Meghalaya, Manipur, Mizoram, Nagaland, and Tripura. Except for Assam, all these states are on an international border with either Burma, China, or Bangladesh. They therefore occupy a special position in the sphere of national politics. They contain 11 percent of the total tribal population. The remaining 89 percent of the Scheduled Tribes are distributed over most of the states, although they are concentrated in large numbers in Madhya Pradesh, Orissa, Rajasthan, Bihar, Gujarat, Dadra Nagar Haveli, and the Laccadive Islands. There are more than seven hundred tribes. Some are very large, running into several thousands, and some are small, having fewer than one hundred members.

Only 16 percent of the population of Scheduled Tribes were literate in 1981. As many as 97 percent reside in rural areas. They live in hilly tracts and forests but are no longer isolated from the market forces and the administrative and political structure of the country. Their main source of livelihood is still agriculture and forest products. The land of the tribal areas is rocky and without irrigation facilities. The majority of the Adivasis (about 80 percent) are small, marginal farmers having less than 5 acres of unirrigated land. Many of them work in forests during the lean season as laborers in various types of work such as timber-cutting, charcoal making, and plantation labor. Thirty-three percent of Scheduled Tribe workers are agricultural laborers, although not all of them are landless.

A few tribals forming a small stratum own more than 5 acres of land per household. They can be called middle or rich farmers, particularly those who also have infrastructural facilities to increase agricultural production. A few of them produce surplus for sale in the market. As a result

[14] See S. P. Punalekar, "Caste Ideology And Class Interests: Reflections on Violence in Marathawada Region," and Pradip Kumar Bose, "Social Mobility and Caste Violence: A Study of the Gujarat Riots," in *Caste, Caste-Conflict and Reservation* (n. 10).

of increased education and the reservation of jobs in government offices, a tiny middle class has emerged among the Scheduled Tribes. The members of this class are educated and employed in white-collar jobs in government offices, schools, semigovernment organizations, and industries. There are also among them petty traders, contractors, and self-employed professionals such as lawyers, engineers, and doctors. However, not all of those who acquire school and college educations can find office jobs. They join the army of the unemployed with the Scheduled Castes and others.

There were a number of tribal revolts against the British administration and against moneylenders and nontribal landlords during British rule. Many of the struggles were messianic movements led by tribal leaders who used religious idioms and symbols to mobilize the tribals against economic exploitation and the penetration of alien administrations. Some of these struggles subsided, whereas others continued and have taken the form of movements. According to one survey, there were 36 tribal movements at different stages in different parts of the country in 1976.[15] A few of them were revivalist movements, aiming at reviving tribal culture, but a majority of the movements dealt with economic and political issues. These latter can be divided into 1) movements for political autonomy; 2) agrarian and forest-based movements; and 3) middle class movements. We call them tribal movements only because the participants were tribals who perceived that their struggle was against nontribals rather than against exploiters per se.

During the last three decades, tribals in various parts of the country have launched movements demanding separate states either within or outside the Indian union. The tribals of the northeast frontier, particularly the Nagas, have repeatedly demanded a state for the Nagas outside the Indian union. The Naga National Council (NNC) formed in 1946 demanded a separate electorate for the Nagas and local autonomy for the Nagas within Assam, a state of free India. After a few months, they changed their stand and demanded an autonomous state with cofederation status with the Indian union. Just before independence, in May 1947, the NNC demanded that an interim government for the Naga people should be set up for ten years under "the guardian power" of the Indian government with full legislative, judicial, and executive powers, except defence, after which they would choose their own government. An extremist group of the Nagas went further and demanded a Naga sovereign state. On the eve of independence, the Nagas expressed their apprehension that the Indians, that is, the caste Hindus, would introduce their laws and customs to supersede the customary laws of the tribals. The NNC conducted a plebiscite in

---

[15] K. S. Singh, *Tribal Movements in India*, 2 vols., Delhi: Manohar, 1983.

1951 to ascertain whether the Nagas would like to join the Indian union or form an independent Naga state. The Nagas boycotted the first general election in 1952 as they would have nothing to do with the union government or the state government in Assam. In 1954, the NNC announced the formation of the Hongkin government. It was called Khunk Kautang Ngeukhum, that is, the People's Sovereign Republic of Free Nagaland, often referred to as the Naga Federal Government (NFG). In 1956, an elaborate structure for this government, with a parliament, president, ministers, and army, was set up.

The government of India used armed force against the Naga rebels and repressed the secessionist activities. The rebels' retaliation resulted in many casualties. Some of the NNC leaders went underground and some, who were against violent activities, left the organization. The Naga Peace Organizing Committee was formed in 1957. With the efforts of the Naga leaders and the Indian government, peace was restored and the first Naga People's Convention was called. It demanded that the Naga Hills district and the Tuersand district should be merged and the new unit called "Naga Hills and Tuersang Area" should be formed. The government accepted the convention's demand and the new unit came into existence in 1957. In 1963, to satisfy the political aspirations of the Nagas, a separate state called Nagaland was formed. Simultaneously, the government conducted several rounds of talks with the underground Naga leaders. In 1975 in the Shillong talks, the Nagas agreed to "accept the Indian Constitution, give up violence and surrender arms." The government of India suspended the operation of the Unlawful Activities Act by which the NNC, the NFG, and the Naga Federal Army (NFA) were outlawed. Several underground rebels laid down arms. In the 1978 elections, over 80 percent of the Naga voters exercised their voting rights. For the time being, peace has been restored in Nagaland.[16]

Not all the Nagas, however, have abandoned the demand for an independent Nagaland. Although the government of India has spent several hundred million rupees for the development of Nagaland, the development has not benefited all sections of Naga society equally. Unemployment among the Nagas has increased. Such a situation is favorable to those Naga rebels who have not laid down their arms. They disapprove of the Shillong agreement and are still working for the achievement of an independent Nagaland. Although the NNC is not particularly powerful, new groups of young persons have become active. One such group is the

[16] For details, see V. K. Anand, *Conflict in Nagaland*, Delhi: Chanakya, 1980; Udayon Mishra, "The Naga Question," *Economic and Political Weekly*, 8 April 1978, pp. 618–624; and Ghanshyam Shah, *Minorities and Nation Building: A Case of Muslims and Scheduled Tribes in India*, Banaras: Banaras Hindu University, 1983.

National Socialist Council of Nagaland (NSCN). Its leaders are Thungalin Muivah and Isak Chishi Swu, who received their training in China and are now based in Burma. The NSCN has gone further than the NNC in two respects. One, it stands for a greater Nagaland consisting of Manipur, Arunachal Pradesh, Nagaland, Assam, and also that part of Burma where the Nagas reside. Two, in addition to political independence, its programs have an economic content. It attacks exploitation of Nagas by Nagas. The manifesto of the NSCN asserts that "Indian capital and Indian nationals" have made inroads into Nagaland and created a "comprador elite," or a class of "reactionary traitors," in Nagaland. It asks the Nagas to fight against the Indian forces indefinitely and appeals to Nagas to "ask not what the maker has in store for us. We have chosen Nagaland and her freedom forever; we will never part with them. . . . it is the war we have to win. . . . praise the lord. We hold promises of history."[17]

The NSCN has continued its armed struggle. There are four other groups: the People's Liberation Army (PLA), the People's Revolutionary party of Kangleipak (PREPAK), the Red Army of PREPAK and its armed wing; and the Red Army. Recently the Indian government has banned these groups. The Disturbed Areas Act has been extended along the border of Nagaland and Arunachal Pradesh, so that the Indian army can operate unfettered in the area, arresting, interrogating, and even raiding the homes of suspected insurgents. The Indian government has also sought the cooperation of the Burmese government in wiping out the insurgent groups operating on the India-Burma border.[18]

Some other tribes in the frontier region also launched "separatist" political movements in the 1960s. In 1963, a number of Kukichin tribes of the Mizo hills, now identified as the Mizo tribe, demanded a separate state for the Mizos outside the Indian union. They asserted that the Mizos differed from the Indians in their religion and that the Hindu Indians were against Christianity and therefore not interested in the prosperity of the Mizo Hills. The Mizo National Army was formed, which resorted to armed struggle. The Indian government, using a mixture of cooperation and oppression to control the Mizo insurgency, signed a peace accord in 1976 with the rebel Mizos. Many underground Mizos surrendered their arms, and some of the rebel leaders have been co-opted by the Congress party.[19] Notwithstanding the peace accord, repression, and co-option, the demand for an independent Mizoram has been frequently revived by var-

[17] *Probe India* 4 (September 1982).
[18] *India Today*, 30 November 1985.
[19] B. B. Goswami and D. P. Mukherjee, "The Mizo Political Movement," in *Tribal Movements in India* (n. 15), vol. 1, pp. 129–150.

ious sections of the Mizos. The Mizo Hills are treated by the Indian government as a "disturbed area."[20]

The nonfrontier tribes do not ask for independent states outside the Indian union; however, many of them have demanded separate districts or states within the union. The Jharkhand movement is one such movement. It began in the late 1920s, when a few educated Christian tribals of the Chota Nagpur region of the present Bihar state organized the Unnati Samaj in 1928. Later, in 1938, the Adivasi Mahasabha was formed. It had as its main objectives statehood for Jharkhand, the area that includes Chota Nagpur and the Santhal Parganas, and the protection of the tribals against the exploitive tactics of the *dikus*, outsiders. Both Christians and non-Christians joined the sabha, although the former dominated the organization. During the 1940s, the sabha supported the Congress party. It demanded, without success, representation of the tribals in the Bihar Pradesh Congress Committee and its working committee. It also demanded the reservation of seats for the local tribals for admission to higher education and employment. The sabha pleaded that "only Chota Nagpurias should be given employment in the industries of the region. It was made clear that fulfilment of these needs and demands would decide the question of Chota Nagpur—whether it would remain with Bihar or be separated from it."[21]

In 1949 the Jharkhand party was formed. It fought the first general elections in 1952 and emerged as the major opposition party in the state. It also made an impressive performance in the 1957 elections, capturing twenty-five seats in the state assembly. Its influence declined, however, in the 1962 elections. The party merged with the Congress in 1963, with its members hoping that they could put pressure on the government and thus succeed in securing a Jharkhand state through working within the Congress party. Later, on the initiative of the Jharkhand party leader, the Birsa Seva Dal was organized in 1967. It took up the cause of tribal students and tried to see that tribal boys and girls gained admission to schools and colleges and received their scholarships on time.[22]

[20] The various clauses under the Assam Maintenance of Public Order Act of 1953, the Assam Disturbed Areas Act of 1955, the Armed Forces (Special Powers) Act of 1958, as amended by the Armed Forces (Assam and Manipur) Special Powers (Amendment) Act of 1972, empower a virtual carte blanche to the army to conduct search and destroy operations, to enter private premises and search them, to arrest individuals without warrant, and even to shoot and to kill. See Amritha Rangasami, "Mizoram: Tragedy of Our Own Making," *Economic and Political Weekly*, 15 April 1978, pp. 653–662. As the book goes to press, Rajiv Gandhi has reached a new accord with Laldenga that will result in the creation of Mizoram as a state of the Indian union and Laldenge as its first chief minister.

[21] K. L. Sharma, "Jharkhand Movement In Bihar," *Economic and Political Weekly*, 10 January 1976, pp. 37–43.

[22] Ibid.

As a result of the rise in unemployment among the educated and the fast deteriorating economic condition of the urban and rural tribal workers in the Chota Nagpur industrial belt, a militant tribal organization was formed in 1973 known as the Jharkhand Mukti Morcha (JMM). Unlike the earlier movements, it does not represent tribals alone but takes all Jharkhandis—the local people who have settled there for generations—into its fold. Its main objectives are to form a separate Jharkhand state to end the exploitation of local tribals and Harijans by nontribals and to give preferential treatment to a large number of the tribals in government offices and industries. The leaders of the JMM argue that, although their region is rich, the local people are poor because they have been exploited by outside landlords and capitalists. A. K. Roy, one of the leaders of the JMM, wrote that "Darkness in the midst of light is Jharkhand. . . . The area contains almost all the steel plants—Bokaro, Rourkela, Jamshedpur, all the power plants of the Damodar Valley project and the Hirakund Dam of Orissa. There is no dearth of development but (they are) only at the cost of the people there. Industries displace them, dams drown them, afforestation starves them."[23] The JMM has launched a movement to recover the land that tribals, Harijans, and poor Muslims of the region have lost to landlords and moneylenders. At the same time, the JMM has undertaken programs for cultural revivalism to strengthen the bond uniting the various tribal groups. Its demands include that school instruction be in the Santhali language and that holidays be declared for festivals celebrated in Jharkhand.

In the course of the struggle on various issues, the economic differentiations among the tribals have come to the surface. The better-off strata of the JMM supporters have opposed the Communist section of the JMM, raising the slogan, "the green flag (the JMM flag) cannot go with the red flag (the Marxist coordination committee flag)."[24] One of the powerful leaders of the JMM joined the Congress party in 1980. However, both the right and left wings of the JMM are active in attempting to carve out a Jharkhand state consisting of fifteen districts that include seven districts from Bihar, two from Madhya Pradesh, three from Orissa, and three from West Bengal.[25]

Thus, the Jharkhand movement, which was originally a tribal movement against nontribals, now includes all the nontribals of the region. It has become a regional movement centered on economic issues. The tribals in the area have also launched agitations over several other economic issues, which we shall discuss in the next section.

[23] A. K. Roy, "Jharkhand: Internal Colonialism," *Frontier* 14 (24 April 1982).
[24] Hiranmay Dhar, "Split in Jharkhand Mukti Morcha," *Economic and Political Weekly*, 2 August 1980, pp. 1299–1300.
[25] Ghanshyam Shah (n. 7).

Mobilization on Economic Problems

In this section, we shall examine political mobilization around economic issues in rural India. We shall deal mainly with the collective action of agricultural laborers, poor peasant-tenants, sharecroppers, small and marginal farmers, and other poor sections of rural society such as forest dwellers and fishermen. Although there are many common issues on which agricultural laborers and poor peasants together launched struggles, some struggles have been primarily confined to the laborers alone.

laborers and peasants

Agricultural Laborers

Landless agricultural laborers, who constitute 25 percent of the work force, belong mainly to the Scheduled Castes, backward castes, Scheduled Tribes, and Muslim community. Their absolute number is around 55 million. They are unorganized except in Kerala and in some pockets of Tamil Nadu. They have nothing but their labor to sell for their survival, and most of them are able to find work for about 180 days in a year. On the average, they are paid Rs. 4 per day for agricultural operations. Although all the state governments have enacted and revised the Minimum Wage Act, it is rarely enforced. In addition to these casual laborers, a few laborers work on a yearly basis and are attached to one master. Their wages are lower than those earned by casual laborers, although their jobs are secure and they get other perquisites such as cloth and shelter. At the same time they are at the beck and call of the master, and they work more than thirteen to fourteen hours a day. A few agricultural laborers are bonded to the master and work for him against the debt incurred for marriage or other day-to-day expenses. Some of these bonded laborers work for the same master for several years or, in a few cases, for life. They live a wretched life. The condition of female agricultural laborers is even worse. In several regions, landlords enjoy customary rights over the wives and daughters of their laborers. They are "taken as common property by the rich landlords, to be thrashed, toyed with, raped, offered to friends as a sign of 'hospitality'. . . . Not only [have] the pleasure-seekers made sport of them but the police [have] behaved the same way when crying, crestfallen women [have] reached the police station to complain."[26]

The agricultural laborers are unorganized, subdued, and fear-striken. Generally they suffer the tyranny of the landlords and the rich or middle peasants who have prospered during the postindependence period. Occasionally they revolt. Most of these revolts are sporadic and spontaneous reactions to immediate provocations. The reasons for provocation vary

[26] Anjali Despande, "Bihar Landless Fight Back," *Mainstream* 20 (17 December 1981).

and may include payment of wages lower than those stipulated by the Minimum Wages Act, excessive work, harrassment and beating, the removal or burning of workers' huts, molestation or rape of their women, and murder of a laborer by the landlords, farmer employers, or their henchmen. The laborers may retaliate by killing the landlords and their *goondas*, by destroying crops and other property, including tractors and other agricultural implements, or by refusing to work. Many of the revolts, though not all, are localized, unorganized, unplanned, and are largely guided by impulse. Their unity is eroded by the landed class by bribing, flattering, and intimidating the leaders. The state machinery invariably works against the laborers. Some laborers are arrested and others beaten by the police to spread terror. A few are bribed and flattered. The revolts subside.

Most of these localized revolts challenge the local power structure but make no sustained efforts to change it. A few of the revolts continue for longer periods resulting in longer-lasting struggles against the landed class. This is possible because of the intervention of a number of ideologically varied voluntary groups and political parties, some of which work among the agricultural laborers. Among these groups are the Gandhian organizations. The Gandhian organizations do not all have an identical approach to the problems of the agricultural laborers and the conflict between the laborers and the landed class. What is common among them is that they call themselves "Gandhians," eschew violence, ignore the class nature of the conflict, and hesitate to challenge the power structure of the state. The Halpathi Seva Sangh of south Gujarat and the Chatra Yuva Sangharsh Vahini of Bodh Gaya in Bihar are illustrations of Gandhian organizations of different approaches engaged in the mobilization of agricultural laborers. The Halpatis, or the Dublas, are one of the tribes in south Gujarat. Almost all of them are agricultural laborers, and in the past, some of them were bonded laborers. During the 1920s, some Gandhian workers started a school for the children of the Halpatis, but their efforts were obstructed by the landowning class. They also tried to persuade the landlords to free the Halpatis from bondage and to raise their wages, but without success. Later, in 1961, Gandhian workers formed the Halpati Seva Sangh (HSS) for the uplift of the Halpatis. The activities of the HSS have included educational activities—basic literacy and vocational training—legal and medical aid, the encouragement of social and cultural activities, temperance advice, the construction of huts and wells, and pressure for the implementation of the Minimum Wages Act.[27] Occasionally the HSS has organized strikes of laborers demanding higher

---

[27] William Ekka and A. K. Danda, "The Halpati Movement among the Dublas of South Gujarat," in *Tribal Movements in India*, (n. 15) vol. 2, pp. 273–283.

wages. Although these strikes have raised the level of militancy among the laborers, the primary concern of the leaders of the HSS has been to keep the conflict under control. They believe in class collaboration and peaceful negotiations and have tried to pacify the militants among the Halpatis. Jan Breman observes, "The HSS advocated higher wages for the landless proletariat. But when agricultural labourers go on strike somewhere to reinforce their claims, the social workers intervene in order to prevent rising tensions and to reach a compromise. Self-respect and class-consciousness are not taught. On the contrary, the organisation does not aim at making the Halpatis capable of standing up for themselves, aware of their exploitation and oppression, but envisages their adjustment to the social system without any fundamental change in their dependence."[28] Consequently, the HSS has remained primarily a welfare organization, although the laborers on their own resort to strikes and protests against low wages and harassment by the landed class. Spontaneous confrontations between the Halpatis and the landowning class are common in this region.

In 1978, the Chatra Sangharsh Yuva Vahini (CSYV) of Bihar launched a struggle against the Matha, the Hindu monastery of Bodha Gaya, which illegally holds 12,000 acres of land. The CSYV has been organizing meagerly paid agricultural laborers working on Matha land for the last several decades. In 1978, the association organized demonstrations of laborers, demanding the distribution of the land to the workers cultivating it. In retaliation, the Matha authority burned two agricultural laborers alive to teach them a lesson. The laborers became more militant, organized a procession, and demonstrated before the police stations to register their protest against the indifferent attitude of the authorities. The struggle continued. In thirty-two villages, laborers declared a strike and no one was allowed to plough the land. In 1980 laborers grabbed about 2,000 acres of Matha land and cultivated it. However, with the support of the state machinery, the laborers were not allowed to take away the harvest. The laborers launched a *satyagraha*, retaliating with nonviolent means against the repression of the state, which had killed a number of men and women among the laborers. The leaders were arrested.[29] Because the CSYV does not have an organization outside the area, the movement has so far remained confined to Gaya district. The aspirations of the CSYV, led mainly by the urban middle class, have been frustrated. After a continuous struggle for five years a lull prevails. The laborers are, however, still militant

[28] Jan Breman, "Mobilisation of Landless Labourers: Halpatis of South Gujarat," *Economic and Political Weekly*, 23 March 1974, pp. 489–496.
[29] Manimala, "Bodh Gaya Andolan" (Hindi) *Sangharsha-Rachana*, Patna: Lokayan, Gram Vikas Sansthan, 1981.

and occasionally protest against the government as well as against the Matha.

There are some nonparty Marxist groups also working among the laborers. Several of these have been working in Tamil Nadu and Andhra Pradesh among the Harijan landless laborers since 1974. They have been inspired by the Brazilian leader Paulo Freire's approach in developing "conscientization" among the oppressed, and have tried to develop consciousness with regard to the socio-economic structure and the cultural reality that keeps the oppressed subjugated. They have further encouraged these laborers to wage struggles to change their social reality. The activists identify themselves with the oppressed and are committed to social transformation through political struggle. For them, conscientization is a way of autonomous creation open to the masses themselves. They expect that it will develop hope among the oppressed masses "for their gradual internal transformation, cultural as well as economic, and for their democratic organisation and, eventually, for their taking possession of power."[30] With this approach, a group of Christian youths formed the Rural Community Development Association (RCDA) in Tamil Nadu in 1974. The RCDA concentrated its efforts for four years among the Harijan agricultural laborers in the Chitamoor area of Chingleput district of Tamil Nadu. They selected Chitamoor for its large concentration of Harijans (79 percent of the population as compared with the national percentage of 14 percent) and for the fact that the laborers there were brutally treated by the caste-Hindu landlords. The RCDA thought that such a situation would strategically help them to build a labor movement combining caste and class consciousness. To some extent the RCDA succeeded in organizing the laborers and launching several strikes demanding higher wages. In 1977, the leaders of the RCDA formed another organization, the Rural Harijan Agricultural Development Association with a membership of 3,000. The association launched several struggles related to economic issues dealing with wages and social issues related to untouchability.[31] During these years, the activists realized that their concentration on the Harijans alone detrimentally divided the agricultural laborers between Harijans and non-Harijans. They therefore formed organizations that included agricultural laborers as well as small, marginal farmers who depend primarily on agricultural labor to earn their livelihood. One of these organizations is the Association for the Rural Poor (ARP) working in Sathyavedu taluka of Andhra Pradesh. The ARP came into existence in

[30] Van der Weid and Guy Poitevin, *Roots of a Peasant Movement*, Poona: Subhada-Saraswat, 1981.
[31] Ibid.

1980 and has so far covered eighty villages, although it has concentrated on thirty-four. The ARP has adopted several methods for conscientizing the rural poor. Its animators build rapport with the rural poor and talk with them in their language and idiom. They explain to them the village power structure and the causes for their exploitation. The association also runs literacy or adult education classes, not just to impart the three Rs, but to create self-consciousness among the exploited to fight against injustice. The purpose of this program

> is to prepare them in the process of reflection and action to see the contradictions between their existence and consciousness and resist against the false slogans, myths and patronage of the dominant socio-cultural and socio-political groups, which keep them under fear, ignorance, despair, powerlessness, debts, hunger and bondage. This method does not prescribe any pseudo-revolutionary ideology but it enables (the activists) to analyse the historicity of revolutions based on ideologies and compare them with the present Indian political scenario. This programme of literacy will break the narrow shell of silence and bring out the revolutionary potential of the oppressed class to become militant for creative and concrete action towards restructuring society with new values of self-respect, dignity and common brotherhood.[32]

The ARP has developed cultural programs that include dramas and songs to depict the condition of the poor and to mobilize them for action against their exploiters. The drama is generally divided into four stages. The first stage presents caricatures of the oppressed and the oppressors. The second stage demonstrates how people can, and should, come together to organize themselves on some economic issues. The third stage shows an actual strike by the people to fight against the oppressors. The last stage concludes with the promotion of the people's movement in which all the poor persons join. In the course of these programs liberation songs are sung in chorus. These songs appeal to the rural poor to unite and fight against injustice.

The ARP organized twenty-six struggles in Sathyavedu taluka between 1982 and 1984 demanding higher wages. It launched agitations when agricultural laborers were harrassed or one of their women raped or molested by landlords. It organized processions and *dharana* (sit-ins) for its demands. The ARP has formed village action committees of the village

[32] Ghanshyam Shah and Sujatha de Magry, "Association of Rural Poor," mimeo., Surat: Centre for Social Studies, 1984.

poor, called *sangama*. It has also often lent support to the leftist parties in organizing struggles of the poor.[33]

The leftist parties—the undivided Communist party of India (CPI) until 1964 and now the CPI, the Communist party of India–(Marxist) (CPI[M]), and the Communist party of India–(Marxist-Leninist) (CPI[ML]), the Socialist party, Sanyukta Socialist party (SSP) and Praja Socialist party (PSP)—have mobilized the agricultural laborers for direct action in electoral politics in various parts of the country. Their main strength is found in Kerala, Tamil Nadu, Andhra Pradesh, Punjab, Bihar, and West Bengal. Although the Kisan Sabha was active in mobilizing peasants in the preindependence period, it did not take up the issues of agricultural laborers. The original CPI, however, organized laborers in some parts of Kerala, Tamil Nadu, and Maharashtra. In Kerala the first agricultural laborers' union was formed in 1940. Communist activists belonging to the urban middle class stayed with and organized the laborers, who were dissatisfied with their condition and occasionally protested against the tyranny of the landlords. The urban industrial trade union workers in some parts extended their support to agricultural laborers in their struggle.[34] When economic conditions of agricultural laborers deteriorated further after the war, as prices of essential commodities rose, the laborers demanded higher wages. By and large, these protests were sporadic and spontaneous, but in some places they received support from the Kisan Sabha and the workers belonging to the CPI. The peasants of Telangana of Andhra Pradesh and the agricultural laborers of the Punnapra and Vayalur areas of Kerala, where the CPI was strong, responded to the call of the Communists for an armed revolt in 1946. Several persons from this area left their homes, set up camps, and started preparations for an uprising. The government immediately suppressed the movement, shooting several of the rebels.[35]

Similarly, the Varlis of Umbargaon taluka in Maharashtra struck work in 1944 when the harvesting season began and demanded higher wages of 12 annas per day as against 2 annas per day for agricultural and forest work. The strike was a spontaneous outburst although it was encouraged by a government servant who asked the people "not to do forced labour and to demand higher wages." The strike continued for two months and then fizzled out, for the strikers did not receive support from outside and their capacity to survive without work was very limited. However, the Kisan Sabha organized its conference in the area in 1945. The leaders of

[33] Ibid.
[34] A. V. Jose, "Trade Union Movement Among Agricultural Labourers in Kerala: The Case of Kuttand Region," mimeo., Ulloor: Centre for Development Studies, 1979.
[35] Ibid.

the sabha persuaded the Varlis to attend the conference. The leaders of the conference spoke against self-tenure and forced labor and urged the Varlis to resist their oppressors. The conference formulated the following slogan: "Do not cultivate the private land of the landlord unless he pays in cash the daily wages of Annas 12. Do not render any free service to the landlord. Resist him if he assaults you. You must all unite."

Under the leadership of the Kisan Sabha, the Varlis launched a strike in 1945 and demanded higher wages. The landlords and the police tried to crush the strike. Five laborers were killed and several injured in police firing, but the resistance continued. Consequently, the landlords had to meet the Varlis' demands. Such struggles provided a foothold for the CPI organization,[36] although, for a few years in the early 1950s, the CPI was banned by the government. During the last thirty years the Communist and Socialist parties have organized a number of strikes of agricultural laborers demanding higher wages and the abolition of forced labor. In the 1960s they also demanded distribution of surplus land to landless agricultural laborers. Most of these parties have formed trade unions. The CPI formed the Bharatiya Khet Mazdoor Union (BKMU) in 1968. The CPI(M) formed the All India Agricultural Workers Union (AIAWU) at the national level in 1981. The local leftist unions organize struggles for higher wages and other benefits. They are very strong in Kerala, where the unions have succeeded not only in raising wages but also in reducing working hours and preventing the mechanization of agricultural operations. The BKMU organized a "massive rally" of more than 300,000 agricultural laborers before the Parliament in New Delhi in 1981. The main slogans of the rally were: "We want land. We want work. We want food and shelter. We want atrocities on us to end."

The rally submitted the following list of demands to the prime minister: 1) stop atrocities; 2) implement land reforms and distribute surplus land; 3) enforce the Minimum Wage Act and enact central legislation for agricultural workers; and 4) provide houses and house sites. The agricultural laborers' unions have also organized demonstrations at the state level, particularly in Kerala, Tamil Nadu, and West Bengal. The non-left parties, the Congress, the Bharatiya Janata party, (BJP), the Dravida Munnetra Kazagham (DMK), the All India Dravida Munnetra Kazagham (AIDMK), and so forth, have also organized unions of agricultural laborers. These unions concentrate mainly on welfare activities rather than struggles. Both the CPI and CPI(M), the Socialist parties, and all the non-left parties mobilize the agricultural laborers in elections.

[36] S. V. Parulekar, "The Struggle of 1946," in *Peasant Struggles In India*, edited by A. R. Desai, Delhi: Oxford University Press, 1979, pp. 583–592.

The CPI(ML), however, which is divided into several factions popularly known as Naxalites, does not participate in electoral politics. In fact, it appeals to its followers to keep away from elections, which perpetuate the feudal capitalist structure. The number of Naxalite groups has increased during the last decade. The People's War party (PWP) in Andhra Pradesh came into existence in 1972 and launched a movement in the Karimnagar area on the issue of distributing government wastelands seized by landlords. After 1978, the PWP also undertook to mobilize the agricultural laborers and poor peasants around some social issues. It formed the "praja panchayat," that is, the people's court, in the villages to settle disputes prevailing there. The PWP and other similar groups have developed liberation songs and dramas to mobilize the masses. The Jana Natya Mandali is led by Gaddar, a singer-dancer who has become a legendary figure in Andhra villages. He renders the bitter lives of the poor, their aspirations and hope of a new society, into song and dance. His performances attract huge crowds from among the agricultural laborers and poor peasants. The influence of the JNM can be gauged from the fact that the police department is now training a cultural troupe of its own to counter the Naxalites with songs about mythological themes and about the success of the Twenty Point Program.[37] The police and landlords have used force and have killed militant laborers in so-called encounters, or jailed them, often without trial, for months. Notwithstanding the repression, struggles of laborers against the rural rich are increasing, resulting in confrontations between the two in many parts of the country.

Poor Peasant Mobilization

The Telangana insurrection on the eve of independence was the first major and widespread peasants' struggle. It began in the middle of 1946 and continued until 1951 in the Telangana region of the present Andhra Pradesh, then ruled by the Nizam of Hyderabad. Agricultural laborers and poor, middle, as well as rich peasants participated in the struggle, although the former two were the backbone of the movement and participated from the beginning until the end of the movement. In Andhra and elsewhere, farm wages were low and were not revised upward after the second world war, although prices of essential commodities had increased steeply. The condition of the small peasants was deplorable. They were compelled to do *vetti*, forced labor, by the landlords. In addition, tenants were evicted on a large scale by landlords fearing tenants' acquisition of occupancy rights on their lands. Adivasi lands were misappropriated by

---

[37] Gurbir Singh, "Naxalite Build-Up in Telengana," *Onlooker* 46 (January 1984).

moneylenders and traders, and even rich cultivators were adversely affected by the depression. The CPI, which began its activities in the 1930s, had consolidated its base in certain pockets of the region. In 1948, the party adopted a thesis advocating "guerrilla warfare" to liquidate the state power of the bourgeoisie. The party "advocated a united front, which included the rich peasantry and the middle bourgeoisie as the allies of the proletariat in the people's democratic revolution and asserted that such a wide front of armed struggle could take shape under the leadership of the party and that the objective conditions for realising these were fast maturing."[38]

During the mid-forties, village committees called *sangams* were formed in several villages of Nalgonda district to resist the tyranny of the landlords and of the Nizam's administration. There were sporadic strikes of laborers against forced labor and for securing better wages, and there were isolated instances in which tribals who had lost their land to landlords retook possession of their land. One such violent incident took place in July 1946, when over a thousand poor peasants and laborers, armed with lathis and slings, took out a procession against the landlords in a village in Nalgonda district. The landlords' hired *goondas* who fired at the procession, killing one of the leaders and injuring several others. The procession then turned into an angry crowd and went to burn a landlord's house, which was saved by the police. This incident was the provocation leading to the Telangana insurrection. Soon after this disturbance, the peasants grabbed the land of landlords in more than 300 villages. Initially, the insurrection was spontaneous and unorganized. The Razakar (the organization formed by the landlords belonging to the Muslim religion) added fuel to the fire when it started defending the Nizam, a Muslim ruler. This led the Hindus to organize against the state. The Congress party also launched a *satyagraha* to seek the merger of Hyderabad with the Indian union. As the Communists gained control over the struggle, however, the Congress not only withdrew from it but also saw to it that the struggle petered out. Nevertheless, by mid–1948, the Communists were able to organize six "area-squads" (each with twenty fighters) and about fifty "village squads." Slowly the movement spread and the party established parallel administrations in 4,000 villages in Adilabad, Karimnagar, and Medak districts. At many places they formed *gram-rajyams*, village soviets.

The movement was focused on three programs, which were executed by the village committees: 1) the abolition of forced labor, 2) the abolition of

---

[38] Mohan Ram, "The Telangana Peasant Armed Struggle 1946–51," *Economic and Political Weekly*, 9 June 1973, pp. 1025–1032.

illegal exactions and repayment of negotiated proportions of those exacted in the past, and 3) the return of lands seized illegally from the farmers by the landlords through indebtedness and the manipulation of land records.

The activists seized the land of the landlords, and the village committees distributed the seized land among the peasants and the laborers. The middle and rich peasants who dominated the village committees were the major beneficiaries of the distribution of land.[39]

By the end of August 1948, about 10,000 peasants, students, and party workers actively participated in the village squads and some 2,000 formed the special mobile guerrilla squads. They fought against the police and the military for three years. About 300,000 people were tortured, about 50,000 were arrested and kept in detention camps for periods ranging from a few days to a few months. More than 5,000 were imprisoned for years. In 1952, the CPI was banned. It should be mentioned that "there is no evidence at all from any source whatsoever that caste played any role at all in the movement. On the contrary, all the too scanty evidence suggests that the old social relations began to disintegrate under the impact of the movement, not only in relation to caste but also [in relation to] women."[40]

Almost simultaneously with the Telangana insurrection, the Tebhaga movement broke out in Bengal. It lasted for a year—1946 to 1947—and was a struggle launched by sharecroppers to retain two-thirds of the agricultural produce for themselves and thereby to reduce the rent they paid to the *jotedars*, a class of rich farmers who appropriated from one-half to two-thirds of the agricultural produce as rent. The movement first started in a village in Dinajpur district, where several volunteers harvested the paddy crop and carried it to their own houses instead of to the *jotedar's* residence. Police intervened, causing clashes between the police and sharecroppers, and about 1,000 peasants and volunteers of the Kisan Sabha were arrested. Slowly, under the leadership of the Bengal Provincial Kisan Sabha, the movement spread to eleven districts. The sharecroppers organized processions, refused to pay any share of the crop to the landlords, and attacked public property such as police stations and post offices. In a clash with the police, fifty peasants were killed, and 3,119 persons were arrested. The leaders of the struggles came from the urban middle class. At the grass-roots level, the Kisan Sabha committees were dominated by the middle peasants. The poor peasants participated actively in the movement

[39] D. N. Dhanagare, *Peasant Movement in India 1920–1950*, Delhi: Oxford University Press, 1983.

[40] Barry Pavier, *The Telangana Movement 1944–51*, Delhi: Vikas, 1981, p. 184.

because the "movement was intended to bring to the sharecroppers an additional gain of one-fourth of the total produce; it was the prospect of gain that led them to be champions of the movement."[41] The struggle was not well organized and fizzled out very soon.

The Telangana and Tebhaga movements led to a chain reaction in several parts of the country. Some of the resulting struggles were spontaneous, some were organized by nonparty ethnic organizations, and some were organized by various leftist parties. In north Gujarat, for instance, the Koli Kshatriyas mentioned earlier revolted against the landlords and moneylenders and seized the land that had been usurped by the "outsiders." Similarly, the tribal organization, Sati Pati Panth, mobilized a large number of its followers against the nontribal landed class. They grabbed land and harvested standing crops. The police arrested several agitators and a few persons died in police firing.[42] The leftist parties also organized tenants and sharecroppers against the landlords in Uttar Pradesh, Kerala, Tamil Nadu, and other parts of the country. Tenants staged struggles to increase their share of the produce. In Tanjore in Tamil Nadu, the poor peasants and landless laborers took control of land for several weeks in hundreds of villages. They also struck work during the harvest season, which compelled landlords to reduce rent and increase wages.[43] They also demanded the abolition of the zamindari system. As a result of the various organized and unorganized movements, the Congress party gave priority to land reform and accepted the objective of building a "socialistic pattern of society" in 1956.

The land reform acts remained by and large on paper, however. Hence, sporadic conflicts continued. The major mobilization of the peasants in the sixties was the Naxalbari revolt between 1967 and 1969. A radical section of the CPI had, from the early fifties, concentrated its activities among the tribal peasants of the Naxalbari area in Darjeeling district of West Bengal. As many as 60 percent of the cultivators in this area were sharecroppers. Between 1954 and 1966, they organized several strikes of agricultural laborers demanding higher wages and occupancy rights for tenants evicted by landlords. Village level committees of peasants were formed to conduct the struggles. The radical section of the CPI (by 1964 most of these radicals formed the radical fringe of the newly formed

---

[41] Krishna Kanta Sarkar, "Kakdwip Tebhaga Movement," in *Peasant Struggles in India* (n. 36), p. 478.

[42] Ghanshyam Shah and H. R. Chaturvedi, *Gandhian Approach to Rural Development*, Delhi: Ajanta, 1983.

[43] K. G. Iyer, "Peasant Movements and Organisations in Tamil Nadu and Pondichery" in *Peasant Struggles in Post-Independence India*, edited by A. R. Desai, Delhi: Oxford University Press, 1985.

CPI(M) believed that the "Chinese path is the path of liberation in India; agrarian revolution can be completed through armed struggle; [and it is necessary] to propagate the politics of the agrarian revolution among the workers and peasants and to organise them to build up a secret party organisation."[44] The conference of those who subscribed to the above party line, essentially the CPI(ML), was held in 1965. It debated the ideological issues and decided to 1) seize the lands of the *jotedars*, 2) seize the lands of the plantation workers who had purchased land from poor peasants, 3) cultivate the above-mentioned lands and retain all the produce from lands appropriated from the *jotedars*, but share half of the crop produced on the plantation workers' land, and 4) not seize from the *jotedars'* self-cultivated lands. The uprising began in 1967 in the Buranganj area. The confrontation between the peasants and the landlords-*cum*-police continued. In the early part of the struggle, a large number of agricultural laborers and sharecroppers participated in the struggle against the *jotedars* and united against the police. However, as the CPI(ML) followed the theory of annihilation of individual landlords, the peasants became alienated. There was very little coordination among the various units of the party. In a way, this lack of central direction helped the struggle to continue a little longer, for each unit organized its own struggle spontaneously. The struggle could not be continued, however, in the face of army action, which resulted in the death or arrest of several hundred persons.

The struggle begun in Buraganj was not, however, confined to the Naxalbari area but spread to almost all the states of the country with varying degrees of intensity.[45] It was most intense in Sikakulam of Andhra Pradesh and Muzaffarpur of Bihar. There the struggle against the landlords was organized on class lines and included the poor as well as the rich peasants.[46] Partha Mukherjee has observed that "The social background of the participants in the movement ran from rich peasants through to the laboring classes, and also covered all ethnic and class groups. It was not unusual that Paulos Kujur (Oram) was attacked by tribals, or that Rajbansis were pitted against Rajbansis."[47] Chain reactions of Naxalbari uprisings occured in many different parts of India. According to government reports, there were 5,424 agrarian agitations between 1967 and 1970.[48]

As the Naxalbari movement became popular, the parties of the left—

---

[44] See Sumanta Banerjee, *In the Wake of Naxalbari*, Calcutta: Subarnarekha, 1980 and Biplab Dasgupta, *The Naxalite Movement*, Delhi: Allied, 1974.

[45] Ibid.

[46] Ibid.

[47] Partha Mukherjee, "Naxalbari Movement and the Peasant Revolt in North Bengal," in *Social Movements in India*, edited by M.S.A. Rao, Delhi: Manohar, 1979, p. 77.

[48] K. C. Pant, "Violence in a Period of Social Change," *Young Indian* 3 (1973).

the CPI, CPI(M), SSP, and PSP—which opposed the ideological and tactical lines of the CPI(ML), launched land grab movements in several parts of the country. In 1970, a struggle began "to highlight the fact that land is concentrated in the hands of landlords, former princes, zamindars and monopolists and to alert the public as regards the urgent need for radical agrarian reforms."[49] According to one estimate, about 1,500,000 agricultural laborers and poor as well as middle peasants participated in the struggles and occupied 334,000 acres of land in various states. Twenty-six persons died and 62,000 persons were arrested during confrontations between the agitators and the police or between the agitators and the landlords' *goondas*.[50] There was, however, no uniform pattern to the struggle and the nature of mobilization in different parts of the country. The CPI and CPI(M) organized the struggle against the big landlords and monopoly houses like the Birlas who occupied agricultural land, whereas the PSP and SSP avoided the big landlords. In some places, the struggle was organized on class lines, leading to a united front of the low castes and Muslims, with slogans such as "Harijan-Muslim bhai bhai" raised to forge unity between the two minority groups of mainly poor peasants and agricultural laborers. The Muslim leaders of the parties appealed to their fellow Muslims to unite because "their 'Mazhab' (religion) was in danger," and to "support poor peasants to abolish big farmers, big businessmen and other rich people of the district."[51] In West Bengal, on the other hand, poor peasants belonging to Scheduled Castes and Scheduled Tribes struggled, under the leadership of the CPI(M), against the *jotedars* of their own caste.[52] The land grab movement petered out after a few months because the sponsoring parties were not united in their efforts to launch the movement. Some of the party leaders who themselves owned a large tract of land did not support the struggle enthusiastically. For them, it was a symbolic struggle to raise the issue. The state, on the one hand, used repression to curb the struggle, and the Congress party on the other, raised the radical slogan *Garibi Hatao* (Out with Poverty) in the 1971 elections. Several states enacted land ceiling acts in 1972 and 1973 and promised to distribute the surplus land among the landless.

Some of the nonparty radicals, who were dissatisfied with the reformist and pressure politics of the leftist parties, the CPI and CPI(M), and the in-

---

[49] C. Rajeswara Rao, "Land Struggle and Its Future," *Indian Left Review* 1 (February 1971).

[50] Ibid.

[51] Rajendra Singh, "Agrarian Social Structure and Peasant Unrest: A Study of Land Grab Movement in District Basti," *Sociological Bulletin* 2 (March 1974), pp. 44–70.

[52] Swati Mitter, *Peasant Movements in West Bengal*, Cambridge: University of Cambridge, 1977.

dividual annihilation theory of the CPI(ML), organized the poor cultivators, sharecroppers, and agricultural laborers for a long drawn-out struggle. They emphasized the importance of "mass-line" mobilization of the peasants and the development of political consciousness. The Shahada movement in Maharashtra between 1972 and 1974 was one of the mass-based movements. Various groups, including the Bhil Adivasi Mandal of the Sarvodayis, the Landless Agricultural Laborers and Poor Peasants Union under the leadership of the Lal Nishan (Red Flag) party, and some independent Marxists organized the Bhu Mukti, the Liberation of the Land Conference in 1972 in Shahada. The conference founded the Shramik Sangathana (SS), an organization of landless laborers and poor peasants. It organized the struggle of the poor Adivasi peasants to get their land back from the landlords and succeeded in recovering 4,000 acres. The SS also launched a struggle to abolish the *begari* (forced labor) system and to acquire open cultivable land that was under the control of the forest department. The *begari* laborers organized a meeting in which they decided to refuse *vethbegar*, forced labor. They also resisted the illegal demands of the forest officers. In April 1972, about 500 landless families occupied wastelands and started cultivation; a large-scale *satyagraha* was launched for the cultivation of forest wasteland. The participants were arrested and sentenced to imprisonment for one to two weeks. In March 1972, the SS asked the people to boycott the assembly elections, which, they said, had so far benefited only "the ruling landlord-moneylender class." As a result, only 30 percent of the voters, as compared to an expected 50 or 60 percent, cast their votes. Among those who went to the polling booths, an additional 30 percent cast empty ballots, thus expressing their protest against the elections. In addition, about 15,000 peasants participated in a rally organized by the SS on the first of March. The marchers demanded an increase in the salary of attached laborers, *saldars*, from Rs. 300 to Rs. 900 per year and regular working hours. They also demanded an increase in daily wages for the laborers. This led to a confrontation with the landlords. The casual day laborers and the *saldars* formed the Mazdoor Samiti, which laid down conditions with the landlords. The workers themselves conducted negotiations with the landlords and presented their demands. They organized *gheraos, dharanas*, demonstrations, and processions almost every week in 1973. In 1974, the Adivasis launched a *satyagraha* in several villages and marched to retake possession of their land and standing crops from the landlords. Over 250 satyagrahis were arrested and charge-sheeted for theft and looting. A demonstration was organized at the taluka towns to protest against the arrests. The landlords, in response, organized a private army equipped with a jeep, 100 horses, and 120 guns to curb the demands of the Adivasi peasants. This private army of the landlords and the government police spread terror in the area in 1974. Several Adivasi laborers were arrested. Although the workers were unable to defend themselves against the police and *goondas* of the landlords, they earned the sympathy of the urban middle class. In theory, their demands for the implementation of the Minimum Wages Act and the distribution of the wasteland to the laborers were accepted by the government and the landlords, but they were not implemented. As a result of the struggles, over 4,000 acres of land illegally appropriated by landlords, rich peasants, and moneylenders were returned to the Adivasis between 1971 and 1974.[53] Those who received land gradually became alienated from the struggle, although their condition has not improved, for they lack the resources to effectively cultivate their land. Although local leadership has emerged, the struggle has become dormant for the present, as the leaders are divided into factions fighting against each other.

The Shetkari Mandal, earlier known as the Bhoomi Sena, is another example of a nonparty action group engaged in political mobilization. An offshoot of the land grab movement, it began in 1970 when the Praja Socialist party launched a *satyagraha* to take the land of a trust that owned 2,000 acres. The satyagrahis were arrested, among them an Adivasi leader, Kaluram. During his imprisonment he and his Adivasi colleagues agreed that they should recover their own lands that had been usurped by the moneylenders. This should be done, they felt, by the Adivasis themselves without depending on the leadership of outsiders. After his release from jail, Kaluram went back to his area, Thana district in Maharashtra, and organized several small meetings in a number of villages, explaining to the people their exploitation by moneylenders. This was the area where the Kisan Sabha was active and where the Varlis had revolted against the landlords in 1945–1947. Kaluram and his colleages collected information regarding the land usurped by the moneylenders in their area. The process of investigation made the Adivasis aware of how and to whom they had lost their land. They formed the organization called Bhoomi Sena, Land Army, to launch struggles against injustice. The first struggle, in which 600 Adivasis participated under the leadership of Kaluram, was launched immediately. The Adivasis marched to the fields of the moneylenders and cut the standing crops "as an assertation of the collective will." They then repeated this action. The moneylenders, who were taken aback initially,

[53] See Maria Mies, "The Shahada Movement: A Peasant Movement In Maharashtra (India)—Its Development and Its Perspectives," *The Journal of Peasant Studies* 3 (July 1976), pp. 472–482; and Sulabha Brahme and Ashok Upadhyaya, "A Critical Analysis of the Social Formation and Peasant Resistence in Maharashtra," mimeo., Poona: Shankar Brahme Samaj Vidnyan Granthalaya, 1979.

retaliated when the cutting was repeated. They sought the help of the police to terrorize the Adivasis. The Adivasis told the police that "they were implementing the law and taking the crop from lands which really belonged to them, and that the police were acting in illegal fashion in league with sawkars."[54] The struggle spread to several villages, although it did not continue for long, for those who got land back from the moneylenders refrained from participating in subsequent struggles for collective crop-cutting.

In order to improve the production of the land regained by the farmers, Kaluram formed the Shetkari Mandal in 1972. The organization carried out an economic program for four years with little success, as the larger economic structure was unfavorable to the farmers. Once again, in 1975, Kaluram and his friends followed the path of struggle. Village-level committees, called Tarun Mandals were formed. In order to raise understanding of the problems, the Bhoomi Sena organized camps (*shibirs*) and educational courses for village leaders demanding minimum wages. These efforts succeeded in raising wages.[55]

The Forest Dweller's Struggle

The forest and sea are also important sources of livelihood for the rural poor. Forests cover 753,584 square kilometers of the country. Generally the forest-dwellers are called tribals, although some nontribals also depend on forest-fuel, fodder, and other forest products. In addition, all tribals are not forest-dwellers. Those who have lived in the forest for centuries use forest resources for fuel and shelter as well as to earn their living. In return, they maintain the forest. The British government imposed certain restrictions on forest-dwellers concerning their rights over forest products and allowed private contractors to cut the trees for industry and business. The forest-dwellers protested against the restrictions. Interestingly, the Congress party supported at that time the forest-dwellers' struggle to restore their customary rights to extract timber and collect forest produce for consumption.[56] Ironically, the same Congress party, once in power, has, during the last three decades, increased restrictions on the rights of the forest-dwellers. The tribals of various parts of the country have again protested against the restrictions and in some places have launched struggles. These struggles have been spontaneous and localized. The Kharwars

---

[54] G.V.S. De Silva, Niranjan Mehta, Anisur Rahman, and Poona Vignaraja, "Bhoomi Sena: A Struggle for People's Power," *Development Dialogue* 2 (1979).

[55] Ibid.

[56] K. S. Singh, "A Forest Satyagraha," in *Tribal Movements in India* (n. 15), vol. 2, pp. 187–195.

of Palamau in Bihar and Madhya Pradesh protested in 1957 against the rules and regulations that prevented them from collecting forest products. The police used force against the agitators, and their leaders were arrested.[57] Recently, the tribals of Ranchi and Singhbhum demanded the withdrawal of the Bihar Military Police (BMP) forces from the forests and the restoration of their rights over their own forests. In retaliation the police looted the tribal villages and spread terror. The forest-dwellers have continued to protest against police tyranny and oppression, protests that have frequently led to confrontations. In one of these confrontations, the police fired fifty-eight rounds of bullets into a crowd of Adivasis who were protesting against atrocious behavior by the BMP.[58] The tribals of Thana district, under the leadership of the Bhoomi Sena, also launched struggles in the 1970s against the forest officers and demanded their traditional rights "to collect and sell headload of firewood from the forest."[59]

The bamboo workers, known as burad workers, of Bhandara district, Maharashtra, also launched a struggle against the forest administration in the early 1980s. In the past, they had free access to bamboo, which they use to make mats and baskets to earn their living. The government introduced a rationing system in the 1960s with cards. Each card holder was permitted to purchase for Rs. 90,150 bamboo stalks per month from the forest department depots. The burad workers became victims of corrupt officers who took extra money to give them bamboo stalks. They frequently did not get their quota. Simultaneously, large bamboo tracts were leased out to paper mills and contractors who began indiscriminate cutting. In 1981, the government suddenly stopped supplying bamboo to the workers from the depots and also withdrew permission previously given to cut 75 stalks per year for hut repairs. The workers organized *morchas* and hunger strikes demanding the resumption of the bamboo supply. They organized the "bamboo roko" and "rasta roko" (stop bamboo; stop road) movements in 1982, preventing the contractors' bamboo trucks from taking away bamboo stalks. The police used force to disperse the agitators, and sixty-four persons, including women, were arrested. The government promised to give the bamboo workers a regular supply of bamboo. The workers formed the Bharatiya Burad Kamdar Mahasabha to protect their interests.[60]

The people of Kumaun and Garhwal of Uttar Pradesh have been demanding their rights in the forests, with greater or lesser success, since

[57] Ibid.

[58] *The Hindu*, 29 January 1981.

[59] De Silva (n. 54).

[60] The Second Citizen's Report, *The State of India's Environment, 1984–1985*, New Delhi: Centre for Science and Environment, 1985.

1930. About seventeen persons were killed and several injured when the army opened fire on people agitating against forest restrictions. The movement was revived in the 1960s by workers who formed the Forest Labour Cooperative Society, and in the 1970s they launched struggles against the forest department and contractors for destroying the forests. The women hugged the trees when the workers of the contractors came to cut them, and they appealed to the workers, saying, "Brother, this forest is our maternal home. From this we satisfy so many of our needs. Do not axe it. If you do so, landslides will ruin our homes and fields."[61] The workers, who belonged to a similar region, understood the appeal. They returned. The contractors were therefore helpless. With this began the resistance popularly known as "Chipko Andolan," that is, the movement to hug or embrace, in 1973. The people organized several demonstrations in support of their demands, which included the removal of the contract system of forest exploitation in order to allow the forest-dwellers to participate in the management and administration of the forests.[62]

Similar agitations took place in Karnataka in 1983 in what is known as the Appiko (to hug) Movement. The protest began in late 1983 against the felling of trees by the forest department in Sulkani forest in Sirsi district. Around two hundred forest-dwellers gathered and forced the woodcutters to leave the forest. Slowly the movement spread to adjoining districts where the match manufacturer Wimco cuts trees. The confrontation between Appiko volunteers and the forest department continues.[63]

With the support of outside activists, organizations have been formed in Uttar Pradesh and Karnataka to protect the rights of the forest-dwellers and maintain ecological balances. These struggles are still localized although their activities have expanded. Recently, attempts were made by various nonparty voluntary groups to launch an all-India movement against the proposed Forest Bill, which would further reduce the rights of forest-dwellers over the forest.[64] Leftist parties extend their support to the struggles of forest-dwellers, but they have not yet actively participated in their struggles.

[61] Bharat Dogra, *Forests and People*, New Delhi: Dogra, 1983.

[62] Ibid. See also J. C. Das and R. S. Negi, "The Chipko Movement," in *Tribal Movements in India* (n. 15), vol. 2, pp. 383–392.

[63] The Second Citizen's Report (n. 60).

[64] The proposed Indian Forest Bill seeks to replace the Indian Forest Acts of 1927. The bill reduces in a variety of ways forest-dwellers' rights to the forest and its produce. Forest officers and police are given the widest possible powers. All offenses under the bill are made cognizable. It is feared that the administrative and criminal law powers of the forest officers will be directed in most cases against the poor and the oppressed.

The Fishermen's Struggle

There are about 2,000 fishing villages on India's 6,500-kilometer-long coastline. The main source of livelihood for these villagers is fish, which are traditionally caught from country boats and catamarans. The poverty of these fishermen became acute during the mid-seventies, when fish production declined. The annual marine-fish production of Kerala was 400,000 tons in 1973; it gradually went down to the alarming position of 268,000 tons in 1980–1981.[65] One of the major reasons for the decline in production was the increased mechanization and the unplanned use of mechanized sailing boats. Mechanization followed the adoption of the Indo-Norwegian aid program in the 1950s. Gradually the big industrial houses entered the fishing business.[66] Greedy businessmen have habitually misused the available technology and have violated laws that prohibit coastal fishing by mechanized crafts in depths of less than five fathoms. Instead of going outward into deeper waters, the mechanized boats fish in the shallow waters that are within the reach of human labor. The continuous fishing in shallow waters by mechanized trawlers and purse seines has destroyed the delicate ecological balance, resulting in the killing of fish eggs and the alarming depletion of the fish population. Consequently, there has been a disastrous decline in the traditional fishermen's daily catch, forcing them to keep "their fishing tools unutilised, rendering lakhs of fishing people underemployed, unemployed and impoverished."[67]

The trawlers also occasionally cut the nets of the poor fishermen. This led to a clash between the fishermen and trawler owners in Goa in 1977. The fishermen organized a *dharna*, observed fasts, and formed a procession demanding action against the owners of trawlers for violating the coastal fishing law. They formed a union called the Ramponkars' Ekvott. A twenty-four-hour chain hunger strike was undertaken for more than 200 days. Their efforts met, however, with little success. Similarly, in Kerala, fishermen formed the Kerala Swatantra Matshya Thozhilali Federa-

[65] Thomas Kocherry, "Fishermen Struggle for Survival," *The Otherside* (August 1984).

[66] R. M. Dhawan, director of fisheries, said that most mechanized craft are owned by "moneyed unwanted elements" and not by traditional fishermen. The big business houses found that fishing by mechanized craft provides lucrative returns. Union Carbide has invested one hundred million rupees and owns ten trawlers; Tata Industries has invested approximately twenty million rupees and owns more than four trawlers. Indian Trading Corporation has put in ten million rupees and owns four trawlers; so has Britannia Biscuits. "Four big houses between them cornered 19.26 per cent of Bombay's prawn export in 1977 and five big houses accounted for 12.3 per cent of Madras' total frozen prawn export." Ayesha Kagal, "Matsyanyaya Big Fish Eat Small Fish," *The Illustrated Weekly of India* (Bombay), 8 April 1979.

[67] Christopher Fonseca, Matanhy Saldhanha, and Urban Lobo, "Stepping on the Fishermen's Toes," *Science Today* (August 1980).

tion (Independent Fishermen's Federation) in 1981. The leadership of the struggle came from clergymen. They organized processions and *dharnas* and submitted memoranda demanding a total ban on fishing by trawlers during the fish spawning season. They have formed an all-India organization and their struggle continues, occasionally taking a violent turn.[68] Political parties have not yet become involved in the fishermen's struggles, although the leftist parties highlight fishermen's problems in the Parliament.

Overview

Now let us try to take up the salient points from the foregoing account and discuss the questions raised at the beginning of this chapter. Some of the questions are: what is the nature of the grassroots mobilization of the rural poor that has been taking place during the last four decades? Around which issues do they mobilize? Why do some struggles last, whereas others are short-lived? What impact do the struggles of the rural poor have on the present political system? And to what extent has the political system been able to cope with the issues raised by the mobilization of the rural poor? At the outset, let me confess that the present state of knowledge does not allow us to answer all the above questions satisfactorily. What follows are tentative answers based largely on speculation.

The rural poor are not stupid. They protest and revolt against injustice. A large number of their protests are spontaneous and sporadic and take forms ranging from outcry to so-called "social banditry," from strikes to armed struggle. More often than not, these collective actions are impulsive and lack organizational planning. Unable to sustain themselves against local powers acting in collusion with political bosses and government administrations with access to resources and police power, they peter out in a few days. Local bosses bribe, split, co-opt, mesmerize and terrorize the poor. A few of the protests take the form of struggles that continue for longer periods if they are organized and linked to similar struggles outside their locale.

Grass-roots mobilization in politics has resulted from ethnic as well as economic issues. Although both issues are intermingled in India where the majority of the population belongs to the lower social strata and is also poor, ethnic issues may predominate in some struggles and economic issues in others. Mobilizations around predominantly ethnic issues have

[68] Vishwapriya Iyenger, "In the Shoes of the Fishermen," *Indian Express* (Bombay), 8 September 1985.

taken three forms. First, some of the backward castes that have a large
number of members in which a small section had improved its economic
conditions during the colonial period took an institutional path of, for example, submitting memoranda and passing resolutions, as well as an ex-
trainstitutional course of securing rights and asserting equality with
higher castes. In the postindependence period, leaders of these groups
have been slowly co-opted by nonleft political parties. Their mobilization
has now been largely confined to electoral politics. They show their numerical strength in elections, in which both collectively and individually,
the backward castes put pressure on the government to secure welfare
measures and reservations in government jobs and educational institutions. The welfare programs and reservations primarily benefit the upper
strata of the backward castes, because the majority of the castes' members
are so marginalized that they lack the prerequisites to take advantage of
the reservations. The struggle to secure such demands is, therefore, relatively passive and is confined to institutional procedures. Some of the relatively better-off backward castes who have improved their economic and
political positions through institutional arrangements take the offensive
against the more backward castes and Harijans when these try to assert
their rights. The poor strata of the backward castes take defensive action
when they are cornered, attacked, and humiliated by the upper castes on
the issue of reservations. They also resort to direct collective action when
their emotions are aroused on the issue of *izzat* (dignity and status) when
their women are raped or molested by landlords, rich peasants, or their
henchmen. Second, the small tribes of the frontier states have blurred their
narrow tribal identity and evolved a transtribal identity. They have raised
the issue of the right of self-determination. Third, the struggles of the
Scheduled Castes and Tribes have been increasingly launched over economic rather than ethnic issues. These groups tend to join hands across
ethnic boundaries.

The economic issues cover a wide range—minimum and higher wages
for agricultural laborers, rights over forest products, preservation of forests, land reforms, distribution of surplus land and agricultural infrastructural facilities, and exploitation of fisheries and fishermen. Many of the
struggles are against the local power structure—the landed class, the
administration, and the political bosses—and a few link their struggles for
securing economic relief with the struggles against the ruling class, aiming
at taking over political power.

Struggles on economic issues do not necessarily unite all the poor across
ethnic boundaries on the basis of class. For many, caste/community and
class are synonymous, because their interactions in economic activities
have been limited for centuries within the membership of the same status

group. This situation of course facilitates and sometimes accelerates the process of mobilization by providing a common bond to the agitators. But, at the same time, it tends to keep the struggle localized, which, in turn, weakens it. Caste/community identity also may split the participants in the course of a struggle if class and ideological bonds do not evolve. Wherever political parties or action groups have formed political organizations to lead the struggles and politicize participants to fight for larger political goals, caste/community loyalties have not hindered the struggles. Evidence is available to show that the poor of different social groups have joined hands against exploiters even when the latter have belonged to their own caste or tribe. Thus, ethnic loyalties are not insurmountable obstacles to political mobilization.

The leftist political parties have played a major role in organizing and mobilizing the rural poor. They have provided an organizational network, exposing and providing linkages to the rural poor. The parties provide their members with a wider perspective, linking the problems of the poor with the problems of state power and their economic structure. However, the major leftist parties believe that agricultural laborers or tenants or sharecroppers cannot by themselves sustain these struggles and that they do not possess the potential to capture state power. They therefore form an alliance of agricultural laborers with poor and middle peasants. Sometimes they also include rich peasants in their alliance. Such united mobilization against the landlords and state power has been widespread, generating a chain reaction in society. These relatively broad-based struggles have also continued for longer periods, leaving important marks on the psyche of the rural poor. Ironically, such united struggles, of which agricultural laborers and poor peasants have been the backbone, have proved most advantageous to the middle and rich peasants. The leftist parties thus face a dilemma: the poor alone cannot sustain the struggles; and the struggles of the allied classes do not improve the condition of the poor.

Because for tactical reasons leftist political parties do not pay enough attention to the problems of agricultural laborers and other marginal groups, nonparty voluntary groups often play a large role. A large number of such action groups have come into existence since the mid-sixties and they are engaged in organizing and mobilizing the rural poor for collective action against the injustices they suffer.

Quite a few groups have emerged in the course of the spontaneous struggles of the poor. The leadership of such groups has remained local, although they receive outside support. Some other action groups have been formed by idealistic and committed educated boys and girls from the urban middle class. These groups can be broadly classified as development groups and political groups. The former are engaged in mobilizing the masses to participate in the development programs of the government. They occasionally take up political issues, insisting on the implementation of legislation passed by the government, but they generally avoid direct action. In time, their activities become absorbed in administrative procedures for formulating and implementing projects. They are co-opted by the ruling party and the state for "efficient management" and implementation of government sponsored development programs.

The political groups can be classified as party and nonparty action groups. The party groups include both the front organizations of the "established" national level parties and small parties or groups that have "pre-party political formations."[69] The latter are the critics of the ideological formulations and tactics of the major leftist parties. Like political parties, they also believe in the capturing of state power by the exploited classes of society. According to them, the present state protects the interests of the feudal and bourgeois classes. Their objective is to overthrow these classes and the capitalist state. The nonparty action groups, on the other hand, are either against political party per se or they have no clear ideas about the issue. Some of them have a well-defined political perspective and, unlike the party or pre-party groups, they believe that the state was or could be independent of the economic power structure. Some groups are grappling with the problems of political ideology and decide their political actions on the basis of the issues confronting them. They are localized and organizationally fragmented,[70] but they mobilize the exploited and oppressed people who "were considered unorganisable by the left parties."[71] On the whole, many of the nonparty groups attempt "to open alternative political space outside the usual arenas of party and government, though not outside the state, rather as new forms of organisation and struggle meant to rejuvenate the state and to make it once again an instrument of liberation from exploitative structure (both traditional and modern), in which the underprivileged and the poor are trapped."[72]

The strategies adopted by the ruling class in dealing with the problems raised by the grass-roots movements reveal the contradictions of the system. The members of the ruling class cannot lay their hands on political power through the ballot box without the support of the vast majority of the poor. Yet, in order to meet the demands of the poor, they must endan-

[69] Harsh Sethi, "Groups in a New Politics of Transformation," *Economic and Political Weekly*, 18 February 1984, pp. 305–316.

[70] D. L. Sheth, "Grass-roots Initiatives in India," *Economic and Political Weekly*, 11 February 1984, pp. 259–262.

[71] D. L. Sheth, "Movements," *Seminar*, no. 278 (October 1982), pp. 42–52.

[72] Rajni Kothari, "The Non-Party Political Process," *Economic and Political Weekly*, 4 February 1984, pp. 216–224.

ger their own interests by taking actions that may consequently lead to
loss of power. Hence, populist as well as authoritarian politics have
emerged. The state has adopted the strategy of mesmerizing the poor by
rhetoric, of attempting to keep them satisfied or quiet by nominal welfare
programs, co-option, and physical oppression. These measures are used
simultaneously when the government is faced with numerous protest
movements. In 1956, in response to the Telangana, Tebhaga, Varli, and
other such movements of the late forties and early fifties, the ruling party
promised to build a "socialist pattern of society." The ideology of "sarvodaya" and "change of heart" of the rich people, however, which received verbal support from the ruling class, led to few concrete results for
the poor.[73] Again, to counter Naxalite and land grab movements in an
election year, the Congress advanced in 1972 the slogan *Garibi Hatao*.
The government passed legislation for land reform and minimum wages
for agricultural laborers. However, the land reform legislation, which
caused inconvenience to the middle and rich peasants, has not been sincerely implemented. As late as September 1982, the then agriculture minister Rao Birendra Singh asked the states to set up additional courts and
appoint special legal advisers to speed up the implementation of land reform measures, a component of "the New 20 Point Programme." But this
plea has so far remained unheeded. In fact, the recent rhetoric—*desh ba-
chavo*, technological revolution, and march toward the twenty-first century—underplay land reform even as a political slogan. As an alternative
to change in the economic and political power structure, the state, the government, the industrial houses, religious organizations and philanthropic
groups undertake "income generating programmes" for the rural poor.
The government has launched various programs and established various
agencies such as the Small Farmer Development Agencies (SFDA), the Integrated Rural Development Program (IRDP), the National Rural Employment Program (NREP), Minimum Needs, and the New Twenty Point
Program to "uplift the poor." Increasingly large amounts of money are allocated for the rural development programs (Rs. 2,747 crore were allocated for the New Twenty Point Program in the central sector plan for
1983–1984).[74] Free legal aid agencies in Lok Adalats have been set up by
the state to provide legal help to the rural poor. Funds from Western capitalist societies have poured in to support the activities of the nonparty
voluntary action groups,[75] and reservations in jobs and educational insti-

---

[73] See Ghanshyam Shah, *Protest Movements in Two Indian States*, Delhi: Ajanta, 1977,
pp. 137–158.

[74] A crore is equal to ten million.

[75] According to the home ministry's report, Rs. 1700.8 million were received by voluntary
groups from foreign funding agencies under the Foreign Contributions (Regulation) Act

tutions have been extended, particularly during the seventies, to backward castes. But these programs have not improved the lot of the rural poor.[76] Of course, they do raise hopes and illusions among the poor, for a few of them do receive some benefits. The government, political parties, and the capitalist class co-opt the leaders of the poor by offering them political positions and other benefits. At the same time, the state freely uses repressive measures against those among the poor who press for any betterment of their lot. The terror of the landlords, rich peasants, forest contractors, and industrialists continues unabated. They have formed armies of *goondas* with licensed and unlicensed weapons to terrorize the poor as and when they demand their rights. These armies operate in collusion with the police and government administration and do not hesitate to violate laws. In fact, the rural rich receive protection against the poor whenever they need it. The police and the private armies of the rich selectively pick up the militant leaders of the poor and kill them in so-called encounters.[77] In addition, the government has armed the police and military with wide powers by declaring certain regions "disturbed areas" so that any person may be searched and arrested without legal formalities.[78] The civil and democratic rights of the vast exploited masses are thus legally and effectively curtailed.

1976, in 1979–1980. See Prakash Karat, "Action Groups/Voluntary Organizations: A Factor in Imperialist Strategy," *The Marxist* 2 (April–June 1984).

[76] See M. L. Dantwala, "Rural Development, Investment without Organisation," *Economic and Political Weekly*, 30 April 1983, pp. 686–689; B. M., "Painless Rural Development," *Economic and Political Weekly*, 25 February 1984, pp. 330–331; and Ghanshyam Shah and H. R. Chaturvedi (n. 42).

[77] See B. N. Juyal, "Encounter, Killing of 'Dacoits': The Face of Repression in a Peasant Society," mimeo., Banaras: Gandhian Institute of Studies, 1985.

[78] Some of the undemocratic acts are the Preventive Detention Act (in force from 1950 to 1969); Maintenance of Internal Security Act (MISA) (1971–1977); National Security Act (NSA) (1980 onward), Assam Maintenance of Public Order Act (1953); Assam Disturbed Area Act (1955), and the Armed Forces (Assam and Manipur) Special Powers (Amendment) Act (1972). The People's Union for Civil Liberties (Delhi) observes, "And now, 38 years after Independence, the people of India have been subject to laws which violate all principles of natural justice. In some ways, they are worse than laws under the colonial regime. Not only do they subvert the right to fair trial but they can also be used against individuals and groups working for social and political justice." *Black Laws 1984–85*, Delhi: People's Union for Civil Liberties, 1985.

State-Society Relations
in India's Changing
Democracy

ATUL KOHLI

The essays in this volume describe and explain India's changing state-society relations. The picture that emerges is of a functioning democracy
within the bounds of a multinational society and a poor economy.[1] It is a
picture of a democracy under considerable strain. Indian democracy is
battered by increasing demands from a variety of politicized social groups.
The norms of democracy have, in addition, been weakened by leaders
who do not attach a high premium to institutional constraints on personal
power. Pressures from within both the state and the society have contributed to the emergence of personalized rule, ineffective government, and
violence and corruption in political life. None of the authors in this volume has suggested, or come close to suggesting, that India's democracy is
about to crumble; each has, however, documented and explained the
sources of growing political strains within India.

The eight essays are organized around three related themes. The first
three essays, by Hart, Manor, and Cohen, analyze the changes in India's
important political institutions—leadership, political parties, and the
armed forces—and document and explain aspects of decay within them.
The papers by Das Gupta and Brass focus on the relation between the state
and ethnic activism and highlight the destabilizing consequences of leaders' refusal to democratically accommodate the demands of ethnic groups.
The focus in the last three essays, by Bardhan, Frankel, and Shah, shifts to
the political role of social groups and to the contribution that India's im-

---

[1] I have, in writing this conclusion, attempted to remain as faithful as possible to the views
expressed by the eight authors of the volume. The conclusion, therefore, does not necessarily
represent my own views but, rather, what I think the materials presented above warrant. I
state this caveat because I am currently writing a book-length study on related themes. My
study, tentatively titled *Erosion of Authority in India*, develops an argument that at times
agrees with, but at other times varies from, the positions developed here.

portant castes and classes make to the political process. Taken together, these eight essays help us delineate the changing nature of India's democracy.

The Decay of State Institutions

A recurring theme at the Princeton conference was, and in some of the essays in this volume is, the disintegration of India's dominant political institutions. The shape of the new institutions that may replace these crumbling ones is still far from visible. Strong institutions are simultaneously an expression of the basic agreed-upon norms of a polity and a source of effective government. Their decay generally reflects erosion of norms and contributes to the emergence of governments that do not govern well. How this process has manifested itself in India and why it has occurred are important concerns.

Henry Hart analyzes the apex of the Indian state, its leaders. His main concern is how well India's national leaders have performed. Beyond an assessment of performance, Hart seeks to explain the structural causes of poor performance. What emerges is a masterly essay discussing, on the one hand, the functions of, and the pathways to, national leadership in India and, on the other hand, the conditions under which the leaders are likely to be most effective.

Hart assesses the performance of Indian leaders as they have sought to maintain political institutions, diagnose and solve important problems, and facilitate national integration. Hart notes that India's dominant political institutions—the parties, the bureaucracy, and the police—are in decay. Focusing especially on the decay in the police force, he wonders why Indian leaders have failed to stem the rot. He suggests that, although the solutions to the problem are really quite complex, the leaders also have not helped the matter. Instead of addressing the problem, they have manipulated and politicized the police force for short-term political advantages. Political interference has corroded organizational norms, introduced widespread corruption, and demoralized the force. The result, Hart judges, is that a crucial arm of the state is now rather limp. Leaders who have politicized bureaucratic organizations for short-term benefits find, over the long term, that they lack an effective organization to maintain orderly rule.

As far as attempts to diagnose and solve national problems are concerned, Hart purposely chooses to focus on two failed "wars": Nehru's China war and Indira Gandhi's war on poverty. Hart traces the policy failure in both instances to an institutional characteristic: the relative isolation of leaders in the process of policy making. A crucial insight thus emerges. Tremendous concentration of power in India has had negative consequences on policy performance. Such decision-making institutions as the Cabinet and the Parliament have been made politically impotent. Moreover, leaders have had a tendency to surround themselves with "yes men." The consequence in the two instances discussed was the relative isolation of leaders, leading up to policy failures of heroic magnitude.

A third important insight that emerges from Hart's essay concerns the changing routes to the position of leadership in India. As institutions have generally weakened, such noninstitutional pathways to leadership as political inheritance and other-than-political popularity (as in films) have become significant. There are thus fewer and fewer mechanisms intact in India for filtering out the incompetent from the competent in positions of power.

Hart's essay helps us focus on the crucial issues of leaders and institutions. Because institutions generally constrain the scope of personal power, leaders have often deinstitutionalized the political system for personal power considerations. Weakened institutions, in turn, have had detrimental political consequences: powerful but isolated leaders have not pursued policies effectively, and skilled leaders are not necessarily coming to the fore.

James Manor analyzes the changes that have been occurring within India's dominant party and within the party system, especially since 1977. While also emphasizing the theme of institutional decay, Manor is very helpful in focusing attention on the causes and the consequences of the Congress party's organizational decline. The complex dynamics of institutional breakdown are partly rooted in a socio-economic development that has produced interest-group activism and sharp value changes. These phenomena are analyzed in several chapters of this volume. The process of decay, however, has also been hastened by the role of those who manage India's dominant institutions. Manor focuses on Indira Gandhi and often finds her wanting. He carefully documents how Mrs. Gandhi, in following her personal political ambitions, contributed to the deinstitutionalization of the Congress party. The role of her son and confidant Sanjay further exacerbated the troubles of the Congress party by incorporating criminals and thugs into the heart of the political process.

The Congress party, according to Manor, has become far less an organized institution than it used to be. As a consequence, the institutional capacity for reconciling conflicting interests, generating consensus and legitimacy, and for initiating national development policies has declined. A number of trends within the Indian polity can thus be explained with reference to the process of institutional decay.

Manor argues that one important consequence of the decay of the Congress party is that elections have become difficult to win. In order to secure electoral majorities, therefore, new strategies are being tried. A confrontational attitude toward opposition parties, the personalization of rule, and flirtation with right-wing communalist politics are all part of such experiments. None of these augur well for a stable democratic polity.

Additional consequences of party decay include the fact that policies have become difficult to implement. Manor suggests that there is a general decline in confidence in the state's capacity to solve pressing socio-economic problems. The polity has, furthermore, become quite fluid: The relationship between parties and the social base is undergoing considerable change; preferred policies of parties are not always clear, and there is considerable movement between parties. Although Rajiv Gandhi has made some efforts to reverse this institutional decline, Manor worries that the problems are massive and that Rajiv's determination is not certain. The long-term consequences of a failure to reverse the process of institutional decay are bound to be negative for India's democracy.

The process of institutional decay and the related growing political turmoil direct attention to the role of the armed forces within India's democracy. India's military has in the past been mainly apolitical, a phenomenon that requires explanation. What also requires attention, however, are the more recent and growing political activities of the Indian military. Stephen Cohen's useful essay unravels both these puzzles.

India's armed forces constitute a highly professional group. The past apolitical stance of these soldiers has, according to Cohen, less to do with the nature of India's armed forces than with the relations of the military to other political and social institutions. The military intervenes in politics when the erosion of the established political order threatens its own institutional viability. Cohen holds that, on balance, the military does not like to initiate political change; it reacts to changes in the political environment. Because India's democratic institutions have been relatively stable over the last four decades, the role of the military in India's political process has been limited and generally subordinate to bureaucratic and political controls. As political institutions have in recent years come under increasing strain, there has been a corresponding change in the military's role.

Cohen analyzes as well a series of changes that have occurred within India's armed forces in recent years. The internal composition of the armed forces has altered considerably: the military has grown in size, it has become much more sophisticated in the strategic sense, and its class composition has broadened to include many officers from middle and lower class backgrounds. Cohen maintains, however, that the military remains a very professional group and that these internal changes are not likely to influence its political role in any significant way.

Cohen repeatedly emphasizes that India's armed forces are reluctant to intervene in politics. Several trends, however, are disconcerting. First, promotions within the military have become increasingly politicized. This has had a negative influence on the apolitical and professional ethos of the armed forces. Second, there has been a dramatic increase in the military's role in maintaining civil order. In 1984, Cohen points out, forty million Indians were living under near martial-law conditions. Third, paramilitary forces and their use continues to grow. Fourth, Cohen discovers an occasional and disturbing convergence of values between India's military and political elite: military leaders have expressed specific political commitments and political leaders have espoused militarist postures. Finally, there is the special problem of Punjab, where the open mutiny by some Sikhs and the general disaffection in a sensitive border state now threaten to weaken India's military capacity.

Cumulatively, these trends suggest that India's military is not as apolitical today as it was in the past. It remains, however, a professional service, and, although the repeated dependence on the armed forces to maintain civil order both reflects and contributes to the breakdown of legitimate, constitutional rule, a major military intervention in politics is not, Cohen feels, likely.

The essays by Hart, Manor, and Cohen help us understand the changing nature of India's major political institutions. The causes of this decay are complex. One set of variables consists of social forces that have become politically active as a result of democratically guided economic development. Their role is discussed in the third group of essays and is summarized below. The other important variable that has contributed to the weakening of institutions is the role of the leaders. It is this factor that is repeatedly emphasized in the essays discussed above. Over and over again, the analysts note how the members of the political elite have themselves weakened institutions. It may thus be suggested against conventional wisdom that institutional decay results not only from increasing social pressures on the state.[2] In India, at least, such decay is also generated by the destructive and self-serving actions of leaders who find institutions a constraint on personal power.

[2] I have discussed this position in the introduction above. This general argument is often associated with Samuel Huntington, *Political Order in Changing Societies*, New Haven: Yale University Press, 1968.

THE STATE AND ETHNIC ACTIVISM

The problem of accommodating diverse ethnic demands in a multinational polity like India is a perennial one. The viciousness, however, with which these demands reemerged in Assam and Punjab in the 1980s contrasted sharply with the 1950s and the 1960s. What happened? Although the 1950s and 1960s have often been regarded as the "most dangerous decades" for India's national unity, the fact is that ethnic demands were accommodated relatively successfully under Nehru. Why, then, during Mrs. Gandhi's tenure did ethnic and regional activism reemerge with renewed intensity? The answer has to do, on the one hand, with the changing composition of ethnic groups and the resources they control and, on the other hand, with the manner in which ethnic demands have or have not been met by the central government. The papers by Das Gupta and Brass help focus attention on the role of a recalcitrant center, especially as exemplified by Mrs. Gandhi, in exacerbating ethnic tensions, as well as on the related problem of center-state relations.

Das Gupta discusses the significance of India's ethnic movements in the context of overall democratic development. He conceives of ethnic activism as a type of collective action that conveniently uses emotional affinity to make claims on the state for the benefits of planned development. For Das Gupta, the renewed ethnic activism, and the related demands for reordering center-state relations, must be understood within the specific Indian context, in which the state plays a considerable role in economic development, and in which the state is accessible through democratic means. Ethnic groups are thus "interest groups," competing for valued goods in a democratic polity.

How has the Indian state dealt with ethnic activism and with what consequence? While discussing several types of evidence, Das Gupta develops a provocative insight: whenever the Indian state has democratically incorporated ethnic demands, the results have been positive for both nation building and economic development. Conversely, the attempt to exclude or repress ethnic-based demands has often backfired. Das Gupta discusses the catastrophic consequences of exclusionary strategies with reference to the case of Assam.

In the case of Assam, Das Gupta documents and argues that the insecurity of the "Assamese" movement and Indira Gandhi's exclusionary and manipulative tactics "contributed to a desperation that claimed a massive human price." By contrast, Rajiv's reconciliatory stance and the corresponding change of attitude among leaders of the Assamese movement generated a ready solution. The case for an inclusionary rather than exclusionary strategy vis-a-vis ethnic movements thus seems strong.

A similar conclusion emerges from Paul Brass's essay on the Punjab. Brass juxtaposes the contemporary Punjab crisis with the demands made by Sikh leaders in the 1960s for a "Punjabi Suba." He delineates the differences between the two periods and explains why demands were accommodated during the 1960s, whereas similar claims have generated tragic political turmoil in the 1980s.

Brass's nuanced essay on the step-by-step emergence of the Punjab crisis is critical of Mrs. Gandhi's political strategy. He argues that, "relentless centralization and ruthless, unprincipled intervention by the center in state politics have been the primary causes of the troubles in Punjab." Brass supports this conclusion by developing a number of important points: Bhindrawale and his brand of terrorist politics were initially promoted by Mrs. Gandhi, Sanjay, and even Rajiv as a means to undercut the moderate Akali Dal; in contrast to both Nehru and Rajiv, Mrs. Gandhi withheld support from the moderate Akali leaders in an effort to avoid losing power for the Congress to them. In addition, Mrs. Gandhi failed to provide unequivocal support to a single leader within Punjab, thus eliminating the prospect of decisive, local-level actions to help control the problem. Finally, Mrs. Gandhi departed from Nehru's strategy of the 1960s by conceding some of the religious, but not the more secular, demands of the Sikhs.

Had Rajiv's more conciliatory policy in the mid–1980s been followed by Mrs. Gandhi five or ten years earlier, Brass suggests, the tragic loss of lives that accumulates to this day might have been prevented. The fact that Rajiv's reconciliatory actions have still not solved the Punjab problem draws attention to the point that center-state relations are not the only factors at work within Punjab and to the point that it will now take time and a persistent reconciliatory approach from the center to decompress the highly charged political situation there.

The analysis of ethnic activism, and of the related issue of center-state relations, that Das Gupta and Brass provide lends support to the general argument of the earlier essays. Prior to Mrs. Gandhi, rules for dealing with center-state conflicts had been developed. The institutionalized process during that period favored inclusionary over exclusionary strategies as long as the demands were nonsecessionist, secular in character, and met with the approval of more than one side in conflict. The state, in other words, attempted during those years to accommodate itself to the diverse and plural nature of Indian society. Mrs. Gandhi, by contrast, came to view accommodative strategies as threats to her personal hold on power. She therefore willfully destroyed the norms and rules of political accommodation carefully crafted by her predecessors. Instead, she concentrated power in her person, attempted to mold state and local politics to suit her interests, and unleashed volatile regional opposition that she could not control. It was, thus, not the politicized social forces alone that came to threaten Indian democracy; it was also the actions of those who controlled governmental power.

CLASS, CASTE, AND POLITICS

The essays discussed above place considerable emphasis on the role of central authorities in influencing political change within India. But what has been the role of the politicized socio-economic groups in molding India's democracy? The issue of ethnic groups has already been discussed, but what political role do India's major social classes and castes play in politics? How has this role been changing? The last three essays in this volume, by Bardhan, Frankel, and Shah, shed light on these complex issues.

Bardhan's brief but insightful essay delineates the political role of India's dominant classes. He conceives of the industrialists, rich farmers, and the white-collar workers and professionals as partners in India's ruling coalition. Bardhan suggests that none of these classes is powerful enough individually to impose its will upon India's polity or the economy. The heterogeneous nature of the dominant coalition then, contrary to conventional Marxist wisdom, may in India support rather than detract from a democratic regime. This is because India's democracy has enabled each of these important groups to eke out state patronage and support by establishing complex bargaining networks.

The patronage-based alliance between the state and India's dominant classes is, for Bardhan, not without costs; the alliance generates its own "contradictions." The growing share of patronage within public resources is a primary cause of declining public investments. This decline, in turn, has created serious infrastructural bottlenecks and has thus contributed to low economic growth in general, and to low industrial growth in specific. The politics of patronage creates a further drag on economic performance by contributing to a poorly managed public sector and associated high and growing capital-output ratios. The fiscal and the managerial crises that result have, in turn, political consequences. Frustration with patronage distribution undermines the legitimacy of the political machine, even in the eyes of the members of the dominant coalition. The lower classes have also started clamoring for a greater share of governmental resources. A legitimacy crisis has thus developed within which centralization of power in individuals and weakening support for the state are simultaneous and related political trends.

Bardhan's argument sensitizes us both to the reasons why India's dominant classes may have supported a democratic regime so far, and to the ways in which this tacit alliance of domination has of late contributed to slow economic growth and to the erosion of the state's legitimacy. The irony is that the same groups that benefit from the state's economic intervention may make it difficult for the state to reorient its policies to solve pressing political and economic problems.

Frankel's essay shifts the attention away from the members of the dominant coalition and toward the groups in the "middle" of the socio-economic hierarchy. These intermediate groups, consisting of the backward castes and the lower middle classes, have periodically challenged the domination of elite groups, especially of the Forward Castes over both the state and the society. This challenge has of late intensified. What are the prospects of democratic accommodation of this challenge from the middle? Frankel sheds light on this issue by contrasting the patterns of relatively successful accommodation in parts of South India with the failure of accommodation in such North Indian states as Bihar and Uttar Pradesh.

The important insight that emerges from the detailed historical and comparative analysis employed by Frankel is that the breakdown of law and order in such northern states as Bihar reflects an intense power struggle between the Forward Castes and the Backward Classes. A number of historical reasons help explain why a similar struggle in such South Indian states as Tamil Nadu was resolved rather early and democratically. The Brahman domination in Tamil Nadu was challenged rather early in comparison to the Hindi heartland. The struggle over, and the sharing of, privilege among Brahmans and Vellalas, for example, created a political opening for Tamil Backwards, an opening successfully capitalized on by the Tamil nationalist movement and leading to the creation of the DMK party. With the introduction of universal suffrage after independence, the DMK slowly but surely mobilized the numerically significant Backwards and successfully displaced the Congress party by an anti-Brahman, pro-Tamil ruling alliance. This new ruling group, however, eschewed radical reforms and maintained its support by co-opting the leaders of Backwards through reservations, by implementing populist programs, and by the fortunate presence of charismatic leaders.

The power struggle in North India has been less smooth. The Brahmans in the North are numerically a much larger force. In addition to enjoying high ritual status, they also simultaneously controlled land and power in parts of North India. This historical monopoly of power and privilege of the Forward Castes has been reinforced by the patterns of zamindari settlement undertaken by the British. Until independence, therefore, the Backwards of the North seldom challenged the privileged position of the Forward Castes. With the introduction of universal suffrage, however, and as a result of such reforms as the zamindari abolition, the Backwards have come into their own. They have used the power of their considerable numbers to effectively challenge the hold of the elite-dominated Congress party and when they have succeeded in forming governments, they have implemented both symbolic and substantial policy changes, for example, the reservation policies. Intense struggles have often broken out over these reform policies, contributing to the breakdown of political order in such North Indian states as Bihar.

The last paper in this volume, by Ghanshyam Shah, draws attention to the political role of India's masses. It was Barrington Moore who noted that, irrespective of whether nations followed the Communist or the capitalist route to modernity, poor peasants always seem to be the victims of the great historical transformation.[3] India's "mixed economy" does not seem to provide an exception. The puzzle that India raises, however, is how such victimization has been maintained within the framework of a democratic polity and how long it can be sustained.

Shah's paper describes and categorizes the myriad of political actions undertaken by India's poor. A number of important insights emerge from his masterly survey. First, and most important, is the clear sense of political restiveness at the lowest social level. The restiveness finds expression in actions that vary from social banditry and impulsive collective action to organized support for key economic demands and for left-of-center political parties.

The second important insight that emerges from Shah's paper is an explanation of why this restiveness has not accumulated. Indian society remains highly segmented along lines of local loyalties, caste sentiments, and spoken language. Village society is still relatively isolated. Protest and discontent in one part of the country, therefore, is seldom supported by other communities with similar complaints. There is plenty of rebellion, but in India, it does not easily add up to a revolution.

It would be wrong to assume, however, that because rebellion of the poor in India is noncumulative, it is also politically inconsequential. Shah points out both the local and the larger political consequences of rural restiveness. The more the poor and the downtrodden have made demands, the greater has been local-level repression. Caste wars, hired *goonda* armies by landlords, and even collusion by local police have all contributed to the tragic and growing oppression of the Scheduled Castes and tribals. Bihar is only the extreme example of how the spread of such local atrocities contributes to the breakdown of orderly government. The higher lev-

---

[3] See Barrington Moore, Jr., *Social Origins of Dictatorship and Democracy*, Boston: Beacon, 1966, especially chap. 9.

els of government are also not immune. Elections cannot be won without the support of the poor. Populism has thus become a common ruling strategy, both within the states and nationally. Populism, however, is a short-term solution; it cannot be maintained indefinitely. Sooner or later, either populism must be curtailed in order to pursue more "rational" economic policies—but how does one then gain the support of the poor—or the economy itself will self-destruct, also creating serious pressures for political change.

The essays by Bardhan, Frankel, and Shah document the political activism of India's various social groups. From the very privileged to the downtrodden, everyone wants more, and everyone hopes and expects that the state will provide it. It can be argued that this growing activism has been a "natural" result of the Indian political economy, in which the Indian state plays an important economic role. The state is perceived as a force that can alter economic distribution within the society, but it is also a state that is organized democratically. Those competing for political support promise economic rewards to their prospective supporters, but those who do not share the gains of planned development may be resentful and attempt to express it politically. As an old, hierarchical society is infused with egalitarian ideas and senses that material gain is controlled by mortals, mortals whom the common man can select, the old order is profoundly disturbed. The nature of the new order is far from clear. Social and economic groups are seeking new niches in a new society whose basic outlines are still not drawn. The short-term pressures on maintaining a legitimate political order are severe. If a breakdown is to be avoided, the choices are either to curtail democracy—and thus the legitimacy of the political order—or to find new and creative ways to satisfy the many clamoring groups.

Retrospect and Prospect

The eight essays discussed above describe the changing nature of India's democracy. The general picture is of a functioning but strained democracy. Some of the strains are caused by what may be considered inevitable byproducts of democratic development. Growing political demands by both the privileged and the underprivileged, as well as the corrosive impact of a new generation of political entrants on norms of political life, are examples of such inevitable consequences. The strains, however, have also been exacerbated by forces that can hardly be considered "sociological necessities." Indira Gandhi's recalcitrant and manipulative political style, and the proclivity of her son Sanjay to incorporate criminals and thugs into the political process, are factors that India's democracy could and should have been spared.

When one takes a retrospective look at India's democracy, what is striking is how the problems have changed. A list of India's pressing problems in the 1950s and 1960s would certainly have included the fragility of the Indian state as a political unit and the inadequacy of domestic food production. Today, in spite of the fact that regional tensions within India are considerable and that the distribution of food is highly skewed, India is a viable nation-state that produces ample food for domestic consumption. It is difficult to say whether contemporary problems are "worse" or more "intense" than these earlier problems, but it is clear that they are different. A list of contemporary problems would include the decay of the ruling institutions, the low rate of economic growth, and, of course, the difficulty of distributing the ample food to the underfed.

The changing nature of India's problems highlights what needs to be recognized by a balanced discussion stressing the contemporary political phenomenon of institutional decay: India's political system and India's political elite have consistently been problem solvers of the highest calibre. The fact that the authors in this volume often stress problems and shortcomings does not mean that they fail to recognize India's achievements. The fact is that some of the important problems of the past in India have been tackled successfully; others continue; and yet others have risen anew, in part because the old problems have been solved. The overriding current problem is that of democratic governability. Even with respect to this, it should be noted that India's political problems often seem intractable precisely because it is a democracy; every political problem that exists in the country is splashed across dozens of newspapers and magazines.

None of this, of course, minimizes the seriousness of the political difficulties facing India today; it only puts them in a relative perspective. The question of the survival of democracy in India is a serious one. Social groups press the state from all directions. State institutions are weakened both by actions of the political elite and by growing social pressures. In a society in which most problem solving must be initiated by the state, an ineffective state would be a cause for great alarm. In a political economy that has cherished democratic survival as one of its great achievements, even at the expense of modest economic growth, the failure of democracy would be a tragic failure.

What do the analyses presented above tell us about the prospect of democracy and good government in India? Most of the authors do not doubt the short-term viability of India's democracy. Most of them, however, have also noted the sources of growing strain within India. A similar set of ambivalent sentiments was expressed by a group of eminent panelists—

L. K. Jha, Myron Weiner, Bashiruddin Ahmed, Pran Chora, and Lloyd Rudolph—who were asked to comment on the future of India's democracy at the Princeton conference.[4] With varying degrees of assuredness, they all felt confident that India's functioning democracy is likely to continue into the near future. Beyond the short term, however, they all wondered whether the growing demands and strains could be accommodated within a democratic framework.

The analyses in this volume draw attention, on the one hand, to the role of the state and of the state authorities in molding political change and stress, on the other hand, the political impact of growing interest-group activism. The simultaneous focus on state and societal forces in political change has important analytical and predictive implications. These can be drawn out briefly.

The main analytical conclusion to be drawn from this volume is that the process of institutional decay in a developing country like India is not simply a function of social mobilization generated by economic development. New demands clearly produce pressures for political accommodation. Several essays in this volume highlight this point. They also suggest, however, that these growing demands reflect distributive conflicts between the "haves" and the "have nots." Moreover, whether these pressures will be accommodated, or whether they will be manipulated and repressed, is a function of the actions undertaken by the state authorities. Several of the essays in this volume develop this position. Power-hungry leaders can refuse to share power. They, in turn, seek to undermine institutions that constrain or threaten their political power. Deinstitutionalization, therefore, is a process to which state and social actors can both contribute.

It is both a conservative and an analytically misleading position to hold that institutions weaken primarily as a result of demand overload from society. This analytical and normative position bestows the state with a superior position over social groups as the guarantor of the public good. The Indian empirical materials do not support such a comfortable conclusion. Social groups and state authorities have both contributed to the process of institutional decay in India.

The twin foci on the state and societal variables also suggests that political change in India will remain a function of the nature and the intensity of group demands, on the one hand, and of the institution building tasks undertaken by political authorities, on the other. The demands are likely to grow. It is ironic that growing demands reflect the spread of the same democracy that they threaten. It was easier to maintain India's democracy

---

[4] See *Summary of the Proceedings of the Conference on "India's Democracy,"* Woodrow Wilson School, Princeton University, mimeo, pp. 69–86.

when it was primarily a gift of the elite, yet it is a measure of the success of Indian democracy that so many groups want to participate and so many want more from the state. The question that remains open, however, is: Can the state meet the demands? Can institutions be recreated through which resource conflict can be resolved legitimately?

With many institutions in disarray, the actions of leaders will remain of utmost importance. Leaders have to simultaneously solve short-term problems while laying down the basis for a longer term rejuvenation of the dormant, damaged, or destroyed institutions. Over the long term, effective problem solving is likely only if it is institutionalized. The building of institutions, however, always requires sacrifice of personal power. Leaders create institutions. Creating institutions means putting impersonal rules ahead of personal discretion; in a democracy, it also means delegating power and responsibility to others. Whether or not India's new leaders will prove worthy of this formidable challenge is a question to which answers will emerge only over the next few decades.

India's Democracy Under
Rajiv Gandhi, 1985–1989

ATUL KOHLI

Rajiv Gandhi came to power in India in late 1984, when the essays in this volume were first conceived. He went out of power just as the new edition of the volume goes to press in early 1990. The main purpose of the Epilogue is thus to interpret his term in power within the framework of the volume. Nothing has happened in the intervening five years that would detract from the broad image of India developed in these essays: a functioning but a strained democratic polity. Rajiv Gandhi's attempts to reverse the continuing institutional fragmentation did not succeed, and activism of various socio-economic groups during his term grew. His failure to translate his considerable popular majority into an effective government highlighted the simultaneous tendencies in Indian politics toward centralization and powerlessness. These tendencies, in turn, reflect the continuing weakness of systematic authority links between the Indian state and society.

The following discussion updates the three central state-society themes of the volume: decline of political institutions; ethnic activism; and the growing mobilization of India's major castes and classes. Comments are also made toward the end on the significance of the 1989 national elections for India's changing state-society relations. Prior to the main discussion, however, two caveats should be noted. First, given that this is to be a fairly brief epilogue, the major analytical themes are discussed only with reference to a few empirical materials and, even then, fairly briefly. Thus, for example, the issue of institutional fragmentation is discussed only in relation to Gandhi's failed efforts to rebuild the Congress party; ethnic problems are discussed mainly with reference to the Punjab; and mobilization of social forces is delineated by a focus on two issues: opposition to economic "liberalization" and growing religious conflicts. Detailed discussion of these and other related themes is available elsewhere.[1] The

---

[1] See, for example, Atul Kohli, *Democracy and Disorder: India's Growing Crisis of Governability*, New York: Cambridge University Press, 1990, esp. Part IV.

second caveat concerns the fact that this is a single-authored epilogue to an edited volume. While an attempt is made to update the main themes of the volume, the interpretations here may or may not be consistent with the other contributions. All the contributors are thus absolved of responsibility for the interpretations developed below.

Continuing Institutional Decline

Rajiv Gandhi came to power with a large electoral majority. Soon thereafter he let it be known that his reign would be different from his mother's, and that he would utilize his newly won power to chart a "new" path for India. Among his priorities were rebuilding of the Congress party, settlement of such regional disputes as the Punjab, and liberalization of India's economy. We know in retrospect that his efforts in these areas were not successful. The reasons for policy failures can be traced back to the conflict between maintaining popularity and implementing difficult decisions. This conflict, in turn, reflects the vicious cycle of centralization and powerlessness that weakness of institutions has created in India: because institutions such as parties are weak, elections are won on general mandates; when leaders attempt to translate such mandates into specific policies, potential winners and losers become politically divided, and the link between leaders and their supporters is quickly exposed for what it really is, namely, fragile; and since leaders cannot implement many of their policies, and thus cannot count on policy success as a vehicle for assuring electoral support, they tend to centralize power in their person and utilize leadership appeals and general "mood swings" as means for a new round of electoral competition.

Given the significance of political parties for effective government, it is not surprising that Rajiv Gandhi sought to reinvigorate the Congress party as an organization. Central to this political project was his espoused commitment in 1985 to hold internal party elections. Such elections could have brought forward new and genuine grass-roots Congress leaders at the level of districts and states. We know in early 1990 that these elections have not materialized, at least not so far. The question for analysis is, why not? Why did a popular leader fail to implement one of his own important political goals?

As Henry Hart and James Manor explain in their essays, the Congress party that Rajiv Gandhi inherited was essentially a top-down structure of appointed officers. Many of these appointed individuals were in power in states and districts because they enjoyed the support of those above rather than of those below them. When Gandhi announced that party elections would be held soon, it became readily evident that most party positions would go to those who could muster support of grass-roots party members. This prospect, in turn, generated two types of power conflicts: one involving the appointed officials against those who sought to challenge them in open, intra-party elections; and the other involving the top leadership, who became worried about ensuring their own power in the face of a newly elected party hierarchy. Since party elections became a victim of both these power conflicts, it is important to comment further on these issues.

Party elections, if held, would have had to be supervised by the existing party hierarchy. Those in positions of power, however, were precisely the same individuals whose power was threatened by the proposed elections. These appointed officers thus sought to preserve their power. Their local-level popularity was often doubtful; how could they then win elections? What they sought to manipulate were the resources they controlled, namely, the records of who was a party member and thus who was eligible to vote in the party elections. Since Congress' local-level records concerning party membership are, at best, incomplete, appointed officers came up with a formidable strategy: they started creating "bogus membership" lists, or hastily enlisting assured supporters, real and fictitious, as party members by paying membership dues out of their own pockets.

As "bogus" members grew, it became evident to potential challengers that those who were part of the existing party structure had gained a distinct advantage. Instead of testing a party candidate's true popularity among party members, elections offered incumbents a chance to translate their appointed positions into electoral victories—corrupt victories, but nevertheless victories. Many Congress elite, who were not in positions of power, and who would have liked the opportunity to contest a fair election, thus came to oppose the elections. The conflict finally came out in the open in 1986 over the issue of "bogus membership" lists and came to be led by the old Congressman, Kamlapati Tripathi.[2] Intra-party conflict in some parts of India in 1986 became vitriolic. Party offices had to be put under the protection of armed guards so that lists of party membership could not be altered any further. Clearly, instead of reinvigorating the party, party elections became a major source of intra-party struggle and thus of party weakness.

The other problem created by looming party elections was that they came to threaten Rajiv Gandhi's own power. His initial mass popularity rested in part on his "inheritance" as a member of the "ruling family" and in part on the circumstances of his mother's assassination and the

[2] See, for example, *India Today*, May 15, 1986, pp. 46–48.

subsequent "national mood" of sympathy and fear of political chaos. As long as this mass popularity was intact, Gandhi thought he could use it to effect significant political outcomes, such as restructuring the Congress party. If successful, such an outcome would have meant nothing less than a translation of personal into institutional power. Building such democratic institutions as a party, however, necessarily entails the risk that those who initiate such tasks may turn out to be the eventual losers. This follows because those elected at the lower and the middle levels of the organization may eventually choose a new leader. Reintroduction of elections into the Congress party was thus a risk. Gandhi felt comfortable taking such a risk as long as his mass popularity was secure. Over time, however, as the Congress party lost several state elections during 1986 and 1987, the prospect of a hostile party must have appeared to be one more political liability that he could do without.

Successful elections within the Congress party could have marked the beginning of a reversal of decline in one of India's important political institutions. Strengthening the Congress party, in turn, could have further helped limit the deinstitutionalizing consequences of personal power. This, however, did not come to pass. During 1985 and 1986, Rajiv Gandhi made numerous public statements and undertook some concrete measures that suggested that rebuilding of the Congress party was an important political goal. By 1987, however, this goal was more or less abandoned. This failure highlighted the difficulties of transforming personal into institutional power. Personalistic power rests on diffuse and often fragile support of a leader by the masses; institutional power, by contrast, requires that the links between national leaders and supporters be systematically organized around a political program via intermediate and grass-roots leadership. The logic of personal and of institutional power thus works at cross-purposes: personal power runs top-down and often requires maximizing leadership discretion; institutionalized power, by contrast, especially in democratic parties, has significant bottom-up tendencies and definitely constrains individual discretion.

The theme of institutional decline during Rajiv Gandhi's rule could be easily developed further with reference to institutions other than the Congress party. For reasons of space, however, I will make only passing references. Gandhi's rule was characterized by a high turnover in senior personnel. Much of decision-making power was centralized in the person of the Prime Minister. Senior-level appointments, both political and bureaucratic, thus reflected Gandhi's personal preferences. As a result, cabinet and parliamentary officers on the one hand, and senior civil and police appointments on the other, were often made at the whim of the Prime Minister. Irrespective of the fact that, on occasion, this brought competent individuals to the fore, it is also true that such a mode of conduct contributed further to continuing deinstitutionalization, with long-term adverse consequences. To be fair, it should be added that, reflecting the logic of personal power, many such non-Congress-run states as Andhra Pradersh under N. T. Ramo Rao, and Tamil Nadu under M. G. Rammachandran, also experienced deinstitutionalization in both politics and bureaucracy in the 1980s.

REGIONAL AND ETHNIC ACTIVISM

The essays by Paul Brass and Jyotirindra Das Gupta underline the political content of India's contemporary regional and ethnic conflicts. In both essays the authors further suggest that democratic accommodation of ethinic demands in India tends to reduce ethnically oriented regional conflict. The same theme emerges from an analysis of Rajiv Gandhi's attempts to solve the "Sikh crisis" in Punjab. Soon after coming to power, Gandhi adopted a reconciliatory approach toward the Sikhs and toward the Akali party that claimed to represent them. As a result, terrorist violence declined and elections were held in 1985. Over time, however, the agreements reached during the early reconciliatory phase came apart. Terrorist violence rose once again, the elected government fell in 1987, and when Gandhi went out of power in late 1989, it remained debatable whether the Punjab crisis was any closer to a solution than when he had come to power. The question for analysis in this brief epilogue is, what factors best help explain this continuing failure to deal with ethnic conflict, such as in the Punjab?

By the time Rajiv Gandhi came to power, conflict in the Punjab was already complex and not amenable to any easy solutions. In addition to the political conflict between the Akali Dal and the Congress party, the conflict was being fueled by a number of other factors: (a) socio-economic demands of wealthy jat Sikh farmers and the unemployed Sikh youths; (b) ready availability of guns and other arms via Pakistan; (c) relative ineffectiveness of the regional police; (d) the high premium put on "violence and sacrifice" in the regional political culture; (e) the growing spiral of violence created by terrorism-repression-terrorism; and (f) a genuine and growing distrust on the part of the Sikh community about the willingness of Congress leaders to compromise. And yet, as Paul Brass argues in his essay, and as both Rajiv Gandhi and Akali Dal correctly understood in 1985, the starting point of any solution had to be political accommodation of "Sikh demands."

The Rajiv-Longowal Accord of 1985 that Paul Brass discusses was precisely such a political agreement. It was agreed in this Accord to transfer Chandigarh to the Punjab, to readjust some river irrigation waters in favor of the Punjab, and to widen the scope of the inquiry into the killings of Sikhs in New Delhi. The fact that Rajiv Gandhi made all these concessions—the same ones his mother had refused—reflected a changed political situation.

During 1984–1985, after a massive electoral victory, Gandhi was a lot more politically secure than his mother had been during 1982–1984. Concessions from a position of political strength added to his popularity by highlighting his magnanimity. By contrast, Indira Gandhi's concessions to the Akalis, say in 1983, would only have dramatized the defeat of a beleaguered leader. Rajiv Gandhi's temporary sense of enormous political security thus enabled him to put aside partisan political considerations for the larger national good. Over time, however, as this sense of security diminished, so did his political largesse.

The short-term consequence of Rajiv Gandhi's new approach in 1985 was that the intensity of conflict subsided. For example, only 64 people died in terrorism-related deaths in 1985. This figure contrasts with nearly 300 in 1984, with more than 600 in 1986, and with nearly 1,000 and 3,000 in 1987 and 1988 respectively. State elections that were held in 1985 were by no means free of violence or threats of violence. Longowal, the leader of the Akalis, was assassinated and the elections were held in the presence of one policeman for every ten voters. In spite of this, there was widespread support for both the Rajiv-Longowal accord and the elections. Public opinion polls suggested that educated Sikhs and Hindus of the Punjab supported the accord.[3] The call of the militants for a boycott of the elections was also widely ignored; the turnout for the elections was extremely high—nearly 70 percent of the Punjab electorate.

For a brief moment in late 1985, then, when a newly elected government under Barnala's leadership was formed, it appeared that the Punjab crisis may have turned the corner. We know in retrospect, however, that such was not the case. The question again arises, why not? The main reason was a failure to implement such crucial clauses of the Rajiv-Longowal Accord as the transfer of Chandigarh to Punjab and the adjustment of river waters in favor of the Punjab. While the reasons for this failure are complex, at root of it lay the broader, national political situation in which Gandhi's popularity was declining. The loss of the Punjab elections had already made some within the Congress party wonder whether he was seriously concerned about Congress's political future. The Congress then lost a second important set of elections in Assam in December 1985.

[3] See *India Today*, August 15, 1985, pp. 10–11.

This further encouraged widespread rumblings, both within and outside the Congress party. The common charge hurled at Gandhi during this period was that he did not care enough about the Congress party's electoral fortunes. As he was put more and more on the defensive, he must have decided to give a higher priority to electoral concerns.

Once this decision was made, much of the Punjab accord was doomed. Implementation of the two crucial issues of the Accord—Chandigarh and the river waters—would have affected Haryana adversely; the Punjab's gain was Haryana's loss. When Gandhi's position was strong in the second half of 1985, it is conceivable that he could have pressed the Congress Chief Minister of Haryana, Bhajan Lal, to go along with the Accord; press statements from this period reveal a conciliatory Bhajan Lal. As Gandhi's position weakened, however, Bhajan Lal's stand also hardened. State elections for Haryana were scheduled for June 1987. Having lost both the Punjab and the Assam elections, Gandhi was not in a position to take the additional blame for Haryana. The implementation of the Punjab accord thus became a victim of Congress's electoral interests.

The more it became clear that crucial clauses of the Accord were not being implemented, the more politically pressed Barnala felt within the Punjab. Barnala's legitimacy rested heavily on his continued capacity to gain advantages for the Punjab from New Delhi. New Delhi's failure to implement the Accord weakened Barnala. The Akali Dal was in any case a deeply factionalized party. Leadership weakness encouraged open factionalism, and the government's position weakened further. Barnala increasingly needed the support of Congress legislators within the Punjab to make his government work. The more the Congress propped up Barnala, the worst fears of the militants appeared to come true: Barnala came to represent more the interests of Congress than of those of the Sikhs. This sentiment encouraged terrorism throughout 1986 and 1987.

Since the Accord was not implemented, and terrorist violence increased, Gandhi, in turn, came to refer to the Punjab more and more as a "police problem." Sidhartha Shankar Ray, who had been in charge of West Bengal in the late 1960s during the Naxalite terror, was sent to the Punjab as the new governor. Ribero, with his reputation of being a "tough and honest" police officer, was put in charge of the Punjab police. The Ray-Ribero team highlighted a new approach to the Punjab. The reconciliatory political period was over. From now on, the Punjab was mainly to be dealt with as a "law and order" problem.

The "law and order" approach failed to bring terrorism under control. Numerous competing groups with unclear goals emerged. Some of these groups proclaimed their goal to be the creation of a sovereign state of Khalistan. To this end, they were willing to kill as many Hindus as it would take to drive Hindus out of the Punjab. Other groups were less clear about their eventual goals; they sought to avenge what they perceived to be the insults brought upon the Sikhs by New Delhi. Militant groups of both types were willing to kill, not only Hindus, but also other Sikhs, who were suspected of being informers, or dissenters with knowledge of the terrorist organizations. Throughout 1987, therefore, terrorism-related deaths continued to rise. They climbed to a record high in 1988; nearly 3,000 people, including women and children, were killed by terrorists and by state repression in that one year. Many of those killed were Sikhs suspected of betraying the militants.

Short-term electoral interests of the Congress party and considerations of the personal power of Rajiv Gandhi repeatedly came in the way of resuming a more political approach to the Punjab. Gandhi failed to pursue an investigation into the killings of Sikhs in New Delhi. One suspects this had to do with the fear that an investigation would implicate some senior Congressmen. A similar theme concerning the interests of the Congress party was at the forefront when Gandhi finally dismissed the Barnala government and imposed Presidential rule on the Punjab in May 1987. Haryana elections were scheduled for June 1987. There was growing apprehension within the Congress party that they might lose these elections. In order to assuage the Hindu sentiments in Haryana, therefore, Gandhi made a last-minute effort to appear tough on the Sikhs. That this ploy failed totally and that the Congress was trounced in the Haryana elections do not in any way reduce the significance of the politically motivated dismissal of the Barnala government.

It is too early at the time of this writing to judge the impact of the resumption of electoral politics in the Punjab in late 1989. What is clear is that the failure to Rajiv Gandhi and his government to find a solution to the Punjab problem can be traced back to the numerous political pressures upon him, especially pressures to protect the electoral and other interests of the Congress party. The initial sense of political security enabled Gandhi to make major concessions to the Akalis in 1985. The resulting decline in militancy and the resumption of electoral politics were important pointers toward a solution to the crisis. Soon, however, as the national mood settled down from the trauma of Indira Gandhi's assassination, and "normal" politics resumed, including a decline in Rajiv's popularity, Rajiv Gandhi found it difficult to implement the concessions made during an earlier period of heady euphoria. The failure to implement the Accord delegitimized the Akalis and encouraged terrorism. None of this is to deny that the regional conflict involving the Punjab is complex in origin and now difficult to solve. The fact remains, however, that partisan political interests of India's national leaders have remained an important cause of the continuing turmoil.

CLASS, RELIGION, AND POLITICS

Growing activism of various social and economic groups was a third theme of continuing significance during Rajiv Gandhi's rule. The essays by Pranab Bardhan, Francine Frankel, and Ghanshyam Shah nicely document the political significance of India's various socio-economic groups. Numerous similar examples could be discussed to extend the temporal discussion to the end of the 1980s. Two types of organized political activities are, however, especially revealing of the changing state-society relations in India's democracy. These are, first, the responses of various interest groups to shifts in economic policy and, second, the growing political mobilization along religious lines.

Rajiv Gandhi attempted to shift India's economic policies away from controls and import substitution and toward a more "liberal" direction.[4] Leaving aside the issues of the economic consequences of such a shift, the political dynamics accompanying the attempted shift are noteworthy. Gandhi had some success in lifting controls, lowering taxes, and liberalizing India's restricted trade regime. Very quickly, however, the policy shift mobilized a diverse set of reactions. While all those who opposed the new policies did not succeed in reversing the government's economic orientation, the fear of electoral losses pushed Gandhi back in a more populist direction. When he lost power in 1989, economic policy, though still moving in a "liberal" direction, increasingly came to be couched in the rhetoric of socialism.

The push for liberalization came mainly from Gandhi and from the bureaucratic-technocratic elites that came to control the levers of India's economic policy-making during his rule. The main social support for these policies came from urban groups, especially those in business and industry. Lifting state controls, for example, on such activities of national firms as entry into production, production decisions, and expansion in size were especially welcome by India's various peak business organizations, the Chambers of Commerce. By contrast, however, business groups were, on balance, reluctant to support any major opening of the Indian economy to international competition in goods, services, or capital. Since

[4] For a detailed discussion, see Atul Kohli, "Politics of Economic Liberalization in India," *World Development*, March 1989, pp. 305–328.

government policies closely followed these preferences of businessmen, one is led to underline the growing political significance of Indian business groups, especially big business that produces for the protected domestic market and especially during Rajiv Gandhi's term in power.

The attempts to move economic policy in a more "liberal" direction did not go unopposed. Concerted and direct opposition to the reforms came mainly from three quarters. Significant sections of the Congress party opposed some of the new economic policies, lest the party abandon one of its important vote-catching assets among India's numerous poor, namely, a pro-poor populist orientation. In retrospect, judged by political criteria, political events have borne out the "political rationality" of those who opposed the efforts at "economic rationality." India's left-of-center intellectuals were another source of direct and vocal opposition to the new policies. While it is hard to judge the significance of such opposition, it did provide a seemingly technical and intellectual rationale for those who disagreed with the government's new orientation. And last, an organized working class in the public sector openly opposed the liberalization thrust. Even before any moves toward "privatization" were made, the organized workers let it be known, through memorandums and strikes, what the government may expect if it undertakes "modernization" of the public sector, leading up to layoffs.

More diffuse and, one is tempted to add, more significant opposition also emerged from the numerically significant rural groups. Middle peasants, for example, sensed in the new economic policies—especially in tax concessions that mainly benefit the more prosperous urban dwellers—if not a direct anti-rural bias, then certainly very little for the peasantry. This opposition was expressed in farmer movements demanding subsidized agricultural inputs and higher producer prices, as well as in electoral behavior, such as in the widespread erosion of Congress's popular base in green revolution states like Haryana. The rural poor, by contrast to the middle peasants, seldom react directly to shifts in macro-economic policies; what they do react to, however, is when they suspect that anti-poverty concerns are being abandoned. There is evidence to suggest that Rajiv Gandhi and the Congress party lost some support among the poorest of the poor, the landless laborers of the scheduled castes. This shift was especially evident in the national elections of 1989, when the scheduled castes in such significant states like Uttar Pradesh voted for the first time, not for Congress, but for a new party of their own, the Bahujan Samaj Party.

Both the direct and the diffuse opposition did not succeed in reversing Rajiv Gandhi's "liberalizing" thrust. The "logic of economic efficiency," as interpreted by Gandhi and his advisers and supported by business groups, kept India's economic policy moving away from a state-controlled "socialist" direction. What the diverse opposition did do, however, was, first, chip away at the government's popularity and, second, force Gandhi to abandon the rhetoric of liberalization, readopt that of "socialism," or more accurately populism, and probably reduce both the pace and the scope of intended policy changes.

This highly abbreviated account of political dynamics accompanying Gandhi's attempted "liberalization" of India's economy clarifies two important points. First, as in the discussion above on Congress party reform and the Punjab, Gandhi's halfhearted pursuit of another major policy goal further highlights the limited capacity of his government in translating popular support into concrete outcomes. More important for the present discussion is the second point, namely, the pattern of political mobilization of socio-economic groups. Business and other well-off urban groups provided support for "economic rationalization." Those in the popular sectors, however, rightly or wrongly, were often suspicious of governmental efforts. They interpreted such moves, less from the criteria of what is economically "rational," but more from the standpoint of who may gain and lose from the outcomes. As a result, many in the middle and lower strata opposed Gandhi's policy shifts and constrained his political capacities. The "logic of efficiency" thus came into conflict with the "logic of democracy." This conflict, in turn, is likely to remain an important state-society issue in India's future.

The rise of religious activism was another important political development during Rajiv Gandhi's term in power. While intense religion-oriented political conflicts are nothing new in the subcontinent, the recent electoral successes of such pro-Hindu parties as the Bharatiya Janata Party (BJP) represented an important new trend. Complex in origin, this development is not unrelated to the distributional conflicts discussed above. Both the timing and the locale of the rise of religious politics suggest that its roots lie, not so much in the "sacred," as in the "secular," that is, in the broader political and economic context.

As James Manor suggests in his essay (see especially p. 80), the recent reemergence of religious political themes can be traced back to Indira Gandhi's courting of the Hindu vote in the early 1980s. It is arguable that there was more than a coincidence in the fact that this political shift occurred around the same time when Indira Gandhi quietly gave up on her "socialist" commitments of "poverty alleviation." We know in retrospect that her populism in the 1970s was mainly a mobilization strategy, whose goals were not implemented. If electoral majorities were not (or could not) be mobilized along rich-versus-poor themes in the 1980s, how were elections to be won? One ready mechanism in a multi-ethnic polity is to mobilize majority ethnic groups against minority ones. And this is precisely what happened. The abandonment of populist themes that were aimed at incorporating the popular sectors left open a political vacuum. As a clever politician, Indira Gandhi herself sought to fill this vacuum initially by adopting pro-Hindu themes. The initiative, however, quickly slipped out of her son's grasp. Parties like the BJP, with their longer commitment to pro-Hindu themes and their superior organization, were much better situated to take advantage of the new political situation than was the less skillful Rajiv.

Rajiv Gandhi flirted with pro-Hindu themes but not with great success. Such initiatives in the second half of the 1980s came to be dominated more and more by the BJP and associated organizations. The electoral successes of the BJP cannot all be attributed to the political vacuum created by Congress's failed populism. The BJP's political advantages vary from region to region: in states like Himachal and Madhya Pradesh, the BJP has basically offered an opportunity to all those opposed to the Congress—irrespective of whether their politics are communal or not; in states like Gujarat and Uttar Pradesh, by contrast, militant anti-Muslim mobilization has altered established political alliances in favor of the BJP; and in nearly all northern states, the BJP has benefited from having entered electoral agreements with other non-Congress parties. The rise of BJP is thus a fairly complex issue. There is nevertheless a common theme underlying its national success: the failure of the Congress to incorporate the groups it mobilized in the 1970s has left them available for mobilization by such other better organized parties as the BJP.

THE 1989 NATIONAL ELECTION

Two issues made India's 1989 election a significant one: the Congress party was voted out of power for only the second time in the last 40 years; and for the first time in these 40 years, India in late 1989 came to be governed by a minority government. The elections were also notable for being violent—more than 100 election-related deaths were officially recorded.

The decline in the number of the seats that Congress won in 1989 was dramatic in comparison to the 1984 and even the 1980 elections: 195 seats won in 1989, in contrast to 415 and 353 seats won in 1984 and 1980 respectively. Congress's share of the popular vote, however, did not decline as dramatically. The Congress in the 1989 elections secured nearly 40 percent of the popular vote. This was a drop of roughly 8 percent from the 1984 elections. One needs to keep in mind, however, that Rajiv Gandhi's spectacular victory in 1984 was itself somewhat of an exception; the voter turnout in 1989 was 10 percent lower than in 1984, suggesting that the extra level of politicization engendered by a sense of crisis in 1984 may have now disappeared. Congress's share of popular votes in the 1980 elections, when it had also secured a comfortable majority in the parliament, thus provides a different, and may be even a more appropriate, point of comparison; Congress's share in that year was 43 percent. The decline in its popular support between 1980 and 1989 was thus only 3 percent.

The juxtaposition of the dramatic decline in Congress's parliamentary seats against the less dramatic decline in its popularity leads to two important issues. First, while the days of Congress's unquestioned dominance clearly have long been over, Congress remains a significant political force in India. Even without dramatic changes, Congress could come back to power in the near future. The second issue concerns the factors that really help explain the shift in India from a majority Congress to a minority non-Congress national government. These factors are two: a small but significant decline in Congress's popularity; and the changing nature of India's non-Congress parties, including their capacity to work together against the Congress. Both these factors require some discussion.

One should not look for dramatic failures of Rajiv Gandhi to explain Congress's defeat in the 1989 elections. As the discussion above suggests, there is no need to deny that Gandhi's term in power was hardly exemplary. Policy failures must have contributed to some decline in Congress's popularity. More important, relatively poor performance is what probably lies behind the story of how Gandhi squandered the opportunity to build new coalitions and to consolidate his considerable power base.

Aside from the inability to implement the major goals that Gandhi had defined as his priorities, his government also got marred by charges of corruption. The so-called Bofor's scandal—named after the Swedish company Bofor that allegedly made payments to high officials of Gandhi's government to secure a contract to supply guns to the Indian armed forces—dominated the attention of the media, especially prior to the election. There is little doubt that such charges contributed to the displeasure of some of the Indian urban middle classes toward Gandhi. Whether or not the electoral impact of such corruption scandals was much wider remains unclear.

The opposition to Rajiv Gandhi, led by V. P. Singh, mobilized primarily around issues of corruption, rising prices, and, most important, the ineffectiveness of Gandhi as a leader: he was not a man of the people; he was too westernized; and he did not understand the plight of the ordinary Indian, who is poor and lives in the dusty, hot countryside. It is clear in retrospect that this form of nativistic populism paid political dividends.

The other major factor that helps account for Congress's defeat was the capacity of the opposition parties to work together. India's electoral arithmetic since 1967 has been such that a unified opposition could have kept the Congress out of office for nearly half of the last 22 years. An important component of Congress's defeat in the 1989 elections was thus the simple fact that most of the significant opposition parties reached a prior electoral agreement. This involved a commitment and an arrangement to fight the Congress party in every constituency with one candidate. Since the Congress has in the past characteristically won with less than 50 percent of the vote, a single opposition candidate in every constituency can usually play havoc with Congress's electoral fortunes. And this is precisely what happened: there was a small but significant decline in Congress's "normal" level of support, and the opposition cashed in on the situation by fielding one-on-one contests across much of India.

How does one explain that India's significant non-Congress parties managed to work together in the 1989 elections? The simple and powerful answer is that the rewards of working together were much higher than those of working separately. The inability, however, of these same parties to work together in the past—and possibly again in the future—leads one to suggest that other factors were also at work. Three are especially noteworthy: the acceptance of a new leader, V. P. Singh, by a number of disparate political forces; the political learning that has taken place since the disastrous performance of the opposition parties during 1975–1977; and a changing political situation in the second half of the 1980s in which Congress's declining popularity bolstered the prospect of a non-Congress victory.

The new government in India in early 1990 is a minority government, supported by disparate parties like the BJP and the Communist Party of India, Marxist. Its political stability at the time of writing is uncertain. For our purposes, however, the broader analytical points are relatively clear. During Rajiv Gandhi's term in power, both the decline of India's political institutions and the activism of various socio-economic groups continued. In spite of a large electoral majority, Gandhi failed to provide effective government. Leadership incompetence was only a part of the problem. The larger and more important reasons lay in the nature of state-society relations in India's democracy, especially the weakness of systematic authority links between the state and society. The review of

Gandhi's term in power thus highlights how short-term electoral pressures often led to policy failures. The concluding question is, what does this disjuncture between electoral needs and the capacity to solve problems tell us about the nature of the Indian state at its apex?

The analysis above suggests that the process of how power is won at the highest level has increasingly little bearing on how power is used in India. The personal popularity of elected leaders thus cannot be easily translated into a capacity to solve problems. What is missing here are parties and programs. Without parties and programs, only leaders with great personal appeal, however acquired, are capable of winning majorities in contemporary India. Such majorities provide a modicum of coherence in what is otherwise an extremely heterogeneous polity. These majorities, however, are seldom acquired while mobilizing support for a specific program. Since winning elections does not mean that you stand for anything specific, general mandates are quickly lost. It is impossible to be something to everyone, especially when "big" decisions need to be made. Attempts to implement specific programs thus quickly give rise to opposition. Even those who support a program are difficult to mobilize because of an organizational vacuum. As opposition mounts and ready supporters are few, decisive action is periodically replaced by the recurring tendency to muddle through.

If the role of the Indian state in India's development was minimal, and if many of that country's pressing problems could be solved by social actors without the help of the state, then the state's relative ineffectiveness would not be of near-crisis consequence. The Indian state, however, is highly interventionist. It controls a major portion of India's resources and potential initiative. Under these circumstances, the state's growing ineffectiveness is a matter of considerable concern. India's problems are likely to grow, but the state's capacity to deal with them may not. This could be a long-term recipe for accumulating crises of governability.

CONTRIBUTORS
(Listed Alphabetically)

PRANAB BARDHAN is Professor of Economics at the University of California, Berkeley. He has taught at Massachusetts Institute of Technology, Indian Statistical Institute and Delhi School of Economics. His publications include, *The Political Economy of Development in India* (Basil Blackwell, 1984); *Land, Labor and Rural Poverty* (Columbia University Press, 1984); and *Economic Growth, Development and Foreign Trade: A Study in Pure Theory* (John Wiley, 1970). His forthcoming books include *The Economic Theory of Agrarian Institutions*. He is currently the chief editor of *The Journal of Development Economics*.

PAUL R. BRASS is Professor of Political Science and South Asian Studies in the Jackson School of International Studies at the University of Washington. His major recent publications include *Ethnic Groups and the State* (Croom Helm, 1985), *Caste, Faction and Party in Indian Politics*, Volume I: *Faction and Party* and Volume II: *Election Studies* (Chanakya, 1983 and 1985), and (with Robert S. Anderson *et al.*), *Science, Politics and the Agricultural Revolution in Asia* (Westview, 1982).

STEPHEN P. COHEN is Professor of Political Science and Associate Director of the Program in Arms Control at the University of Illinois. The author of several books on South Asia, including *The Indian Army* (University of California Press, 1971) and *The Pakistan Army* (University of California Press, 1984), Professor Cohen during 1985–1987 served as a member of the Policy Planning Staff of the U.S. Department of State.

JYOTIRINDRA DAS GUPTA is Professor of Political Science at the University of California, Berkeley. He is also involved in the Program in Development Studies, the Center for South and Southeast Asia Studies and the Institute of International Studies at Berkeley. His publications include *Authority, Priority and Human Development* (Oxford University Press, 1981) and *Language Conflict and National Development* (1970) and, as co-author, *Language Planning Processes* (1977).

FRANCINE R. FRANKEL is Professor of Political Science and South Asia Studies at the University of Pennsylvania. Her numerous publications include *India's Political Economy, 1947–1977, The Gradual Revolution* (Princeton, 1978). In collaboration with M.S.A. Rao, she has recently completed a major project on "Caste, Class and Dominance in Modern India." The two-volume study will be published by Oxford University Press in 1987.

HENRY C. HART is Professor Emeritus of Political Science (and former Chairman of the Department of Asian Studies) at the University of Wisconsin, Madison. His publications include *New India's Rivers* (Orient Longmans, 1956); *Campus India* (Michigan State University Press, 1960); *Administrative Aspects of River Valley Development* (Asia Publishing House, 1963); and *Indira Gandhi's India* (ed.), (Westview Press, 1976).

JOHN P. LEWIS is Professor of Economics and Public Affairs at Princeton University. He first visited India for the Brookings Institution in 1959–1960. He wrote *Quiet Crisis in India* (Brookings, 1962), served as the Director of USAID/India during 1964–1969, was a consultant to the Ford Foundation's India program during the 1970s, and continues to visit and write about India as the occasion affords. He is also the former Dean of the Woodrow Wilson School and current Director of the Research Program in Development Studies at Princeton University.

ATUL KOHLI is Associate Professor of Politics and International Affairs at Princeton University. His publications include *The State and Poverty in India: The Politics of Reform* (Cambridge University Press, 1987) and an edited volume, *The State and Development in the Third World* (Princeton University Press, 1986). He is currently writing a book tentatively entitled, *Erosion of Authority in India: A Study of Political Change*. He is the Review Article Editor of *World Politics*.

JAMES MANOR is Professor and Fellow at the Institute of Development Studies in the University of Sussex. He has taught at Yale and Harvard in the U.S. and at London and Leicester Universities in England. His numerous publications include *Political Change in Mysore, 1917–1955* (Australian National University Monograph, 1978) and a coedited volume, *Transfer and Transformation: Political Institutions in the New Commonwealth* (Leicester University Press, 1983). Since 1980, he has edited the *Journal of Commonwealth and Comparative Politics*.

GHANSHYAM SHAH has been associated with the Centre for Social Studies, Surat, India since 1972. He has been the Director of and a Senior Fellow at the Centre since 1977. He has published six books including *Caste Association and Political Process in Gujarat* (1975), *Politics of Scheduled Caste and Tribe* (1975) and *Economic Differentiations and Tribal Identity* (1984).

PUBLICATIONS OF THE CENTER

OF INTERNATIONAL STUDIES

Gabriel A. Almond, *The Appeals of Communism* (Princeton University Press 1954)

William W. Kaufmann, ed., *Military Policy and National Security* (Princeton University Press 1956)

Klaus Knorr, *The War Potential of Nations* (Princeton University Press 1956)

Lucian W. Pye, *Guerrilla Communism in Malaya* (Princeton University Press 1956)

Charles De Visscher, *Theory and Reality in Public International Law*, trans. by P. E. Corbett (Princeton University Press 1957; rev. ed. 1968)

Bernard C. Cohen, *The Political Process and Foreign Policy: The Making of the Japanese Peace Settlement* (Princeton University Press 1957)

Myron Weiner, *Party Politics in India: The Development of a Multi-Party System* (Princeton University Press 1957)

Percy E. Corbett, *Law in Diplomacy* (Princeton University Press 1959)

Rolf Sannwald and Jacques Stohler, *Economic Integration: Theoretical Assumptions and Consequences of European Unification*, trans. by Herman Karreman (Princeton University Press 1959)

Klaus Knorr, ed., *NATO and American Security* (Princeton University Press 1959)

Gabriel A. Almond and James S. Coleman, ed., *The Politics of the Developing Areas* (Princeton University Press 1960)

Herman Kahn, *On Thermonuclear War* (Princeton University Press 1960)

Sidney Verba, *Small Groups and Political Behavior: A Study of Leadership* (Princeton University Press 1961)

Robert J. C. Butow, *Tojo and the Coming of the War* (Princeton University Press 1961)

Glenn H. Snyder, *Deterrence and Defense: Toward a Theory of National Security* (Princeton University Press 1961)

Klaus Knorr and Sidney Verba, eds., *The International System: Theoretical Essays* (Princeton University Press 1961)

Peter Paret and John W. Shy, *Guerrillas in the 1960s* (Praeger 1962)

Geroge Modelski, *A Theory of Foreign Policy* (Praeger 1962)

Klaus Knorr and Thornton Read, eds., *Limited Strategic War* (Praeger 1963)

Frederick S. Dunn, *Peace-Making and the Settlement with Japan* (Princeton University Press 1963)

Arthur L. Burns and Nina Heathcote, *Peace-Keeping by United Nations Forces* (Praeger 1963)

Richard A. Falk, *Law, Morality, and War in the Contemporary World* (Praeger 1963)

James N. Rosenau, *National Leadership and Foreign Policy: A Case Study in the Mobilization of Public Support* (Princeton University Press 1963)

Gabriel A. Almond and Sidney Verba, *The Civic Culture: Political Attitudes and Democracy in Five Nations* (Princeton University Press 1963)

Bernard C. Cohen, *The Press and Foreign Policy* (Princeton University Press 1963)

Richard L. Sklar, *Nigerian Political Parties: Power in an Emergent African Nation* (Princeton University Press 1963)

Peter Paret, *French Revolutionary Warfare from Indochina to Algeria: The Analysis of a Political and Military Doctrine* (Praeger 1964)

Harry Eckstein, ed., *Internal War: Problems and Approaches* (Free Press 1964)

Cyril E. Black and Thomas P. Thornton, eds., *Communism and Revolution: The Strategic Uses of Political Violence* (Princeton University Press 1964)

Miriam Camps, *Britain and the European Community 1955–1963* (Princeton University Press 1964)

Thomas P. Thornton, ed., *The Third World in Soviet Perspective: Studies by Soviet Writers on the Developing Areas* (Princeton University Press 1964)

James N. Rosenau, ed., *International Aspects of Civil Strife* (Princeton University Press 1964)

Sidney I. Ploss, *Conflict and Decision-Making in Soviet Russia: A Case Study of Agricultural Policy, 1953–1963* (Princeton University Press 1965)

Richard A. Falk and Richard J. Barnet, eds., *Security in Disarmament* (Princeton University Press 1965)

Karl von Vorys, *Political Development in Pakistan* (Princeton University Press 1965)

Harold and Margaret Sprout, *The Ecological Perspective on Human Affairs, With Special Reference to International Politics* (Princeton University Press 1965)

Klaus Knorr, *On the Uses of Military Power in the Nuclear Age* (Princeton University Press 1966)

Harry Eckstein, *Division and Cohesion in Democracy: A Study of Norway* (Princeton University Press 1966)

Cyril E. Black, *The Dynamics of Modernization: A Study in Comparative History* (Harper and Row 1966)

Peter Kunstadter, ed., *Southeat Asian Tribes, Minorities, and Nations* (Princeton University Press 1967)

E. Victor Wolfenstein, *The Revolutionary Personality: Lenin, Trotsky, Gandhi* (Princeton University Press 1967)

Leon Gordenker, *The UN Secretary-General and the Maintenance of Peace* (Columbia University Press 1967)

Oran R. Young, *The Intermediaries: Third Parties in International Crises* (Princeton University Press 1967)

James N. Rosenau, ed., *Domestic Sources of Foreign Policy* (Free Press 1967)

Richard F. Hamilton, *Affluence and the French Worker in the Fourth Republic* (Princeton University Press 1967)

Linda B. Miller, *World Order and Local Disorder: The United Nations and Internal Conflicts* (Princeton University Press 1967)

Henry Bienen, *Tanzania: Party Transformation and Economic Development* (Princeton University Press 1967)

Wolfram F. Hanrieder, *West German Foreign Policy, 1949–1963: International Pressures and Domestic Response* (Stanford University Press 1967)

Richard H. Ullman, *Britain and the Russian Civil War: November 1918–February 1920* (Princeton University Press 1968)

Robert Gilpin, *France in the Age of the Scientific State* (Princeton University Press 1968)

William B. Bader, *The United States and the Spread of Nuclear Weapons* (Pegasus 1968)

Richard A. Falk, *Legal Order in a Violent World* (Princeton University Press 1968)

Cyril E. Black, Richard A. Falk, Klaus Knorr and Oran R. Young, *Neutralization and World Politics* (Princeton University Press 1968)

Oran R. Young, *The Politics of Force: Bargaining During International Crises* (Princeton University Press 1969)

Klaus Knorr and James N. Rosenau, eds., *Contending Approaches to International Politics* (Princeton University Press 1969)

James N. Rosenau, ed., *Linkage Politics: Essays on the Convergence of National and International Systems* (Free Press 1969)

John T. McAlister, Jr., *Viet Nam: The Origins of Revolution* (Knopf 1969)

Jean Edward Smith, *Germany Beyond the Wall: People, Politics and Prosperity* (Little, Brown 1969)

James Barros, *Betrayal from Within: Joseph Avenol, Secretary-General of the League of Nations, 1933–1940* (Yale University Press 1969)

Charles Hermann, *Crises in Foreign Policy: A Simulation Analysis* (Bobbs-Merrill 1969)

Robert C. Tucker, *The Marxian Revolutionary Idea: Essays on Marxist Thought and Its Impact on Radical Movements* (W.W. Norton 1969)

Harvey Waterman, *Political Change in Contemporary France: The Politics of an Industrial Democracy* (Charles E. Merrill 1969)

Cyril E. Black and Richard A. Falk, eds., *The Future of the International Legal Order*. Vol. I: *Trends and Patterns* (Princeton University Press 1969)

Ted Robert Gurr, *Why Men Rebel* (Princeton University Press 1969)

C. Sylvester Whitaker, *The Politics of Tradition: Continuity and Change in Northern Nigeria 1946–1966* (Princeton University Press 1970)

Richard A. Falk, *The Status of Law in International Society* (Princeton University Press 1970)

John T. McAlister, Jr., and Paul Mus, *The Vietnamese and Their Revolution* (Harper and Row 1970)

Klaus Knorr, *Military Power and Potential* (D.C. Heath 1970)

Cyril E. Black and Richard A. Falk, eds., *The Future of the International Legal Order*. Vol. II: *Wealth and Resources* (Princeton University Press 1970)

Leon Gordenker, ed., *The United Nations in International Politics* (Princeton University Press 1971)

Cyril E. Black and Richard A. Falk, eds., *The Future of the International Legal Order*. Vol. III: *Conflict Management* (Princeton University Press 1971)

Francine R. Frankel, *India's Green Revolution: Political Costs of Economic Growth* (Princeton University Press 1971)

Harold and Margaret Sprout, *Toward a Politics of the Planet Earth* (Van Nostrand Reinhold 1971)

Cyril E. Black and Richard A. Falk, eds., *The Future of the International Legal Order*. Vol. IV: *The Structure of the International Environment* (Princeton University Press 1972)

Gerald Garvey, *Energy, Ecology, Economy* (W.W. Norton 1972)

Richard Ullman, *The Anglo-Soviet Accord* (Princeton University Press 1973)

Klaus Knorr, *Power and Wealth: The Political Economy of International Power* (Basic Books 1973)

Anton Bebler, *Military Role in Africa: Dahomey, Ghana, Sierra Leone, and Mali* (Praeger 1973)

Robert C. Tucker, *Stalin as Revolutionary 1879–1929: A Study in History and Personality* (W.W. Norton 1973)

Edward L. Morse, *Foreign Policy and Interdependence in Gaullist France* (Princeton University Press 1973)

Henry Bienen, *Kenya: The Politics of Participation and Control* (Princeton University Press 1974)

Gregory J. Massell, *The Surrogate Proletariat: Moslem Women and Revolutionary Strategies in Soviet Central Asia, 1919–1929* (Princeton University Press 1974)

James N. Rosenau, *Citizenship Between Elections: An Inquiry into the Mobilizable American* (Free Press 1974)

Ervin Laszlo, *A Strategy for the Future: The Systems Approach to World Order* (Braziller 1974)

John R. Vincent, *Nonintervention and International Order* (Princeton University Press 1974)

Jan H. Kalicki, *The Pattern of Sino-American Crises: Political-Military Interactions in the 1950s* (Cambridge University Press 1975)

Klaus Knorr, *The Power of Nations: The Political Economy of International Relations* (Basic Books 1975)

James P. Sewell, *UNESCO and World Politics: Engaging in International Relations* (Princeton University Press 1975)

Richard A. Falk, *A Global Approach to National Policy* (Harvard University Press 1975)

Harry Eckstein and Ted Robert Gurr, *Patterns of Authority: A Structural Basis for Political Inquiry* (John Wiley & Sons 1975)

Cyril E. Black, Marius B. Jansen, Herbert S. Levin, Marion J. Levy, Jr., Henry Rosovsky, Gilbert Rozman, Henry D. Smith II, and S. Frederick Starr, *The Modernization of Japan and Russia* (Free Press 1975)

Leon Gordenker, *International Aid and National Decisions: Development Programs in Malawi, Tanzania, and Zambia* (Princeton University Press 1976)

Carl Von Clausewitz, *On War*, ed. and trans. by Michael Howard and Peter Paret (Princeton University Press 1976)

Gerald Garvey and Lou Ann Garvey, eds., *International Resource Flows* (D.C. Heath 1977)

Walter F. Murphy and Joseph Tanenhaus, *Comparative Constitutional Law Cases and Commentaries* (St. Martin's Press 1977)

Gerald Garvey, *Nuclear Power and Social Planning: The City of the Second Sun* (D.C. Heath 1977)

Richard E. Bissell, *Apartheid and International Organizations* (Westview Press 1977)

David P. Forsythe, *Humanitarian Politics: The International Committee of the Red Cross* (Johns Hopkins University Press 1977)

Paul E. Sigmund, *the Overthrow of Allende and the Politics of Chile, 1964–1976* (University of Pittsburgh Press 1977)

Henry S. Bienen, *Armies and Parties in Africa* (Holmes and Meier 1978)

Harold and Margaret Sprout, *The Context of Environmental Politics* (The University Press of Kentucky 1978)

Samuel S. Kim, *China, the United Nations, and World Order* (Princeton University Press 1979)

S. Basheer Ahmed, *Nuclear Fuel and Energy Policy* (D.C. Heath 1979)

Robert C. Johansen, *The National Interest and the Human Interest: An Analysis of U.S. Foreign Policy* (Princeton University Press 1980)

Richard A. Falk and Samuel S. Kim, eds., *The War System: An Interdisciplinary Approach* (Westview Press 1980)

James H. Billington, *Fire in the Minds of Men: Origins of the Revolutionary Faith* (Basic Books, 1980)

Bennett Ramberg, *Destruction of Nuclear Energy Facilities in War: The Problem and the Implications* (D.C. Heath 1980)

Gregory T. Kruglak, *The Politics of United States Decision-Making in United Nations Specialized Agencies: The Case of the International Labor Organization* (University Press of America 1980)

W. P. Davison and Leon Gordenker, eds., *Resolving Nationality Conflicts: The Role of Public Opinion Research* (Praeger 1980)

James C. Hsiung and Samuel S. Kim, eds., *China in the Global Community* (Praeger 1980)

Douglas Kinnard, *The Secretary of Defense* (The University Press of Kentucky 1980)

Richard Falk, *Human Rights and State Sovereignty* (Holmes and Meier 1981)

James H. Mittelman, *Underdevelopment and the Transition to Socialism: Mozambique and Tanzania* (Academic Press 1981)

Gilbert Rozman, ed., *The Modernization of China* (Free Press 1981; paperback edition 1982)

Robert C. Tucker, *Politics as Leadership*. The Paul Anthony Brick Lectures. Eleventh Series (University of Missouri Press 1981)

Robert Gilpin, *War and Change in World Politics* (Cambridge University Press 1981)

Nicholas G. Onuf, ed., *Law-Making in the Global Community* (Carolina Academic Press 1982)

Ali E. Hillal Dessouki, ed., *Islamic Resurgence in the Arab World* (Praeger 1982)

Richard Falk, *The End of World Order* (Holmes and Meier 1983)

Klaus Knorr, ed., *Power, Strategy and Security* (Princeton University Press 1983)

Finn Laursen, *Superpower at Sea* (Praeger 1983)

Samuel S. Kim, *The Quest for a Just World Order* (Westview Press 1984)

Gerald Garvey, *Strategy and the Defense Dilemma* (D.C. Heath 1984)

Peter R. Baehr and Leon Gordenker, *The United Nations: Reality and Ideal* (Praeger 1984)

Joseph M. Grieco, *Between Dependency and Autonomy: India's Experience with the International Computer Industry* (University of California Press 1984)

Jan Hallenberg, *Foreign Policy Change: United States Foreign Policy Toward the Soviet Union and the People's Republic of China, 1961–1980* (University of Stockholm 1984)

Michael Krepon, *Strategic Stalemate: Nuclear Weapons and Arms Control in American Politics* (St. Martin's Press 1984)

Gilbert Rozman, *A Mirror for Socialism: Soviet Criticisms of China* (Princeton University Press 1985)

Henry Bienen, *Political Conflict and Economic Change in Nigeria* (London: Frank Cass 1985)

Kenneth A. Oye, ed., *Cooperation under Anarchy* (Princeton: Princeton University Press 1986)

Richard Falk, *Reviving the World Order* (Virginia: University Press of Virginia 1986)

Ikuo Kabashima and Lynn T. White III, eds., *Political System and Change* (Princeton: Princeton University Press 1986)

Atul Kohli, ed., *The State and Development in the Third World* (Princeton: Princeton University Press 1986)

Cyril E. Black, *Understanding Soviet Politics: The Perspective of Russian History* (Colorado: Westview Press 1986)

INDEX

LIBRARY OF CONGRESS
Library of Congress Cataloging-in-Publication Data

India's democracy: an analysis of changing state-society relations / edited by Atul Kohli:
contributors, Pranab Bardhan . . . [et al.]; foreword by John P. Lewis.

p.   cm.
   "Written under the auspices of the Center of International Studies, Woodrow Wilson
School, Princeton University"—"First presented and discussed at a conference . . . held at
the Woodrow Wilson School of Public and International Affairs, Princeton University, on
March 14 through 16, 1985"—Pref. Includes index.

ISBN 0–691–07760–6

1. Representative government and representation—India—Congresses. 2. India—Politics
and government—1947—Congresses. 3. Democracy—Congresses. I. Kohli, Atul. II. Bardhan, Pranab K. III. Woodrow Wilson School of Public and International Affairs. Center of
International Studies.
JQ281.I53 1988   320.954—dc19   87–27390 CIP

ATUL KOHLI is Associate Professor, Department of Politics and the Woodrow Wilson
School, Princeton University.